The UNSC Permanent Members Resolution of International Conflicts with Soft Law Agreements

International Humanitarian Law Series

Editor-in-Chief

VOLUME 77

The International Humanitarian Law Series is a series of monographs and edited volumes which aims to promote scholarly analysis and discussion of both the theory and practice of the international legal regulation of armed conflict.

The series explores substantive issues of International Humanitarian Law, including:

- Protection for victims of armed conflict and regulation of the means and method of warfare
- Questions of application of the various legal regimes for the conduct of armed conflict
- Issues relating to the implementation of International Humanitarian Law obligations
- National and international approaches to the enforcement of the law and
- The interactions between International Humanitarian Law and other related areas of international law such as Human Rights, Refugee Law, Arms Control and Disarmament Law, and International Criminal Law.

The titles published in this series are listed at *brill.com/ihul*

The UNSC Permanent Members Resolution of International Conflicts with Soft Law Agreements

By

Attila Nagy

BRILL | NIJHOFF

This book was initially a PhD thesis defended by the author at The Faculty of Law, University in Jena, with a title: *Informal Rules in Post-Conflict Development.*

ISSN 1389-6776
ISBN 978-90-04-74608-4
ISBN 978-90-04-74609-1 (PDF)
DOI https://doi.org/10.1163/9789004746091

Library of Congress Control Number: 2026935186

Brill Nijhoff and Koninklijke Brill BV are part of De Gruyter Brill.
www.degruyterbrill.com

Questions about General Product Safety Regulation: productsafety@degruyterbrill.com.

Cover illustration: Security Council Debates Protection of Civilians in Armed Conflict – Photo credit: UN Photo/Loey Felipe.

Contents

Abbreviations

A/C	Association/Community of Serbian municipalities
BRI	Belt and Road Initiative
BiH	Bosnia and Herzegovina
BrExit	United Kingdom withdrawal from The European Union
BA	Brussels Agreement 2013
CEFTA	Central European Free Trade Agreement
CEEC	Central and Eastern European Countries
CNPC	China National Petroleum Corporation
CSDP	Common Security and Defense Policy
DDR	Disarmament, Demobilization, and Reintegration
ETIM	East Turkestan Islamic Movement
EU	European Union
EULEX	European Union Rule of Law Mission in Kosovo
IGOs	Intergovernmental Organizations
ISO	Internal Organization for Standardization
ICL	International Common Law
ICJ	International Court of Justice
ICC	International Criminal Court
ICTY	International Criminal Tribunal for the Former Yugoslavia
UNIDROIT	International Institute for the Unification of Private Law
IS	Islamic State
KFOR	Kosovo Force
KSC	Kosovo Specialist Chambers and Specialist Prosecutor's Office
NIS	Naftna Industrija Srbije
NK	Nagorno-Karabakh
NGO	Non-Governmental Organizations
NATO	North Atlantic Treaty Organization
OBOR	One Belt One Road initiative
OSCE	Organization for Security and Co-operation in Europe
PRC	People's Republic of China
PICC	Principles for International Commercial Contracts
SC	Security Council
SAA	Stabilization and Accession Agreement
SDGs	Sustainable Development Goals
UK	United Kingdom of Great Britain and Northern Ireland
UN	United Nations
UNCITRAL	United Nations Commission on International Trade Law

CISG	United Nations Convention on Contracts for the International Sale of Goods
UNMIK	United Nations Interim Administration Mission in Kosovo
UNSC	United Nations Security Council
USA	United States of America
WA	Washington Agreement 2020
WRM	Water Resources Management
WTO	World Trade Organization

Introduction

The obviously rising number of conflicts globally has made the necessity for this research, where we are aiming to make a comparative analysis of some most recent post-conflicts agreements. In this regard we will research the agreements as related to Kosovo, Nagorno-Karabakh and Afghanistan. Such agreements are coming from various influential global and regional stakeholders, which are also interestingly the permanent members of the UN Security Council. All the mentioned societies have been a ground of some recent conflicts but also stepped recently into the direction of reconciliation process and they have established some basics for their future development in these agreements. While all three mentioned conflicts are coming from geographically different regions and perspectives, they are all interconnected and also have the potential influence on similar future post-conflict developments. These conflicts also fall into the primary interest spheres of the UN Security Council permanent member states and are therefore representing their ultimate aims and goals in the given region and conflict, which can ultimately differ from the viewpoints of other states.

Regarding Kosovo we will research the Brussels Agreement from 2013, which is made according to the EU standpoints regarding Kosovo and its future development where the most important aspects are the integration of the Serbian majority from North Kosovo and the establishment of the Association/Community of Serbian Municipalities in Kosovo. This new and complex form of autonomy for Serbs in Kosovo foresees the membership of the Serbian majority municipalities from all Kosovo; also we will approach the case of the Serbian *de facto* recognition of Kosovo in this regard. Another agreement regarding Kosovo is the USA supported Washington Agreement from 2020, which has made both the Serbian and Kosovo governments agree about various cooperation models and human rights aspects. Still the most notable outcome of this agreement is definitely the mutual recognition between Israel and Kosovo. Regarding Serbia this agreement also requests the relocation of the Serbian embassy to Jerusalem, which is contrary to the EU standpoints and overall the UN Resolutions in regard to this conflict. This Agreement is coming from the broader framework of The Abrahamic Accords Agreements, which are all aiming to establish friendly connections and cooperation between Israel and various Muslim majority states in The Middle East and North Africa. In specific, it is interesting to research how such agreements will cover the overall conflict between Israel and Palestine considering its future possible resolution mechanisms.

 | HTTPS://DOI.ORG/10.1163/9789004746091-002

The decades-long conflict in Nagorno-Karabakh has recently been instantly reshaped by a new Agreement or, as it is formally called, the Statement from 2020, supported by The Russian Federation. Interestingly, very shortly after that, in 2023 the situation changed and this change meant the end of the idea of an independent or semi-recognized Nagorno-Karabakh (Artsakh) Armenian Republic inside the sovereign Azerbaijani territory. These changes were all coming after the Russian invasion in Ukraine and as an outcome of the surprisingly very good Russian relationship with Turkey. At the moment it is hard to determine what agreements there are to be applied regarding Nagorno-Karabakh and to what extent the various stakeholders including Armenia and Azerbaijan support the peace efforts, human rights and their mutual cooperation after all. 'Conflict Resolution Documents for Nagorno-Karabakh Conflict'[1] serve as a good example of how conflict resolution has developed in the perspective of Russia, with obvious shortcomings regarding the legality of post-conflict enforcement mechanisms. Therefore, in this case we will also observe how regional geopolitics influence smaller nations and in fact diminish both human and minority rights, reshaping them into completely new frameworks and understandings. Such agreements also cover the possibilities of better regional interconnectedness, which is a necessity for all including Russia, Turkey and even China aiming to reach Europe and The Middle East by developing trade opportunities. Finally, Nagorno-Karabakh has in 2023 lost the capacity to be a Republic in any possible form and it is still to be seen what kind of presumable autonomy, human and minority rights protection Armenians will have inside Azerbaijan, if any.

Researching Afghanistan is important since recently it has been serving us with many interesting and crucial turning points, of which the most challenging ones are the agreements China has reached with and the officially not recognized Taliban government by the UN. The very complex but mutually satisfying agreements are for now not lowering the refugee waves from Afghanistan towards Europe, but in the future that might change. It is also necessary to observe how China makes its BRI Initiative develop and secure more alternative roads, which could be used to transport goods towards the West, but also source necessary raw materials back into China, which are needed for the constant maintenance of its industry.

As all the three case studies cover almost all the UN Security Council permanent member states we can observe what priorities regarding post-conflict

1 International Center on Conflict and Negotiation, 'Conflict Resolution Documents for Nagorno-Karabakh Conflict' (2023) <http://iccn.ge/index.php?article_id=331&clang=1> accessed 25 March 2026.

administration, human rights and development potentials they have and can enforce. Since all the agreements are signed in an informal setting they are treated therefore as soft law, which can't be enforced or at least not without the use of military intervention in such post-conflict societies. The overall research and its developments are done with an aim to support and give valuable feedback to the efforts regarding transitional justice and reconciliation in post-conflict settings from a legal perspective, for which the best initial options are such informal agreements. While there are many challenges, such as the depopulation of post-conflict areas they are all bringing a lasting development-related pressure on societies which are trying to help them. 'Once located in the context of Palestine–Israel, the dynamic between the self as the landscape, and the self on the landscape, becomes one, for as long as both are subject to contestation, the passing of time will not diminish the connection between (and to) the land, the landscape, and the depopulated sites.'[2] The removal, expulsion and in some cases even genocide over a certain nation is not the path the societies should aim at and want to follow in this new century. The rising number of challenges is from recently reaching its peak and the possibilities of finding a real legal answer is at the moment pretty complex. Regarding the conflict in Ukraine it is also evident that the need for stopping and limiting the conflict is a necessity, more and more quoted by all the parties involved. While the informal agreements are a new tool in solving post-conflict development concerns they are also the only possibility to make the first steps towards them and while they are not perfect, they are already being supported and cherished by many states concerned.

2 Luisa Gandolfo, 'Ruins, Resistance and Pluritemporality in Palestine-Israel' in Natascha Mueller-Hirth and Sandra Rios Oyola (ed), *Time and Temporality in Transitional and Post-conflict Societies* (Routledge 2018).

CHAPTER 1

The Role of Informal Rules in General and in Post-conflict Environments

1 Defining and Understanding Informal Rules (Soft Law)

Defining and understanding informal rules, while also taking into consideration the recent trend in the rising number of post-conflict agreements, is necessary in order to understand their role and capacity overall, in specific, their form and application regarding their possible successful post-conflict development potentials. For a better understanding, we look into the peace agreements in their present form as informal rules or treaties which formally best fit into the understanding of international soft law as a new hybrid form of international regulations. The non-formal agreements in international law, which are made in the framework of post-conflict development, are usually made under the auspices of a certain UNSC permanent member state. In order to be able to understand these specific regulations at the beginning of the 21st century, we will accordingly aim to define them using the most recent theories and practices.

Probably, one of the most important aspects of soft laws is to regulate issues which would otherwise be out of law[1] and left to the free will of the parties, without any possible involvement and approval from any authority. It is evident that informal rules are being used by many, but in the framework of post-conflict development, only the ones stemming from the most influential states can prevail. These states are almost exclusively the five permanent member states of the UN Security Council. To better understand them, we will try to build up on conclusions from previous researchers and depart from where they have concluded. 'The case studies on non-binding international instruments suggest that the source for developing the norms must be viewed as legitimate by the international community.'[2] Therefore, not every act can be seen as a valid non-formal act in post-conflict environments or ultimately also to have a certain effect on the development and potential for its own future

1 Matthias Knauff, *Der Regelungsverbund : Recht Und Soft Law Im Mehrebenensystem* (Mohr Siebeck 2010).

2 Edith Brown Weiss, 'Conclusions: Understanding Compliance with Soft Law' in Dinah Shelton (ed), *Commitment and Compliance: The Role of Non-binding Norms in the International Legal System* (Oxford University Press 2000).

HTTPS://DOI.ORG/10.1163/9789004746091-003

implementation. Non-formal acts in a form of soft law certainly have some power, and this power is not derived from them but from their creators, after all.

The post-conflict agreements enforcement is similar to that of customs, where the parties can't change the form and understanding of such laws or practices. 'However, mere custom cannot explain why customary law is law, nor can it explain the belief in its legally binding character.'[3] Accordingly, calling for a solution to which the parties have not clearly agreed to and apply it is more complex and even more questionable when there is no one to stand behind that, except morality of course. Now, when we split with morality, as it is not something very influential and used in post-conflict societies and international law overall, we continue with the understanding of the idea of customs as such. They are deeply incorporated into the human mind and of course the legal profession as well. Customs are therefore something which correspond to expectations. Overall, customs are something that need to be respected and achieved, while the path and the personal understanding of it can be changed, e.g. by the parties. 'There does not seem to be any need for a specific definition of soft law as a whole which would neatly distinguish it from *travaux préparatoires* or from documents lacking any legal effects.'[4] Such *travaux préparatoires* are made with an intention to showcase what needs to be achieved; in our case, it is mainly the conflict-resolution- and development-related actions. Therefore, if we say that the main idea of the parties is conflict resolution and development, it is evident that it can't be reached without cooperation, from which the most necessary step is the obvious cooperation with neighbours. In such cases, resolutions of conflicts have to be reached and societies should reconcile in order to re-establish their own potentials for their common development.

It is also necessary to understand how a society or a government which just came out of a conflict can guarantee anything, when it can also be seen as a perpetrator of some crimes, which is actually a fact in many cases. For such cases therefore, it is necessary to have the agreements which can be seen as basic ones and in the best interest of the majority of citizens, but hopefully, ultimately, for everyone. Also, it is the case when the idea or an agreement in post-conflict development is agreed to by the parties, while in fact it is also

---

3 Bart van Klink and Oliver W. Lembcke, 'A Fuller Understanding of Legal Validity and Soft Law' in Pauline Westerman, Jaap Hage, Stephan Kirste and Anne Ruth Mackor, *Legal Validity and Soft Law* (Springer 2018).

4 Allan Rosas, 'Soft Law and the European Court of Justice' in Julia Iliopoulos-Strangas and Jean-François Flauss (ed), *Das soft law der europäischen Organisationen – The Soft Law of European Organisations – La soft law des organisations européennes* (Nomos 2012).

supported by a wider array of stakeholders from inside the given societies and the international community. 'The term soft law might give extra legitimacy to instruments that lack formal legal status.'[5] In agreements, such law-related aspects are the will of people to go further and achieve development; the actual path in a given moment might not be seen, but certainly it is a wish which gets a form of a promise in such cases. So, the value of such a promise in harsh times gets a higher level of importance; it is also given to a wider level of audience which counts on it and its future implementation. Finally, the written form of such agreements, although being informal or at least not in a form of an international treaty but agreed to between the highest possible level of political actors, is what ultimately gives them the necessary 'legal' authority.

The presence and acknowledgement coming from a certain part of the international community, with a direct involvement of some UNSC permanent member states, gives to a certain post-conflict agreement, an additional power and capacity for its respect, if not full enforcement guarantees, after all. 'Consequently, it seems inappropriate and unhelpful to use the term soft law to describe norms and normative instruments which are clearly not in legal form, not intended to be legally binding, and thus not, in any of the usual sense in which we use the word, law at all.'[6] When a wide array of stakeholders makes a promise and formalizes it in some document, it is, in that case, hard to say that all what has been agreed is finally not binding. In the case of post-conflict development, the actual situation is what makes impossible the signing of a document of any other type impossible, and therefore such informal agreements are treated as law or better to say informal or soft law agreements, accordingly. 'The origin of soft law is context specific and different actors are likely to promote binding or non-binding instruments in different circumstances according to their political, economic, and military interests.'[7] In post-conflict agreements, it is context-specific that actors are promoting the agreements and are actually the ones which are choosing its final form, which many times tend to have the form of an informal agreement, for various and obvious practical reasons. Influential actors and states, such as the UNSC permanent

5 Andrea K. Bjorklund, 'Assessing the Effectiveness of Soft Law Instruments in International Investment Law' in Andrea K. Bjorklund and August Reinisch (ed), *International Investment Law and Soft Law* (Edward Elgar Publishing 2012).

6 Richard B. Bilder, 'Beyond Compliance: Helping Nations Cooperate' in Dinah Shelton (ed), *Commitment and Compliance: The Role of Non-binding Norms in the International Legal System* (Oxford University Press 2000).

7 Christine Chinkin, 'Normative Development in the International Legal System' in Dinah Shelton (ed), *Commitment and Compliance: The Role of Non-binding Norms in the International Legal System* (Oxford University Press 2000).

member states, do not want to be blamed for an agreement which could fail; in such instances, they tend to find a solution which could bring them back and keep them on to the safe side, while they can fully claim that such agreements have been agreed by the parties themselves.

This dimension is very important, as we will see later how soft laws are becoming hard laws and how they broaden their potential field of application. It can be observed that soft law is a pre-runner for hard law,[8] and in many instances directly corresponds to the final framework of the soft law regulated area. For now, we will look into the phases where soft laws are still considered laws in a wider sense. 'It is widely accepted that soft law refers to norms that are neither law nor mere political or moral statements, but lie somewhere in between.'[9] Even when the intention of stakeholders is that a soft law agreement will be once hard law, for a certain period of time it is not, while leaving soft law still not enforceable upon parties. As mentioned earlier and in order to round up the capacity of soft law agreements, we tend to call and treat them as some legal frameworks from the beginning. 'Notwithstanding the lack of legal force behind such documents, non-binding normative standards can possess moral, ethical, political or persuasive value, potentially greater than that of formal legal texts.'[10] It is the actual situation, as mentioned earlier, which makes such agreements authoritative and also the fact that they are known, respected and finally their application is expected by many. Such agreements being general ones are later used to discuss more in detail some of their aspects and also able of going back and forth discussing their priorities for now and later.

Such informality is also beneficial for the framework of post-conflict development, where time has already been wasted and huge steps are necessary to be made in the direction towards development. When we talk about necessary and vital steps in law-making, it is needed to mention the trends of other levels of governance that are used in post-conflict states. 'Nowadays, even state organs create their own soft law or have soft law created for them.'[11] The benefits of soft law in making quick and useful solutions are widely accepted.

---

8 Matthias Knauff, *Der Regelungsverbund: Recht Und Soft Law Im Mehrebenensystem* (Mohr Siebeck 2010).

9 Doron Goldbarsht, *Global Counter-Terrorist Financing and Soft Law: Multi-layered Approaches* (Edward Elgar 2020).

10 Dug Cubie, 'An Analysis of Soft Law Applicable to Humanitarian Assistance: Relative Normativity in Action?' (2011) 2 International Humanitarian Legal Studies 177.

11 Anne Ruth Mackor, 'What Is Legal Validity and Is It Important? Some Critical Remarks about the Legal Status of Soft Law' in Pauline Westerman, Jaap Hage, Stephan Kirste and Anne Ruth Mackor, *Legal Validity and Soft Law* (Springer 2018).

Finally, it is not a surprise that even the EU has accepted this model of governance and used it for decades where some of its non-bonding decisions like Recommendations and Opinions[12] are indeed treated as soft law. 'Soft law instruments do not need ratification at the national level and for politically controversial issues, adopting a soft law instrument may be the answer.'[13] Soft law solutions have been reached by an agreement with an obvious will and support of a certain (in)formal authority. Additionally, the organs and bodies subordinated to the agreement will take its direction and make a decision in compliance with it, by respecting how to fully apply it, for which they have not been obliged to but only advised by the soft law to do so. Obviously, soft law as an agreement or a solution need not stay in a form that has been agreed, it can be somehow reshaped by the parties but also re-regulated and influenced by the authority which is supporting its implementation. In some later phases of implementation, soft law can also become a hard law, as mentioned, which we will research more broadly in the following chapters.

On the EU level, states can detour from the soft law regulations of the EU and also bring their own, sometimes opposite solutions for a certain period of time, which can also be at some instances indefinite. Similarly, in the framework of the post-conflict agreements, some solutions can be changed by the parties, their understanding reshaped and ultimately some agreements or, more frequently, some of their parts simply forgotten, of course with no consequences. Therefore, the need to understand and regulate them is coming from an external factor and is crucial in informal rules and post-conflict development where the power which gives the highest level of authority to such agreements is not coming solely from the parties signing it but from the authority which has initiated its final birth. 'Soft law is not a declaration of intentions or an individual resolution stating s specific decision, but an exteriorized will to regulate.'[14] This exteriorized will is lying in authoritative as an outside factor, which does not want to include its own sovereign right to regulate but neither wants to request anyone to use its own sovereign right to obey but still somehow remains liable for its ultimate implementation. It can

12 European Center for Constitutional and Human Rights, 'Hard law/Soft Law' <https://www.ecchr.eu/en/glossary/hard-law-soft-law/> accessed 22 March 2026.

13 Sumudu Atapattu, 'International Environmental Law and Soft Law: A New Direction or a Contradiction?' in Cecilia M. Bailliet, *Non-state actors, soft law, and protective regimes : from the margins* (Cambridge University Press 2012).

14 Daniel Sarmiento, 'European Soft Law and National Authorities: Incorporation, Enforcement and Interference' in Julia Iliopoulos-Strangas and Jean-François Flauss (ed), *Das soft law der europäischen Organisationen – The Soft Law of European Organisations – La soft law des organisations européennes* (Nomos 2012).

be seen that soft law has a very strong capacity to influence the will of states[15] in which it can achieve more smooth declarative but later rather more binding soft law resolutions. Finally, the agreements in post-conflict resolution and development remain informal due to the actual will of the external actors, but fully in a form of a treaty, as perceived by the local stakeholders. So that is what is taking its final shape following the more in-depth formulation of its actual solutions by the parties, ultimately leading to many, if not all, of its articles and chapters applied or potentially becoming future hard law.

2 Terminology Concerns and Understandings of the Agreements

In this research, we are dealing with a comparative analysis of acts made in the process of peace talks in various post-conflict societies. Such final acts are the outcomes and arrangements made in order to make cooperation and development possible. These acts are achieved in the process and interaction of many stakeholders and present the final agreements of the given post-conflict society. While we are researching three case studies, our aim is to overall include the standpoints and practices of the most influential states and their approach in regard to post-conflict resolution and development capacities. Accordingly, we are comparing the standpoints of all the five United Nations Security Council permanent member states. It is interestingly at this moment very possible since recently there have been activities in regard to conflict resolution mechanism establishment by all the five UNSC permanent member states.

First we approach the US perspective, as visible in The Abrahamic Accords from 2020, where one of the agreements was dealing in specific with the conflict resolution between Serbia and Kosovo. This act is titled as Economic Normalization[16] agreement but deals with various issues in regard to this region from the US perspective. The Economic Normalization agreement is understood to advance the cooperation between Serbia and Kosovo in general but also their mutual relationship with Israel. It overall concludes with the mutual recognition between Israel and Kosovo and the moving of the Serbian

---

15 Matthias Knauff, *Der Regelungsverbund: Recht Und Soft Law Im Mehrebenensystem* (Mohr Siebeck 2010).

16 Washington Agreement, 'Economic Normalization' (2020) <https://www.peacefare.net/2020/09/04/much-ado-about-nothing/> also available at <https://exit.al/en/2020/09/04/kosovo-and-serbia-signed-separate-pledges-not-an-agreement/> accessed 22 March 2026.

Embassy in Israel to Jerusalem, which is against the common EU understanding of not moving Israeli embassies to Jerusalem.

The most debated agreement in the framework of post-conflict resolutions in Kosovo is the Brussels Agreement[17] from 2013. The First Agreement of Principles Governing the Normalization of Relations is commonly referred to as The Brussels Agreement. It was signed between the governments of Serbia and Kosovo, while its implementation is facilitated by the EU. In the agreement, Serbia has given up some of its parallel structures in Kosovo, in exchange for the establishment of the Association/Community of Serbian Municipalities. While this institution still has not been formed or initiated in any form so far by the Kosovo authorities, its importance is vital for the existence of the Serbian minority. One of the biggest successes of this agreement is definitely the possibility for the collection of electricity bills in North Kosovo, and the establishment of the relevant and specific companies dealing with electricity-related issues in North Kosovo. This agreement was signed under the supervision of Catherine Ashton from The United Kingdom, at that time the EU High Representative. Therefore, we consider this agreement as a common approach from both the UK and all other EU member states. Finally, we have also a more specific French approach in regard to this conflict, as it is the remaining UNSC permanent member state in the EU. This is the support formed in the Ohrid Agreement,[18] which is commonly referred to as the Franco-German proposal. While the Ohrid Agreement itself was not signed by the parties, it represents the soft power exercised in regard to the future relationship and cooperation between Serbia and Kosovo.

The Statement[19] achieved by The Russian Federation in the framework of the war in Nagorno-Karabakh in 2020 is serving us with the Russian perspec-

17 Brussels Agreement, 'First Agreement of Principles Governing the Normalization of Relations' (2013) <https://www.peaceagreements.org/media/documents/ag2022_5bdc31b326555.pdf> also available at <https://www.srbija.gov.rs/cinjenice/en/120394> and <https://gzk.rks-gov.net/ActDetail.aspx?ActID=8892&langid=2> accessed 22 March 2026.

18 European Union External Action, 'Belgrade-Pristina Dialogue: Agreement on the path to normalisation between Kosovo and Serbia' (2023) <https://www.eeas.europa.eu/eeas/belgrade-pristina-dialogue-agreement-path-normalisation-between-kosovo-and-serbia_en> accessed 22 March 2026.

19 President of Russian Federation, 'Statement by President of the Republic of Azerbaijan, Prime Minister of the Republic of Armenia and President of the Russian Federation' (2020) <http://en.kremlin.ru/events/president/news/64384> also available at <https://documents-dds-ny.un.org/doc/UNDOC/GEN/N20/307/34/PDF/N2030734.pdf?OpenElement> accessed 22 March 2026.

tive of conflict resolution mechanisms. While initially this agreement has taken into consideration many different aspects and requests by both Azerbaijan and Armenia, it has very quickly lost importance after the final dissolution of the Nagorno-Karabakh Republic, as controlled by Armenia in 2023. This agreement is very important in order to understand and see what to expect as future Russian standpoints in regard to conflict resolution mechanisms and priorities. In particular, this is valuable in the framework of the future potentials solving the conflict in Ukraine. While drafting, The Statement Russia did take into consideration the requests from its new ally Turkey, and also Iran, which is also bordering both Azerbaijan and Armenia. In this Statement, a broader idea of interconnectedness was agreed, which is necessary by all the states in the region but primarily on the decades-long closed borders between Azerbaijan and Armenia. While the idea of Nagorno-Karabakh has failed, the idea and necessity for regional connectivity remained. Further, Iran also borders Afghanistan, which introduces to us another case study and the relevant Chinese approach in regard to post-conflict resolutions.

While China is also an UNSC permanent member-state, it is very new in the agenda of peace-making and post-conflict development efforts. The sudden leave of the US forces from Afghanistan and the quick takeover of the entire country by the Taliban forces has made China act. In general, this change has not surprised China and it was able to intervene, also by including all the neighbouring countries of Afghanistan. It offered some solutions, which are in more detail explained in two separate acts. The first act is the Joint Statement[20] of the Third Foreign Ministers' Meeting Among the Neighboring Countries of Afghanistan and the second is called The Tunxi Initiative[21] of the Neighboring Countries of Afghanistan on Supporting Economic Reconstruction in and Practical Cooperation with Afghanistan. The Taliban Government in Afghanistan has not taken part in the drafting of these agreements but can

20 Embassy of the People's Republic of China in the Kingdom of the Netherlands, 'Joint Statement of the Third Foreign Ministers' Meeting Among the Neighboring Countries of Afghanistan' (31 March 2022) <http://nl.china-embassy.gov.cn/eng/zgyw/202203/t20220331_10658230.htm> also accessible on <http://lawinfochina.com/display.aspx?id=8253&lib=tax&SearchKeyword=&SearchCKeyword=> accessed 22 March 2026.

21 Ministry of Foreign Affairs of the People's Republic of China, 'The Tunxi Initiative of the Neighboring Countries of Afghanistan on Supporting Economic Reconstruction in and Practical Cooperation with Afghanistan' (1 April 2022) <https://www.fmprc.gov.cn/mfa_eng/gjhdq_665435/2675_665437/2676_663356/2677_663358/202204/t20220401_10662024.html> also available on <https://lawinfochina.com/display.aspx?id=8251&lib=tax&SearchKeyword=&SearchCKeyword=> accessed 22 March 2026.

still count on the relevant achievements incorporated into them. Such a model of incorporating solutions into the framework of a post-conflict society is similar to the one used by the EU in the Ohrid Agreement and the use of its relevant soft power. The priority is therefore always to stabilise a certain society and make the necessary steps in regard to its future development potentials possible. As the Taliban government did not receive any recognition so far, such acts are serving as its main focal points in foreign policy it can surely rely on.

The terms and formulations used in all these agreements use various concepts while dealing with the same issue, post-conflict peace establishment and development. The usage and understanding of informal rules and soft law in agreements is therefore used solely by the given authority. Overall, they do have the tendency to mean the same thing, but are not necessarily synonyms. Therefore, informal rules as a concept used are norms which have been either agreed or to some extent forced on by some UNSC permanent member-state on the given post-conflict societies. They do not come in the form of an exact International agreement and the requirement for them to be accepted in the local parliaments does not exist. Also, they have many aspects which are usually not in accordance with the relevant local constitutional frameworks. Their importance lies in the fact that they are solving informally a conflict which has been unresolved for a longer period of time. Such informal agreements are also necessary to make parties agree between each other in some form, while otherwise they would not recognise each other's claims or the relevant statehood at all. The parties do agree about certain issues but with a clear and obvious lack of enforcement capacity and control body. The UN itself is unable to control such agreements since they are concluded outside its framework by the most powerful UNSC permanent member-states. They accordingly represent the divides present in the UNSC regarding some post-conflict resolution mechanisms, while this is a division line present in it for decades. Finally, for some agreements, the term Statement has been used, which, in this sense, does not mean a different idea and does not change the concept of using various names for the same activity in regard to solving international conflicts.

3 The Application of Informal Rules in Post-conflict Settings

When we go one step further and try to understand the roles of post-conflict peace agreements and their influence and capacity in shaping post-conflict societies, it is necessary to look deeper into different correlations in such societies and their applicable development potentials. Whereas the solving of the conflicts without an involvement of a third party[22] is very limited today, it is in some instances still possible where the parties have more freedom to regulate their mutual relationships. As we have outlined in the previous chapter, a post-conflict agreement does tend to be informal but nevertheless its power to shape and influence stands and remains. 'Even if they are not ultimate peace agreements, written commitments that remain at the negotiation table unless a settlement is achieved can be productive signs of good will and also stop some violent activities.'[23] Such agreements are there to finish with the hostilities and start a new chapter in the peace process, which means the start of the reconciliation process and the establishment of the legal framework for future constitutionalism. 'If all parties feel fairly treated in the process of negotiating the compromise, they will tend to accept it as fair, although the material outcome will not fully comply with any party's standards of justice.'[24] The agreements we are researching are trying to incorporate a big volume of transitional justice matters and get the most possible benefits for both parties involved, but obviously, such development-related agreements can't serve fully the final purpose of justice.

With the introduction of the system of post-conflict criminal proceedings and the 'universal' application of the International Criminal Court (ICC), we see no reason to mention its application specifically. While the ICC tends to have universal jurisdiction per se, its actual jurisdiction is very limited; it has not been applied to any of the parties in conflicts we are going to research further. In this sense, it is not just that the bigger states, but also the smaller ones want to influence their own future and in particular, the idea of being responsible for their own acts in any possible future situation. 'The question is rather, given that there are non-state, informal resolution mechanisms, whether the state system always influences the informal solutions for conflicts and is necessary as a back-up to those solutions.'[25] Obviously, states do not fully control what will be included and how the agreements will look like

---

22 Matthias Knauff, 'Soft Law im europäischen Und internationalen Verwaltungsrecht' in Wolfgang Kahl und Markus Ludwigs (ed), *Band 2: Grundstrukturen des europäischen und internationalen Verwaltungsrechts* (C.F. Müller 2021).

23 Martin Leiner, 'Introduction to Negotiation' in Martin Leiner and Christine Schliesser (ed), *Alternative Approaches in Conflict Resolution* (Palgrave Macmillan 2018).

24 Rudolf Schuessler, 'Justice in Negotiations and Conflict Resolution' in Martin Leiner and Christine Schliesser (ed), *Alternative Approaches in Conflict Resolution* (Palgrave Macmillan 2018).

25 Sanne Taekema, 'The Point of Law: The Interdependent Functionality of State and Non-state Regulation' in Hanneke van Schooten and Jonathan Verschuuren (ed), *International Governance and Law: State Regulation and Non-state Law* (Edward Elgar 2008).

on the end; they are more like an actor setting the red lines and requirements which are more realistic and acceptable to the other side as well.

While the inevitable influence of a bigger influential state which supports and introduces the agreements are such that they can expect the agreed terms to be respected and also align their own future policies accordingly. One of the main characteristics of the agreements is definitely guaranteeing lasting peace, which as one of their first outcomes later also brings other valuable future potentials. 'However, together with other instruments that the international community and the parties to the conflict possess, the peace agreement may be used to achieve economic development and long-lasting peace.'[26] It is hard to understand why societies choose conflict instead of cooperation and mutual development, but certainly there are reasons which force them at some moment to do so. Lastly, even after concluding an agreement, there are forces on both sides which would be ready to cancel any agreement and even return to hostilities after all. This is why the role of the international community and the specific UNSC permanent member-state or in this case, a patron country is important, not to mention the economic and military power of such states which are able to influence and support others. 'The lack of criteria for recognising an entity as a government of a state – as well as the lack of a clear idea of how much recognition is required – can, in turn, facilitate the practice of international actors in securing the international legal authority of their preferred domestic actors.'[27] This very interesting form and perspective of democracy on the domestic level means that people can choose any government they like, but only with a single requirement that it should follow the foreign policy in regard to the given post-conflict agreement.

Many times, even the patron state can change the government, which then places a focus on some particular parts of the agreement, while some others are treated as not so important and many times excluded or even completely ignored. 'Hence, in the area of armed conflict, it might provocatively be argued that soft law plays the role of a *normexcluder* rather than a norm-filler or norm-creator.'[28] Indeed, in the sense of a post-conflict development, such

26 Marcia A. Dawes, 'Considerations for Determining When to Include Natural Resources in Peace Agreements Ending Internal Armed Conflicts' in Carl Bruch, Carroll Muffett and Sandra S. Nichols (ed), *Governance, Natural Resources, and Post-conflict Peacebuilding* (Routledge 2016).

27 Matthew Saul, 'International Law and the Identification of an Interim Government to Lead Post-conflict Reconstruction' in Matthew Saul and James A Sweeney (ed), *International Law and Post-conflict Reconstruction Policy* (Routledge 2015).

28 Peter Vedel Kessing, 'The Use of Soft Law in Regulating Armed Conflict: From Jus in Bello to "Soft Law in Bello"?' in Stéphanie Lagoutte, Thomas Gammeltoft-Hansen and John

agreements tend to take a big part of sovereign rights and powers of the states which have been guaranteed for previously. Such an approach is necessary, since states usually establish themselves as a sovereign of a certain territory for which they have or claim rights to, but the post-conflict procedures simply can't accommodate such requests and demands after all. One very interesting example for this is Israel, which in fact has re-established its sovereignty today on the territory of the historic Israel, after more millennia, but having its sovereignty primarily deriving from others military power than its own. 'In this perspective, law has a necessary connection to the state, at least as soon as there is one.'[29] One of the main characteristics of post-conflict agreements before, and now as well, is their capacity to form and protect the sovereignty of states. If there is a state, there can be law, usually both are being formed on soft grounds primarily and, by time, transferring themselves into 'hard' and applicable forms.

It is therefore somewhat absurd that a certain great power would, for example, support the sovereignty of a smaller state instead of spreading its own, but certainly this has been an established trend recently from one side, while from the other, the influence on such a newly sovereign state and its inner and foreign policies can be seen as some form of neocolonialism[30] today. While larger states and, in specific, UNSC permanent member states have the ability to influence and control smaller states, it still is a *terra incognita* when they clash between themselves. 'A number of new soft law instruments have been adopted in the last two decades regulating areas of armed conflict that states have been unwilling or unable to regulate in treaty law.'[31] As was seen earlier, such regulations only apply to smaller states while the permanent members of the UNSC would not be so keen to submit their sovereignty to any kind of such possible limitations. When we mention *terra incognita* in the correlation between states, we will see it in the following chapters how states behave

Cerone (ed), *Tracing the Roles of Soft Law in Human Rights* (Oxford University Press 2016).

29 Bart van Klink, 'Can There Be Law without the State? The Ehrlich-Kelsen Debate Revisited in a Globalizing Setting' in Hanneke van Schooten and Jonathan Verschuuren (ed), *International Governance and Law: State Regulation and Non-state Law* (Edward Elgar 2008).

30 Oseni Taiwo Afisi, 'Neocolonialism' <https://iep.utm.edu/neocolon/> accessed 22 March 2026.

31 Peter Vedel Kessing, 'The Use of Soft Law in Regulating Armed Conflict: From Jus in Bello to "Soft Law in Bello"?' in Stéphanie Lagoutte, Thomas Gammeltoft-Hansen and John Cerone (ed), *Tracing the Roles of Soft Law in Human Rights* (Oxford University Press 2016).

today in such environments, namely in their mutual relationship regarding, e.g. the Antarctica and the research of the Outer Space.

Finally, as reciprocity in general does exist between UNSC member-states in the framework of post-conflict development, they tend to refute the influence of each other in various societies; they also tend to cooperate in areas where they can benefit proportionally the most to the amount of the resources they have invested in a given process. Similarly to this, the same reciprocity applies to each and every citizen of a post-conflict society where they are asked to give up certain rights in order to be able to benefit from a greater goal of peace, reconciliation and development, which is entailed in the implementation of every post-conflict agreement. 'A thicker version of reconciliation is "democratic reciprocity," in which former enemies come to respect one another as fellow citizens with whom they now deliberate over the future of their country.'[32] This is the final and ultimate aim of such agreements to re-establish the trust between former enemies to such a level that they are able to build their future together and see how a certain agreement is serving their own good, therefore it has to be respected, protected and cherished by everyone after all.

32 Daniel Philpott, *The Politics of Past Evil: Religion, Reconciliation, and the Dilemmas of Transitional Justice* (University of Notre Dame Press 2006).

CHAPTER 2

Forms of Informal Rules in the International Arena

The most important actor and factor in the development of soft law instruments is the authority which is issuing or supporting a certain solution agreed (in)formally by the parties. In the framework of post-conflict resolution and development, it is the patron state which is able to successfully influence both parties. While it is not necessary for the patron state to be directly involved and be a signatory to the agreed terms, it would suffice to acknowledge its existence in some direct or indirect way, which is usually coming through its political acknowledgement. In a later phase it can be outlined and quoted directly regarding some of its agreed terms, which are deemed necessary to be strengthened, clarified or finally implemented. 'Across specifications, we find that strong recommendations had statistically and substantively significant effects, whereas weak recommendations made no difference.'[1] Therefore, when an authority 'strongly' recommends some acts it makes a difference than when it is just recommended as a simple path to be taken in a given direction. Also, when the UN Secretary General is 'deeply concerned'[2] in certain situations it can possibly also trigger the action of some other UN bodies. In a framework of local politics it can be seen as a critique, which is not producing legal but solely political effects and responsibilities. 'At this stage, however, I want to suggest that the non-binding directives of international authorities can be seen as a form of authoritative advice.'[3] Such authoritative advices are not to be followed immediately and exactly as stated, but they are meant to give some hints of what needs to be achieved in the future or regarding a certain issue which is going to happen. Again the lack of legal tools is obvious and parties can only have political responsibility in such cases after all.

Accordingly, when we approach the timeframes and possible legal outcomes regarding agreements which have been agreed by the parties them-

1 Katerina Linos and Tom Pegram, 'The Language of Compromise in International Agreements' (2016) 70 International Organization 587.

2 United Nations, 'Secretary-General Deeply Concerned about Continued Clashes in Sudan, Strongly Condemns Deaths, Injuries of Civilians' (16 April 2023) <https://press.un.org/en/2023/sgsm21764.doc.htm> accessed 22 March 2026.

3 Andrei Marmor, 'Soft Law, Authoritative Advice and Non-binding Agreements' (2019) 39 Oxford Journal of Legal Studies 507.

selves the situation is similar. 'So we might think that the non-binding agreement between the parties is essentially a commitment to try, not a commitment to do or to accomplish.'[4] Therefore, the clear commitment to achieve a certain goal and outcome is not fully and legally guaranteed, it is rather a path to be followed. Certainly it does not consist of just one try and in the case of failure the cancellation of the final obligation. The mere act to try is a prolonged situation when in a longer period of time an outcome has to be achieved and everything needs to be done in order to do so. Regarding this issue of making a try, one of the main components is also the harmonization of acts with other stakeholders among which there is also the other party of the given post-conflict agreement. 'In the absence of specific legal forms available for this kind of coordination, soft law is almost inevitably the chosen vehicle through which coordination is ensured.'[5] The soft law application and implementation phase consists of more soft law acts in sum, and all the acts on the path and before a certain agreement and solution are achieved do not become hard law automatically.

It is also a characteristic of such soft laws that they might have different forms in coming both from the authoritative body issuing them and the local framework of implementation. Locally for instance an actor might conform to the request of the soft law and regulate the issue accordingly while the other authority might still be completely unaware of its existence, which does not lower its need to implement it after all. Also, local authorities might have different forms of applying the same requirement, which might be often unclear and confusing but certainly producing the same legal effects on the end. 'The role of reason as a governor of action varies, and so then does the extent to which action is arbitrary.'[6] Such actions can be free and arbitrary as long as it is reasonable and they do not produce contrary effects in specific to other articles of the given agreement. Implementing a certain article in various phases or the full agreement's implementation does not allow a party to lower the importance of other articles and disrespect them, also to make the application of some requirements impossible in the future.

4 Ibid.

5 Matthias Knauff, 'Coronavirus and Soft Law in Germany: Business as Usual?' (2021) 12 European Journal of Risk Regulation 45.

6 Martin Krygier, 'Philip Selznick: Incipient Law, State Law and the Rule of Law' in Hanneke van Schooten and Jonathan Verschuuren (ed), *International Governance and Law: State Regulation and Non-state Law* (Edward Elgar 2008).

1 Informal Rules and Sovereignty

The influence of soft law agreements on some components of state sovereignties are very actual and important to understand. While the most important step in informal rule-making is the fact that sovereignty is not in any form taken from a state but an obligation or a commitment to revise its sovereignty, in certain aspects, it is what is given. It can be observed that after the conflict it is the best possible moment to make or revise a given state's future constitution, which in that case can better conform to various requests and the given post-conflict agreement. 'For the constitutions to contribute to societal cohesion rather than conflict, peace must be brokered outside of the constitution-making process, and remedial measures must be undertaken to increase broad public engagement and support for the constitutions among major constituencies.'[7] Accordingly, states have to be able to step into the stadium of peace development where they can fully guarantee development to their own citizens and also possibly have guarantees from outside that they have the sovereignty, which is necessary to establish their own constitutional frameworks in this regard.

In the sense of the EU and the future EU membership, sovereignty is the key factor, while also some interesting exceptions can be observed, such as in Cyprus. In this case, the exception is that Cyprus is in fact not controlling the northern part of its territory. Since Cyprus was invaded from the north by Turkey, a few decades ago, this military act has established a specific and unrecognized Turkish Republic in Northern Cyprus. On the other side, Turkey was very keen to support Azerbaijan in suppressing the unrecognized Nagorno-Karabakh Republic and overall push towards shrinking the Armenian statehood in any possible form. Finally, Turkey will most likely cooperate with the new *de facto* states made by Russia in the Black Sea region primarily in Ukraine, which will be making Turkey the most important security player on the EU borders towards the Middle East. In the following chapters we will discuss Turkey, its importance and influence in more detail regarding The Nagorno-Karabakh final agreement, its resolution and the possible future status of Armenians inside Azerbaijan.

The main characteristic of soft law therefore remains its application regarding unfinished political resolutions of some post-conflict situations. 'In addition to facilitating low-cost collaboration, soft law serves as a driver for a collective approach to international engagement; countries can tackle complex,

7 Darin E.W. Johnson, 'Post-conflict Constitution-Making' in Paul R. Williams and Milena Sterio (ed), *Research Handbook on Post-conflict State Building* (Edward Elgar 2020).

quickly evolving global problems that cannot be addressed unilaterally.'[8] Accordingly, soft law and informal rules are a good mechanism for achieving quick and long-lasting solutions, which are agreed and have a consensus from the highest possible number of stakeholders, especially in the framework of post-conflict societies. Many times such agreements can even accommodate changes for the future, but by now it has been established that what needs to be hardly changed is better to be left outside the agreement or just mentioned for future reference as a potential. Soft law is evidently a phase in developing a solution which incorporates other future steps, if not more than the final outcome of the soft law becoming hard law on the end. All this proves that the process of international treaty making is not easy, it has in fact never been, and it is in particular true for the post-conflict societies where some sort of solution or 'law' needs to be achieved very quickly. 'A plethora of agreement forms are emerging to fill the void left by the decline in treaty making: charters, codes of conduct, declarations, etc.'[9] It is also evident that post-conflict agreements have a very specific name, which does not directly follow what has been agreed or even what the real intention of the parties has been to agree about. Why a certain agreement is a post-conflict peace agreement is the fact that there is a certain international stakeholder, a so-called patron state, which deems such an agreement necessary. Such an influential state is also guaranteeing by its authority that the animosities have ended, and that the parties have actually reached an agreement, which will ultimately stop the conflict.

It has been in many instances characteristic for post-conflict agreements that they are using a wording in their own text, which is more unclear and not easily determinable in what kind of final outcome the parties have agreed. 'At the very minimum, one must reckon with "general" and "specific" obligations, the "tripartite classification" of state obligations ("respect", "protect", "fulfil"), "minimum core obligations", as well as obligations of "conduct" and "outcome", and violations "through act of commission" or "through omission".'[10] As we are trying to round up the discussion on what is written and what needs

8 Chris Brummer, *Soft Law and the Global Financial System: Rule Making in the 21st Century* (Cambridge University Press 2015).

9 Joanne Irene Gabrynowicz, 'The UN Principles Relating to Remote Sensing of the Earth from Outer Space and Soft Law' in Irmgard Marboe (ed), *Soft Law in Outer Space: The Function of Non-binding Norms in International Space Law* (Böhlau Verlag 2012).

10 Mátyás Bódig, 'Soft Law, Doctrinal Development, and the General Comments of the UN Committee on Economic, Social and Cultural Rights' in Stéphanie Lagoutte, Thomas Gammeltoft-Hansen and John Cerone (ed), *Tracing the Roles of Soft Law in Human Rights* (Oxford University Press 2016).

to be achieved, we can conclude that the intention is the key requirement and the bare wording does not have any power or a fixed outcome. Just as flexible the wording of the agreements is, the same is true to the fact that something might be a political declaration rather than a soft law agreement. Also, it is important to mention that politically some things can't be promised or expected without a partnership, e.g. peace in a certain region can't be achieved without having an agreement with all in the conflict-participating countries. Guaranteeing to every state the same equal treatment and also to every individual the same level of human rights usually needs many compromises, which can be achieved by hard cuts for what the most appropriate tools are informal agreements. The level of power of such guarantees is in the fact that a wide array of people follow it, have trust in it and expect it to be respected, putting it high on the political agenda of a certain society, state and region. 'Within the human rights field, soft law has often played a norm filling or a norm-creating role.'[11] It brings up to the level of a law something that was not respected and completely ignored previously, although was expected to be regulated and also is a human right in general, but without a enforcement mechanism in the present local circumstances.

Therefore, soft law agreements do tend to include and shape some sovereign rights and are obviously able to do so in a very transparent and presumably democratic way. When we say democratic it necessarily entails the right of all and everyone to do so and follow such a pattern, while in international law it applies to states, which can act similarly as another state did previously. Many times such acts can be problematic but more than welcome by others since they see it as a good example, or excuse, to achieve something they otherwise wouldn't be able to. 'The fluidity of custom is demonstrated by the present debate over whether NATO's intervention in Kosovo has formed the basis for an emerging customary right to unilateral humanitarian intervention.'[12] In this regard this intervention has nullified the importance of the UN as a dominant post-conflict player and regulator and has let the five UNSC permanent member states regulate their own domains and interests globally according to their own present needs. As we can see it today Russia does not see any illegitimacy in intervening in Ukraine while also China does not see any legal obstacle of a possible future intervention in Taiwan. Obviously acts in the framework of international politics are making informal rules

11 Peter Vendel Kessing, 'Soft Law Instruments Regulating Armed Conflict: Are International Human Rights Standards Reflected' (2018) 12 Hum Rts & Int'l Legal Discourse 79.

12 Anthea Elizabeth Roberts, 'Traditional and Modern Approaches to Customary International Law: A Reconciliation' (2001) 95 The American Journal of International Law 757.

that have the capacity of becoming customs in a form of a soft law primarily, which can later be accordingly invoked by others in similar situations.

2 Antarctica and the Outer Space

2.1 Antarctica and the Arctic

When we try to understand the practicalities of post-conflict development and make some logical conclusions we are evidently in a need to have some corresponding arguments, which can support our ideas and claims. Why certain laws are being made in such a way they are, who and how is influencing them and finally is there a chance for a success for all the informal rules in the framework of post-conflict resolution and development? There are certainly some other aspects of not-so-legally regulated territories in the sphere of international law and we can't find a better word than to call them *terra incognita* or *terra nullius* of International Law. In this category we definitely need to mention two areas or territories, which are the continent of Antarctica and the endless area of the Outer Space. 'Outer Space and the frozen continent, Antarctica, have been widely perceived as areas reserved for peace and science.'[13] Due to their specific location, distance and technical requirements to reach them, research them and finally be able to use them they are considered as *terra nullius* at the moment. It is not the case that no one would like to own them and have sovereignty over them but their value and the need to primarily research them before is much more complex, than just establishing a certain state's sovereignty. As these two areas of the globe and the universe are reserved for peace and science they are able to give us many answers of what and how can be regulated while achieving a situation without conflicts or any form of interest enforcement or will to own them. Obviously these two parts of the globe or the universe are, for now, regulated by some kind of International (Soft) Law.

It is also worth mentioning here that the area covered by the Arctic, which is not a land mass but an ice mass covering the territory of the Northern Pole, is to be regulated as well. Strategically lying between the USA and Russia this area has an obvious importance, but again the harsh weather conditions make it less attractive. 'Despite the common grounds on sustainable development,

13 Steven Freeland and Anja Nakarada Pecujlic, 'How Do You like Your Regulation – Hard or Soft? The Antarctic Treaty and the Outer Space Treaty Compared' (2018) 30 National Law School of India Review 11.

the present-day Arctic is still far from the vision of a completely integrated region that is shaped by common interests and aims.'[14] While it is not just the harsh weather conditions that make such places not attractive it is also the cost–value parity, which makes any endeavour here financially unstable, for now. 'Equally, the economic opportunities in the Arctic come with great risks and potential negative impacts that affect other regions beyond the Arctic.'[15] As long as there is no obvious economical or strategic benefit of controlling such offshore destinations there is very little interest in investing both efforts and resources in owing something which can't be turned into an economic or military advantage. Cooperation in such regions is essential and the need to protect them for future generations is of a vital and primary importance. The regulation of such areas can again be influenced by various means of non-formal acts present today becoming potentially a custom while also the future potentials of technology and science in correlation to the specific needs have to be preserved.

2.2 The Outer Space

Probably one of the biggest successes of reconciliation between the two biggest nuclear powers, being USA and The Soviet Union previously, is definitely the area of the Outer Space. After the space race and many controversial actions, including the moon landing, this area remains largely out of reach to humanity for now. It is either the unavailability of this area or the simple high cost of using it as both a warfare area and exploitation area that for now it has been put under strict control. Due to financial and technological issues the Earth's orbit is for now more economically viable to exploit and share, mainly using it for satellite technology development needed for communication purposes.

Some practices which are again rooted in their economic feasibility have produced as an outcome a very peaceful use of the Outer Space without the need to further regulate it for now. Such practices of using the Outer Space can be deemed now to be as a soft law of space activities, which is in a constant phase of development and following the most recent technological advances. 'However, as a consequence of State practice and compliance with them they

---

14 Kong Soon Lim, 'Soft Law Instruments on Arctic Investment and Sustainable Development' (2020) 56 Polar Record 1.

15 Ibid.

may turn into rules of customary law.'[16] Even if a certain document is signed and becomes law in any sense regulating Outer Space it could be a technological advance or simply the time which opens up other uncovered areas, which then again need to be regulated or covered by some future agreements. Just as it is the case in the Outer Space regulations so is the case with the changes in any post-conflict framework where time can play an important role and make some articles less applicable, while some new ones much needed. 'Treaties properly ratified and having entered into force are of course binding upon the States concerned as "hard law", but what if they provide for obligations too general or too vague to be useful in any particular dispute?'[17] As long as there is no authority to oversee and judge them in the cases of disrespecting some Outer Space clauses it is necessary for states to use them in the best interest of the humankind and the benefit of all.

Here we also need to add that the status of the UN has changed in the previous decades and it has lost its importance as an arena for discussing the most burning issues of today's societies, concerning both the post-conflict territories but also potentially the Outer Space issues as well. 'That said, as noted, the adoption of recommendations and resolutions by the UN marked a transition in developing international space law from hard to soft law, by the body principally regarded as being responsible for the "creation" of space law.'[18] This level of freedom allowed by the UN, which has been using its democratic nature and let actors shape their acts and legal frameworks according to their own will. This is similar to post-conflict areas where actors are again having a free hand to regulate and shape the societies according to their own will, while respecting the most basic provisions coming from the UN and the general necessity to respect human rights. 'The nonbinding nature of the Space Principles Declaration is further emphasised by the very next Resolution passed on the same day by the United Nations General Assembly.'[19] The UN has understood that it can't control all aspects of the Outer

---

16 Fabio Tronchetti, 'A Soft Law Approach to Prevent the Weaponisation of Outer Space' in Irmgard Marboe (ed), *Soft Law in Outer Space: The Function of Non-binding Norms in International Space Law* (Böhlau Verlag 2012).

17 Frans von der Dunk, 'Contradictio in Terminis or Realpolitik ? A Qualified Plea for a Role of "Soft Law" in the Context of Space Activities' in Irmgard Marboe (ed), *Soft Law in Outer Space: The Function of Non-binding Norms in International Space Law* (Böhlau Verlag 2012).

18 Steven Freeland and Anja Nakarada Pecujlic, 'How Do You Like Your Regulation – Hard or Soft? The Antarctic Treaty and the Outer Space Treaty Compared' (2018) 30 National Law School of India Review 11.

19 Steven Freeland, 'The Role of "Soft Law" in Public International Law and Its Relevance to the International Legal Regulation of Outer Space' in Irmgard Marboe (ed), *Soft Law in*

Space explorations and foresee each and every situation. It has accordingly left it to the parties interested in such explorations while it has remained the observer, having in fact the authority to finally comment and request regarding any potential future misuse – similarly to the authority which is being established by a patron state observing the implementation of a given non-formal agreement in the framework of post-conflict development. 'Addressing highly technical issues, it is preferable that guidelines regulating such activities should exclude political compromise as much as possible and should be expeditiously updated and amended according to the latest scientific developments and technological progress.'[20] There is a need to remain as an observer to the development and technological advances to which the UN would not in any case have the required technical knowledge and capabilities to understand.

The UN is still there to observe and raise its voice in case something is going wrong or there is a misuse of power or a position of some space exploring states. 'Many emerging and future space States are concerned that if a process is taken outside the United Nations, they will have significantly less influence in the direction and content of such an initiative.'[21] We can observe that as much as there is no need to interfere or control the given situation, there is definitely the need to observe and have common sense, which will be able to raise a voice or simply serve as the place where disagreements can be further discussed. Obviously there is a parallel structure of an observing authority being present in Outer Space research and post-conflict resolution and development where authorities are needed to control and align various positions keeping the necessary distance and neutrality.

Further there is another perspective, which is important to mention and again functions the same way in Outer Space and post-conflict environments where the majority of informal expert organizations are in a position to positively comment, advise and influence such acts and situations. 'With so many non-governmental entities involved in space activities today, it may be challenging for a government to exercise authorisation and continuing supervi-

---

Outer Space: The Function of Non-binding Norms in International Space Law (Böhlau Verlag 2012).

20 Setsuko Aoki, 'The Function of "Soft Law" in the Development of International Space Law' in Irmgard Marboe (ed), *Soft Law in Outer Space: The Function of Non-binding Norms in International Space Law* (Böhlau Verlag 2012).

21 Ben Baseley-Walker, 'Analysing International Reactions to Soft Law Initiatives on Space Security' in Irmgard Marboe (ed), *Soft Law in Outer Space: The Function of Non-binding Norms in International Space Law* (Böhlau Verlag 2012).

sion, particularly if that country is new to space activities.'[22] When we come back to the cost-effective maintenance of certain research areas where there is a need to have expert organizations, the cost-benefit correlation proves that it is again better to cooperate and have resources gathered in one centre from where they can be used and redistributed for both the present and future use.

Accordingly, when there is a contact point it is easier to have it as a place to discuss misunderstandings and reach agreements, and again such agreements would be highly informal but very technically and practically applicable to the given problem. 'In the case of an accident involving a space nuclear power source, the global public as well as the media would likely make little difference whether the safety guidance the main actors had not followed was contained in a binding document or in an internationally agreed, though non-binding safety framework.'[23] Ultimately there is one more similarity between these agreements related to spaces where there is the highest priority given to the fact that conflicts and accidents need to be as a matter of prevention fully excluded and for this the form of informal regulations are perfectly enough for now. In the sense of technical developments it is simply impossible to use the legal ways of long discussions of giving power and authority to a certain body while there is a need to act in a matter of hours and minutes in order to solve potential future problems or some potential accidents. This time constraint is the most necessary factor that will help understand and see why some professional bodies and actors have the power to make informal rules and how in a short term such regulations can become hard law without initially having an intention to become one. 'These functions prove that the practice of soft law in space activities is a generally recognised system resulting from common interests and goals.'[24] It can be concluded that there is an obvious connection between the Outer Space law development and post-conflict law development where the initial phase of having an informal rule quickly, as a matter of need represents the urgent law making capacity for both areas. Both areas tend to be regulated using universal principles of equality and technical

22 Werner Balogh, 'The Role of Binding and Non-binding Norms in the Implementation of Small Satellite Programmes' in Irmgard Marboe (ed), *Soft Law in Outer Space: The Function of Non-binding Norms in International Space Law* (Böhlau Verlag 2012).

23 Leopold Summerer and Ulrike M. Bohlmann, 'The STSC/IAEA Safety Framework for Space Nuclear Power Source Applications: Influence of Non-binding Recommendations' in Irmgard Marboe (ed), *Soft Law in Outer Space: The Function of Non-binding Norms in International Space Law* (Böhlau Verlag 2012).

24 Marco Ferrazzani, 'Soft Law in Space Activities: An Updated View' in Irmgard Marboe (ed), *Soft Law in Outer Space: The Function of Non-binding Norms in International Space Law* (Böhlau Verlag 2012).

advance corresponding to the needs and the capacity of the whole human race and civilization as such.

3 Nuclear Power and Weapons Regulation

The rising demand and possible shortages of energy are making us face the new challenge of how to use and regulate nuclear power in the future. The traditional gas-and-oil-run economy is seriously challenged and its imports endangered. A major disturbance can occur from the whole borderline between EU towards Russia but also including Turkey and the Russian-controlled Caucasus. 'In many cases, nuclear energy and natural gas has been substituted by coal, an outcome that clearly was not the intention of Europe's climate policies.'[25] In this regard we are facing a double challenge where the question is whether nuclear energy can be claimed to be green? Since it is not a renewable energy source it is in our opinion hard to be conceived as green, while some might argue differently. While we are not aiming at defining and discussing its nature we certainly need to research its application and potentials in the rising trend of energy demand. 'Because soft law instruments such as principles are not legally binding, they are expressed in general terms which are flexible and can be easily adapted to different needs, encouraging States to adhere to the notions embodied within without making States feel coerced.'[26] Logically in this sphere just as in many other fields in which it is hard to regulate, such as post-conflict societies or space exploration and the like, we have the soft law regulation of nuclear energy as well. 'As has been shown, the Principles are, essentially, a soft law instrument drafted in such a way as to be as vague and general as possible so no-one would see any reason not to comply with the provisions contained therein.'[27] The dangers in nuclear power are commonly

25 Brenda Shaffer, 'European Union Energy Policy: The Role of the South Caucasus' in Kornely Kakachia, Stefan Meister and Benjamin Fricke (ed), *Geopolitics and Security: A New Strategy for the South Caucasus* (Konrad-Adenauer-Stiftung 2018).

26 Daniel A. Porras, 'The United Nations Principles Relevant to the Use of Nuclear Power Sources in Outer Space : The Significance of a Soft Law Instrument after Nearly 20 Years in Force' in Irmgard Marboe (ed), *Soft Law in Outer Space: The Function of Non-binding Norms in International Space Law* (Böhlau Verlag 2012).

27 Daniel A. Porras, 'The United Nations Principles Relevant to the Use of Nuclear Power Sources in Outer Space : The Significance of a Soft Law Instrument after Nearly 20 Years in Force' in Irmgard Marboe (ed), *Soft Law in Outer Space: The Function of Non-binding Norms in International Space Law* (Böhlau Verlag 2012).

known to everyone and are such that no one sees an interest in breaching such soft law regulations, while in some other cases this can't be claimed.

While some general aspects of nuclear use and regulations might be found in soft law forms, the overall need and control over it is highly formalized and accordingly followed by all the relevant stakeholders. The various phases and acts in this regard need approval, which is a more formal process, usually implying a written permission for an operator to perform specified activities.[28] In regard to soft laws in nuclear energy regulation, there is no such divide in the international community like elsewhere. It can be stated that the nuclear regulation itself and the follow-up on it is more serious and includes the widest possible array of stakeholders. At some instances it is more serious than in fact the issue of recognizing or not recognizing a certain post-conflict society, where the division and the frozen conflict can last even for decades. As we are approaching another possibility of a conflict resolution in Ukraine it is necessary to mention the previously established norms and in particular soft law norms in this regard. A Memorandum from 2014 signed in Budapest deals in particular with the status of Ukraine in regard its nuclear weapons. At that time Ukraine had given up its arsenal for a common good and security guarantees in a multiparty agreement including Russia. As the situation has changed in the past 30 years we need to see how and why such Memorandums in a soft law form has limited application or is completely inapplicable. The commitment of Ukraine to eliminate all nuclear weapons from its territory,[29] some 30 years ago certainly did not foresee a full military attack by Russia on its soil. In particular, it is necessary to outline the guarantees Ukraine has received at that time in regard the respect of the independence and sovereignty and the existing borders of Ukraine.[30] Russia has interfered in Ukraine claiming a very specific role and it is hard to see what future relationship these two countries might have.

28 Leopold Summerer and Ulrike M. Bohlmann, 'The STSC/IAEA Safety Framework for Space Nuclear Power Source Applications: Influence of Non-binding Recommendations' in Irmgard Marboe (ed), *Soft Law in Outer Space: The Function of Non-binding Norms in International Space Law* (Böhlau Verlag 2012).

29 Ukraine, Russian Federation, United Kingdom of Great Britain and Northern Ireland and United States of America, 'Memorandum on security assurances in connection with Ukraine's accession to the Treaty on the Non-proliferation of Nuclear Weapons' (1994) Budapest, 5 December 1994, No. 52,241 <https://treaties.un.org/Pages/showDetails.aspx?objid=080000028040 1fbb > accessed 22 March 2026.

30 Ibid.

It is not just Ukraine, which has the issue of nuclear threat included in the conflict; some aspects in this regard can connect us also to Afghanistan. President Biden explained that the US military withdrawal was necessary because in Afghanistan other strategic challenges have emerged such as the intensifying competition with China and Russia and the threat of cyberattacks and nuclear proliferation.[31] We can see that the issue of controlling and potentially using nuclear weapons does influence the resolution and developments in some post-conflict societies. 'These interests in what happens within Afghanistan are closely related to the key U.S. interest in South Asia of preventing nuclear war between Pakistan and India and preventing nuclear terrorism as a result of Pakistan's nuclear weapons falling into the hands of a terrorist group.'[32] While it is possible that China has used Pakistan as a proxy to influence and disturb the US presence in Afghanistan, it is not likely that any kind of nuclear threat has really been included in this case. USA has left Afghanistan with an aim to strengthen its positions in other more important regions in regard its foreign policy overall.

Russia was overall keen to comply with various laws and standards coming from international organizations before. Unfortunately, recently it is not the case and it does not seem to have an interest to do so any longer, especially regarding the environment where no hard laws were introduced ever globally. There is the case of Russia's failure to report on dumping of decommissioned nuclear submarines core reactors in coastal waters and whaling catches,[33] which is just an example of how the environment is ignored and money saved for some presumably more important activities. While the protection of nature is commonly being sidelined more and more by many stakeholders globally, it is still to be seen how the deepening division in world politics can regulate the use of nuclear power and weapons in the future. Due to the flexible nature of soft law instruments, technical disagreements were willingly sidestepped so as to permit the continuation of work without all parties hav-

---

31 Kurita Masahiro, 'Great Power Politics over Afghanistan after the U.S. Withdrawal' [2022] NIDS East Asian Strategic Review <http://www.nids.mod.go.jp/english/publication/east-asian/pdf/2022/e01.pdf> accessed 22 March 2026.

32 Vanda Felbab-Brown, 'A bri(dge) too far: The Unfulfilled promise and limitations of China's Involvement in Afghanistan' [2020] Global China: Regional influence and strategy <https://www.brookings.edu/wp-content/uploads/2020/06/FP_20200615_china_afghanistan_felbab_brown.pdf> accessed 22 March 2026.

33 Peter M. Haas, 'Choosing to Comply: Theorizing from International Relations and Comparative Politics' in Dinah Shelton (ed), *Commitment and Compliance: The Role of Non-Binding Norms in the International Legal System* (Oxford University Press 2000).

ing to dig in their heels for each and every discussion.[34] In global politics connected to soft law regulations we can conclude that cherry-picking will be the most commonly used path of dealing with problems and using the relevant rules just to the extent one feels comfortable. Finally, it remains to see what exactly and in which form Ukraine is ready to agree with Russia and with which guarantees, since the sole fact of concluding agreements in a soft law form did not prove to be an efficient tool in the past.

4 Other Non-formal Law Authorities and Their Aspects

For a better understanding of some general non-formal authoritative documents which do have some extent or capacity to be enforced we will list now some examples and practices in this chapter. It should be outlined that frequently a certain non-formal law or requirement has more different phases of being made and developed; such phases and corresponding documents characterizing it could also have different names. 'Put another way: the document is soft law and the Principles and Guidelines are evidence of law and sometimes policy or practice.'[35] Such principles and guidelines do not necessarily be the same for all parties, or at least their path of execution can be very different whereas they tend to ultimately guarantee the same outcome. In many instances there are specific bodies whose advices and practices need to be followed in order to achieve a certain goal, they serve the alignment purposes and are frequently covering very important aspects of both implementing the law and also explaining its actual nature. 'If the link is not made carefully in legislation, the non-state organization can easily be seen as an administrative authority to which all kinds of public regulations apply.'[36] Accordingly it should not be the case that a specific body in any moment and aspect overtakes the regular authority and the mandate of state bodies,

---

34 Daniel A. Porras, 'The United Nations Principles Relevant to the Use of Nuclear Power Sources in Outer Space : The Significance of a Soft Law Instrument after Nearly 20 Years in Force' in Irmgard Marboe (ed), *Soft Law in Outer Space: The Function of Non-binding Norms in International Space Law* (Böhlau Verlag 2012).

35 Bruce 'Ossie' Oswald, 'The Copenhagen Process: Some Reflections Concerning Soft Law' in Stéphanie Lagoutte, Thomas Gammeltoft-Hansen and John Cerone (ed), *Tracing the Roles of Soft Law in Human Rights* (Oxford University Press 2016).

36 Hans Peters, 'The Influence of Court Judgements on Non-state Law' in Hanneke van Schooten and Jonathan Verschuuren (ed), *International Governance and Law: State Regulation and Non-state Law* (Edward Elgar 2008).

while in many instances it can form and shape it in what it sees would be the best way and applicable for its future development.

4.1 Trade Regulation

Apart from scientific, security, health[37] and other purposes there is a very important sphere of life where many organizations are reshaping the actual trends of business – those are obviously all the companies in their wide variety of forms present today in different jurisdiction globally. Such companies are using the same excuses as the scientific ones are and aim at reshaping and forming the world to do business according to their needs and expectations, before state authorities can even understand such changes. 'The polycentric nature of governance means that there is much greater emphasis on the exercise of power by private actors, eg, corporations and insurance companies.'[38] The constant need and necessity to develop and make profit and business elsewhere in the world pushed companies supported by their respective governments to find alternative ways to do business.

One of the best examples of this is the Chinese made BRI[39] Initiative. This project reflects largely the critical idea behind the whole Chinese economy of finding alternative ways to get resources and sell products globally. This Initiative will be later explained into more detail in further chapters and also how China treats its needs and efforts to connect better the East to the West by the means of trade. The Chinese Government is doing everything to make the implementation of its Initiative as smooth as possible and also resilient to possible local legal requirements, authorities and changes. 'For example, soft law that is incorporated by reference would be subject to all mandatory rules of local law, whereas soft law chosen as governing law would only be subject to "overriding" mandatory rules of local law.'[40] Also, it is necessary to mention here the Arbitrations since they are also able to make certain solutions, which do have an authority of a state but are initially not coming from a body having the authority of a state.

---

37 Fruzsina Molnár-Gábor, 'Soft Law: Bindung Ohne Fesseln?' [2022] Weich & Hart <https://heiup.uni-heidelberg.de/journals/rupertocarola/article/view/24585/18481> accessed 22 March 2026.

38 Imelda Maher, 'Revisiting Soft Law: Governance, Regulation and Networks' in Mariolina Eliantonio, Emilia Korkea-aho and Oana Ştefan (ed), *EU Soft Law in the Member States: Theoretical Findings and Empirical Evidence* (Hart 2021).

39 Office of the Leading Group for Promoting the Belt and Road Initiative, 'Belt and Road Portal' <https://eng.yidaiyilu.gov.cn/> accessed 22 March 2026.

40 Steven L. Schwarcz, 'Soft Law as Governing Law' (2020) 104 Minnesota Law Review 247.

4.2 Arbitration Aspects

It is evident that as close a certain party is to a certain arbitral institution it raises its chances of being awarded a decision, which would comfort better to its needs. In this regard we can also find some solutions of how to achieve a just and fairer decision by choosing or even changing a relevant arbitration institution after it has not been determined but is determinable by some informal rules. 'Soft law can also be used as a tool for uniform interpretation of the rules of arbitral institution, that are often drafted without any connection to the seat of the institution, because their character should be international since the seat of arbitration is usually determined by the parties.'[41] Such aspects of the Arbitration are a very important actor in the conflict and dispute resolution mechanism system of the business world and are also worth mentioning here as we are witnessing various aspects of rules being invented after an agreement has been reached. Obviously arbitrations also gain their authority from the agreements or a treaty, which at the time of ratification or signing did not have clear rules and paths to follow. 'That the parties, in the frame of arbitration, may choose to replace the governing law with soft sources, however, is not sufficient to ensure a harmonization of the general contract law.'[42] Arbitration can be considered in the business world as a trend which is rising similarly to the trend of how informal rules and their importance are rising in the world of post-conflict development.

4.3 The Open Balkan Initiative

Here it is worth mentioning an interesting solution or system being made in the framework of some Western Balkan countries which are not members of the EU but are keen to become, one day. This is the Open Balkan[43] initiative, which makes EU-like solutions of trade liberalization possible in some coun-

41 Miluše Hrnčiříková, 'The Meaning of Soft Law in International Commercial Arbitration' (2016) 16 International and Comparative Law Review 97.

42 Giuditta Cordero-Moss, 'Soft Law Codifications in the Area of Commercial Law' in Andrea K. Bjorklund and August Reinisch (ed), *International Investment Law and Soft Law* (Edward Elgar Publishing 2012).

43 Albanian Government, 'Important Cooperation Agreements Signed at Open Balkan Summit' (2 September 2022) <https://www.kryeministria.al/en/newsroom/nenshkruhen-marreveshje-te-rendesishme-bashkepunimi-ne-samitin-per-ballkanin-e-hapur-beograd/> accessed 22 March 2026.
Accessible also in a Serbian source: <https://en.pks.rs/open-balkan>
Accessible also in a North Macedonian source: https://customs.gov.mk/en-GB/otvoren-balkan.nspx.

tries, which in fact do not have this as a priority of their future economic development but see it as a good tool to align their policies now with their neighbours, which will ultimately lead to an easier alignment to EU standards and requirements. At this point we approach the issue of what is more important to countries outside the EU and also the post-conflict ones, business development or human rights protection and how they are interconnected by a requirement for any kind of future development.

4.4 The UN Understanding

We also have such a similar system in the framework of the UN and its developments of soft law instruments. 'In consequence the integration of the business human rights responsibility discourse into a UN soft law instrument has inevitably led to the abandonment of any pretence that business enterprises should have actual human rights obligations.'[44] Now having this in mind it is obvious that the UN is not going to request any kind of responsibility on enterprises regarding human rights, but nevertheless regarding post-conflict peace agreements it will and probably this is one of their most important aspects. 'In contrast to this, the SDGs, by not taking the form of a legally binding document, allow for the options of becoming more inclusive and referring to a wider group of stakeholders than states only.'[45] Also at this moment it is necessary to mention the concerns UN and its member states do have regarding this correlation, so instead of bringing a mandatory or better said more authoritative UN treaty they have chosen a path of introducing Sustainable Development Goals (SDGs). While it is obvious how important SDGs are for the development of post-conflict societies at this moment, we are not going to explain them in more detail or apply them to our case studies later. It is nevertheless necessary to mention that actually every treaty and also post-conflict agreement is presumably taking SDGs into consideration and is having in it the possibility of being changed and aligned in the future according to certain SDG ideas and requirements. We can claim that SDGs are a real soft law made for the better understanding of post-conflict agreements

44 Stéphanie Lagoutte, 'The UN Guiding Principles on Business and Human Rights: A Confusing "Smart Mix" of Soft and Hard International Human Rights Law' in Stéphanie Lagoutte, Thomas Gammeltoft-Hansen and John Cerone (ed), *Tracing the Roles of Soft Law in Human Rights* (Oxford University Press 2016).

45 Marcel M. T. A. Brus, 'Soft Law in Public International Law: A Pragmatic or a Principled Choice? Comparing the Sustainable Development Goals and the Paris Agreement' in Pauline Westerman, Jaap Hage, Stephan Kirste and Anne Ruth Mackor, *Legal Validity and Soft Law* (Springer 2018).

as well, among others. While the directions of development in post-conflict societies can't be fully envisaged, neither can it be done for the business requirements or SDG applications after all.

4.5 Internet Regulation

The trend of having new business opportunities which are at the time of their implementation not legally regulated brings us to another important dimension of informal rules development. 'Most discussions about the new *lex mercatoria* and Internet law focus on non-state law *beyond* the national state.'[46] Internet is another aspect of human everyday life which can't be regulated or as said before foreseen in all of its future possible aspects. Internet is seen as freedom, which is used by humans in order to make their life and well-being easier to achieve. Although it would not be realistic to compare internet to a post-conflict environment while in fact it does have many aspects which need to be regulated informally before a formal agreement or solution can be achieved. It is both necessary to mention and understand the Internet in its technical and broader sense since it does now, and will also in the future, influence our lives and everyday activities to a greater extent. The importance of internet to influence businesses and also other aspects of life we are researching, like human rights, brings us to a conclusion that the Internet will be inevitably more and more the creator of the technical and artificial intelligence soft law of the future.

4.6 ISO Regulations

Another very important future concern, which has recently gained importance in the business world and is concerning consumer rights are The Internal Organization for Standardization (ISO) regulations, while they are being highly appreciated and also the key of success of many companies. Businesses have recognized and consumers are highly valuing such standards, which are helping them to make a decision in an informed manner when they are able to decide by not just knowing the price of a certain product but also by knowing its various qualities and in specific the conditions under which it was produced. Still the inclusion of ISO standards in a certain company or process has a cost and it has to be valued on a long term basis, which makes

46 Marc Hertogh, 'What Is Non-state Law? Mapping the Other Hemisphere of the Legal World' in Hanneke van Schooten and Jonathan Verschuuren (ed), *International Governance and Law: State Regulation and Non-state Law* (Edward Elgar 2008).

that important cost-to-benefit ratio a big concern. 'Thus many corporations, especially in the U.S., are taking a "wait-and-see" attitude toward ISO conformance.'[47] Since ISO is not a mandatory standard, its inclusion in a producing process is free to be taken, and the most important value it can have is the possible penetration into other markets where final consumers and more importantly distributors will be able to source goods of a certain kind and guarantee that it conforms to certain standards, requirements and expectations without even being present or controlling its production process. It is necessary to mention that ISO is a non-state related standardization or requirement where an independent body is giving a credit for a certain process or procedure. Obviously by respecting such non-state and non-mandatory regulations companies are having a better position on the market, which also ultimately guarantees higher revenues. 'It would seem that non-state law works when things are going well but is not effective on its own in the business world when there is deliberate non-compliance.'[48] We can assume that both in the business world and post-conflict development soft regulations apply and function as long as there is a common wide understanding for their necessity and benefit for all. In cases of disagreements the situation is more complex and it is hard to find a general solution for this as it is a fact that such informal rules are generally non-enforceable and that they are always missing the system of finding and applying the necessary enforcement mechanisms.

---

47 Naomi Roht-Arriaza, '"Soft Law" in a "Hybrid" Organization: The International Organization for Standardization' in Dinah Shelton (ed), *Commitment and Compliance: The Role of Non-Binding Norms in the International Legal System* (Oxford University Press 2000).

48 Jenny Job, 'Barristers beyond the Law: State and Non-state Actors Work in Partnership to Enforce Legal and Moral Norms' in Hanneke van Schooten and Jonathan Verschuuren (ed), *International Governance and Law: State Regulation and Non-state Law* (Edward Elgar 2008).

CHAPTER 3

Transformation of the Soft Law into Hard Law

1 What Paths Are to Be Taken for Soft Law to Become Hard Law

When we try to define soft law and its transition into hard law, it is necessary to take into consideration whether soft law has inherently such intentions at all. Considering the reasons why soft law has been made, it is obvious that there were some limitations to make it a hard law initially, accordingly soft law is just a step in regulating a certain legal problem in its broadest understanding, with a connection which is inevitably stemming from various political interests and decisions. While political decisions and priorities are changing, so is the case with the law which tries to accommodate the most recent needs and aspirations of humans and their societies, respectively. 'While *lex lata* is synonymous with existing law, the term *lex ferenda* is not identical to the proposed definition of soft law.'[1] Lex ferenda is the aim of what a certain society or system wants to achieve, what they are aiming at as an outcome or final solution; it is more like an idea which is being regulated, taking into consideration all the possibilities. In general, *lex lata* is a fact which should be or which could be achieved in the future, also in which regard, it is not possible now to determine exactly what way a law should take at the given moment. Overall, in this regard soft law is just a try by which something should be achieved obviously without any guarantees that it will be in fact achieved on the end.

In the same way, hard law does not guarantee its full application but has a system of punishments and sanctions behind them as a tool in helping in achieving its goals. 'There is no way to know with absolute certainty, at the adoption stage, which form a soft law instrument is likely to take in the future, and what kind of legal obligations could arise from it.'[2] So, as questionable now it is of how to implement a soft law, the same applies to its possible future

1 John Cerone, 'A Taxonomy of Soft Law: Stipulating a Definition' in Stéphanie Lagoutte, Thomas Gammeltoft-Hansen and John Cerone (ed), *Tracing the Roles of Soft Law in Human Rights* (Oxford University Press 2016).

2 Léticia Villeneuve, 'Could the Progressive "Hardening" of Human Rights Soft Law Impair Its Further Expansion?: Insights from the UN Declaration on the Rights of Indigenous Peoples' in Stéphanie Lagoutte, Thomas Gammeltoft-Hansen and John Cerone (ed), *Tracing the Roles of Soft Law in Human Rights* (Oxford University Press 2016).

enforcement or finally its existence after all. Not applying a soft law bares the risk of future possible sanctions, whereas applying it also risks that efforts could have been made in a wrong direction and accordingly wasted or not properly used. Many times, soft law does not give an exact path of its execution and is therefore giving freedom to try to implement. 'At the same time, light should be shed upon the fact that extra-legal requirements supporting arguments in legal interpretation will not necessarily become soft law just because it plays a role in the interpretation of a legal rule.'[3] So, as if there is a desire to implement a soft law, there is no authority which could align the acts necessary to confirm the requirements stemming out of such a soft law regulation.

There can be no court, professional body or an authority in any form which can say whether a soft law act has been implemented or applied. The actors to which the soft law applies can be various organizations, from which many can fall outside the forms required by statutory requirements and possibilities. 'Soft law which is considered soft only because the participants in the regime are not all nation-states or inter-governmental organizations is likely to be the first to be re-categorized, when nongovernmental organizations, and others join the legal system as full members.'[4] The actors in a soft law framework can be uncategorized and in this case, be soft actors, as they do not have the necessary legal acknowledgement.

Here, we come again to the most important point of our future work and research when we try to categorize and legalize various forms of governments present in unrecognized post-conflict settings. 'Most importantly, in the globalisation process the concept of soft law has increasingly been used to develop instruments and regimes that rely primarily on non-state actors in their making, implementation and enforcement.'[5] As there is a need to regulate and control some informal entities, there was also an obvious necessity to shape regulations which can't be hard law but obviously had to have more power and influence than bare political statements. Also, as applying international law to entities which are not part or able to represent themselves as bodies recognized by such law could not be possible, there is a need to find a solution which should keep such societies and entities outside the legal vacuum. Also,

3 László Blutman, 'In the Trap of a Legal Metaphor: International Soft Law' (2010) 59 The International and Comparative Law Quarterly 605.

4 Mary Ellen O'Connell, 'The Role of Soft Law in a Global Order' in Dinah Shelton (ed), *Commitment and Compliance: The Role of Non-Binding Norms in the International Legal System* (Oxford University Press 2000).

5 Ilhami Alkan Olsson, 'Four Competing Approaches to International Soft Law' (2013) 58 Scandinavian Studies In Law 177.

as they can't be treated according to the norms of international law, they are to be treated consequently by soft law norms. The norms and bodies which usually have the power to make hard law decisions are, in such post-conflict frameworks, making soft law decisions, which are then slowly transitioned into hard law. A prominent role here belongs to the connecting capacity between hierarchical norms,[6] when and where there is a need to align them more and make them more consistent.

Once a certain post-conflict society evolves to a stage where it is lawful and just enough to be part of the international community, its soft laws can become hard laws. In such cases of evolution, it is not necessarily post-conflict soft laws which evolve, they in fact disappear and do not apply directly any more. Their effects are what matters in that case and what brings the society into a stadium of a potential full recognition. Ultimately, we can say that it is in the best interest and the most paying off situation for a certain society to respect soft law regulations on its transitioning path from a post-conflict society to a prospective member of the international community. There can be no punishment in a legal sense for post-conflict societies but more in a moral sense, and of course political sanctions and critiques can also be applied.

Such examples can be seen as one alternative to soft law development, changes and transitions altogether within the society, for which it is made for and bind according to international laws. 'Soft law is largely used in international law as a working alternative to hard law'[7]. It also gives flexibility to actors in the framework of international law to develop, experiment and try finding a solution where they regulate a certain area on a step-by-step basis. Certainly, one of the biggest similarities which brings international soft and hard law closer is their thin line of enforcement, as hard laws made by international organizations also struggle many times to be applied. In the following chapters, we will be dealing with this problem in more detail and see how the enforcement mechanisms are working and functioning in regulating this thin line between soft and hard law enforcement solutions.

---

6 Matthias Knauff, 'Soft Law im europäischen Und internationalen Verwaltungsrecht' in Wolfgang Kahl und Markus Ludwigs (ed), *Band 2: Grundstrukturen des europäischen und internationalen Verwaltungsrechts* (C.F. Müller 2021).

7 Enzo Cannizzaro and Emanuele Rebasti, 'Soft Law in the EU Legal Order' in Julia Iliopoulos-Strangas and Jean-François Flauss (ed), *Das soft law der europäischen Organisationen – The Soft Law of European Organisations – La soft law des organisations européennes* (Nomos 2012).

2 Connections between Soft Law, Hard Law and the International Law

To finally try to define and understand better the existence and application of post-conflict agreements and their character, we will see how such norms are being made in the framework of international law. Soft law itself has been present in international law for a very long period of time, but only since recently has it gained importance in the framework of post-conflict development. We can therefore state that such soft law shaped non-formal post-conflict agreements have been a new category in international law, representing a new form of governance for non-recognized entities in the form of international (soft) law creations. 'Soft law is now a well-established legal category, and contemporary international law has to accommodate it within the varied processes for creating and implementing international norms.'[8] Previously, there was no need for norms regulating post-conflict societies, in the sense that there were not many places unknown and unoccupied such as *terra nullius,* since every civilization was aiming to gain and control as much territory as possible.

In order to balance out such situations and previous confrontations, there has been a need to temporarily regulate certain important aspects of life and human rights in post-conflict frameworks. 'Interestingly, unlike hard law treaties which, at the end of their Preambles, use the term "have agreed", the Principles uses the term "Adopts", as do all five of the United Nations Declarations and Legal Principles, signalling that something less than "agreement" was achieved.'[9] Whereas such non-formal (adoptions) agreements can be named differently and even have very strong titles, their function still remains that of a soft law and in this case, in the framework of international law. Various similar tools like soft laws have been present in the development of international law before as well, but it never got such publicity as in recent times, since people are more and more concerned and informed about certain global conflicts and their conclusions, potentials and possibilities. 'First, a significant majority of the scholars who have published on the subject recognize that soft law plays some role in the making, interpretation and develop-

8 Felipe Gómez Isa, 'The Role of Soft Law in the Progressive Development of Indigenous Peoples' Rights' in Stéphanie Lagoutte, Thomas Gammeltoft-Hansen and John Cerone (ed), *Tracing the Roles of Soft Law in Human Rights* (Oxford University Press 2016).

9 Daniel A. Porras, 'The United Nations Principles Relevant to the Use of Nuclear Power Sources in Outer Space : The Significance of a Soft Law Instrument after Nearly 20 Years in Force' in Irmgard Marboe (ed), *Soft Law in Outer Space: The Function of Non-binding Norms in International Space Law* (Böhlau Verlag 2012).

ment of international law.'[10] The new forms and expressions in recent conflicts and their agreements which have gained publicity are not new, neither are they more innovative than their predecessors; they are just more popular and the demand and observance of their implementation is much stronger. This also gives a very interesting and new moment, as the public is also able to influence the implementation, and request certain parts of the agreements to be either implemented or even changed. 'Moreover, we cannot depend solely on the passage of international treaties because of the delays in negotiation, the problems with ratification, and the control of the process by diplomats rather than experts.'[11] As the administration is becoming more and more burdensome and complicated in various aspects of life, so is the case with the development of international law and its solutions.

There is also a need and big demand for development possibilities in post-conflict societies, which due to their unclear legal status, can't be part of the international treaty-making and the international community as such. 'Despite objections and criticisms, which ultimately reduce to differing views about the costs of sovereignty and whether sovereignty is better conceived of as a diachronic rather than synchronic concept, international law and relations have moved markedly in the direction of soft law.'[12] Following on this, we can observe that with a lack of internationally recognized sovereignty, a certain entity can't take part in the international law-making or be a party in it. Obviously, it can be represented in various forms during treaty-making and also as we can see it here, be a party to certain agreements which have a rather soft law character in the framework of international laws. Soft law provides a basis for efficient international contracts, and it helps create normative covenants and discourses that can reshape international politics.[13] In this regard, we necessarily again face the problem of enforcement, which is already a problematic issue when it comes to international treaties.

It is hard to imagine who and how could enforce something against the will of a member of the UN and even harder to imagine it altogether for all the five permanent members of the UN Security Council. 'Lastly, soft enforcement

10 Melaku Geboye Desta, 'Soft Law in International Law: An Overview' in Andrea K. Bjorklund and August Reinisch (ed), *International Investment Law and Soft Law* (Edward Elgar Publishing 2012).

11 Jean Galbraith and David Zaring, 'Soft Law as Foreign Relations Law' (2014) 99 Cornell Law Review 735.

12 Christopher R. Rossi, 'Nagorno-Karabakh and the Minsk Group: The Imperfect Appeal of Soft Law in an Overlapping Neighborhood' (2017) 52 Texas International Law Journal 45.

13 Kenneth W. Abbott and Duncan Snidal, 'Hard and Soft Law in International Governance' (2000) 54 International Organization 421.

typically facilitates more readily than judicial processes the necessary input of scientific and technical expertise required to deal with issues of compliance under agreements of this kind.'[14] When making an international treaty and even more, a soft law agreement meant to regulate relations in the framework of international law, a special focus has to be given to the idea that it should be beneficial for all, or at least not harm anyone. This aspect is also covering the scientific and technical solutions which are being developed, and their future implementation would benefit everyone. Some of such aspects we have more broadly already explained in some previous chapters, such as the outer space sharing and development.

Finally, we should not forget the implementation phases for soft law and how parties can deliberately choose the right means of doing so. 'This introduces a difference with a system of Soft Rule of Law where the actions of a government can be legally valid but fail to conform to the law and its general principles.'[15] In such cases, it is obvious that governments can choose various means of not implementing soft law requirements and obviously still be inside their legal capabilities. Such acts can be observed and easily proved by any other subject of law or state, and in case it is necessary, they can also revise the outcomes and potentials of such acts. In a case that there is a need for a body to determine facts regarding the implementation of soft law, there are also various means to do so. 'Soft adjudication sometimes serves as a second-best form of accountability, where "hard" adjudication is appropriate but is practically impossible.'[16] So, as much as soft law is independent, the adjudication of its norms is accordingly easier to apply and implement. It has to be taken into consideration when breaching soft law requirements that breaching such soft law clauses do have their own legal consequences, since in the end, soft law is a law in fact. 'A better normative claim to defend the use of soft law is that it furthers the Rule of Law by supplementing the underlying law.'[17] In most instances, the clauses of soft law are needed by all the stakeholders and parties of international law, while their implementation is finally under no question and becomes much smoother. International actors overall will not engage in a debate in which they will ultimately not find a solution or a certain final agreement, be it in a free form or even of a soft law character. Such agreements are

14 Alan E. Boyle, 'Some Reflections on the Relationship of Treaties and Soft Law' (1999) 48 The International and Comparative Law Quarterly 901.
15 Rubén Méndez Reátegui and Oscar Sumar Albujar, 'Rule of Law Versus Soft Rule of Law' (2020) 109 Revista de Derecho Político 373.
16 Paul MacMahon, 'Soft Adjudication' (2017) 69 Administrative Law Review 529.
17 Stephen Daly, 'The Rule of (Soft) Law' (2021) 32 King's Law Journal 3.

meant to regulate and encircle a legal or technical path in which a development of a certain area of economy or social life will develop in the future.

3 Enforcement as a Benchmark between Soft and Hard Law

A very important and distinctive feature between soft and hard laws is their capability or incapability for enforcement. While it is evident that the main feature of soft law is in fact its non-enforcement character, whereas one of the most important features of hard law is the fact that there are tools with which they can be somehow enforced. The fact is that even hard law enforcement many times can't be guaranteed or achieved and there is a certain duty of state organs, among which are most importantly courts, as their main duty is to prosecute, judge and finally enforce their own decisions. Opposite to this, there is the no duty on the courts side to enforce soft law regulations. Accordingly, it does not mean that parties do not have the duty to respect them, after all, actually they can and have to do. 'The second understanding of duty is therefore the legal duty that, for various reasons, may not be enforceable in a court of law.'[18] Regular courts therefore do not deal with soft law, but they are in fact more and exclusively concerned about hard law, which ultimately does not mean that no one cares about the implementation and potential results prescribed by soft laws. There are various bodies which do reflect on some soft law implementation phases and even if they find a potential disrespect, they are able to inform and advise the parties about it. But ultimately, they are not able to enforce it, while in this case, their opinion is of great concern. So, when the parties ask for an advice or are informed about certain issues, they should aim at changing or applying their actions as a rather voluntary act, without a real enforcement system or capability present. 'Reflecting this soft law concern, most national laws and policies use the word "voluntary" in relation to settlement options.'[19] Even when an authority is present or appointed by the parties regarding adjudicating soft law cases their final acts still can't be forced or pressured. It can be therefore stated that soft law is very much a moral

18 Beate Sjåfjell, 'Quo Vadis, Europe? The Significance of Sustainable Development as Objective, Principle and Rule of EU Law' in Cecilia M. Bailliet, *Non-state actors, soft law, and protective regimes : from the margins* (Cambridge University Press 2012).

19 Megan Bradley and Angela Sherwood, 'Addressing and Resolving Internal Displacement: Reflections on a Soft Law "Success Story"' in Stéphanie Lagoutte, Thomas Gammeltoft-Hansen and John Cerone (ed), *Tracing the Roles of Soft Law in Human Rights* (Oxford University Press 2016).

obligation and has to be respected because of such values, but there is more value and importance in soft law than that.

When we talk about soft law, it is also necessary to understand that it includes a deeper obligation where a party is not just a simple actor but in fact a beneficiary of the whole process; this is in particular important for post-conflict agreements. Such agreements are having a very strong soft law character due to their non-enforceability and at the same time, huge interest for implementing what has been agreed and achieved, while also necessarily respecting each other in the process. In such post-conflict development frameworks also, together with implementing the agreement a more complex and important system of correlation is born and it includes respecting the other with the establishment of new and improved ties between each other. Such ties are meant to last, while no party in such a relationship is having an interest to break that chain of cooperation, which, by time, is creating some kind of custom of good and friendly relationship. 'This advantage flows from the capacity of soft law instruments to be both "non-binding" and "norm-creating."'[20] We are coming to the most important characteristic of the soft law and its definition, which is that it is being non-binding, having a strong norm creating character, which ultimately makes it to be a law without an enforcement capacity. Norms and laws are in any case not meant to last forever and in fact they last as long as there is someone to judge upon them and later are also able to enforce and accept them. As long as there is a missing link between judging and enforcing, a norm it can't be stated to be a hard law any more, therefore it ceases to exist, but does it become soft law in that case?

We are of the opinion that hard norms cannot become soft law just as their judiciary or enforcement authority ceases to exist; ultimately, this will lead to a wide disintegration of the system of hard norms where ultimately people will see no interest in applying and respecting them. So, it is not possible to simply change the role of norms from soft to hard or vice versa. There is an important interest in parties which are making soft law agreements and a greater importance than just simple agreements or political declarations. 'At its core, soft law does not bind, rather it influences.'[21] Soft law is therefore more an idea that is followed than a norm; it exists until it can be used to fill in gaps in the future and also provide solutions for future problems which

20 Jack M. Beard, 'Soft Law's Failure on the Horizon: The International Code of Conduct for Outer Space Activities' (2017) 38U. Pa. J. Int'l L. 335.

21 Doron Goldbarsht, *Global Counter-Terrorist Financing and Soft Law: Multi-layered Approaches* (Edward Elgar 2020).

might not exist in the present time or parties might be unaware of their possible existence in the future. Soft and hard laws are, in their deep understanding, completely different forms and ideas of regulating the everyday activities of a certain person or society. 'And the other way round, the harder it is to show a rule to be binding, the softer is that rule.'[22] As soon as a soft law norm is covered by all the characteristics of a hard law it transforms accordingly, while it is not necessary to change its form, since it is a law in the end and is accepted as such by all. It only becomes more formal and melts into the environment more easily. In post-conflict societies, it is due to the development of the society and it becomes more formal with more authority and responsibilities given to it, where one of the responsibilities is also to have a system of adjudication and enforcement included. 'Recent inclusion of soft law commitments in hard law instruments suggests that both form and content are relevant to the sense of legal obligation.'[23] Some parts of soft laws can be also separately transferred into hard laws and be more applicable and enforceable. It is also the intention of the parties to push for some kind of enforceability of agreement clauses since it is hard at some moments to count on the goodwill of the other party, in particular taking into consideration political turbulences upon what soft law is hugely dependent on. A change in the political arena can also change the implementation of soft laws, and in some cases, block its partial or full implementation as well, which also triggers many other legal consequences.

22 Jaap Hage, 'What Is Legal Validity? Lessons from Soft Law' in Pauline Westerman, Jaap Hage, Stephan Kirste and Anne Ruth Mackor, *Legal Validity and Soft Law* (Springer 2018).

23 Dinah Shelton, 'Introduction: Law, Non-law and the Problem of "Soft Law"' in Dinah Shelton (ed), *Commitment and Compliance: The Role of Non-Binding Norms in the International Legal System* (Oxford University Press 2000).

CHAPTER 4

The Legal and Conflict Resolution Capacity of Informal Rules

The legal capacity of informal rules in general can't be exactly predetermined and it is more on a case-by-case basis that one can value its real capacity and capabilities. While the sole determination of the understanding of such informal rules in the case studies of our post-conflict societies depends on their patron country primarily, their application can finally be very different when applied into various local circumstances. 'Context matters, and while there is a clear idea of what durable peace looks like in the international community, with legitimate, effective governance and inclusive development, there is no privileged pathway from conflict to durable peace that will work in all contexts.'[1] Post-conflict development requests not just a particular standpoint and the implementation of standards but also it requires the respect of local needs and demands, which can also ultimately produce friction. Friction as a correlation and mutual influence of local and international needs and demands, which will be explained in the following chapters in more detail is a fact which can't be set or predetermined. 'It is implementation rather than design that matters for the success of projects in post-war environment.'[2] So a perfectly designed restructuring plan with poor implementation capacity is inevitably set to fail, as we will see it later on some of our case studies. It is not just the UN and other various stakeholders which are unable to offer a unique, one fits all solution, it is also us who are making theories and are unable to offer solutions or steps for which we can guarantee that steps forward can be achieved. 'Statistical research on peacebuilding does not give any clear evidence on which reforms are most likely to promote long-term democratization.'[3] Overall, it is not just the legal and social sciences which are unable to

1 Graham K. Brown and Arnim Langer, 'Timing and Sequencing of Peacebuilding Reforms and Policies: People-Centred Prioritization for Post-conflict Peacebuilding' in Arnim Langer and Graham K. Brown (ed), *Building Sustainable Peace: Timing and Sequencing of Post-conflict Reconstruction and Peacebuilding* (Oxford University Press 2016).

2 Lisa Chauvet, Paul Collier and Marguerite Duponchel, 'What Explains Aid Project Success in Post-conflict Situations?' (2010) 5,418 Policy Research Working Paper <https://documents1.worldbank.org/curated/en/713121468323979859/pdf/WPS5418.pdf> accessed 22 March 2026.

3 Anna Jarstad, 'Democratization after Civil War: Timing and Sequencing of Peacebuilding Reforms' in Arnim Langer and Graham K. Brown (ed), *Building Sustainable Peace: Timing*

 | HTTPS://DOI.ORG/10.1163/9789004746091-006

properly handle and align peacebuilding; it is also statistics, which are usually taken as granted in the sphere of mathematics and accounting.

Finally in the process of peacebuilding, one plus one does not necessarily give two, as some might expect, and the permanently changing social factors can even further deny such a calculation. 'The lack of critical thinking about peacebuilding theory has generated a series of policy prescriptions that address only a truncated subset of the problems with the international community's peacebuilding practice.'[4] The existence of UN standards and treaties with various definitions does not produce the same outcomes or have the same expectations in different cultural connotations. There are terms stemming from Western democracies which are set in some treaties with an expectation to produce certain effects, but in fact such standards have different understandings in some developing countries and in particular the post-conflict ones. 'Even if those notions are widely used, it is unclear what "inhuman" or "best interests" mean.'[5] Such standards are hard to implement after the conflict and in particular taking into consideration the revenge-like feelings in societies which are also many times supported silently by the UN observer missions and other similar peacebuilding envoys.

Accordingly, not just that words have different meanings in various languages it is also the case that standards such as 'inhuman' can be differently understood and seen in various cultures. So it is not just that ideas can be missing from a certain language; it is also a concept, which can be new and previously unseen as the following example shows. Interpreters and Russian-speaking members of the US delegation were left to guess at an appropriate translation of 'rule of law' into Russian, because the concept simply did not exist under soviet or even Czarist law.[6] While the whole concept might be missing it does not mean that some standards or outcomes it requires are not present. We need to outline that it is not the wording of a certain treaty that makes and incorporates standards, it is more its application by the international and local stakeholders overall. The expectations and in particular

---

and Sequencing of Post-conflict Reconstruction and Peacebuilding (Oxford University Press 2016).

4 Naazneen H. Barma, *The Peacebuilding Puzzle: Political Order in Post-conflict States* (Cambridge University Press 2017).

5 Angelika Nußberger, 'Hard Law or Soft Law – Does It Matter?: Distinction Between Different Sources of International Law in the Jurisprudence of the ECtHR' in Anne van Aaken and Iulia Motoc (ed), *The European Convention on Human Rights and General International Law* (Oxford Academic 2018).

6 Erika B. Schlager, 'A Hard Look at Compliance with "Soft" Law: The Case of the OSCE' in Dinah Shelton (ed), *Commitment and Compliance: The Role of Non-Binding Norms in the International Legal System* (Oxford University Press 2000).

timeframes of achieving standards can be very different and also ultimately inapplicable into the local frameworks of peace development. 'Crucially, from the point of view of this chapter, everyday peace may operate according to a very different time dimension than the "capital city peace" of signing ceremonies.'[7] Obviously, it is not just the UN system that is unable to guarantee standards or its Security Council permanent member states, which are to some extent able to imply decisions into local frameworks.

Another benefit of informal rules is that although they request a certain standard, its final application can be later changed and reformulated and in this way serve to a higher extent the local conflict resolution capacity. It is able to make such changes, which are more in line with the frequently changing local circumstances. 'While this may occur top-down after ratification of a treaty, it may also develop bottom-up, as on the-ground actors identify soft law norms as useful in guiding their work and ascertain how best to adapt and implement them in their contexts.'[8] Therefore the bottom-up approach and its influence can be seen as a more perfect match in post-conflict development, while its quick reshaping and reformulation can be in this case beneficial and also legal as being part of the informal rules governance framework in a certain post-conflict area. It is also very specific for the informal rules in post-conflict development that they apply solutions, which would not be otherwise applicable according to local or even international laws and standards. 'By choosing the specific soft law to govern the transaction, parties override the otherwise applicable law that would govern the transaction and thereby limit the application of the soft law to themselves.'[9] It is of utmost importance to find out how and why such informal rules could or could not be applied in similar frameworks coming from the same patron and why such solutions can't be more broadly applied internationally in similar contexts. In fact, it is evident and very important to mention that the patron states which support a certain framework or agreement are usually against a broader application of such *sui generis* solutions. The UN can also be against some solutions would really disturb the otherwise long-accepted and established norms in peace-building practice and post-conflict development. 'The frustration that the

7 Roger Mac Ginty, 'Political Versus Sociological Time: The Fraught World of Timelines and Deadlines' in Arnim Langer and Graham K. Brown (ed), *Building Sustainable Peace: Timing and Sequencing of Post-conflict Reconstruction and Peacebuilding* (Oxford University Press 2016).

8 Elena Baylis, 'The International Law Commission's Soft Law Influence' (2019) 13 FIU L. Rev. 1007.

9 Henry Deeb Gabriel, 'The Use of Soft Law in the Creation of Legal Norms in International Commercial Law: How Successful Has It Been' (2019) 40 Mich J Int'l L 413.

aggressor is "rewarded", since the law favours the consolidation of the unlawful territorial status quo, is understandable and legitimate.'[10] It is normally not one side which is coming out of a certain conflict as victorious but also the patron state, which is usually by rule a permanent member state of the UN Security Council.

It can be also observed that regarding timing and the steps made in the process of melting a frozen conflict it only happens then and in such circumstances which are favourable for a certain patron state. This has been clearly seen for example in the Nagorno-Karabakh conflict where a new solution was achieved only after Russia came closer with Turkey, so such a shift or favour was seen as a possible move. 'When considering the institutions and mechanisms of transitional justice and peacebuilding from a temporal perspective, we can become alert not only to the power to impose deadlines but also the power to assert a particular temporality and transitional justice imaginary.'[11] Obviously to end a certain conflict or just to imagine how it could be ended is more dependent on the imagination of the patron state. This can now be seen very clearly from the US view of the future Israeli position in the Middle East as it is surrounded by friendly Muslim countries, also envisaged accordingly in the Abrahamic Accords. In this regard and in particular the future relationship between Israel and Palestine is seen as fully dependent on foreign needs and expectations and absolutely not on the local ones. Also in a broader context it is necessary to observe the fact that it is more and more complicated to reach common understandings and solutions regarding self-determination, as the most crucial fact stemming from conflicts in the framework of post-conflict development and its agreements.

There are so many present divides in the UN regarding some statehood related issues and in particular the recognition of the new states. It is therefore not realistic to expect that a common solution can be reached regarding the most important cases but also the ones we are dealing with, namely Kosovo, Nagorno-Karabakh and the Taliban-governed Afghanistan. 'Recently, the existence of the right to external self-determination for colonial peoples and peoples under alien subjugation was confirmed in the Advisory Opinion of the

10 Tom Ruys and Felipe Rodríguez Silvestre, 'Illegal: The Recourse to Force to Recover Occupied Territory and the Second Nagorno-Karabakh War' (2021) 32 EJIL 1287.

11 Natascha Mueller-Hirth and Sandra Rios Oyola, 'Conclusion: Defusing Time Bombs: Towards an Understanding of Time and Temporality in Peacebuilding' in Natascha Mueller-Hirth and Sandra Rios Oyola (ed), *Time and Temporality in Transitional and Post-conflict Societies* (Routledge 2018).

International Court of Justice regarding Kosovo.'[12] We don't wish here to elaborate more regarding the International Court of Justice (ICJ) decisions, which are many times given in an informal and advisory character only. So they might have a form of a decision but their enforcement or wider acceptance can't be guaranteed, but just expected as such in the future. The ICJ can be seen as a court, which is many times bringing decisions that are not enforceable, contrary to the International Criminal Court (ICC) and other *ad hoc* War Crimes Tribunals. These courts do have some limited enforcement capacity although still not a universal one. Some of the most evident division lines can be observed in both ICJ and ICC where the interests of the UNSC permanent member states inevitably frequently clash.

The legal ambiguity regarding post-conflict states and their recognition is deeply dividing the states globally. While it is not coming as a surprise that not just new recognitions are happening but also de-recognitions. This fact brings us into a very challenging legal and political stance in international statebuilding overall. 'Derecognitions usually take place against states with partial international recognition, which are not part of the UN and which do not have international support.'[13] This fact can be observed on the case of Kosovo more broadly where not just the Serbian foreign policy agitates for de-recognition but is wholeheartedly assisted by the Russian and Chinese non-recognizers. They are in this way undermining the US efforts for a wider Kosovo recognition and its possible future UN membership. Even if Kosovo presumably becomes a UN member state it is going to be a sui generis case. Although we need to be aware of the fact that in the international law as a fact and by the definition of the sovereignty and self-government they are a changing category in both their definition and practical understanding. 'However, there are still no clear criteria for what constitutes, as a matter of international law, genuine self-government.'[14] As long as there are five UNSC permanent member states, which form two different world policies and interests, there will be divides. Such divides will be supported and fuelled by their respective own interests, divisions and disagreements regarding mainly post-conflict development, recognition and sovereignties overall.

---

12 Daniella Dam-de Jong, *International Law and Governance of Natural Resources in Conflict and Post-conflict Situations* (Cambridge University Press 2015).

13 Eugen Cakolli, 'KOSOVO: Between Universal Non-Recognition and "Derecognitions"' [2020] Kosova Democratic Institute (KDI) and the Konrad Adenauer Foundation <https://www.kas.de/documents/286052/0/Policy+brief+20-09-13+Kosovo+Between+universal+non-recognition+and+derecognitions+(Eng).pdf.> accessed 22 March 2026.

14 Matthew Saul, *Popular Governance of Post-conflict Reconstruction: The Role of International Law* (Cambridge University Press 2014).

CHAPTER 5

Other Capacities Applicable to Informal Rules

1 The Political Dimension of Informal Rules, Changeable or Not Changeable

As we have mentioned before, it is necessary to explain the influence which politics have or could have on international law. It is obvious that the international informal and soft law clauses are very much influenced by politics. In particular, we have the UNSC permanent member-states which are dominating politically in their respective geographical areas of interest. 'International law has always been surrounded by politics, informality, and unilateralism.'[1] Before a certain international law standard is accepted, it necessarily needs to go through a long process of discussion in various political forums. Politics stand very close to informal law-making in many aspects, and political decisions can be changed and reshaped very quickly in the same manner as ordinary politics, where no one really needs to clarify and explain why such changes were deemed necessary. It is important to note that political settings can determine what soft laws will be made and even more importantly, how much such soft laws will be implemented and understood in certain settings. 'Soft law instruments do not contain legally binding obligations, but they can and often do convey political commitments by states.'[2] Finally, such an informal way of making laws or, in this case, soft laws can be very beneficial, as without any formal engagement, states can set a standard and accordingly request its enforcement by a certain entity, claiming that it is the 'law' in fact.

There is a wide array of tools and documents which have such an informal form but have the highest level of priority for some states which are also very keen on their enforcement and also request it accordingly. 'The so-called "political treaties", which refer to those treaties that are concluded with no expectation of effective enforcement, are traditionally classified as legal soft law.'[3] It is also possible, contrary to what was previously stated, that a certain treaty is having a soft law form, with a reason not to make it enforceable or in

1 Nico Krisch, 'The Decay of Consent: International Law in an Age of Global Public Goods' (2014) 108 The American Journal of International Law 1.

2 Jack M. Beard, 'Soft Law's Failure on the Horizon: The International Code of Conduct for Outer Space Activities' (2017) 38 U. Pa. J. Int'l L. 335.

3 Ilhami Alkan Olsson, 'Four Competing Approaches to International Soft Law' (2013) 58 Scandinavian Studies In Law 177.

 | HTTPS://DOI.ORG/10.1163/9789004746091-007

some form active, while still giving a certain promise, which is thus leaving it pending in the air. That is also the case when an obligation is formed in a soft law treaty form and stands against the interest of a bigger and more influential state, where smaller states or possibly more of them have no means of enforcement. While giving a promise that some policies will develop in a certain direction, it is still possible that they will never do and that the treaty-like form will just remain as a reminder of their initial form and nothing more than that. A very typical characteristic of big words, such as eradicate hunger globally or to stop the climate change, are very unclear, while governments have very limited capacities of changing such complex problems outside their respective sovereign borders. 'Some agreements refer to soft law instruments in their preamble, with the purpose of positioning the new treaty regime within the general political cooperation among the parties or of identifying critical issues which merited attention during the negotiations.'[4] Preambles and White Papers are also a very important forms and sources of informal rules or better to say, the way they should be understood or looked at in the future.

One of the most interesting preambles we can mention here is definitely the one found in the Serbian Constitution,[5] which states that the Province of Kosovo and Metohija is an integral part of the Republic of Serbia. Such a *de jure* statement from the Preamble is hardly following the *de facto* situation on the ground. Obviously, such a preamble has just a declarative character without any real present or future meaning to actually enforce it on the ground, also due to the existence of the United Nations Resolution 1244[6] and its UNMIK[7] mission present in Kosovo. 'Often, it is only soft law that can maintain the momentum of normative development in the face of shifting political and institutional challenges.'[8] So, to be in the line with normative requirements, certain decisions are made in the form of soft law, whereas such solutions are

4 Giovanna Adinolfi, 'Soft Law in International Investment Law and Arbitration' (2021) 1 The Italian Review of International and Comparative Law 86.

5 The National Assembly of the Republic of Serbia, 'Constitution of the Republic of Serbia' (30 September 2006) <https://www.parlament.gov.rs/upload/documents/Constitution_%20of_Serbia_F.pdf> accessed 22 March 2026.

6 United Nations, 'Resolution 1244 (1999)' (10 June 1999) <https://unmik.unmissions.org/sites/default/files/old_dnn/Res1244ENG.pdf> accessed 22 March 2026.

7 United Nations, 'United Nations Interim Administration Mission in Kosovo' <https://peacekeeping.un.org/en/mission/unmik> accessed 22 March 2026.

8 Mátyás Bódig, 'Legal Validity, Soft Law, and International Human Rights Law' in Pauline Westerman, Jaap Hage, Stephan Kirste and Anne Ruth Mackor, *Legal Validity and Soft Law* (Springer 2018).

declared to be law, while their actual enforcement will never be requested or even be possible after all.

Soft law is therefore standing in a perfect limbo between politics and law, leaning towards one or the other, depending on the present need coming from a certain political elite which uses it to legalize its own actions. 'In practice, the right to choose a durable solution is often pared down to the "right" to accept the particular solution that is most politically acceptable, materially feasible, and enforceable within domestic legal systems.'[9] Soft law can be also seen as part of the political agreement to put certain requirements into the form of the law, but in fact exclude them from the possibility of enforcement due to the lack of the relevant political will. Ultimately, the final word of whether a certain soft law treaty will be enforced depends solely on the political will of certain states. Whereas bigger states are able to influence and in fact force smaller states to align their policies with the requirements coming from a soft law treaty, in the case of some relationships between more powerful and influential states, such norms are accordingly more declarative and their final enforcement depends solely on the present political will of such states. 'Coming back to the specific case of the actors/subjects debate, soft law mechanisms have the capacity to translate the factual power of certain actors on the international level into normative terms.'[10] As we will see it later on our case studies, such a political power is very important in the process of peace building and conflict resolution.

While the main characteristic of such processes is that they stay in line within the previously prescribed norms and requests coming from influential states and are enforced as such on the parties. It is also important to note that such soft law agreements in post-conflict settings have the possibility to be again reshaped accordingly and to the newly established political authorities in a patron state. They can even be changed as a counteroffer in an agreement with other states which are able to offer something in exchange, which could be more valuable in the present or future political settings. An obvious example of this is Nagorno-Karabakh, which had two phases of change; while

9 Megan Bradley and Angela Sherwood, 'Addressing and Resolving Internal Displacement: Reflections on a Soft Law "Success Story"' in Stéphanie Lagoutte, Thomas Gammeltoft-Hansen and John Cerone (ed), *Tracing the Roles of Soft Law in Human Rights* (Oxford University Press 2016).

10 Christoph Good, 'Mission Creeps: The (Unintended) Re-Enforcement of the Actor's Discussion in International Law through the Expansion of Soft Law Instruments in the Business and Human Rights Nexus' in Stéphanie Lagoutte, Thomas Gammeltoft-Hansen and John Cerone (ed), *Tracing the Roles of Soft Law in Human Rights* (Oxford University Press 2016).

both were informal, the last one, which has completely eliminated the Armenian governance, was in a form of a simple political and military action on the ground, in line with the Azerbaijani sovereignty. 'On the other hand, transitional justice practice and scholarship associates resistance with specific actors: those who have something to lose in the political transition and are powerful enough to visibly block transitional justice processes.'[11] The soft law form is therefore the best possible manner in solving and regulating challenges in the post-conflict frameworks, where no guarantees regarding enforcement or its possible future timeframe can be reached.

There is a clear need to revise or rethink constitutional frameworks in post-conflict societies, where the democracy, with its standards and institutions, is still very fragile and highly dependent on foreign aid and political support. It is also not a surprise that in such cases, constitutions can only serve a limited function where foreign states limit their respective responsibility in enforcing human and minority rights, which, by rule, can't be fully guaranteed or acceptable by international norms. 'However, where the constitution marks the culmination of the transition and the point at which the international community "exits", the adoption of the constitution can mark the end rather than the beginning of the state's commitment to the implementation of international law.'[12] In such transitional societies, the implementation of international norms is rather an exception to a rule and this fact can't be changed until institutions in such states do not gain real power. Once institutions finally gain on strength, it is not sure in which direction they will have their focus on, as there are obviously various challenges in post-conflict societies which are also present in other more advanced ones.

Even one of the most developed systems of human rights protection, like the EU, has its inner challenges, where not every policy has the same priority or protection available. 'The EU's institutional complexity implies "political deals", a system of political checks and balances impeding effectiveness and efficiency of individual policies.'[13] Certainly, one of the biggest challenges is

11 Julie Bernath, Djané Dit Fatogoma Adou and Briony Jones, 'Understanding "Resistance" to Transitional Justice' in Martin Leiner and Christine Schliesser (ed), *Alternative Approaches in Conflict Resolution* (Palgrave Macmillan 2018).

12 Catherine Turner and Ruth Houghton, 'Constitution Making and Post-conflict Reconstruction' in Matthew Saul and James A Sweeney (ed), *International Law and Post-conflict Reconstruction Policy* (Routledge 2015).

13 Ingo Peters, Enver Ferhatovic, Rabea Heinemann and Sofia Sturm, 'The Effectiveness of EU Crisis Response in Afghanistan, Iraq and Mali' in Roger Mac Ginty, Sandra Pogodda, and Oliver P. Richmond (ed), *The EU and crisis response* (Manchester University Press 2021).

whether the focus will be more on the development and economic incentives or human and social rights, which are rarely in opposing positions. It is a matter of fact and a completely political decision to decide which area will be prioritized and in such cases, the formal or informal explanation or norm creation can be used. In this regard, we can observe a similar pattern in the EU foreign policies. It is not a surprise that the EU struggles to implement the Brussels Agreement (BA)[14] of 2013, while overall it has a status neutral position towards Kosovo's independence, due to its own inner political divides. We will elaborate in more detail in regard these phenomena in later chapters, which are dealing with the agreements regarding Kosovo in more detail. 'Nevertheless, in international relations, the EU often underlines their nonlegally binding nature by stating that they are of 'political nature only.'[15] Such international agreements are not spared of being relativized and sometimes even ignored by the most prominent systems of human rights protection mechanisms today, as it is the EU itself. As a conclusion to this chapter, we will outline once again that soft law norms can be debated on to what level they are or are not laws, but it is necessary to outline that they all certainly have a very strong political character and dimension incorporated.

2 The Social Dimension of Informal Rules, Changeable or Not Changeable

When we deal with the social dimension of informal rules and soft laws, we can see that there is a very important aspect, in the sense of various social requests and movements which do tend to push for a wider understanding and implementation of such norms. Social conditions are, in this regard, lawmaking and are going hand in hand with the political will, while they are also one of the main factors to formulate or change relevant policies. The examples demonstrate that soft law is not a more or less inefficient alternative to hard law but that it has developed towards an inevitable instrument to bring about

14 Brussels Agreement, 'First Agreement of Principles Governing the Normalization of Relations' (2013) <https://www.peaceagreements.org/media/documents/ag2022_5bdc31b326555.pdf> also available at <https://www.srbija.gov.rs/cinjenice/en/120394> and <https://gzk.rks-gov.net/ActDetail.aspx?ActID=8892&langid=2> accessed 22 March 2026. Further will be cited as BA 2013.

15 Ramses A. Wessel, 'Normative Transformations in EU External Relations: The Phenomenon of "Soft" International Agreements' (2021) 44 West European Politics 72.

desired social conditions and to avoid undesired ones.[16] It is also true in the vice versa correlation where soft law is forming and shaping social conditions, as they are more and more able to accommodate certain changes or even future ones as requested by relevant soft laws. This mutual relationship is a key element in the development and correlation of the society and soft laws where mutual influences are not just clearly visible but also could be projected into the future. In one sentence, the core of the social movements is the way of how they form future behaviours, for what soft law is a necessary tool.

Now, as we had this very basic introductory part, we now step to a more complex area of social conditions and their influence in post-conflict societies. 'To the extent that peacebuilding continues to be viewed as an increasingly professionalized domain of intrepid foreigners, the liberal peacebuilding project will remain an inadequate response to the challenges posed by contemporary conflict.'[17] A very important influence in post-conflict development is given to the actual interests and the social dimensions coming outside of the framework of conflict societies. It is very important to note that even the start, duration and the time when a certain conflict will finish has more to do with outside social factors than the real inner ones. This is also due to the very huge dependence of smaller societies on bigger ones and the need of the bigger ones to regulate the smaller ones. This needs to happen in such a manner that they are in line with their own political will and in this case, even more importantly the social understanding they have at home. 'National reconciliation efforts include the disarmament, demobilization, and reintegration (DDR) of former combatants and other groups affected by the war as well as the rehabilitation of basic services and infrastructure.'[18] This process also depends on the foreign factors which either see an interest to do so or continue to support the combat-like activities before, during and after the open conflict. An example of this can be clearly observed in the case of Nagorno-Karabakh, where Russia has supported and also sold weapons to both the Armenian and Azerbaijani side simultaneously. In such situations, it is very hard to achieve long-term peace, although it would be one of the highest priorities of local societies which are being devastated for decades, but is obviously not a priority for a certain foreign power.

---

16 Christian Brünner and Georg Königsberger, '"Regulatory Impact Assessment" – A Tool to Strengthen Soft Law Regulations' in Irmgard Marboe (ed), *Soft Law in Outer Space: The Function of Non-binding Norms in International Space Law* (Böhlau Verlag 2012).

17 Timothy Donais, *Peacebuilding and Local Ownership: Post-conflict Consensus-Building* (Routledge 2012).

18 Graciana del Castillo, *Rebuilding War-Torn States: The Challenge of Post-conflict Economic Reconstruction* (Oxford University Press 2008).

Smaller societies and, in particular, minorities in post-conflict settings suffer the most, their voice and social demands are either not heard or when even heard, they fall outside the agenda of the bigger stakeholders in the overall conflict resolution agenda. 'Debate in elaborating the Guidelines centred on whether minorities should be singled out as having a "responsibility" or (stronger) "duty" to integrate and on what exactly those responsibilities should entail.'[19] In this case, we aim at understanding and defining the word integrate in many instances and when it would mean assimilate, in the end. When it comes to the EU understanding of integration, it allows more freedom and social interaction, but also costs more efforts, for which the majority of post-conflict states do not have or are not willing to use resources. Many times, in such cases, a certain authority can ask for time and patience to be given, which again can be understood differently in such specific settings. So patience, something that is often asked of people in transitional and post-conflict societies, is a cultural value that arguably loses its significance with the development of modernity and the inevitable compression of time.[20] In fact, the issue of time, economic hardships and also social ignorance, all brings minorities into a harsh position where many times, the answer and solution accessible is emigration, which is anyway the most characteristic phenomena in every post-conflict society, overall.

3 Economic Aspects of Informal Rules, Changeable or Not Changeable

Another important aspect to take into consideration when understanding informal rules and soft law in post-conflict development is their economical dimension. Overall, this aspect and their conflict resolution connotations are also one of the focal points of our work; therefore apart from the basic guidelines explained in this chapter, we will also aim to go into more details in the following ones. In particular, it will be important to research how by various soft law means, some powerful states can or can't influence the development

19 Sally Holt, Zdenka Machnyikova, and John Packer, 'The Role of Soft Law in Minority Rights Protection and Diversity Management: Reflections from Practice' in Stéphanie Lagoutte, Thomas Gammeltoft-Hansen and John Cerone (ed), *Tracing the Roles of Soft Law in Human Rights* (Oxford University Press 2016).

20 Natascha Mueller-Hirth and Sandra Rios Oyola, 'Introduction: Temporal Perspectives on Transitional and Post-conflict Societies' in Natascha Mueller-Hirth and Sandra Rios Oyola (ed), *Time and Temporality in Transitional and Post-conflict Societies* (Routledge 2018).

of some post-conflict ones. 'Major business operations and deals in post-conflict countries are certainly likely to be highly "political", but the proposal is not that peace operations act as interim national investment approval institutions.'[21] So when we step into this very challenging sphere of development studies, we can see that a single document, agreement or anything agreed in an informal form is to serve as a tool for developing a certain society, but is after all, not an almighty tool, while the previously mentioned frameworks and patterns, as outlined in such documents, do serve as guidelines for everyone in and outside the conflict.

Potential economic dominance is the priority in all the societies we will research later, where EU and USA claim exclusivity regarding Kosovo, Russia regarding Nagorno-Karabakh and China over Afghanistan. 'Controversial initiatives such as concession reviews and land reforms are avoided or delayed until after the most lucrative natural resource rights are issued to powerful players.'[22] These phenomena of natural resources share can be seen as a form of post-colonialism where the most vulnerable societies are used for the benefit of some influential ones. Still, the main aim of our work is not to claim that post-colonialism is a fact but to see how various informal agreements can bring development and thus lower the pressure and demand for foreign aid. Also, when we talk about development, it is obvious that there will be various demands locally and interests internationally. Many times, the regional, local and also some tribal differences will be visible in the agreements and even more, in their various phases of implementation. 'For natural resources, central and local governments sometimes share revenue-collecting authority, and certain local areas with more natural resources sometimes have arrangements for receiving a greater share of the corresponding revenue.'[23] This revenue share can be also the source of the conflict previously and with the final agreement, it can be more just or reasoned as well.

A very unique solution of establishing new entities, or in some instances states, can solve the problems regarding revenue collection and spending. There can also be some companies specialized in revenue management, which have a more balanced and just management structures and are also

21 Jolyon Ford, *Regulating Business for Peace: The United Nations, the Private Sector and Post-conflict Recovery* (Cambridge University Press 2015).

22 Emily E. Harwell, 'Building Momentum and Constituencies for Peace: The Role of Natural Resources in Transitional Justice and Peacebuilding' in Carl Bruch, Carroll Muffett and Sandra S. Nichols (ed), *Governance, Natural Resources, and Post-conflict Peacebuilding* (Routledge 2016).

23 Margaux J. Day, 'Fiscal Arrangements' in Paul R. Williams and Milena Sterio (ed), *Research Handbook on Post-conflict State Building* (Edward Elgar 2020).

more socially responsible, politically correct and economically viable. 'International financial law thus carries with it a general sense of obligation, and investors, markets, national regulators, and international organizations routinely impose penalties on noncompliant financial authorities, companies, and firms for derogating from established best practices.'[24] In this aspect, the checks and balances regarding companies and investments in post-conflict societies can also be, in many instances, best protected and overseen by some informal mechanisms where an authority can be more flexible.

Regarding investments, development and the establishment of new companies, the Brussels Agreement[25] in Kosovo can be a very valuable document. In this document, it is elaborated which companies should be formed in order to protect the economic interests of the Serbian community in Kosovo, in particular, telecommunications and electricity trade and distribution. While the formation and the work of such companies will be further elaborated in the following chapters regarding Kosovo, it is necessary to mention here some limiting factors regarding their future. Namely, in the Washington Agreement[26] from 2020 related to Kosovo, it was outlined that the whole idea of Serbian sovereignty in the fields of energy and telecommunications in Kosovo has to be distanced from other foreign influences, in this case Russian energy and Chinese telecommunication sectors in Serbia, respectively. Also, regarding the financing of various projects, it was outlined that Serbia and Kosovo will work with the US International Development Finance Corporation[27] on financial mechanisms for some infrastructure projects. The financial or borrowing capacity of a certain society depends many times on the goodwill of countries which are able to credit them, but such arrangements often come in line with the crediting countries political, social and economic interests. Overall, in post-conflict societies, similarly to the states in the developing world, credits and financial arrangements are given only to those who are politically ready to follow the political and economic interest of the donor country. This can be seen today as the main clash between economically stable countries, where they are aiming at securing markets by investing into infrastructure

24 Chris Brummer, *Soft Law and the Global Financial System: Rule Making in the 21st Century* (Cambridge University Press 2015).

25 BA 2013.

26 Washington Agreement, 'Economic Normalization' (2020) <https://www.peacefare.net/2020/09/04/much-ado-about-nothing/> also available at <https://exit.al/en/2020/09/04/kosovo-and-serbia-signed-separate-pledges-not-an-agreement/> accessed 22 March 2026. Further will be cited as WA 2020.

27 Ibid.

projects, while by doing so, they also spread their economy, politics and not rarely military power as well.

In the capitalistic systems, giving or borrowing money is not an activity which depends on an absolute free will of a certain government, it does have to follow some profit-making patterns. 'Consequently, although not formally binding on borrowing country governments, the Bank's operational standards are likely to have significant legal and practical implications for borrowers, both internationally and domestically.'[28] Governments have to take care that money is spent according to some rules and guidelines and that also such investments do correspond to the investing countries guidelines. It is also very similar with donations, in which case, they are made in such a way that they follow both the investing state priorities and the recipient states interests.

As a conclusion in this regard, we can underline once again that economic incentives are a necessary and vital tool for every post-conflict society and the ultimate path to its future development and political stability. It is also important to note that economic growth itself does not always guarantee advancement in the fields of law, human rights and constitutionalism overall. 'Just as economic growth alone proved insufficient for building democracy, reinstating property rights is not enough to foster economic and social stability.'[29] Even when it is a prerequisite for development and all the other democracy-related patterns economic incentives are not a magic wand, and are not able to change societies just by investing and spending more on them. Unfortunately, the best example for this is Afghanistan, which has received donations for almost two decades while finally falling back again to its pre-intervention stadium, without even having traces of the previously established democratic patterns, principles and standards. Such an economic failure and the case of Afghanistan and its status today with limited access to global investments will be further elaborated in the chapter dedicated to Afghanistan and its new Chinese model of development.

---

28 David A. Wirth, 'Compliance with Non-binding Norms of Trade and Finance' in Dinah Shelton (ed), *Commitment and Compliance: The Role of Non-Binding Norms in the International Legal System* (Oxford University Press 2000).

29 Megan J. Ballard, 'Post-conflict Property Restitution: Flawed Legal and Theoretical Foundations' (2010) 28 Berkeley Journal of International Law 462.

4 Water-Related Concerns and Their Regulation by Informal Agreements

In this chapter, we will deal with the water-related concerns in post-conflict societies and in particular, the informal rules regulating this important source of life. We will not deal with water as a commodity but as a free access resource, which has recently seen some very important changes, as it is being more and more used and in some instances, also depleted. While water can't be owned and its use limited or controlled, there are still some exceptions to this. It is not a hard law which regulates the use of water as is the case with electricity, oil supplies or even telecommunications capacities. Water is seen as a source of life and in places where it is scarce or non-existent, such areas are not capable of sustaining larger human settlements. By following on this idea, it brings us to the post-conflict societies and their certain need for stable water supplies. 'Both the overview and the case studies indicate that natural resources play a role in peace agreements, but they are generally not the back breakers in the agreement that security and power-sharing issues tend to be.'[30] In the sense of some post-conflict agreements, water has been treated as a resource which can be valued, measured and shared as well.

Even in cities or conglomerates where water management is important and where there are established ways of decision-making of what will be prioritized, water spending in case of scarcity regulation is unclear. The principle of people's participation, invoked in relation to the national strategies, is vague; the obligation to integrate a right to participate in decision-making processes for affected individuals and groups in any policy, programme or strategy concerning water is considerably stronger.[31] While many successful human development ideas were linked to water and its abundance, it has recently become evident that conflicts for or around water do exist and have the tendency to be more frequent in the future. 'Engaging business and other stakeholders on problematic landholding or water use issues of a major mine, for example, may hold far greater long-term peacebuilding significance than the typical pattern of repeated capacity-building workshops involving only civil society

30 Simon J. A. Mason, Damiano A. Sguaitamatti and María del and Pilar Ramírez Gröbli, 'Stepping Stones to Peace? Natural Resource Provisions in Peace Agreements' in Carl Bruch, Carroll Muffett and Sandra S. Nichols (ed), *Governance, Natural Resources, and Post-conflict Peacebuilding* (Routledge 2016).

31 Anette Faye Jacobsen, 'Soft Law within Participation Rights: Tools in Development' in Stéphanie Lagoutte, Thomas Gammeltoft-Hansen and John Cerone (ed), *Tracing the Roles of Soft Law in Human Rights* (Oxford University Press 2016).

actors.'[32] Therefore, water management can never be successfully managed on a local level, since its accumulation on one place will immediately produce shortages on another level.

It is important to have a wider regional cooperation or agreements regarding water management, and this is, in particular, important for post-conflict societies where peace is fragile and any disturbance in economic activities can bring out conflicts. 'A major challenge for peacebuilding projects, particularly in the Middle East, is how to manage the critical natural resource base such as freshwater and pursue sustainable policies of growth and development.'[33] At this moment, we will not aim at going deeper into this topic and bring up various case studies but just mention that we will deal with water management practices in post-conflict environments in our coming chapters. In particular, we will deal with the water management solutions achieved in the Washington Agreement[34] of 2020 regarding the Gazivode/Ujmani Lake in North Kosovo. This lake is important since its water source is in fact coming from Serbia, while the water itself is used in Kosovo for many different purposes, starting from drinking water, agriculture, industry and especially as an important resource for energy production.

Another important aspect regarding water is also its recent importance by the Chinese in the restructuring[35] of the new Taliban-led economy in Afghanistan. 'It seems plausible to assume that the success of natural resource management in creating sustainable post-conflict peace depends on knowledge about the mechanisms linking resources to conflict.'[36] The scarce water resources leave fewer opportunities for economy and local communities might get more engaged in illegal activities which are giving them opportunities. In Nagorno-Karabakh, there was also a water-related problem after the 2020 war concluded. Stepanakert had to develop a new plan for its water, long supplied from a reservoir near Shusha, which was at that time in Azerbaijani hands.[37] It will be interesting to see how water supplies will be developed

32 Jolyon Ford, *Regulating Business for Peace: The United Nations, the Private Sector and Post-conflict Recovery* (Cambridge University Press 2015).

33 Ashok Swain, 'Water and Post-conflict Peacebuilding' (2016) Vol. 61, No. 7 Hydrological Sciences Journal 1313.

34 WA 2020.

35 Lynne O'Donnell, 'The Water Wars Are Coming to Central Asia' (31 July 2023) <https://foreignpolicy.com/2023/07/31/afghanistan-uzbekistan-water-war-central-asia/> accessed 22 March 2026.

36 Siri Aas Rustad and Helga Malmin Binningsbø, 'A Price Worth Fighting for? Natural Resources and Conflict Recurrence' (2012) 49(4) Journal of Peace Research 531.

37 International Crisis Group, 'Improving Prospects for Peace after the Nagorno-Karabakh War' (2020) 91 Crisis Group Europe Briefing <https://www.crisisgroup.org/europe

and controlled overall and who and how responsible they will be for the future development of cities, and also what will happen when water cuts become necessary and how such shortages will be managed in a democratic or not-so-democratic manner in the future.

By concluding this short chapter on water, it is hard to determine what role water will have in the future regarding the modern societies and the development of post-conflict societies as well. 'But, at the same time, there is no golden principle to managing freshwater resources in post-conflict societies.'[38] Water is, for now, seen as a common good which can't be owned or controlled by someone, just as the outer space, for example. Sources like water can't be owned, controlled or depleted by someone; they are there to be managed for the common good, what exactly many times post-conflict agreements tend to do.

-central-asia/caucasus/nagorno-karabakh-conflict/b91-improving-prospects-peace-after-nagorno-karabakh-war> accessed 22 March 2026.

38 Ashok Swain, 'Water and Post-conflict Peacebuilding' (2016) Vol. 61, No. 7 Hydrological Sciences Journal 1313.

CHAPTER 6

Informal Rules Today, Positive Examples and Their Applicability

After the first few initial chapters where we went deep into the understanding of informal rules, their sources, applicability and potentials we will now briefly turn to see what potentials are left in the framework of modern lawmaking and its capabilities. As we have pointed it out earlier that while certain UN Security Council permanent member states have shown the most activity in making informal rules in the post-conflict settings it is still the UN, which has or should have the mandate to make the final hard law in this regard. 'However, we have relatively little knowledge, especially with regard to UN peacekeeping, as to what qualities or characteristics of interventions lead to durable peace.'[1] While there were many good and positive examples where a durable and long-lasting peace has been achieved it is still unknown what tools and means we exactly need to achieve them. It can also be said that monetary incentives and guarantees are not that one key aspect or a magic wand by which peace can be achieved. As an evidence to this we can observe EU, which is eager and able to invest into peace, specifically on its borderlands whereas it is still failing to achieve some standards, unfortunately even more obviously visible now than any time before.

Due to the strong and pertinent division line between East and West clashing in the EU neighbourhood area the conflict has never discontinued, and the USA vs. Russia (Soviet) conflict obviously still exists today. 'The West (the more patient party) was not prepared to recognize Soviet dominance in Eastern and Central Europe on a legally binding basis, but it was willing to do so in less precise and explicitly nonlegally binding terms – if in return the Soviets would accept a soft human rights framework that turned out to have an unexpectedly significant bite over the longer term.'[2] The remains of democracy and the pouring in of human rights from the West into the Soviet-dominated area has influenced not just local societies but the Soviet society as well, making it finally more human. The main question posed here is whether Russian will be

1 Lisa Hultman, Jacob D. Kathman and Megan Shannon, 'United Nations Peacekeeping Dynamics and the Duration of Post-civil Conflict Peace' (2016) 33(3) Conflict Management and Peace Science 231.

2 Kenneth W. Abbott and Duncan Snidal, 'Hard and Soft Law in International Governance' (2000) 54 International Organization 421.

a banned language in Ukraine after the conflict ends and how it could be legally achieved keeping in mind all the EU frameworks for the protection of minorities.

To outline it once again, the EU is on the crossroads and such powerful states as the USA and Russia do not prioritize EU interests at all. The only safeguard for EU interests could be an agreement, in any form, which can be reached and guaranteed only by the UN and its Security Council. 'The Security Council's future practice in mandate-creation will very likely continue to be marked by a discretionary case-by-case approach.'[3] Overall while there is no common interest in making stable or hard rules the soft lawmaking capacity of some powerful states will be blooming just as it is the case today. When we turn back to the European continent and try to research and understand its position, while having two UNSC member states in it, it is still exposed to the will of others without being able to influence, prevent or even stop the most challenging problems in its neighbourhood. Even without mentioning them all we can see that EU is struggling with the refugee crisis for decades, now even without having any initial sign that it can stop and put an end to the pressure on the EU external borders. What the EU can expect and in particular what the societies from where the refugees are coming in huge numbers can expect, is obviously the amount of such a huge brain drain as a big challenge for their future. The refugees are coming primarily from war-hit zones, which would definitely need some strong post-conflict reconstruction agenda. 'The experience of the last two decades has proved that reintegration is the most complex, challenging, expensive, and long-term activity relating to post-conflict reconstruction and the one in which the political and economic objectives of reconstruction are most intertwined for national reconciliation.'[4] Therefore, researchers together with the EU and the whole of the international community are facing a problem that there will be areas in the post-conflict frameworks where there will be no people to build for or wishing to come back. This is such a global challenge and while every economy can always welcome cheap labour it is another aspect that depopulation and the centralization of various economic activities will just prolong this agony, and could not solve anything in the future.

---

3 Jolyon Ford, *Regulating Business for Peace: The United Nations, the Private Sector and Post-conflict Recovery* (Cambridge University Press 2015).

4 Graciana del Castillo, 'Economic Reconstruction and Reforms in Post-conflict Countries' in Arnim Langer and Graham K. Brown (ed), *Building Sustainable Peace: Timing and Sequencing of Post-conflict Reconstruction and Peacebuilding* (Oxford University Press 2016).

Finally we will now try to explain a very interesting principle present in the EU where it has a very prominent role, the Precautionary Principle.[5] It is very unclear regarding goals and settings where it exists and what exactly it regulates, which makes it a perfect informal or soft law-related mechanism. Accordingly it is very interesting to observe that this principle combines science into policymaking, which makes again a very important correlation for future hard law but most importantly soft law-making. 'Sustainable development, intergenerational equity, or the precautionary principle, are all more convincingly seen in this sense: not as binding obligations which must be complied with, but as principles, considerations or objectives to be taken account of-they may be soft, but they are still law.'[6] The whole idea of development, economy, human rights and environment are all intertwined by this principle and certainly meant to prevent any harm, which might occur due to the selfish behaviour of some states, companies or individuals who might misuse the dominant position they presently pose. There are also scientific arguments, which can be different and even contrary to each other, so it is in such cases necessary to maintain a system which does not harm today nor will do it in the future. 'It is therefore not imaginable that a proper invocation, implementation and application of the precautionary principle would be based solely on a "perceived" risk.'[7] Many times the risk can be real and actual, but the system of laws can't be ready to stand up in the defence of a certain system. It is important to have soft laws, which could be quickly used without activating the whole system of the state apparatus. Informal or soft laws present a very important aspect of every hard law system where time and institutional challenges can be easily overcome due to them.

1 Courts and Informal Rules

Courts themselves are not soft lawmakers while they certainly have a considerable role in accepting and applying them; still their most important role is determining which law to apply, whereas many times they could also apply soft laws. More importantly courts are able to see what institutions and organ-

5 European Parliament, 'The Precautionary Principle: Definitions, Applications and Governance' (9 December 2015) <https://www.europarl.europa.eu/thinktank/en/document/EPRS_IDA(2015)573876> accessed 22 March 2026.

6 Alan E. Boyle, 'Some Reflections on the Relationship of Treaties and Soft Law' (1999) 48 The International and Comparative Law Quarterly 901.

7 Rene Von Schomberg, 'The Precautionary Principle: Its Use Within Hard and Soft Law' (2012) 2 EJRR 147.

izations have the right to form laws and also decide which institutional laws they will apply as a matter of priority. 'They raise questions of whether or not an institution or mechanism is intended to create binding rules or non-legal norms; whether it contains precise, highly elaborated rules or vague principles; and whether or not it is envisaged that there will be a role for a legal institution such as an international court.'[8] As an addition to rule-making institutions there could be various rule-interpreting institutions such as reconciliation and mediating bodies, while arbitrations would have a more prominent role as institutions with harder rules and regulation capacity available. Once again we come to the most important issue where it has to be determined if an institution applying a certain law to solve cases has the capacity and if someone is willing or able to accept and finally enforce its decision. This is one of the most important and key questions, since during or after the conflict there are not so many authorities which can approach the parties and offer them applicable solutions to their disagreements. Regarding post-conflict agreements it is very important to note who is making and supporting such an agreement, while obviously the state will be responsible to also guarantee the enforcement of what has been agreed. Such a role of mediating between parties and supporting a certain agreement is present in our work as well; namely we will deal with such agreements which have been reached under the supervision of the EU high representative of the Union for Foreign Affairs and Security Policy, the US president, the Russian president and also the Chinese government.

The rule-making authority always has a prominent role and the interpreting capacity, which also explains and elaborates it regarding its potential implementation. 'The prohibitive status of the norm through reiterated interpretations by hard and soft courts in tandem enables soft courts to act as meaningful sites for accountability, at least in Europe.'[9] Where it is necessary to only determine the level of accountability for a certain act and no punitive intentions are present it is possible to have an extraordinary court or authority make such a decision. Often decisions can't be enforced but are able to serve as authoritative guidelines, just as it is the case in the EU. There are other important international bodies, which are able to make an authoritative decision of which the most prominent one is the International Court of Justice

8 Elizabeth Craig, 'From Soft to Hard Law? Culture, Identity, and Language Issues within the Northern Ireland Bill of Rights Process' (2010) 56 Focaal – Journal of Global and Historical Anthropology 35.

9 Başak Çalı, Cathryn Costello and Stewart Cunningham, 'Hard Protection through Soft Courts? Non-refoulement before the United Nations Treaty Bodies' (2020) 21 German Law Journal 355.

(ICJ).[10] The United Nations Charter gave the ICJ little clear guidance, so the court often had no choice but to engage in a form of judicial rule-making.[11] An independent and professional body has always the relevant capacities which are necessary to make it function and be completely independent of both outside institutional support or even the input of some norms, which are necessary for rule-making.

Similarly to the authority of the ICJ there was another court with an important role and specific jurisdiction. 'Ex hypothesi, the conflicting jurisprudence between the ICTY and the ICJ could have been avoided if the ICTY had not overstepped its institutional setting as a criminal court and instead confined itself to the issue of conflict categorization.'[12] ICTY has been an ad hoc tribunal and while its existence was necessary at that time it is unclear how after the formation of the ICC such a tribunal can exist. In particular for the territory of ex-Yugoslavia[13] and now in either Serbia or even Kosovo as a non-UN member state. 'Unfortunately, the ICTY has fallen far short of its task.'[14] The challenging establishment of a new court, which will be dealing with war crimes originating from Kosovo, while this territory has already had the ICTY mandate and its work in this territory regarding war crimes, now makes a very interesting and challenging legal ambiguity in this regard.

The Kosovo Specialist Chambers and Specialist Prosecutor's Office (KSC)[15] has been newly established and meant to be a local court with local legal framework while having international judges and its seat in the Hague. One of the main questions is how a local court can deal with cases which might even include crimes which fall under the exclusive jurisdiction of the ICC. 'Victims of aggression could be the entire population of a state, and they might present to the ICC personal claims for matters that have traditionally

10 International Court of Justice, 'How the Court Works' (2023) <https://www.icj-cij.org/how-the-court-works> accessed 22 March 2026.

11 Andrew T. Guzman and Timothy L. Meyer, 'International Soft Law' (2010) 2 Journal of Legal Analysis 171.

12 Ke Song and Xuechan Ma, 'Individual Opinions as an Agent of International Legal Development?' (2022) 13 Journal of International Dispute Settlement 54.

13 Julia Marquier, 'Soft law : das Beispiel des OSZE-Prozesses ; ein Beitrag zur völkerrechtlichen Rechtsquellenlehre' (Inaugural-Dissertation zur Erlangung des Grades eines Doktors der Rechte, Rheinische Friedrich-Wilhelms-Universität 2003).

14 Jamie Rowen, 'Reconciliation in Divided Societies: Considerations for Timing and Sequencing' in Arnim Langer and Graham K. Brown (ed), *Building Sustainable Peace: Timing and Sequencing of Post-conflict Reconstruction and Peacebuilding* (Oxford University Press 2016).

15 Kosovo Specialist Chambers & Specialist Prosecutor's Office, 'Kosovo Specialist Chambers & Specialist Prosecutor's Office' <https://www.scp-ks.org/en> accessed 22 March 2026.

fallen within the purview of states to settle through interstate agreements or resolve with the help of the UN.'[16] It is therefore a huge challenge which remains of how to deal with cases for which a certain court have an exclusive jurisdiction and if some other courts might deal with such cases how their decisions could be treated in the local and international contexts. Overall how to treat laws of unrecognized states and their court decisions also remains a challenge; can they be treated as soft laws after all? Such challenges of determining what can be a law and how can it be established is a question for the future, while we can define some valuable institutions which can take up a role to determine what can be a law and in particular soft law in the framework on international law, adjudication and conflict resolution.

2 The International Court of Justice and Informal Agreements

2.1 ICJ and Its Role Regarding the Interpretation of Informal Agreements

The very challenging issue of interpreting informal agreements offers us an insight into the practice of the states, and the role of courts in cases where they are hesitant or simply not able to sign binding agreements. 'Nonbinding soft law obligations allow states to realize more value from their commitments by reducing the losses in the event of undeterrable violations.'[17] Even when states at a certain moment change their mind it is not possible to completely ignore an obligation, and that is why the area of understanding and enforcing such informal agreements are on the rise today. The influence and the application capacity of various understandings of adjudication bodies is changing and shaping the mutual relationships between states in both formal and informal aspects. Some court decisions such as the ICJ, can produce unclear, confusing and legally non-applicable decisions. 'There is some concern that, beyond Kosovo, other groups aspiring to statehood or seeking to consolidate their statehood claims may be encouraged by the advisory opinion – among them, Turkish Cypriots, Bosnian Serbs, Iraqi Kurds, Somalilanders, Abkhaz

16 Edda Kristjansdottir, 'Who Is Most Able and Willing? Complementarity and Victim Reparations at the International Criminal Court' in Cecilia M. Bailliet, *Non-state actors, soft law, and protective regimes : from the margins* (Cambridge University Press 2012).

17 Andrew T. Guzman and Timothy L. Meyer, 'International Soft Law' (2010) 2 Journal of Legal Analysis 171.

and South Ossetians.'[18] This proves that the advisory opinion of the ICJ has tremendously influenced and also changed the understanding of sovereignty, where everyone sees it through its own lenses. This decision has been seen as very influential for various independence struggles worldwide, what again brings in the possibility for new post-conflict agreements.

While the international common law (ICL) is a new concept that falls outside the purview of many discussions of soft law[19] it is evitable how these two aspects and spheres of legal life are mutually shaping and influencing each other. It is also true that soft law allows states to tap into a more efficient method of amending legal rules as circumstances change[20] and this is one of their core and vital values. The arena of international law is therefore permanently changing, and this has also been outlined and described at the time when the ICJ mandate has been established and outlined regarding which norms are binding. 'Binding refers to instruments that, on the international stage, fall within the sources of law as defined in article 38 of the ICJ Statute and UNSC resolutions under Chapter VII of the UN Charter.'[21] It is not the form that matters, but the binding character of an act, which is being decided by the ICJ on the highest possible international level.

When we look at the variety of norms we can see that the intentions of parties also change, as well as the form in which they are shaping and putting in their mutual relationships. Mandatory rules can be placed into international conventions, whether general or particular, establishing rules expressly recognized by the contesting states.[22] With informal rules states can in later phases understand and interpret the norms differently, while naturally maximally outlining and defending their own standpoints and interests. It is not different with the application and interpretation of various court decisions as long as there is place to do so. In this lasting struggle it is possible that more states accept a certain pattern or behaviour, which can, by the force of international customary law, become mandatory for other countries as well. An international custom, as evidence of a general practice is accepted as law[23]

---

18 Richard Caplan, 'The ICJ's Advisory Opinion on Kosovo' (2010) 55 PEACEBRIEF <https://www.usip.org/sites/default/files/PB55%20The%20ICJs%20Advisory%20Opinion%20on%20Kosovo.pdf> accessed 22 March 2026.

19 Andrew T. Guzman and Timothy L. Meyer, 'International Soft Law' (2010) 2 Journal of Legal Analysis 171.

20 Ibid.

21 Doron Goldbarsht, *Global Counter-Terrorist Financing and Soft Law: Multi-layered Approaches* (Edward Elgar 2020).

22 United Nations, 'Statute of the International Court of Justice' (18 April 1946) <https://www.icj-cij.org/statute> accessed 22 March 2026.

23 Ibid.

and so it is treated and being challenged in front of various tribunals including the ICJ.

2.2 ICJ and Its Conflict Resolution Capacity

When signing an agreement in any of its possible forms states are also mutually agreeing to resolve various conflicts. 'Reciprocity offers one reason why states might opt for a soft law agreement rather than a treaty.'[24] In soft law agreements there are no sanctions and the possibility to suffer harm outside the framework of the given agreement is also very low. Another benefit is that by violating an agreement it can be a tool to spur change in a partner's behaviour[25] and to re-establish reciprocity.

While we speak about reciprocity it is very important to have acts, which can maintain such a balance and not disturb it further or misinterpret it. 'Undoubtedly, the ICJ Advisory Opinion on Kosovo's independence has played a role in shaping the public discourse towards Europe by the Moscow discourse.'[26] In fact Russia is using it to promote its own interests and agenda in its sphere of influence, obviously according to its own needs and benefits. While in Ukraine, Russia supports the establishment of new republics, it has for some political reasons recently supported the instant dissolution of the Nagorno-Karabakh Republic in 2023. The previous agreement supported by Russia in 2020 between Armenia and Azerbaijan has solved some important aspects of life in the South Caucasus it soon ceased to exist. Will Russia still partly support this agreement or some of its outcomes after all? 'If Russia subsequently violates that agreement, countries around the world will observe that violation and Russia's reputation for compliance with international law will suffer.'[27] The Russian behaviour and standpoints can be used in the future to determine its understanding of soft laws and its approaches towards their future use and interpretation.

Every single agreement, in any form, signed in the framework of international law between two independent states or entities has the capacity to be in

24 Andrew T. Guzman and Timothy L. Meyer, 'International Soft Law' (2010) 2 Journal of Legal Analysis 171.

25 Ibid.

26 Pëllumb Kallaba, 'Russian Interference in Kosovo: How and Why?' (2017) 9 Kosovar Centre for Security Studies <https://qkss.org/images/uploads/files/Russian_interference_in_Kosovo_finale_2_735070.pdf> accessed 22 March 2026.

27 Andrew T. Guzman and Timothy L. Meyer, 'International Soft Law' (2010) 2 Journal of Legal Analysis 171.

the future interpreted by the ICJ. This is what the article 38 of the ICJ Statute[28] allows the court to do and allows it to have a very wide interpretative capacity. The ICJ is the principal neutral arbiter of customary international law.[29] One of the main questions we are facing today is regarding sovereignty and the forever lasting struggle to define it and determine who can have a claim for it and who doesn't. One prominent case where sovereignty was approached was Malaysia v. Singapore where the parties had agreed to discontinue the proceedings[30] so we could not get a valuable answer out of it. Definitely, the most prominent case today is the case concerning Kosovo and its self-declared independence. In this regard, the ICJ was of the opinion that the declaration of independence of Kosovo adopted on 17 February 2008 did not violate international law[31] and has ultimately missed the opportunity to narrow down in which situations independence can be declared.

Regarding sovereignty an important role also belongs to the case concerning Nicaragua v. United States of America where sovereignty protection was described in more detail. 'The right to sovereignty and to political independence possessed by the Republic of Nicaragua, like any Other State of the region or of the world, should be fully respected and should not in any way be jeopardized by any military and paramilitary activities which are prohibited by the principles of international law.'[32] This conclusion, as being almost four decades old could be easily interpreted today after so many actual and present breaches of sovereignty, which have happened and are happening more frequently recently.

2.3 ICJ Cases and Their Application to Informal Agreements

In order to define and better understand the future possible cases before the ICJ regarding informal agreements, and in particular the ones we are researching, it is necessary to point out some important aspects stemming out of them and also to apply the relevant previous practice of the ICJ. Regarding sover-

28 United Nations, 'Statute of the International Court of Justice' (18 April 1946) <https://www.icj-cij.org/statute> accessed 22 March 2026.

29 Andrew T. Guzman and Timothy L. Meyer, 'International Soft Law' (2010) 2 Journal of Legal Analysis 171.

30 *Request for Interpretation of the Judgment of 23 May 2008 in the Case concerning Sovereignty over Pedra Branca/Pulau Batu Puteh, Middle Rocks and South Ledge (Malaysia/Singapore) (Malaysia v Singapore), Order* [2018] ICJ Reports 2018 288.

31 *Accordance with International Law of the Unilateral Declaration of Independence in Respect of Kosovo, Advisory Opinion* [2010] ICJ Reports 2010 403.

32 *Military and Paramilitary Activities in and against Nicaragua (Nicaragua v United States of America), Provisional Measures Order* [1984] ICJ Reports 1984 169.

eignty it can be seen that the NATO bombing and its presence in Kosovo suspended the effective exercise of Serbian sovereignty over the territory of Kosovo as of 10 June 1999, a fact recognized clearly by the International Court of Justice.[33] The question remains what, how and who can limit a certain state's sovereignty and in which instances secession can occur in accordance with international law and the ICJ doctrine. It is legally accurate to conclude that the ICJ Kosovo Advisory Opinion does not establish a positive right of secession.[34] 'Historically, questions submitted to the ICJ have been quite broad but this particular one that the Court was asked to consider was a very narrow one.'[35] Therefore even by not answering this question fully the world politics in this aspect have been still tremendously influenced. After many decades of post-colonialism we have now stepped into the era of conflicts and the rising number of various post-conflicts societies, which are either not recognized or just function as semi-recognized entities. 'However, despite challenging the legality of the declaration of independence by Serbia before ICJ, Kosovo managed to secure 69 recognitions, from the declaration of independence until the publication of the Court's opinion in 2010, which is more than half the total number of recognitions.'[36] Such an outcome showed us that the independence declaration was more of a political act than a legal act per se, and so was the rushed recognition campaign initially led by the United States. Despite expectations that the ICJ opinion would pave the way for new recognitions[37] it was just partially true, and Kosovo has until now remained a semi-recognized entity with very little potential to ever become a UN member state. On the other side, such an outcome has initiated the rising number of conflicts which were supported by various UNSC permanent member states globally. 'It may be argued that the ICJ determined in the Kosovo case that secession is permissible under international law, because it is not expressly

---

33 Enver Hasani, 'The Role of the Constitutional Court in the Development of the Rule of Law in Kosovo' (2018) 43 Rev Cent & E Eur L 274.

34 Milena Sterio, 'Self-Determination and Secession under International Law: Nagorno-Karabakh' (2016) 59 German YB Int'l L 81.

35 Richard Caplan, 'The ICJ's Advisory Opinion on Kosovo' (2010) 55 PEACEBRIEF <https://www.usip.org/sites/default/files/PB55%20The%20ICJs%20Advisory%20Opinion%20on%20Kosovo.pdf> accessed 22 March 2026.

36 Eugen Cakolli, 'KOSOVO: Between Universal Non-recognition and "Derecognitions"' [2020] Kosova Democratic Institute (KDI) and the Konrad Adenauer Foundation <https://www.kas.de/documents/286052/0/Policy+brief+20-09-13+Kosovo+Between+universal+non-recognition+and+derecognitions+(Eng).pdf> accessed 22 March 2026.

37 Ibid.

prohibited.'[38] The peaceful reintegration of Kosovo into Serbia is an impossibility and independent statehood therefore represents the only plausible way forward.[39] While such claims undoubtedly and necessarily claim independence it is a bit more complex to fully achieve them, when it comes to legal possibilities in the previously established understanding of sovereignty concepts.

Post-colonialism can still be seen today as it makes challenges in the sense of sovereignty issues even now in the 21st century. One of the main questions is whether before colonialism certain territories belonged to anyone and if possible to be determined to whom exactly. 'Western Sahara (Rio de Oro and Sakiet El Hamra) at the time of colonization by Spain was not a territory belonging to no-one (terra nullius)'.[40] So the ICJ concludes that 'there were legal ties between this territory and the Kingdom of Morocco'[41] and also that 'there were legal ties between this territory and the Mauritanian entity,'[42] which both are in fact bordering Western Sahara until today and potentially also claiming its territory respectively. While there is no final and widely acceptable solution for this region, such a situation also hinders its development, as also the human and minority rights protection. Another case study from post-colonialism is the exercise of Portuguese sovereignty over the enclaves[43] in India, where it was allowed to keep contact with them by passing through Indian territory.

The issue of how to establish and especially how to protect sovereignty was also one of the first challenges and cases in front of the ICJ. This case was concerned by the fact that the United Kingdom violated the sovereignty of the People's Republic of Albania.[44] There were no specific damages in this case apart from establishing the fact that a breach of the sovereignty had occurred. Now all such arguments put us in front of a more challenging case today where the ICJ is to decide regarding the Israeli occupation of East Jerusalem and/or Palestine overall? Finally, the recent war in Nagorno-Karabakh has also started some interesting sovereignty and human rights related ques-

38 Milena Sterio, 'Self-Determination and Secession under International Law: Nagorno-Karabakh' (2016) 59 German YB Int'l L 81.

39 Richard Caplan, 'The ICJ's Advisory Opinion on Kosovo' (2010) 55 PEACEBRIEF <https://www.usip.org/sites/default/files/PB55%20The%20ICJs%20Advisory%20Opinion%20on%20Kosovo.pdf> accessed 22 March 2026.

40 *Western Sahara, Advisory Opinion* [1975] ICJ Reports 1975 12.

41 Ibid.

42 Ibid.

43 *Case Concerning Right of passage over Indian Territory (Portugal v India) Merits* [1960] ICJ Reports 1960 6.

44 *Corfu Channel case, Judgment* [1949] ICJ Reports 1949 4.

tions. 'Both Parties shall refrain from any action which might aggravate or extend the dispute before the Court or make it more difficult to resolve.'[45] While it is very difficult we are still facing many challenges regarding various post-conflict societies and their presumable future sovereignty challenges in front of the ICJ and also broader.

As a last aspect regarding the work of the ICJ we will see some recent cases and their potentials regarding our case studies and agreements, which will be researched in the following chapters more specifically. One very famous investment-related cases in the Gabčikovo-Nagymaros Project was also a case between Hungary and Slovakia in front of ICJ. It was concluded that 'Hungary and Slovakia must negotiate in good faith in the light of the prevailing situation, and must take all necessary measures to ensure the achievement of the objectives of the Treaty.'[46] The ICJ has accordingly a prevailed pro-investment and pro-development priority with refuting possible local and national interests. The court continues stating that 'unless the Parties otherwise agree, a joint operational régime must be established in accordance with the Treaty.'[47] Obviously this idea of investment protection can be expected in the future and at least for now it overrules other aspects stemming from investment treaties. We conclude by the finding that rulings are, of course, not accepted in their entirety by all states[48] posing therefore an ever-lasting challenge of how to enforce ICJ decisions where there is no such tool, which could guarantee their enforcement, just as it does not exist regarding any other informal and soft law regulation.

3 The Role of Courts in Interpreting Soft Law in the EU

It is very challenging to find out and interpret soft laws as a set of not finally set rules when it comes to court proceedings and relevant interpretations. Still it can be seen that the Courts overall in the EU are already experienced with such dubious questions but what still remains is the fact that a court will always be challenged by new legal problems, which are always more and more innovative. Actual problems are such as how to interpret the acts or the no acts of certain parties when it comes to the implementation of soft

45 *Application of the International Convention on the Elimination of All Forms of Racial Discrimination (Azerbaijan v Armenia), Provisional Measures* [2021] ICJ Reports 2021 405.

46 *Gabčikovo-Nagymaros Project (Hungary/Slovakia), Judgment* [1997] ICJ Reports 1997 7.

47 Ibid.

48 Andrew T. Guzman and Timothy L. Meyer, 'International Soft Law' (2010) 2 Journal of Legal Analysis 171.

laws. 'The courts would consider the actual intentions of the author to the extent that these can be discovered by looking at the institution's external behaviour and associated objective evidence.'[49] In such cases where the final implementation phase of a certain soft law is not present or either not possible, it is the steps made towards a certain goal which matter the most. Such steps made do not necessarily bring a certain party closer to the actual implementation of the required norm; in such cases even the level of none performance can be measured.

In general soft law norms are there to fill and guide in the case of law ambiguity where the answers to such questions should be found in previous cases or even soft laws, which could offer new, innovative and unofficial solutions to such problems, in short soft law regulations. 'Such conclusions are interesting and suggest that the Court indeed applies double standards: while it does not consider itself bound by soft law, they urge national courts to take soft law into consideration when judging cases.'[50] This is atypical behaviour or in the case of soft laws more likely a typical behaviour, where a key component of a soft law is its enforcing authority as long as there is an authority to back up a certain regulation, it will be applied and respected. As low the authority to enforce soft law is, similarly the lower is the will to even take its application into consideration by any concerned party. 'Finally, the "must consider" obligation stops short before becoming a duty of consistent interpretation, since reasoned deviation is allowed and no obligation to interpret national law in the light of Union soft law is foreseen.'[51] For courts it has to be a very shortcut whereas they must decide whether such a norm of soft law applies or does not. Ultimately such a decision can bring a very different outcome concerning the differences of its application, or not. In case of institutions, companies and similar bodies it is more different as they have to, or are bound to make steps which are necessary to incorporate and implement some norms of soft law.

Finally, the role soft laws have in the EU legal framework is much more important and developed than in some other jurisdictions; that is also why they have to be researched and understood better in this work and its possible

49 Napoleon Xanthoulis, 'Legal Effects and Reviewability of EU Acts: Between Institutional Intentions and Perceptions of Concerned Parties' in Mariolina Eliantonio, Emilia Korkea-aho and Oana Ştefan (ed), *EU Soft Law in the Member States: Theoretical Findings and Empirical Evidence* (Hart 2021).

50 Mariolina Eliantonio and Oana Stefan, 'Soft Law Before the European Courts: Discovering a "Common Pattern?"' (2018) 37 Yearbook of European Law 457.

51 Petra Lea Láncos, 'A Hard Core Under the Soft Shell: How Binding Is Union Soft Law for Member States?' (2018) 24 European Public Law 755.

future wider implementation. 'A factor in this debate is that current and future EU soft law would remain persuasive whether incorporated or not and decision-makers or courts could still avail themselves of it where relevant if they so wished.'[52] This finally brings us again to the actual determination of the real power of courts and in particular the very vague presence they and their enforcement mechanism can have in post-conflict settings. It is also necessary to mention the very influential and in some cases more influential power of politics in such post-conflict settings, where courts are either influenced or directly set to implement in a certain manner actual soft law regulations. The very complex setting and understanding of soft laws makes it more a law in regulated systems and less than a law regulation in post-conflict settings in particular.

4 International Organizations and Their Informal Rules-Making Capacity

The role of various organizations in post-conflict development is very important and it is necessary to research and explain the most important ones and their activities regarding their informal and soft law interpretation capacity. Such organizations could be international, inter-governmental, governmental, non-governmental and also private ones such as companies. All such institutions have their inner rules, which are then applied to various cases in which they are engaged; this way they can influence the local developments and also shape present and future policies. 'Finally, many international instruments emanating from non-state actors have emerged in the past decades and are often considered as soft law standards for these actors (e.g. international agreements on corporate social responsibility, framework agreements or codes of conduct signed by international trade union organizations, employers' organizations, companies, etc.).'[53] For post-conflict settings it is important to have some intergovernmental organizations (IGOs), which are able to oversee situations and quickly act as conflict resolution and solution-offering mecha-

52 Mary Dobbs and Oana Ştefan, 'EU Soft Law in the UK on the Eve of Brexit: (Not) Much Ado about Nothing?' in Mariolina Eliantonio, Emilia Korkea-aho and Oana Ştefan (ed), *EU Soft Law in the Member States: Theoretical Findings and Empirical Evidence* (Hart 2021).

53 Thomas Gammeltoft-Hansen, Stéphanie Lagoutte and John Cerone, 'Tracing the Roles of Soft Law in Human Rights' in Stéphanie Lagoutte, Thomas Gammeltoft-Hansen and John Cerone (ed), *Tracing the Roles of Soft Law in Human Rights* (Oxford University Press 2016).

nisms. Such organizations have been widely used as observing and implementing missions; probably the most important ones in Europe today are UNMIK[54] and EULEX[55] in regard to Kosovo. 'In the post-conflict setting it would also require IGOs to fully consider the context of their administration rather than merely taking a "one-size fits all approach" that entirely relies on reactive due diligence to remedy violations.'[56] Such organizations are forced to be creative in the implementation of their capacity while still limited by their mandate and also various and changing local contexts. These organizations can be limited by the various interests of their own structures; their founders' priorities might also differ.

A very prominent feature stemming from the UN itself is that some decisions simply can't be agreed by all its member states. 'When Western states, under the leadership of the United States, started to lose their initially dominant position within the UN, many Western non-governmental organizations (NGOs) had to take sides in order to secure funding from Western states and institutions.'[57] As previously mentioned, funding is never happening without making some priorities first, they are aimed at reaching certain outcomes in every post-conflict setting. The fact that NGOs do not belong to a certain government but still depend on their funding makes their position as a neutral and independent stakeholders a bit more complex. Many times some acts of organizations engaged in peacebuilding and also infrastructure-building are not meant just for the benefit of locals, but also serve as an important profit making tool for foreign companies and investors. In such societies where there is a dearth of institutions which are able to do quality checks money is not spent according to international norms and standards and this is more visible and prominent in the sphere of infrastructure-building. 'Although being a soft law that lacks stringent enforcing mechanism, the principles of quality infrastructure represent the collective intent of rule-setting under G20.'[58] While

54 United Nations, 'United Nations Interim Administration Mission in Kosovo' <https://peacekeeping.un.org/en/mission/unmik> accessed 22 March 2026.

55 European Union Rule of Law Mission in Kosovo, 'About EULEX' <https://www.eulex-kosovo.eu/?page=2,60> accessed 22 March 2026.

56 Aoife O'Donoghue, 'The Exercise of Governance Authority by International Organisations: The Role of Due Diligence Obligations after Conflict' in Matthew Saul and James A Sweeney (ed), *International Law and Post-conflict Reconstruction Policy* (Routledge 2015).

57 Jochen von Bernstorff, 'New Responses to the Legitimacy Crisis of International Institutions: The Role of "Civil Society" and the Rise of the Principle of Participation of "The Most Affected" in International Institutional Law' (2021) 32 EJIL 125.

58 Umirdinov Alisher, 'Generating a Reform of the BRI from the Inside: Japan's Contribution Via Soft Law Diplomacy' [2019] RIETI Discussion Paper Series <https://www.rieti.go.jp/jp/publications/dp/19e076.pdf> accessed 22 March 2026.

standards might still exist their implementation as everything else in post-conflicts societies can lack important steps and also serve as a tool for corruption locally, but also internationally.

When it comes to trade and the important trade liberalization necessities in post-conflict settings we need to mention some important international standards and tools. Probably one of the most important institutions in this regard today is the United Nations Commission on International Trade Law (UNCITRAL). Interestingly, one of the features of UNCITRAL is that it is not a mandatory rules-making organization, accordingly its standards can't be forced upon anyone. 'As a consequence of their prominence, the UNCITRAL Arbitration Rules and the UNCITRAL Model Law on International Commercial Arbitration represent particularly powerful co-ordinating soft-law documents.'[59] While its most important feature is the Arbitration and solving problems of such a nature it is necessary to have some previous trade established.

In this regard, specifically there is an important convention, The United Nations Convention on Contracts for the International Sale of Goods (CISG). 'Since there is no real uniform interpretation of the CISG, there is no certainty as to which approach a court will follow and if it will find there to be a choice of law or not.'[60] So apart from the bare existence of tools for trade they are bringing an extra challenge to post-conflict societies as the disagreements and confrontations can be to an extent that trade is restricted and blocked in many different ways. In Kosovo for instance the government has for some time applied a 100% tax on Serbian goods,[61] which has literally blocked all the imports in this territory. Free trade is still seen as a benefit and an evolutionary principle of free societies, which are able to trade between each other for their mutual benefit, but also for the benefit of their own citizens. 'Moreover, the CISG widely permits private parties otherwise subject to its terms to simply decide that they do not like its provisions and thus opt out by saying as much in their contracts.'[62] So while it is very hard to establish free trade and also

59 Bryan H. Druzin, 'Why Does Soft Law Have Any Power Anyway?' (2017) 7 Asian Journal of International Law 361.

60 Brooke Marshall, 'The Hague Choice of Law Principles, CISG, and PICC: A Hard Look at a Choice of Soft Law' (2018) 66 American Journal of Comparative Law 175.

61 European Parliament, 'Kosovo: MEPs Welcome Lifting Tariffs on Goods from Serbia and Bosnia and Herzegovina' (4 February 2020) <https://www.europarl.europa.eu/news/en/press-room/20200402IPR76410/meps-welcome-lifting-tariffs-on-goods-from-serbia-and-bosnia-and-herzegovina> accessed 22 March 2026.

62 Susan Block-Lieb, 'Soft and Hard Strategies: The Role of Business in the Crafting of International Commercial Law' (2019) 40 Mich. J. Int'l L. 433.

once it is made it can be easily blocked and disturbed by other factors, such as the ones we have mentioned earlier, political, social and the permanently confronting economic interests of the local communities against imports overall.

It is not a surprise that trade-related norms are hard to establish on a higher level and that is also why the Principles for International Commercial Contracts (PICCs) have been developed by UNIDROIT. Organizations such as UNIDROIT are having a capacity to form some trade-related aspects but still have not developed and strengthened so much to be able to put on some mandatory provisions in such cases as our cases studies of post-conflict societies. 'Even more interesting, however, is the circumstance that in half of the collected decisions the PICC are cited by either arbitral tribunals or, increasingly, domestic courts, as an aid to interpret or supplement the applicable domestic law (including CISG).'[63] Overall trade is still the most important and necessary achievement of post-conflict societies and their development. Also as we will see it later many Agreements focus on trade and its various aspects while also try to strengthen its initial implementation.

Obviously, trade is a very important conflict prevention mechanism and international trade is under very strict scrutiny regarding the biggest global economies, which do not want to lose their share or present dominant positions anywhere. In this regard the system of the World Trade Organization (WTO) is under constant revision since disturbances and changes in the global trade patterns can have a very negative impact on some of its member states. 'China's persistent trade surpluses with Europe and the United States are increasingly perceived as a systemic WTO problem.'[64] It is therefore not coming as a surprise that some key high-tech trade areas such as telecommunications are already producing conflicts. The recent restrictions placed on the Chinese Huawei[65] company by the US government is showing the burning problems of today where investments, technology and its trade can serve as a

63 Anna Veneziano, 'The Soft Law Approach to Unification of International Commercial Contract Law: Future Perspectives in Light of Unidroit's Experience' (2013) 58 Vill. L. Rev. 521.

64 Petersmann, Ernst-Ulrich, 'From Integration Through Law to Global Community Law? Between Arbitration, Adjudication, and Judicial Overreach' in Giuliana Ziccardi Capaldo (ed), *The Global Community Yearbook of International Law and Jurisprudence 2020* (Oxford University Press 2021).

65 Michael R. Pompeo, 'The United States Further Restricts Huawei Access to U.S. Technology' (17 August 2020) <https://2017-2021.state.gov/the-united-states-further-restricts-huawei-access-to-u-s-technology/> accessed 22 March 2026.

conflict-boosting reason as well. Ultimately various soft laws and their vague understanding and implementation can also cause trade limitations and disturbances where the unavailability of their judicial interpretation and the enforcement of such decisions can be seen as one of the biggest threats in the framework of post-conflict development overall.

CHAPTER 7

The Application of Informal Rules in the EU Framework

1 The EU Legislative Mechanism and Its Understanding of Informal Rules

The very specific relationship between EU and its member states has also produced a big amount of ambiguities of who and how to regulate what in the complex system of post-conflict resolution, where a very prominent role belongs to various forms of informal rules. It is also interesting to observe that the EU and its institutions are very active in responding to various legal challenges, while they are concerned about such acts their role might still be absent in a given case and also their problem-solving capacity be limited. EU and its institutions prefer when their voice is heard. Also, this way they are aiming at promoting and presenting their political standpoints. It is very important in turbulent times regarding some actual political issues or eventually some legal challenges. 'This is the case in particular as regards communications, in respect of which a distinction must be made between informative communications, interpretative communications and decisional communications.'[1] While there are many EU official languages and the communications can accordingly have different translations and, by that, also meanings, such a variety of forms in communications can give more linguistic and legal challenges also. It has highlighted that EU soft law does not follow a predefined format,[2] so when mentioning soft law, we should not forget about any kind of document which is issued by EU regarding some legal or political challenge it faces. In this regard, it is very challenging to determine what role a certain EU act has, whether it is a legal or just a political document.

There are also very frequent documents and texts which merely 'name and shame' human rights violations,[3] which again have an informative character about some acts which might be even sanctioned in the future. It is also a very

1 Linda Senden, *Soft Law in European Community Law* (Hart 2004).

2 Andreas Hofmann, 'Types of EU Soft Law and Their National Impact' in Mariolina Eliantonio, Emilia Korkea-aho and Oana Ştefan (ed), *EU Soft Law in the Member States: Theoretical Findings and Empirical Evidence* (Hart 2021).

3 Guenter Schirmer, 'Goals and Functions of European Soft Law – Statement –' in Julia Iliopoulos-Strangas and Jean-François Flauss (ed), *Das soft law der europäischen Organisa-*

 | HTTPS://DOI.ORG/10.1163/9789004746091-009

characteristic feature of the EU that it shows its future intentions in different ways and in that way, tries to shape and align the acts of its institutions, citizens and companies in a required manner. The role and application of soft laws in the EU is very prominent, and it is also required that the EU continue such an activity for the legal safety of its own system and its proper functioning. There are some very important challenges in this regard 'connected with interpretation and discretion'[4] since it is hard to finally interpret a soft law document and also, many times, challenge and prioritize their supremacy over one another. Many times, different EU institutions can have different and opposing interests and standpoints, while their soft law outputs can also raise different applications in practice. It is not just that the well-known recommendations and opinions have a soft law character in the EU. 'While Article 288 TFEU refers to recommendations and opinions, EU primary and secondary law as well as practice know of a number of other notions to designate instruments of a soft law character, such as "guidelines", "code of conduct", "conclusions", "communication" and "notice".'[5] This wide array of tools enables EU institutions to disperse its will into different aspects of everyday life of EU citizens, companies and institutions. Accordingly, while having no legally binding force, it does not imply that recommendations can't impose certain obligations.[6] They certainly do impose obligations but necessarily lack their enforceability character. In such a moral and legally regulated system, just as it would be a case in any similar real-life family, recommendations do need to be respected and followed. The actual enforcement in such cases is not important, as the meaning of the system is not to enforce but ultimately regulate potential relationships.

So, as always, the biggest challenge regarding soft law presence everywhere and likewise in the EU, is its potential to be enforced. EU itself does not have a mechanism and sometimes even lacks the interest to actually enforce some soft laws, while courts are an exception to this, although, in this case, it is not soft law any longer, but a formal court decision. 'Therefore, in principle, EU soft law may be found to have "legal effects" or "legally binding effects" (or

---

tionen – The Soft Law of European Organisations – La soft law des organisations européennes (Nomos 2012).

4 Mirko Pečarič, 'Soft Law – The Intermediate Stage Between Freedom and Control' (2022) 13 Danube 42.

5 Allan Rosas, 'Soft Law and the European Court of Justice' in Julia Iliopoulos-Strangas and Jean-François Flauss (ed), *Das soft law der europäischen Organisationen – The Soft Law of European Organisations – La soft law des organisations européennes* (Nomos 2012).

6 Corina Andone and Sara Greco, 'Evading the Burden of Proof in European Union Soft Law Instruments: The Case of Commission Recommendations' (2018) 31 Int J Semiot Law 79.

none) depending on the action brought, and against whom the effects of EU soft law are tested.'[7] It is evident that the EU overall makes soft laws as important guidelines and advice-making mechanism, which fill in a very important aspect of legal (un)certainties in the EU framework. Also, it can introduce or give a notice of a future change, so a bigger system can accordingly rearrange itself in due time and manner. 'Even though a soft law instrument might not seem to introduce new legal obligations, it might promote a radical interpretation of an obligation provided in a regulation or a directive, thus having significant effects in practice on the legal situation of individuals or Member States.'[8] Nevertheless, legal changes can't happen on a daily, weekly or monthly basis in the EU. The whole process needs time and the proper interpretation of professional bodies regarding a possible legal challenge is quicker and more accurate when it is shown the way forward.

It is not surprising at all that everyone in the EU tends to follow such soft law regulations and accept them as they would be laws. 'Soft law may not be law in the full sense of the term (hard law), but it is law, albeit in a rather incomplete form.'[9] Such a complex and complicated system, as the EU, therefore requires all its stakeholders to be more attentive and follow the detailed regulations which might have different forms, from which many have a soft law character. This also brings up various challenges where some soft law regulations can change, alter or diminish the actual laws of certain member states. This brings out the problem of 'Member State efforts aimed to limit EU-level action even more strictly'[10] and requiring that EU stays with it soft laws in the borders of its legislative domain, while in fact not challenging or requiring the removal of soft laws as an instrument overall. 'Soft law may be intended to serve as either a temporary or a permanent alternative to legislation.'[11] This conclusion brings us to the end of describing and understanding

7 Giulia Gentile, 'Ensuring Effective Judicial Review of EU Soft Law via the Action for Annulment before the EU Courts: A Plea for a Liberal-Constitutional Approach' (2020) 16 European Constitutional Law Review 466.

8 Oana Ştefan, 'Soft Law and the Promise of Transparency in the Member States' in Mariolina Eliantonio, Emilia Korkea-aho and Oana Ştefan (ed), *EU Soft Law in the Member States: Theoretical Findings and Empirical Evidence* (Hart 2021).

9 Fabien Terpan, 'Soft Law in the European Union – The Changing Nature of EU Law' (2015) 21 European Law Journal 68.

10 Laura Gyeney, 'Hard and Soft Law in EU's Integration Policy' (2018) 1 Hungarian Y.B. Int'l L. & Eur. L. 149.

11 Marloes van Rijsbergen, *Legitimacy and Effectiveness of ESMA's Soft Law* (Edward Elgar 2021).

the role of soft laws in the EU and broadly, its role and understanding certainly does not differ in the framework of post-conflict developments, as seen from the EU perspective.

Evidently, the most influential tool EU can have in post-conflict development is soft law, as its power in this regard is also a soft political power that it has actually successfully used for decades by now. EU has the most success in its neighbourhood where such standards can be more successfully applied due to the strong political ties and economic dependency of the given states. In the following chapters, we will focus more on the EU soft power in the case of Kosovo and its role in its development and potential influence in other similar post-conflict societies. At the moment, we will not deal with the case of Ukraine, since it is still in the middle of the conflict, but we will mention some guiding principles of how the future of this EU neighbouring country could look like in the future in the eyes of the EU.

2 Case Studies of EU Informal Rules

While we research the EU, it is also necessary to mention some other sources of soft law from which EU itself has learned and from whose experience it has developed itself as well. It is definitely the UN Universal Declaration of Human Rights, upon which the most basic rights and standards are based and which are also directly applicable in the EU. 'It should be noted that the ECJ has also referred to genuine soft law instruments such as the Universal Declaration of Human Rights of 1948, the Community Charter of 1989 and the Charter of Fundamental Rights 2000–2009.'[12] While such UN documents are widely applicable in many parts of the globe, it is necessary to mention that EU has also developed the most complex system of human rights protection, and apart from the UN standards, has its own ones which are broader and more developed.

Such a level of human and minority rights development also poses many challenges to the EU, from which the most prominent one now is the refugee crisis and the human rights violations coming with it. Additionally, there are the various post-conflict societies in the EU neighbourhood in which EU also

12 Allan Rosas, 'Soft Law and the European Court of Justice' in Julia Iliopoulos-Strangas and Jean-François Flauss (ed), *Das soft law der europäischen Organisationen – The Soft Law of European Organisations – La soft law des organisations européennes* (Nomos 2012).

struggles to enforce some basic human and minority rights. Such challenges do divide EU from inside where some member states simply disagree while some are even directly against some standards that EU is aiming to achieve. 'Soft law instruments, in particular those enacted during crisis, are deemed particularly suitable to deal with the complexity and diversity of European affairs in a rapidly changing situation.'[13] It is not just that some soft law standards are being changed and challenged in the EU today, there are also many laws such as the Dublin Regulation[14] itself, which is today practically inapplicable. While the EU got divided in regards the refugee crisis some years ago, it is divided now regarding the war in Ukraine and its final conflict resolution. This is all ultimately leading to the unchangeable divide regarding the recognition of the Kosovo self-proclaimed independence, which five EU member states can't accept, mainly due to their own inner autonomy-related problems. This all shows us that there are many 'no go' areas in the EU legal and political life, which even such soft law approaches can't change; an important one is the EU's proclaimed status neutral position towards the self-proclaimed independence of Kosovo.

Following on the division lines in the EU, we can also observe some patterns of behaviours which are very country-, culture- and politics-specific. This can be connected to the local interests but also can mirror the political power of certain states in the EU where they are able to push their own political interests from above upon smaller states, which can simply not correlate and find an interest in such decisions. While the EU has a common foreign policy in general, it can't reach a consensus in some other aspects. 'At the same time, there are strong country-specific patterns, with some member states frequently following recommendations (for example Germany), while others almost never do so (for example Denmark or the UK).'[15] Since the UK has left the EU, it also gives us hints about the path it has followed before the BrExit happened. Some states are eager to follow up on every EU action and request;

13 Corina Andone and Florin Coman-Kund, 'Persuasive rather than 'binding' EU soft law? An argumentative perspective on the European Commission's soft law instruments in times of crisis' (2022) VOL. 10, NO. 1, The Theory and Practice of Legislation 22.

14 European Commission, 'Country Responsible for Asylum Application (Dublin Regulation)' (23 September 2020) <https://home-affairs.ec.europa.eu/policies/migration-and-asylum/asylum-eu/determining-member-state-responsible-asylum-application_en> accessed 22 March 2026.

15 Gerda Falkner, Oliver Treib, Miriam Hartlapp and Simone Leiber, *Complying with Europe: EU Harmonisation and Soft Law in the Member States* (Cambridge University Press 2005).

they are not just ready to take it into consideration but certainly do a certain level of efforts to research, understand and finally either apply or refuse it. 'Even those legal systems which apply the most restrictive test, namely Italy and Germany, allow actions against soft law measures when they are not purely internal measures, but rather acts with external relevance.'[16] On the other side, we have a rising number of countries which start feeling some discomfort by not applying EU soft laws and recently, even some EU laws. EU itself does not really have a ready mechanism for such cases, since it is simply unable to use any kind of force against its own member states. 'As a whole, the data seems to confirm the hypothesis that the perception of EU soft law as an "external" source and the low awareness of these norms contribute to the non-application of EU soft law in Hungary.'[17] The idea of such an external mechanism of the law is therefore not characteristic of soft laws but in this case, in the EU regarding many laws which either put EU in a dominant position regarding regulating some aspects of life or simply because some states, such as Hungary, do not see any interest in applying EU laws. Together, with this challenge, there is also the previously mentioned BrExit, for what EU was not completely ready. Overall, such challenges are just making it more complex to find a real and applicable solution in regards the various post-conflict agreements that EU is concluding or is aiming to conclude in the future, keeping on mind that it also lacks the real enforcement capacity. This is bringing the EU to a very harsh position outside of the Union as well, and in particular, regarding the application and enforcement of its soft laws.

When it comes to the implementation of EU foreign policies and their role in post-conflict societies, it is necessary to mention Afghanistan, which has been one of its priorities earlier. While the USA was more involved with its military presence in Afghanistan, the EU was more active in the field of development. 'Since 2002, the EU has provided Afghanistan with more than €4 billion in development aid, making the country the biggest recipient of EU development aid in the world.'[18] As it is still unclear what development

---

16 Mariolina Eliantonio, 'Judicial Review of Soft Law before the European and the National Courts: A Wind of Change Blowing from the Member States?' in Mariolina Eliantonio, Emilia Korkea-aho and Oana Ştefan (ed), *EU Soft Law in the Member States: Theoretical Findings and Empirical Evidence* (Hart 2021).

17 Petra Lea Láncos, 'The Approach of Hungarian Authorities to Soft Law: On the Road to Where?' in Mariolina Eliantonio, Emilia Korkea-aho and Oana Ştefan (ed), *EU Soft Law in the Member States: Theoretical Findings and Empirical Evidence* (Hart 2021).

18 Beatrix Immenkamp and Tania Latici, 'Security Situation in Afghanistan: Implications for Europe' [2021] European Parliamentary Research Service <https://www.europarl.europa.eu/thinktank/en/document/EPRS_BRI(2021)698771> accessed 22 March 2026.

projects were prioritized by the EU in Afghanistan, it is clearer what the Chinese are focusing on now and they are clearly not ready to waste any money or do investments with loss. Interestingly, the same pattern is used in the EU neighbourhood in which it produces some benefits, whereas in many aspects, it has shown no potential for development in other distant countries, such as Afghanistan. 'In theory, Afghanistan has access to the EU's market; however, in practice, the country has little to sell in the market, and the sides have adopted different food standards.'[19] The implementation of the same rules and standards in the EU neighbourhood and their benefits for both the EU and local communities are accordingly not possible in such distant and different countries like Afghanistan. It also has to be mentioned that there are many spoilers to the EU foreign policy implementation, such as the Russian and Chinese interests, which are accordingly very present in Afghanistan today. The previous cooperation patterns between EU and USA on one side and Russia and China on the other are now shifting, and the EU will have a limited or more controlled access regarding investments from now on. 'The EU should ensure that any cooperation with Russia on Afghanistan is not used to undermine Western values or commitments elsewhere, in particular regarding the many other conflicts in the post-Soviet space.'[20] While the conflicts in the EU neighbourhood, and in particular in Ukraine, are able to take all the attention and funds from the EU, it still sees Afghanistan as a necessary focal point due to its year-long role in the migration crisis.

Even when many countries in the EU have a more neutral position regarding the refugee crisis, the German government, in particular, has an interest to have some kind of control over it. It is also the biggest recipient of migrants from the East and ultimately their final destination country. 'But this position has also drawn attention to the outsized involvement of particular EU member states in Afghan affairs, including Germany, and their parallel role as bilateral donors – even their aspirational role as brokers in the peace process.'[21] While EU aims to have a single foreign policy, the interest of some member

19 Angela Stanzel, 'Fear and Loathing on the New Silk Road: Chinese Security in Afghanistan and Beyond' [2018] European Council on Foreign Relations <https://ecfr.eu/wp-content/uploads/ECFR-264-Chinese_Security_in_Afghanistan_2.pdf> accessed 22 March 2026.

20 Diana Janse, 'Russian Interests in Afghanistan' (2021) 1 SCEEUS Reports <https://www.ui.se/globalassets/ui.se-eng/publications/sceeus/russian-interests-in-afghanistan-sceeus-report-no1-2021.pdf> accessed 22 March 2026.

21 Andrew Watkins and Timor Sharan, 'Europe's Engagement in Afghanistan Post-2021: Uncertainty, Pragmatism, and Continued Partnership' [2020] Friedrich Ebert-Stiftung (FES) Afghanistan <https://library.fes.de/pdf-files/bueros/kabul/16900.pdf> accessed 22 March 2026.

states can differ and also their will to get involved more in certain conflicts can be present in many instances. In the EU neighbourhood, such differences stemming from the EU might be present, but more likely they are to melt in the process of the overall EU integration processes.

It is not just Afghanistan, Kosovo or Ukraine where EU member countries interests differ; it is also the divide regarding the most problematic global conflict, the Israeli-Palestinian conflict. 'At the level of EU member states, frequent distinctions are made between EU countries that, for political and historic reasons, are biased towards Israel and countries that are more willing to defend European values and Palestinian rights.'[22] While many have already taken sides and decided how to proceed in the future, this specific conflict has gained another dimension when it was included in the Washington Agreement[23] (WA), according to which Israel and Kosovo have also mutually recognized each other. This surprising act by the Israeli government has not just outlined the influence of the USA and other UNSC permanent member states in such cases, but even more the absolute vulnerability and exposure of post-conflict countries. Additionally, Kosovo, but Serbia primarily will open their respective Israeli embassies in Jerusalem, which is completely against the EU foreign policies and the UN Resolutions regarding this active (frozen) conflict.

Finally, it is not just Serbia which does not align its foreign policies with EU when it does not impose sanctions on Russia, but it is also Kosovo which deteriorates its foreign policies from the EU guidelines. 'Parallels in their critiques reveal inconsistencies between the rhetoric and practice of the EU's approach to Kosovo and would be an indication of the intention–implementation gap.'[24] When the EU took over the implementation of development agenda in Kosovo from the UN, it probably did not count that the whole idea of Kosovo independence comes from the USA, and that the main military force in Kosovo comes from the USA through NATO and its military presence. Definitely, the position of a post-conflict country, such as Israel or Kosovo, which have received support from the USA, can't deviate much from the US support and standpoints. Their foreign policies remain even when they would like to have them to be more likely aligned with the EU policies, for instance.

22 Patrick Müller, 'Normative Power Europe and the Israeli- Palestinian Conflict: The EU's Peacebuilding Narrative Meets Local Narratives' (2019) 28 European Security 251.

23 WA 2020.

24 Kari M. Osland & Mateja Peter, 'The Double Proximity Paradox in Peacebuilding: Implementation and Perception of the EU Rule of Law Mission in Kosovo' (2019) 28 European Security 493.

3 Soft Law from a French Perspective

3.1 The General Understanding of Soft Law in France

It is important to research the French perspective in regard to soft law and especially their role in shaping various post-conflict agreements as France is a sole UNSC permanent member state in the EU. Economically, France shares roles in many post-conflict societies with Germany. While on the Eastern neighbourhood areas of the EU, this influence also includes cooperation regarding security, military and their overall role in shaping and democratizing societies. After the UK left the EU, it became evident that France is the only power which can in fact defend EU interests politically, legally and also militarily.

Taking into consideration the role of the French Republic in various conflicts and in specific regarding Kosovo, Nagorno-Karabakh and Afghanistan, we can follow how this influence fluctuates and depends on other global powers. Recently, at many instances, the French influence has lost on importance and therefore we are still facing the problem of how to interpret some agreements and make it legally possible for the French administration to recognize and act. 'In the French system, the divide between hard law and soft law remains controversial in the academic literature and case law.'[25] One of the most challenging situations in this regard is the fact that after the very generous legal and political help that France has invested in the Nagorno-Karabakh Republic, it has been dissolved without leaving much trace of its former territory. While for the EU overall, the dissolution of the NK Republic was not so much of a failure, for France it was. The EU itself was not part of the OSCE Minsk Group, but France was.[26] France was not legally or politically involved in the drafting or implementation of the Agreement under Russian supervision. While some limited role was given to Turkey, its final implementation never happened and Azerbaijan extended its full sovereignty, it could not be challenged by the UNSC in any aspect. Possibly, some French or Human Rights courts will find a basis to legally challenge some acts of the Azeri state but the final enforcement will still remain questionable. In such

---

25 Giulia Gentile, '*Verba Volant, Quoque* (*Soft Law*) *Scripta ?*' An Analysis of the Legal Effects of National Soft Law Implementing EU Soft Law in France and the UK' in Mariolina Eliantonio, Emilia Korkea-aho and Oana Ştefan (ed), *EU Soft Law in the Member States: Theoretical Findings and Empirical Evidence* (Hart 2021).

26 András Rácz, 'War in Nagorno- Karabakh: A Two-Track Strategy for the EU' (2020) 30 DGAP Commentary <https://dgap.org/sites/default/files/article_pdfs/dgap-commentary-2020-30-en.pdf> accessed 22 March 2026.

cases, the OSCE and the French role in it cannot help much, especially if we know that the whole OSCE mission and its mandate in EU overall is questionable after the recent conflict with Russia, which OSCE was meant to prevent for decades.

Therefore, it is still necessary to see how France will respond to future challenges, as it is for now the only UNSC permanent member state which recently did not use its power to resolve a conflict with an informal agreement. 'To sum up, if we would like to effectively introduce sustainable development rules both from an international and national perspective, we have to dispose of a broad scope of regulatory intervention tools.'[27] Such tools have recently been mainly coming in the form of soft regulations, for which the authority and some provisional mandate from UNCS permanent members was extensively used. 'The greatest problem is that the wording of soft law measures does not correspond to the way in which these acts are used in practice.'[28] The wording and the ultimate effects of such measures are both very challenging, and in neither aspect, they are gaining full legal and practical application but serve mainly and primarily as a conflict-resolution mechanism.

3.2 French and Other Approaches towards the Understanding of Soft Law in the EU

Regarding the overall EU agenda in the sphere of soft law and its modest development potentials by relevant agreements, at least in our case studies, it is necessary to mention the common efforts of French and UK, and their achievements. While UK was still part of the EU at the time the Brussels Agreement was achieved in 2013, it is hard to see if anything has changed since then. 'The lack of soft law in France and the UK giving effects to the same EU soft law measure is a testament to the fragmented implementation of EU soft law in the Member States.'[29] EU members can be seen as more divided ever since, while their interests clash in the most recent active conflicts, and it is still a challenge to expect that they can achieve or agree about a certain common policy to be followed. 'During Mogherini's term, the direct

27 Michał Mariański, 'The potential role of soft law rules and the French concept of regulations with the force of law (ordonnance) in achieving sustainable development goals' (2024) 66 Studia Prawnoustrojowe 301.

28 Giulia Gentile, ''Verba Volant, Quoque (Soft Law) Scripta?' An Analysis of the Legal Effects of National Soft Law Implementing EU Soft Law in France and the UK' in Mariolina Eliantonio, Emilia Korkea-aho and Oana Ştefan (ed), *EU Soft Law in the Member States: Theoretical Findings and Empirical Evidence* (Hart 2021).

29 Ibid.

involvement of two member states, namely Germany and France, was marked, which aimed at taking under their umbrella this process by organizing Summits in their capitals.'[30] It also made visible that the whole process of solving the Kosovo conflict is not an EU matter but a matter of foreign policies and serves more the interests of some influential states. They will then later ask for some sort of acknowledgement and support in this regard from other EU member-states.

While the division lines in the EU are being strongly marked, it is also evident that not everyone has the same interest, especially when a certain agreement gets reflected to some of their domestic challenges. It also gets very complex politically and legally when member-states on the Eastern and Southern borders are challenged by various security threats, for which a common EU strategy is necessary but still falls out. Member-states such as France, Italy, Germany and the UK have big economic interests in Azerbaijan and tend to avoid publicly criticizing Azerbaijan.[31] Although they have never managed to achieve a satisfactory level of human rights protection in Azerbaijan, they certainly have a more flexible understanding when it comes to business, and especially maintaining sustainability for their energy sector. In this regard, an important role belongs to the Southern stream coming through Turkey and is meant to severe the influence of Russia in the energy sector, but at a certain cost as well.

Apart from requiring some human-rights-related standards in the NK conflict, Western countries did not care much, as their trade interests did not get interrupted. 'The United States and to a lesser degree the European Union (specifically France) have invested little in the Minsk process in recent years.'[32] While the USA was struggling in Afghanistan and finally also left this country, it showed little interest in the NK conflict, which was also located close to the Russian borderlands. Finally, the Ukrainian conflict has taken all the attention, but in this case, we see little will on any side to give up easily on its interest and reach a compromise, legally binding or not.

30 Jeta Krasniqi, 'EU-Mediated Kosovo-Serbia Dialogue: A New Attempt or Resumption with the Old Approach?' [2020] Kosova Democratic Institute (KDI) and the Konrad Adenauer Foundation <https://kdi-kosova.org/wp-content/uploads/2020/10/Policy-Brief-20-07-24-EU-mediated-Kosovo-Serbia-dialogue-ENG.pdf> accessed 22 March 2026.

31 Jana Kobzova and Leila Alieva, 'The EU and Azerbaijan: Beyond Oil' [2012] European Council on Foreign Relations Policy Memo <https://ecfr.eu/wp-content/uploads/ECFR57_EU_AZERBAIJAN_MEMO_AW.pdf> accessed 22 March 2026.

32 Mark Anstey, Paul Meerts, Mikhail Troitskiy and I. William Zartman, 'The Conflict over Artsakh – Nagorno-Karabakh' (2020) 1 oPINion <https://assets.ctfassets.net/mvajnncmgvdq/1fPT78KfLANItgII8kRIbm/04dc0c24f46f468d7dce284a6e17fe1d/oPINion_Dez_2020.pdf> accessed 22 March 2026.

3.3 The French Approach towards International Soft Law

While we see that France is very active in resolving conflicts in its vicinity, mainly focusing on Kosovo and Nagorno-Karabakh,[33] it is more challenging to see what standpoints and legal documents it can apply in cases such as Afghanistan or in the future, regarding Ukraine and Israel. France is joining the efforts in implementing agreements reached in the EU framework and to some extent, the ones reached under the US supervision, while its standpoints are completely missing from some other conflicts. 'The United States and France had lost most of their influence over the dispute by the end of the 45-day war between Azerbaijan and Armenian forces in early November 2020.'[34] This momentum was a key in losing dominance over this conflict area and while the absence of their consent for resolving this conflict does not look so important, it is still necessary to see how they will respond to it, once the conflicts in the Middle East gets a new shape and share of influences. The agreements have envisaged a certain connection line between two parts of Azerbaijan, which will to some extent, cut off Iran from Russia. In geopolitical terms, this solution could serve some Western interests, for which they can additionally support Azerbaijan in the future, despite the lack of human rights standards implementation.

While the French UNSC membership is not enough to shape conflicts as far as Afghanistan[35] is concerned, it certainly was in their long established role in the NK conflict. 'The war and its resolution, which will shape the region for years to come, thus clearly showed the combined lack of interest and ineffectiveness of the US, France and the EU, the failure of the Minsk Group, the lasting power of Russia, and Turkey's increasing ambitions.'[36] This specific relationship and the alignment of interest in the Middle East between Russia and Turkey is probably going to be one of the determining factors of who and how they will solve other similar conflicts. As we can see, the Syrian regime

33 Anar Valiyev, 'Karabakh After the 44-Day War: Russian Peacekeepers and Patterns' (2021) 705 PONARS Eurasia Policy Memo <https://www.ponarseurasia.org/wp-content/uploads/2021/08/Pepm705_Valiyev_August2021.pdf> accessed 22 March 2026.

34 Güney Yıldız, 'Turkish-Russian Adversarial Collaboration in Syria, Libya, and Nagorno-Karabakh' [2021] SWP Comment <https://www.swp-berlin.org/publications/products/comments/2021C22_Turkish-Russian_Collaboration.pdf> accessed 22 March 2026.

35 Khushal Jawad and Zahid Ullah Saidi, 'Obstacles to Implementing Foreign Law: A Comparative Study of Afghan and French Laws' (2024) 1 Al-Taqwa Journal of Social Sciences 30 DOI: https://atjss.at.edu.af/index.php/atjss/article/view/62.

36 Tracey German, 'Russia and the South Caucasus: The China Challenge' (2022) 74 Europe-Asia Studies 1596.

lead by Assad also collapsed in a matter of days, leaving the path to new administration and future legal challenges.

4 Soft Law from the UK Perspective

4.1 The General Understanding of Soft Law in the UK

The UK has been a very active player in forming the EU foreign policy in as much as Baroness Catherine Ashton was also in charge of the EU common foreign policy when the BA was signed in 2013. It can't be excluded that the agreement itself corresponds to the British interest in the Balkans and in specific this conflict between Serbia and Kosovo. When we approach such unclear acts like the BA without knowing who is responsible for its full implementation or quality check, it is necessary to mention the role and importance of the UK courts in some similar situations. The UK courts have many times stepped in and answered the calls of various organizations, entities and unrecognized states to determine what is the law. One of the most interesting cases is definitely Western Sahara where the UK has a prominent role, although it was not the colonizer of this territory. 'The contribution that soft law can have towards clarifying certain aspects of the law, thus also fostering transparency, appears to be acknowledged as well by UK judges.'[37] With BrExit and without the future necessity of binding the UK legislation to the EU common policy, it can be conceived that the UK can see and establish a different viewpoint than the EU regarding the BA, for example. 'If a superior court refers positively to a soft law instrument in a case and relies on it in its reasoning for example, to help justify the outcome or in noting that the decision-maker must consider the soft law instrument then this can become interwoven into the precedent.'[38] This hypothesis entails the most important question stemming from this work and that is, what kind of power, soft or hard, is held by the agreements signed between the parties in conflict under the auspices of a certain UNSC permanent member-state.

Finally, with BrExit, we will witness a more differentiated approach towards the understanding of international laws, including soft laws as well. Overall, the application of norms coming from higher instances will be implemented

---

37 Mary Dobbs and Oana Ştefan, 'EU Soft Law in the UK on the Eve of Brexit: (Not) Much Ado about Nothing?' in Mariolina Eliantonio, Emilia Korkea-aho and Oana Ştefan (ed), *EU Soft Law in the Member States: Theoretical Findings and Empirical Evidence* (Hart 2021).

38 Ibid.

differently in the UK than in the EU. One of the examples is already present in the sense of environmental standards. The UK soft law acts implementing the EU environmental soft law may be considered as having binding effects, while the original EU soft law is not binding.[39] This difference is due to the various understanding of soft laws and the necessity for their implementation.

4.2 UK Approaches towards the Understanding of EU Soft Laws

The aim of this work is not to research BrExit and its consequences but to critically approach the future relationship between the UK and EU, especially regarding their possible common approaches towards soft laws. Accordingly, it is not expected that the UK will have major cuts in regard the most common EU post-conflict agendas, in whose formation it also participated. Brexit is not disastrous for the various facets of the EU's power,[40] in specific to its soft power and regarding its various post-conflict agendas. UK is still sharing its support towards the various conflicts that EU is engaged with and is an active player in Kosovo, and now in the efforts to solve the conflict in Ukraine. Overall, the whole challenge in regard to security on the European continent and its disturbance by Russia is a common problem where the EU can count on the UK as a partner. 'The Western Balkans are part and parcel of Russia's strategy to establish itself as a first rate player in European security affairs, along with other major states such as Germany, France, and the UK.'[41] It is hard to expect that the UK will not support the EU-achieved agreements regarding Kosovo.

Apart from the overall Russian influence, there is also the rising Chinese influence, especially on the Eastern borders of the EU. The Belt and Road initiative is aiming at connecting China to the EU and this idea is complete as soon as the BRI infrastructure reaches the well-developed transportation networks interconnecting Europe from the East towards the West. 'The EU has been relatively slow in reacting to the BRI, with Member States formulat-

39 Giulia Gentile, ''Verba Volant, Quoque (Soft Law) Scripta?' An Analysis of the Legal Effects of National Soft Law Implementing EU Soft Law in France and the UK' in Mariolina Eliantonio, Emilia Korkea-aho and Oana Ştefan (ed), *EU Soft Law in the Member States: Theoretical Findings and Empirical Evidence* (Hart 2021).

40 Scott A.W. Brown, 'The EU's 'strategic partnership' with China in a post-Brexit world: Recalibrating internal dynamics and facing up to external challenges' (2020) 4 Europe and the World: A Law Review 1.

41 Dimitar Bechev, 'Russia's Strategic Interests and Tools of Influence in the Western Balkans' [2019] NATO Strategic Communications Centre of Excellence <https://stratcomcoe.org/cuploads/pfiles/russias_strategic_interests_in_balkans_11dec.pdf> accessed 22 March 2026.

ing their own positions.'[42] It is hard to imagine that the development of BRI will be at any moment interrupted, but if so, the whole idea will be regulated from the USA, then through the UK and passed over to the EU. This could cause another polarization of the world where the presently more-divided UK and EU standpoints will certainly get more unified.

4.3 The UK Approach towards International Soft Laws

At the moment, it is very hard to divide and specify what approaches, different than the EU, the UK might have as related to the application and understanding of the post-conflict agreements, from our case studies. It is still on the same line and stands firmly between the USA and EU in backing up their ideas and interests. The role of the UK as a UNSC permanent member-state has been long fitted into this position and since its departure from the EU, this did not show any tendency to change in the future. As it was, the case also before the EU's substantial soft power advantage over China is largely thanks to the resources and status of member-states, including the UK.[43] Despite being outside of the Union, it still shares the majority of the EU interests regard security, trade and development. The UK has generally been supportive of China's efforts with the BRI,[44] which has been, in many ways, built to ease trade and is financed solely by the Chinese side. The only remaining challenge is how to deal with the rising trade imbalance, for which neither the EU nor the UK can offer an answer. Presently, a limited number of solutions are coming from the USA in the form of policies requiring higher taxation of Chinese goods.

Further, the role of the UK is accordingly in line with the EU and its French partners when it comes to the NK, and specifically their future relationship with Azerbaijan. Also, it is in line with the US understanding when it comes to their future relationship with Afghanistan. While the situation is very complex regarding the (non)recognition of the Taliban government, there is also a humanitarian aspect in which both countries are active participants. Maybe indirectly, but they still support in some sense, the development of Afghanistan. 'Most aid donors, including the UK and US, have sought for aid to be delivered to Afghans via neutral NGOs and UN agencies, rather than via the

42 Scott A.W. Brown, 'The EU's 'strategic partnership' with China in a post-Brexit world: Recalibrating internal dynamics and facing up to external challenges' (2020) 4 Europe and the World: A Law Review 1.

43 Ibid.

44 Ibid.

Taliban-controlled Government.'[45] This very new and extreme situation also brings many moral and legal challenges, for which again soft law regulations pose the most viable solutions. Accordingly, even before regular regulations can be applied, there is a need for intermediary solutions, usually in an informal manner. 'The United Kingdom, United States and European Union have subsequently amended sanctions legislation to support the delivery of humanitarian aid.'[46] Humanitarian aid is delivered to Afghanistan in order to somehow stabilize the country and in that way, also limit the migration flow towards Europe. So far, the migration crisis has proved to be one of the most challenging common issues of our societies, for which no viable solution has been proposed so far.

5 Soft Law from a German Perspective

5.1 The General Understanding of Soft Law in Germany

Researching the available literature on the German language, we can also outline many important aspects of soft law and its applications in this jurisdiction. It is very important to outline firstly the importance of soft law as a solution for legally controversial issues[47] where no final solution can be reached for various reasons. While it is still helpful and beneficial to have a certain area regulated and form the lines of mandatory application of the law[48] and the general understanding of what should not be done, while still not knowing what should be, it is giving hints and serves us as a guideline, showing the direction and also aims to exclude middle or second solutions,[49] which are not wished in certain legally challenging situations.

45 Philip Loft, 'Aid to Taliban-Controlled Afghanistan' (2022) 9,343 The House of Commons Library <https://researchbriefings.files.parliament.uk/documents/CBP-9343/CBP-9343.pdf> accessed 22 March 2026.

46 Ibid.

47 Matthias Knauff, 'Soft Law im europäischen Und internationalen Verwaltungsrecht' in Wolfgang Kahl und Markus Ludwigs (ed), *Band 2: Grundstrukturen des europäischen und internationalen Verwaltungsrechts* (C.F. Müller 2021).

48 Fiona Karl, 'Rechtsschutz Gegen Soft Law Der EU' [2023] Geprägte Freiheit <https://journals.ub.uni-heidelberg.de/index.php/hfst/article/view/92640/87248> accessed 22 March 2026.

49 Marie-Christin Sommer, 'Die Bedeutung des internationalen Soft Law der Vereinten Nationen und des Europarates für den deutschen Strafvollzug: am Beispiel des Vollzugs der Freiheitsstrafe an erwachsenen Männern' (Dissertation, Friedrich-Schiller-Universität Jena 2022).

There is also a very important integrative function of soft law[50] where it can overall coherently integrate and help by applying various forms of norms. Also, by connecting norms, they can often come from various levels while they can serve in better connecting different levels of law[51] together. The function of connecting the norms is important since the bodies making them are usually not consulting each other and in that way, the gap in understanding such acts is widening. This important aspect is necessary in overcoming legal uncertainties and is mostly used by various stakeholders to regulate their relationships, which are now and also in the future meant to remain fully legal. In this regard, it can be claimed that soft law can be interpreted and so implemented by the party it was aimed at,[52] and also more broadly by other relevant stakeholders. Many times, profession-specific regulations can't be achieved and understood on time, so it is left for such professional bodies and companies to position themselves accordingly in the system. This system of inter-institutional regulations can also apply to the wider public.[53] It can be observed that professional bodies do tend to influence and to some extent regulate areas by taking authority from soft law regulations, applying and understanding them for the benefit of the wider society.

When it comes to the limiting capacities of soft laws and their role as a restricting and punitive mechanism, it can be seen that it is very limited in such aspects. This is obviously coming out of its enforceable character by which soft law is widely recognized; in this case, we will look at the German understanding. 'In the present context, with respect to restrictions on fundamental rights authorised by the legislation, administrative directions have served to ensure the uniform application by enforcement authorities of what the German legal system refers to as "undetermined legal concepts" (unbestimmte Rechtsbegriffe), namely terms such as "appropriate" or "necessary".'[54] Accordingly, only in cases of appropriateness and necessity, some norms have

50 Sebastian Scholz, 'Integration Durch Soft Law – Eine Rechtsstaatliche Herausforderung' in Jörn Axel Kämmerer, Markus Kotzur and Jacques Ziller (ed), *Integration und Desintegration in Europa* (Nomos 2019).

51 Matthias Knauff, *Der Regelungsverbund: Recht Und Soft Law Im Mehrebenensystem* (Mohr Siebeck 2010).

52 Fiona Karl, 'Rechtsschutz Gegen Soft Law Der EU' [2023] Geprägte Freiheit <https://journals.ub.uni-heidelberg.de/index.php/hfst/article/view/92640/87248> accessed 22 March 2026.

53 Emanuel Grießer, '„Soft Law“ in der Europäischen Union und Österreich' (Dissertation zur Erlangung des Akademischen Grades Dr.iur, Leopold-Franzens-Universität Innsbruck 2016).

54 Matthias Knauff, 'Coronavirus and Soft Law in Germany: Business as Usual?' (2021) 12 European Journal of Risk Regulation 45.

to be enforced, in which case, their role can also be changed and replaced by other non-soft law regulations. Apart from the very typical non-enforcement character, the not fully developed potential regarding penalties in soft law[55] can be observed, and while locally, there could be some limiting capacities, in the framework of international law, it is completely absent.

While aiming at understanding the various state-level applications of soft law, it can be seen that many of its aspects are accordingly applicable into its presence in the international framework as well. Many times, the complex system of international relations and politics requires a tool to overcoming obstacles and building up networks of interconnectedness. Especially in the framework of human rights, rule of law, democracy and legality, overall,[56] the importance of various forms and norms, with a soft law character can be outlined. We can also observe that apart from local and international, the need and capacity to fill in loopholes in the legal system exists, and the very prominent role of soft law can be accordingly also used in the framework of international post-conflict agreements, while the absence of enforcement and punitive capacity of the soft law and its role in regulating relationships in the framework of law is undisputed and soft law and law are undividable[57] in this sense.

5.2 German and Other Literatures towards the Understanding of Soft Law in the EU

The research of German authors also points to the inevitable and necessary role of soft law regulations in the EU system. It functions as a tool for coordination between the EU member-states[58] where there is a need to achieve some kind of harmony and universal legal certainty. In the EU, there is a practical applicability of soft law norms towards the member-states,[59] while

---

55 Marie-Christin Sommer, 'Die Bedeutung des internationalen Soft Law der Vereinten Nationen und des Europarates für den deutschen Strafvollzug: am Beispiel des Vollzugs der Freiheitsstrafe an erwachsenen Männern' (Dissertation, Friedrich-Schiller-Universität Jena 2022).

56 Julia Marquier, 'Soft law : das Beispiel des OSZE-Prozesses; ein Beitrag zur völkerrechtlichen Rechtsquellenlehre' (Inaugural-Dissertation zur Erlangung des Grades eines Doktors der Rechte, Rheinische Friedrich-Wilhelms-Universität 2003).

57 Matthias Knauff, 'Soft Law im europäischen Und internationalen Verwaltungsrecht' in Wolfgang Kahl und Markus Ludwigs (ed), *Band 2: Grundstrukturen des europäischen und internationalen Verwaltungsrechts* (C.F. Müller 2021).

58 Ibid.

59 Marie-Christin Sommer, 'Die Bedeutung des internationalen Soft Law der Vereinten Nationen und des Europarates für den deutschen Strafvollzug : am Beispiel des Vollzugs

their necessity and recognition is not challenged. Accordingly, it achieves the idea of regulating EU matters without the necessary approval from the member-states[60] directly. Another important aspect is the role of filling in light lines of areas not covered by EU regulations,[61] where such an application is necessary, relevant and applicable. Such a broad and important role of soft laws in the EU framework of its institutions and member-states shows the overall need of soft laws and their implementation and future development.

Soft laws are regulations coming outside of the parliament[62] since the acts of the parliament, while various in nature, all have its authoritative character. The specific role of soft law in sending messages, ideas and future plans to each other is also observable in the EU bodies such as the Commission, which can send messages to others in areas they can't regulate themselves.[63] It can also be outlined that by using soft law, the institutions achieve reciprocity,[64] which is a specific stadium where areas of regulating matters complement rather than challenge each other. The idea of soft law follows the idea of various jurisdictions without endangering each other's regulatory spheres, probably the most important aspect is the understanding, according to which judges in the EU are treating such regulations. 'Judges also explicitly pointed out the non-binding nature of soft law, whilst simultaneously acknowledging its efficiency-enhancing potential.'[65] So while such acts are not mandatory or enforceable, their role serves up to the level of efficiency that proper regulations would have otherwise. The actual need to have soft laws also corresponds to their capacity and need in such situations where a legal uncertainty or need is present and where a certain regulation can't be accordingly applied.

By looking into jurisdictions other than German, we can have a very similar conclusion, which again proves the EU's unity in regards to the making and

---

der Freiheitsstrafe an erwachsenen Männern' (Dissertation, Friedrich-Schiller-Universität Jena 2022).

60 Matthias Rossi, 'Soft Law im Europarecht' (2020) 1 Zeitschrift für Gesetzgebung 1.

61 Matthias Knauff, 'Soft Law im europäischen Und internationalen Verwaltungsrecht' in Wolfgang Kahl und Markus Ludwigs (ed), *Band 2: Grundstrukturen des europäischen und internationalen Verwaltungsrechts* (C.F. Müller 2021).

62 Matthias Rossi, 'Soft Law im Europarecht' (2020) 1 Zeitschrift für Gesetzgebung 1.

63 Ibid.

64 Emanuel Grießer, '„Soft Law" in der Europäischen Union und Österreich' (Dissertation zur Erlangung des Akademischen Grades Dr.iur, Leopold-Franzens-Universität Innsbruck 2016).

65 Miriam Hartlapp, Andreas Hofmann and Matthias Knauff, 'Soft Law in Germany: Still Opposing Dynamics in Status and Effect' in Mariolina Eliantonio, Emilia Korkea-aho and Oana Ştefan (ed), *EU Soft Law in the Member States: Theoretical Findings and Empirical Evidence* (Hart 2021).

applying laws and soft-laws altogether. 'It is also highly unlikely that the pandemic plan would have been more effective in a legally binding form.'[66] Therefore, a very typical German discipline has been applied here and overall in the EU regarding respecting the Corona regulations, but mainly the relevant recommendations in general.

While there are some member-states in which soft law is not so popular, it is extensively popular in Austria[67] just as is the case in Germany, definitely due to the similar legal frameworks and shared scientific developments and understandings. 'Pursuant to the German legal tradition, key decisions have, however, been made in a legally binding form.'[68] Even if not enforceable, soft law can cover wide areas, such as administrative tasks, for example. On the other side, like in France, soft law is defined as an instrument in the law of administrative processes[69] while and when there is a need to better understand such processes.

Soft law plays a crucial role in solving norm collisions in multilevel governances[70] such as it is in the EU, where norms can be easily misunderstood or even misapplied. It is important to observe that solutions and scientific research on the local level, such as in the German scientific research, do echo in the EU as well. 'In sum, the growing importance of soft law as well as the willingness among many relevant protagonists in German legal circles to engage with soft law – with the possible exception of the courts – is strongly related to developments at the EU level.'[71] It is not just in the EU that solutions complement but they also have influences and relationships related to both EU and its member-states, and also with states outside of the EU. Finally, there

66 Matthias Knauff, 'Coronavirus and Soft Law in Germany: Business as Usual?' (2021) 12 European Journal of Risk Regulation 45.

67 Emanuel Grießer, '„Soft Law“ in der Europäischen Union und Österreich' (Dissertation zur Erlangung des Akademischen Grades Dr.iur, Leopold-Franzens-Universität Innsbruck 2016).

68 Matthias Knauff, 'Coronavirus and Soft Law in Germany: Business as Usual?' (2021) 12 European Journal of Risk Regulation 45.

69 Fiona Karl, 'Rechtsschutz Gegen Soft Law Der EU' [2023] Geprägte Freiheit <https://journals.ub.uni-heidelberg.de/index.php/hfst/article/view/92640/87248> accessed 22 March 2026.

70 Matthias Knauff, *Der Regelungsverbund: Recht Und Soft Law Im Mehrebenensystem* (Mohr Siebeck 2010).

71 Miriam Hartlapp, Andreas Hofmann and Matthias Knauff, 'Soft Law in Germany: Still Opposing Dynamics in Status and Effect' in Mariolina Eliantonio, Emilia Korkea-aho and Oana Ştefan (ed), *EU Soft Law in the Member States: Theoretical Findings and Empirical Evidence* (Hart 2021).

is a great potential in solving problems regarding EU integration[72] and also post-conflict resolutions just as we will see it in our case studies regarding EU and its understanding of future relationship between Serbia and Kosovo in the framework of post-conflict resolution and development.

5.3 The German Literature towards International Soft Law

When we approach the role of soft law on the international level, it is necessary to mention its prominent role in the international public law,[73] regulating various relationships between states. While the challenge of enforcing international law is permanent, we can still say that the law on that level is de facto enforceable.[74] The norms which can be stated to be soft law in international law are also the various post-conflict agreements, just as we will research them later and see how their enforcement develops in regard to various legal systems. Therefore, such agreements can be deemed to be sources of law just as contracts[75] signed between states on the international level regulating various issues in international frameworks. It is not that just soft law norms that lack enforcement capacity in the frame of international legal order, but many contracts and agreements signed between independent states also do.

In order to research possibilities regarding conflicts and post-conflict resolutions, it is necessary to mention OSCE,[76] which is the very well-known system of preventing and regulating reconstruction in the broader area of Europe. The relevance of OSCE has also been outlined by Knauff[77] and many other

72 Sebastian Scholz, 'Integration Durch Soft Law – Eine Rechtsstaatliche Herausforderung' in Jörn Axel Kämmerer, Markus Kotzur and Jacques Ziller (ed), *Integration und Desintegration in Europa* (Nomos 2019).

73 Fruzsina Molnár-Gábor, 'Soft Law: Bindung Ohne Fesseln?' [2022] Weich & Hart <https://heiup.uni-heidelberg.de/journals/rupertocarola/article/view/24585/18481> accessed 22 March 2026.

74 Matthias Knauff, 'Soft Law im europäischen Und internationalen Verwaltungsrecht' in Wolfgang Kahl und Markus Ludwigs (ed), *Band 2: Grundstrukturen des europäischen und internationalen Verwaltungsrechts* (C.F. Müller 2021).

75 Fruzsina Molnár-Gábor, 'Soft Law: Bindung Ohne Fesseln?' [2022] Weich & Hart <https://heiup.uni-heidelberg.de/journals/rupertocarola/article/view/24585/18481> accessed 22 March 2026.

76 Carey Cavanaugh, 'OSCE and the Nagorno-Karabakh Peace Process' (2016) 27 s & Hum Rts 422.

77 Matthias Knauff, 'Soft Law im europäischen Und internationalen Verwaltungsrecht' in Wolfgang Kahl und Markus Ludwigs (ed), *Band 2: Grundstrukturen des europäischen und internationalen Verwaltungsrechts* (C.F. Müller 2021).

authors, describing its work and processes.[78] While the importance of OSCE is very high, it is still the UN Resolutions[79] which have the final and most influential say in every post-conflict development, and can be seen as the system of conflict resolutions on the highest possible level. Overall, the acceptance and implementation of Resolutions is not problematic; it still happens that many times they are not or just partially implemented. This is again posing a challenge to the idea of global law enforcement and conflict prevention. The weak system of respect and application of UN Resolutions sometimes causes the rising in the number of conflicts globally, and also opens the door for the implementation of more informal agreements regarding such post-conflict societies.

Lastly, one of the most important aspects of soft laws in the international arena is their capacity for conflict solutions.[80] While it is necessary to regulate and define in more detail human rights,[81] in which a prominent role also belongs to soft law, it also has an important role in the process of building up the rule of law[82] framework in developed societies, but in particular in the post-conflict ones. We can observe that the most prominent role in regulating conflict resolution[83] belongs to soft law in the form of post-conflict agreements, which are widely accepted as the most influential tool for such activities. While all the five UN Security Council (UNSC)[84] permanent member-states use it in solving various conflicts over which they have influence and are able to swiftly reshape conflict situation into more stable and development ready societies, the most important and prominent role in the appli-

78 Julia Marquier, 'Soft law: das Beispiel des OSZE-Prozesses; ein Beitrag zur völkerrechtlichen Rechtsquellenlehre' (Inaugural-Dissertation zur Erlangung des Grades eines Doktors der Rechte, Rheinische Friedrich-Wilhelms-Universität 2003).

79 Matthias Knauff, 'Soft Law im europäischen Und internationalen Verwaltungsrecht' in Wolfgang Kahl und Markus Ludwigs (ed), *Band 2: Grundstrukturen des europäischen und internationalen Verwaltungsrechts* (C.F. Müller 2021).

80 Matthias Knauff, *Der Regelungsverbund: Recht Und Soft Law Im Mehrebenensystem* (Mohr Siebeck 2010).

81 Fruzsina Molnár-Gábor, 'Soft Law: Bindung Ohne Fesseln?' [2022] Weich & Hart <https://heiup.uni-heidelberg.de/journals/rupertocarola/article/view/24585/18481> accessed 24 March 2026.

82 Sebastian Scholz, 'Integration Durch Soft Law – Eine Rechtsstaatliche Herausforderung' in Jörn Axel Kämmerer, Markus Kotzur and Jacques Ziller (ed), *Integration und Desintegration in Europa* (Nomos 2019).

83 Matthias Knauff, 'Soft Law im europäischen Und internationalen Verwaltungsrecht' in Wolfgang Kahl und Markus Ludwigs (ed), *Band 2: Grundstrukturen des europäischen und internationalen Verwaltungsrechts* (C.F. Müller 2021).

84 United Nations, 'United Nations Security Council' <https://www.un.org/securitycouncil/> accessed 24 March 2026.

cation of development efforts definitely belongs to their capacity for trade[85] which develops societies and serves as the most stable ground for the future implementation and improvements in regard to societies' capacity for human rights[86] protection overall.

6 The Application of Soft Laws in the EU Foreign Policy and Development

The EU diplomatic power is always keeping in mind that it is itself not a military power and is therefore not able to compete with other such great powers, nevertheless it still positions itself very well in the arena of the overall global economy and diplomacy. While it is active in many regions of the world, and in particular our focus regions, we will deal now with its position in Kosovo, for which we will in particular go into more detail in the coming chapters. 'Using soft diplomacy tools, including prevention, it stands a great chance of playing the role of a mediator between the parties in the conflict.'[87] The role of the EU might be many times unclear, but certainly it gets to use its soft power in order to regulate a conflict situation which does not benefit its own agenda and the local communities. It is also important to note that similar to its inner agenda settings, the EU communicates with the outside world and sends messages about its intentions in different forms. 'Soft law instruments in EU external relations may bear various labels, including Joint Communications, Joint Letters, Strategies, Arrangements, Progress Reports, Programmes or Memoranda of Understanding.'[88] There are also many acts related to Serbia-Kosovo conflict, from which probably the most important one is the Brussels Agreement,[89] which in fact does not have a particular form and can't be determined exactly what level of final act it is. In fact, the Brussels Agreement is not an act made by the EU but is supported by the EU and its institutions, for what some kind of a legal argumentation is necessary. Regarding the BA, we will be discussing it and researching it more deeply in the following chapter dedicated to the post-conflict resolutions and developments in Kosovo.

---

85 Matthias Knauff, *Der Regelungsverbund: Recht Und Soft Law Im Mehrebenensystem* (Mohr Siebeck 2010).

86 Ibid.

87 Mirza Sabawoon, 'The European Union's Strategy on Afghanistan. Selected Issues' (2019) 3 Central European Political Studies 181.

88 Ramses A. Wessel, 'Normative Transformations in EU External Relations: The Phenomenon of "Soft" International Agreements' (2021) 44 West European Politics 72.

89 BA 2013.

It is very hard to shape and align the EU soft laws in its foreign relations, since the interests of the EU can change, while the member-states' interests are also shifting from time to time. It is also possible that regarding a certain foreign state or area, a particular member-state has a specific interest, which is sometimes connected to its colonial past. 'Compliance with EU soft law seems to depend on the interaction between characteristics of the policy instrument in question and national-level interests and processes.'[90] National-level interests are usually not so general and focused on achieving a certain democratic standard or the promotion of human and minority rights, they are usually more business oriented and supporting the initiatives of their own companies. If we look back to the agendas being implemented on various levels, we can also observe that 'national representations of the member-states often cooperate poorly with one another and the EU delegations'.[91] It can also be beneficial that some states take a primary role in some areas, as they can respond to challenges quicker and more swiftly than the slow and bureaucratic system of the EU itself.

This also brings some more broader opportunities to states, as they can in fact act also on their own as long as they do not confront the interests and priorities of the EU overall. 'This suggests that the EU is generally open to allow its missions to cooperate with the respective de facto states even though such an engagement is not always explicitly mentioned in the documents constituting the legal basis for its actions.'[92] The core achievement of the EU foreign policy relationship is definitely with Kosovo. Although towards Kosovo, the EU itself has a neutral status position, some EU member-states are its biggest foreign supporters in both diplomatic and financial aspects. Such a division places additional challenges regarding the relationship of the EU with other similar post-conflict societies. Here, we can finally also outline some cases like the one in Nagorno-Karabakh, Afghanistan and now in Ukraine and Israel, which are all further dividing EU member-states and their respective approaches.

---

90 Miriam Hartlapp and Emilia Korkea-aho, '"Whatever-Law" and Teenage Member States?: The National Reception of EU Soft Law and How to Study It' in Mariolina Eliantonio, Emilia Korkea-aho and Oana Ştefan (ed), *EU Soft Law in the Member States: Theoretical Findings and Empirical Evidence* (Hart 2021).

91 Joanna Buckley, 'Can the EU Be More Effective in Afghanistan?' [2010] Centre for European Reform <https://www.cer.org.uk/sites/default/files/publications/attachments/pdf/2011/pb_afhganistan_27apr10-223.pdf> accessed 24 March 2026.

92 Stefania Kolarz, 'The European Union's Engagement with the "de-Facto States" in the Eastern Partnership' (2020) 8 EU Diplomacy Papers <https://www.coleurope.eu/sites/default/files/research-paper/edp_8_2020_kolarz_0.pdf> accessed 24 March 2026.

To align all the foreign policies of the EU and to achieve a consensus such as is the requirement for some inner decisions, it is recently becoming almost impossible. EU is being divided from inside and the freedom to act separately in foreign relations brings some kind of necessary democratic balance into it. Also, asking for unity and permanently looking for a consensus would make actions outside the EU impossible, while we also need to keep in mind that the 'participation of actors in all stages of the development of soft law measures is not possible'.[93] The acceptance of some general agreements, from which further development in various other and different policies can be achieved, is becoming one of the light motives of the EU and a characteristic of its foreign policies. 'In addition, the ambiguity of its legal status enables all three parties to continuously produce and reproduce the "Agreement" in different, and at times, contradictory ways.'[94] Such a reproductive ambiguity brings probably some stability to the relationship between states inside the EU but produces more harm to both the EU and the local communities. This is a very obvious threat to the EU where its soft law agreements finally fail, endangering the overall concept of the EU as a soft power. There are many reasons and possible explanations for such behaviour from the side of the EU as well.

6.1 The Brussels Agreements or the First Agreement of Principles Governing the Normalization of Relations

In fact, initially, the EU itself did not want to publicize the Brussels Agreements 'hoping to enhance ownership over the agreements'.[95] This is not a problem at all as long the countries concerned, namely Serbia and Kosovo, have the same interpretation of such agreements, but it has turned out that they don't. The BA can be considered as a success for the EU foreign policy, in the sense that an agreement has been achieved while its actual implementation or even a possible failure of the agreement ultimately does not concern the EU. While a clear benefit and power of the EU soft power is to make

93 Danai Petropoulou Ionescu and Mariolina Eliantonio, 'Democratic Legitimacy and Soft Law in the EU Legal Order: A Theoretical Perspective' (2021) 17(1) Journal of Contemporary European Research 43.

94 Krenar Gashi, Vjosa Musliu and Jan Orbie, 'Mediation Through Recontextualization: The European Union and The Dialogue Between Kosovo and Serbia' (2017) 22 European Foreign Affairs Review 533.

95 Florian Bieber, 'The Serbia-Kosovo Agreements: An Eu Success Story?' (2015) 40 Review of Central and East European Law 285.

parties sign an agreement, 'the EU lacks credible incentives to motivate the parties to take a more constructive stance in the dialogue'.[96] It is a benefit for the EU that it has the capacity to make the parties sign an agreement but after that, it unfortunately lacks the incentives to make them comply accordingly.

While formality is one of the main characteristics of the EU, informal rules are a novelty with which the EU is supporting some informal post-conflicts agreements, such as the BA itself. In some aspects, the EU supports even the enforcement of the BA but it does not oblige itself to achieve any guaranteed goals, leaving complete freedom to the parties to even conditionally refute the agreement as it is. 'With the use of vague language and constructive ambiguity, the EU has succeeded in maintaining engagement, avoiding at the same time to specify thorny operational details.'[97] The whole implementation and supporting procedure the EU has towards the BA is hiding a deeper agenda of the whole EULEX[98] mission, which has failed in many aspects previously to comply with its own strategy and mission objectives. For this, we can blame its questionable takeover of its mandate from the UNMIK and the years-long criminal proceedings in Kosovo, which have now been taken over by the Kosovo Specialist Chambers and Specialist Prosecutors Office in the Hague. The idea behind this is that the parties and their governments can be blamed for anything and everything, which certainly can't be a standard in post-conflict resolution processes. 'It creates an atmosphere of "constructive ambiguity" but neither side is particularly happy with the result.'[99] The agreed terms need to have a stronger institution, above which they will be able to control and enforce, such as is the case in Bosnia and Herzegovina with the Office of the High Representative,[100] which can quickly respond to any legal challenge on the ground. 'The European Union's use of "constructive ambiguity," while understandable as a negotiating tool, has made it difficult for

96 Wouter Zweers and Myrthe de Boon, 'Overcoming EU Internal Dividing Policy Brief Lines in the Belgrade-Pristina Dialogue' [2022] Clingendael <https://www.clingendael.org/sites/default/files/2022-04/Policy_brief_Overcoming_EU_internal_dividing_lines_Belgrado_Pristine_Dialogue.pdf> accessed 24 March 2026.

97 Argyro Kartsonaki, 'Playing with Fire: An Assessment of the EU's Approach of Constructive Ambiguity on Kosovo's Blended Conflict' (2020) 22 Journal of Balkan and Near Eastern Studies 103.

98 European Union Rule of Law Mission in Kosovo, 'About EULEX' <https://www.eulex-kosovo.eu/?page=2,60> accessed 24 March 2026.

99 Peter Van Elsuwege, 'Legal Creativity in EU External Relations: The Stabilization and Association Agreement Between the EU and Kosovo' (2017) 22 European Foreign Affairs Review 393.

100 Office of the High Representative, 'General Information' <https://www.ohr.int/about-ohr/general-information/> accessed 24 March 2026.

citizens to discern what has been agreed upon and where implementation stands.'[101] It is unclear why EU is not using the EULEX mission[102] according to its mandate, where it can be efficient in solving interethnic conflicts more successfully. Such a practice and a mission which is able to act, but is failing to act, is a big stake for the future EU conflict resolution capacity and neighbourhood policy overall.

It can't be expected that the EU will be capable of doing and implementing a similar mission in Ukraine in any possible form, as that conflict is already dominated by the divided interests of the USA and Russia, as they are positioned in the EU borderlands. 'Due to the image of it being a leading actor in certain dimensions, the EU's weak record in managing conflicts and establishing peaceful zones beyond its borders seems disappointing.'[103] While EU has been an important player in the transitions and economic development earlier, its real capacity to control and solve conflicts has turned out to be very limited. The research of the BA in all of its aspects is very important, since it was outlined that the full implementation of this agreement will be facilitated[104] by the EU.

6.2 The Ohrid Agreement or the Agreement on the Path to Normalization between Kosovo and Serbia

After a decade-long ambiguous situation and the obvious non-application of the Brussels Agreement from 2013, the EU has decided to make the parties agree (sign) another agreement. This time, the representatives of Serbia and Kosovo have met in Ohrid, North Macedonia, to agree about this new agreement,[105] potentially normalizing their mutual relationship to a greater extent, at this occasion. Although the BA, which was signed 10 years ago, or other agreements have not been fully implemented and respected until now, this

---

101 Heather A. Conley and Dejana Saric, 'The Serbia-Kosovo Normalization Process: A Temporary U.S. Decoupling' [2021] CSIS BRIEFS <https://csis-website-prod.s3.amazonaws.com/s3fs-public/publication/210527_Conley_Serbia_Kosovo_Normalization.pdf?VersionId=.21Hry3HPFOAwZTCoBbJaZjcVSMfTGqF> accessed 24 March 2026.

102 European Union Rule of Law Mission in Kosovo, 'About EULEX' <https://www.eulex-kosovo.eu/?page=2,60> accessed 24 March 2026.

103 Rok Zupančič and Nina Pejič, *Limits to the European Union's Normative Power in a Post-conflict Society: EULEX and Peacebuilding in Kosovo* (Springer 2018).

104 BA 2013.

105 European Union External Action, 'Belgrade-Pristina Dialogue: Agreement on the path to normalisation between Kosovo and Serbia' (2023) <https://www.eeas.europa.eu/eeas/belgrade-pristina-dialogue-agreement-path-normalisation-between-kosovo-and-serbia_en> accessed 24 March 2026.

new agreement requests much broader and higher level of cooperation between Serbia and Kosovo, with the final aim of joining the EU, for which this agreement is, as stated, the ultimate path to be followed. Apart from many interesting and legally challenging articles in the agreement, which at this moment we will not research in detail, the agreement quotes and declares itself not to be a legally binding agreement. In its article 6, it states the following 'while the present Agreement constitutes an important step of normalization, both Parties will continue with new impetus the EU-led Dialogue process which should lead to a legally binding agreement on comprehensive normalization of their relations.'[106] While the Agreement itself has not been properly signed, the EU still requires its implementation, which therefore puts this agreement into the long line of informal rules regulating the relationship between Serbia and Kosovo. 'These opposing reactions to the agreement in Ohrid were already discernible by the two sides' stances towards the EU proposal: Kosovo was ready to sign the agreement, while Serbia was not (the ultimate solution was for the sides to 'tacitly agree').'[107] The overall EU enforcement capacity in regard to the agreement is in any case very limited, since the final word regarding a possible future EU integration lies primarily in the hands of the respective EU member-states. The EU institutions can in this regard just follow, advise, recommend and criticize the parties in regard to their implementation efforts. One of the obvious requirements of the agreement and its challenges is the requirement that parties do recognize their passports mutually, which is more than a challenge for the five EU member-states which do not recognize the independence of Kosovo.

The Ohrid agreement also entails an Annex,[108] which details more in depth the requirements imposed on the parties and serves as a roadmap for its implementation. In the annex, a very new formation of an overseeing body is pre-

106 European Union External Action, 'Belgrade-Pristina Dialogue: Agreement on the path to normalisation between Kosovo and Serbia' (2023) <https://www.eeas.europa.eu/eeas/belgrade-pristina-dialogue-agreement-path-normalisation-between-kosovo-and-serbia_en> accessed 24 March 2026.

107 Branislav Stanicek, 'Belgrade-Pristina Dialogue: The Rocky Road towards a Comprehensive Normalisation Agreement' [2023] European Parliamentary Research Service <https://www.europarl.europa.eu/thinktank/en/document/EPRS_BRI(2025)779231> accessed 24 March 2026.

108 European Union External Action, 'Belgrade-Pristina Dialogue: Implementation Annex to the Agreement on the Path to Normalisation of Relations between Kosovo and Serbia' (2023) <https://www.eeas.europa.eu/eeas/belgrade-pristina-dialogue-implementation-annex-agreement-path-normalisation-relations-between_en> accessed 24 March 2026.

scribed, a new 'Joint Monitoring Committee'[109] will be formed in order to oversee the implementation of all the provisions agreed terms. It is not that other agreements, such as the BA, were left without an appropriate overseeing mechanism. In the BA, there was also an implementation committee agreed with an EU facilitation, still this agreement is neither fully applied nor in any way enforced by the respective EU facilitation mechanisms. 'Kosovo and Serbia recognise that any failure to honour their obligations from the Agreement, this Annex or the past Dialogue Agreements may have direct negative consequences for their respective EU accession processes and the financial aid they receive from the EU.'[110] Such a wide elaboration of possible sanctions in fact opens the door for many potential sanction-like measures to be imposed, while the likeliness that some will really happen puts them into a great disparity. The EU accession process is, as mentioned earlier, a much more complex issue where the final say is with the EU member-states, where the five non-recognizers can hardly be influenced by the application of the respective (informal) agreements. We can conclude that this agreement and its annex are very general and declarative documents, which are placing a tremendous burden of their implementation on the parties. Overall, they are lagging behind with the more simple but important steps in regard to human rights protection and the general hardships of everyday life in Kosovo.

---

109 Ibid.

110 European Union External Action, 'Belgrade-Pristina Dialogue: Implementation Annex to the Agreement on the Path to Normalisation of Relations between Kosovo and Serbia' (2023) <https://www.eeas.europa.eu/eeas/belgrade-pristina-dialogue-implementation-annex-agreement-path-normalisation-relations-between_en> accessed 24 March 2026.

CHAPTER 8

The Application of Informal Rules in the US Framework

1 The US Legislative Mechanisms and Their Understanding of Informal Rules

In foreign relations it is very hard to achieve strong results using soft law mechanisms and there are not so many examples globally where it has produced more positive results than the actual bare use of force. Although the use of force has been a dominant factor in global politics until recently, there are still some interesting past examples of how tremendous changes have been made in the world politics without the use of power. 'It was a brilliant stroke in 1971, when Nixon and Kissinger took advantage of China's fears of the USSR with the historic U.S. opening to China.'[1] It is hard to imagine how the world politics would have developed in some other circumstances and how the world would look like without this act; certainly for now this trade relationship between the USA and China has been dominating the world scene in many aspects for decades. While USA is in fact more stable and independent from Chinese products it is not the case with the EU and also in some post-conflict societies where China is raising its presence globally. Specifically when we look at the Balkans[2] we see the posed threat here coming from the Chinese goods and investments but also from the high dependence on Russian energy supplies. The Western understanding of post-conflict development is different and there are so many opposing interests visible in the USA and EU approaches when compared.

While the USA and the EU overall cooperate in many conflict settings and function perfectly inside NATO and its military actions, their interests differ when it comes to the peaceful implementation of their various agendas. 'Despite talk of the United States and its more militaristic approach undermining the EU's civilian ones, one should keep in mind the EU's inten-

1 Mathew Burrows and Robert A. Manning, 'Kissinger's Nightmare: How an Inverted US–China–Russia May Be Game-Changer' (2015) 33 Valdai Papers <https://valdaiclub.com/files/11410/> accessed 24 March 2026.

2 Rok Zupančič and Nina Pejič, *Limits to the European Union's Normative Power in a Post-conflict Society: EULEX and Peacebuilding in Kosovo* (Springer 2018).

 | HTTPS://DOI.ORG/10.1163/9789004746091-010

tions to contrary to what they saw the United States doing conflict resolution.'[3] This can also be visible in many cases and the one we will mention here is Kosovo, where USA has a dominant military presence via NATO while the EU is more active in civilian matters with its EULEX mission.[4] This means that achieving common goals differs and such differences can also cause additional misunderstandings in the local communities where peacebuilding is being implemented and meant to function and comply with various stakeholders standards.

2 Case Studies of US Informal Rules

There is presently a very big imbalance between the implementation of soft and hard laws regarding foreign diplomacy and post-conflict development among the most influential members of the UN Security Council. While the EU is overall not represented as an important stakeholder in global security policies, it certainly is a very important stakeholder in its geographic region and neighbourhood. It also has a very prominent role in regard the implementation and functioning of post-conflict economic development frameworks. When EU does not succeed in finding the right informal regulation of the given area there is always USA to back it up in their then mutual efforts. While our aim is not to remain exclusively on the legal field and see what legal mechanisms there are to change the behaviour of the parties, here it is necessary to mention the US soft law approach. 'For the time being, it is more important to note that the (apparent) success of the US in un-locking the blocked dialogue laid bare the structural weaknesses of the European Union as a diplomatic actor.'[5] It is not that USA has supported the EU efforts regarding peace activities in Kosovo but it had also added some of its viewpoints and interests into this relationship, which were also somewhat surprising.

---

3 Morten Bøås, Bård Drange, Dlawer Ala'Aldeen, and Abdoul Wahab Cissé and Qayoom Suroush, 'The Paradoxes of EU Crisis Response in Afghanistan, Iraq and Mali' in Roger Mac Ginty, Sandra Pogodda, and Oliver P. Richmond (ed), *The EU and crisis response* (Manchester University Press 2021).

4 European Union Rule of Law Mission in Kosovo, 'About EULEX' <https://www.eulex-kosovo.eu/?page=2,60> accessed 24 March 2026.

5 Vladimir Medović, 'The Potential and Limits of the European Union as a Mediator in the Dialogue Between Serbia and Kosovo*' (2022) 3 Istituto Affari Internazionali (IAI) Papers <https://www.iai.it/sites/default/files/iaip2203.pdf> accessed 24 March 2026.

The US-made agreement on economic normalization[6] has introduced and supported many trade and transportation related issues between Serbia and Kosovo. 'The rest of the WA is almost entirely (except art. 15–16) designed to curb China's and Russia's influence in the energy sector and to contribute to Trump's campaign.'[7] Interestingly the WA was signed in a very interesting time period, which is timewise during the US presidential campaign in 2020, but also together as a part of the bigger framework of agreements signed between Israel and some Arab countries, which are aiming to be friendlier towards the Jewish state in the Middle East.

Apart from the recent US involvement in Kosovo there is an even more interesting case of the US foreign politics in Afghanistan, which has also been a failure in some sense after its recent 2021 withdrawal. Regarding military presence it can be noted that USA has lost Afghanistan, but regarding development potentials and foreign support it looks like Afghanistan has not lost very much. China became even more active in the sphere of investing into Afghanistan and has in some sense maximized its efforts to invest into Afghanistan in all possible fields. This also stands in line with the previous Chinese interests and investments, which were also welcome in the era of the US dominance in Afghanistan. 'As the US and NATO provided security, Chinese companies have been making inroads into the troubled country.'[8] It is still very unclear why all such efforts made in Afghanistan have finally failed. Unfortunately, before Afghanistan even got a chance to become a democratic country it fell back to tribal wars and divided political fractions. 'On 29 February 2020, the US signed a bilateral peace agreement with the Taliban, who had 'refused to engage in talks' with the Afghan government.'[9] Such a deal has secured the various interests of the USA inside and in particular outside of Afghanistan, but has also left the previous government, which it had supported, without any chances of being a factor in the present-day Afghani politics.

Lastly, in another very important conflict just on the border between Asia and Europe in Nagorno-Karabakh, the USA has been completely left out from

6 WA 2020.

7 Andrej Semenov, 'The Washington Agreement: A Supplementary Document to the EU Efforts in Kosovo?' (2021) 23 Insight Turkey 259.

8 Loro Horta, 'US Afghan Withdrawal: Enter China and Taliban?' (2021) 120 RSIS Commentary <https://rsis.edu.sg/wp-content/uploads/2021/08/CO21120.pdf> accessed 24 March 2026.

9 Beatrix Immenkamp and Tania Latici, 'Security Situation in Afghanistan: Implications for Europe' [2021] European Parliamentary Research Service <https://www.europarl.europa.eu/RegData/etudes/BRIE/2021/698771/EPRS_BRI(2021)698771_EN.pdf(2021)698771_EN.pdf> ac cessed 24 March 2026.

the final peace agreement between Armenia and Azerbaijan. Interestingly, the USA was included in this conflict for decades via its proxy in the Middle East, Turkey. As Turkey has reached a very interesting compromise with Russia they now have an even more similar common interest in this region, but obviously such interest does not correspond to the US priorities in this regard. 'For the time being, it is not clear to what extent the two co-chairs of the Minsk Group, namely the US and France, will be ready to support Russia's decision to play the main role in ensuring peace in Nagorno-Karabakh.'[10] The USA will in this case have to align its policies and interests in this region with its allies, which will most likely be shaped in such a way to confront the Russian and Iranian interests as much as possible. Also, it will have to follow the Israeli standpoints regarding this conflict as it has been seen that Israel did have an active role in this recent war in Nagorno-Karabakh, which also means that it certainly has an interest to shape this conflict according to its needs and viewpoints, but mainly to confront Iranian interests in this area.

3 The Application of Soft Laws in US Foreign Policy and Development

The application of US interests over soft law regulations and especially their intelligence and military engagements with NATO is very complex. Our aim is to research how USA behaves or what tools it uses when it feels that its expectations can't be achieved otherwise; in particular it is important to mention the dominant position of the USA in both the UN and NATO. USA tries to use its dominant position in the UN to achieve certain outcomes, and also frequently tends to use NATO in order to intervene where it feels such an intervention would benefit its own agenda. As NATO was not used in the recent conflict in Ukraine it can be concluded that soft law diplomacy will prevail and USA is more than ready to use it regarding Ukraine as previously in Israel and some other conflicts. 'It pushed for improved relations between Israel and Muslim majority countries, encouraged natural resource diversification away from Russia, and denied China a significant 5 G influence in Serbia and Kosovo.'[11] The USA does try to establish itself in many various areas

10 Kerim Has, Vali Kaleji and Sergey Markedonov, 'The Breakdown of the Status Quo and the International Dimension of the Nagorno-Karabakh Crisis' [2020] Valdai Discussion Club Report <https://valdaiclub.com/files/32745/> accessed 24 March 2026.

11 Leonardo Dinic, 'Huawei Targeted by Trump's Recent Serbia-Kosovo Meeting?' (28 October 2020) <https://www.chinausfocus.com/finance-economy/huawei-targeted-by-trumps-recent-serbia-kosovo-meeting> accessed 24 March 2026.

and also has some priorities, while it most definitely has a dominant position regarding the conflicts in Kosovo and the Middle East, specifically in the area surrounding Israel.

The US withdrawal from Afghanistan has put on a completely different picture about US interests, which shrunk in Asia leaving place for the Russian and Chinese common domination. 'Furthermore, state-building in Afghanistan was done on the basis of a simplified interpretation of what the state is and does, and prioritised the capacity building of executive powers over other aspects of development and change.'[12] Our priority is not to research how and why the USA has failed, but to see how it positions itself in this regard and what behaviour we can expect in some similar situations worldwide. It still can't be understood why USA has failed so badly in Afghanistan and what was their true intention, knowing that they have not used their full capacity and therefore left an open gate for the Taliban to fully take it over. What USA did in Afghanistan and whether it is good for its position and reputation among its present allies remains an open question. Also, the US administration has decided not to leave money to the new Taliban regime and decided to revoke '$7 billion-plus to 9/11 plaintiffs',[13] which will finally somehow compensate and potentially establish the new relationship regime between the US and the new Taliban government in the future.

4 Abrahamic Accords

While we are researching the understanding and application of soft law by the USA, it is necessary to mention its very recent issue of many Accords concerning the relationship between Israel and some predominantly Muslim countries, in the Middle East and the North African region. When we say accords we necessarily mean in this case some documents, which are in-between political declarations and informal rules (soft law) but mainly regulating relationships where USA is not an active but a more passive party to such agreements. Since the accords have a very general and descriptive character they do have some hard focal points strictly requesting a certain behav-

12 Jaïr van der Lijn, 'Frictions in Illusionstan: Engagement between the "Global" and the "Local" in Afghanistan's Imagination-Building' in Annika Björkdahl and others (ed), *Peacebuilding and Friction: Global and local encounters in post-conflict societies* (Routledge 2016).

13 William Byrd, 'Afghanistan's Frozen Foreign Exchange Reserves: What Happened, What's Next' (1 March 2022) <https://reliefweb.int/report/afghanistan/afghanistans-frozen-foreign-exchange-reserves-what-happened-whats-next> accessed 24 March 2026.

iour. 'We support science, art, medicine, and commerce to inspire humankind, maximize human potential and bring nations closer together.'[14] One of the main ideas covered in the Abrahamic Accords is the peace and cooperation between Israel and its neighbours in the Middle East and North Africa (MENA) region. The main idea for supporting the Accords by the USA is accordingly to guarantee a 'shared commitment to advancing peace and security in the Middle East stressing the importance of embracing the vision of the Abraham Accords'.[15] This is coming at the moment when many states are turning for cooperation in trade but also militarily towards Russia and China, in particular in this critical MENA region.

While Israel represents US interests in the MENA it was necessary to strengthen its position and also make the US allies coming from Muslim countries have stronger cooperation ties with Israel but also ultimately recognize its existence as a state. 'In this spirit, we warmly welcome and are encouraged by the progress already made in establishing diplomatic relations between Israel and its neighbours in the region under the principles of the Abraham Accords.'[16] Some states have signed a cooperation agreement with Israel, which also came as a surprise to many to see that USA is able to influence them to such an extent that they give up some of their common interests and agendas, for better cooperation and support from the USA. The agreements usually also cover an interesting and important aspect of political and legal life of given states where, in some critical aspects, USA is giving them support regarding some of their local problematic issues and that way is winning their sympathies. 'The United States recognizes Moroccan sovereignty over the entire Western Sahara territory and reaffirms its support for Morocco.'[17] This support for Morocco is coming as an answer to a conflict which it has with its neighbours over a territory, which was previously held by the colonial

14 U.S. Department of State, 'The Abraham Accords Declaration' (2020) <https://www.state.gov/wp-content/uploads/2020/10/Abraham-Accords-signed-FINAL-15-Sept-2020-508-1.pdf> accessed 24 March 2026.

15 U.S. Department of State, 'Abraham Accords: Declaration of Peace, Cooperation, and Constructive Diplomatic and Friendly Relations' (2020) <https://www.state.gov/wp-content/uploads/2020/09/Bahrain_Israel-Agreement-signed-FINAL-15-Sept-2020-508.pdf> accessed 24 March 2026.

16 U.S. Department of State, 'The Abraham Accords Declaration' (2020) <https://www.state.gov/wp-content/uploads/2020/10/Abraham-Accords-signed-FINAL-15-Sept-2020-508-1.pdf> accessed 24 March 2026.

17 U.S. Department of State, 'Joint Declaration' (2020) <https://www.state.gov/wp-content/uploads/2021/01/Joint-Declaration-US-Morrocco-Israel.pdf> accessed 24 March 2026.

Spain. Western Sahara, a territory on the north-west coast of Africa bordered by Morocco, Mauritania and Algeria[18] is contested and under UN supervision but without a final settlement for decades after the ceasefire has been agreed. For Morocco, it is very important to have the support of a UN Security Council member state in this case and overall for every African state it is similarly important, while all great powers including Russia and China also have their various interests in this region.

Regarding formal requirements, The Abrahamic Accords are very different and also use various names in titles, but still stay in the field of mostly political and legal arrangements. This is also the case with the Washington Agreement, which is in fact titled as an agreement of 'economic normalization'.[19] With the Washington Agreement the Serbian and Kosovo sides have signed two slightly different documents, where the difference is mainly concerning the mutual recognition between Israel and Kosovo, while Serbia has a duty to move its embassy to Jerusalem. Except this requirement the agreement contains mutual obligations between the parties but towards the USA as well. Interestingly for the Republic of Sudan[20] The Abrahamic Accords document was signed unilaterally by a government official without even quoting who it was. This declaration does not lower the status of the document where the USA can quote it as a soft law obligation regarding the Sudanese state, which accordingly needs to comply with it.

When it comes to the United Arab Emirates, they have signed a more formal treaty with Israel with an aim to fully formalize it in the future. 'This Treaty shall be transmitted to the Secretary-General of the United Nations for registration in accordance with the provisions of Article 102 of the Charter of the United Nations.'[21] Therefore we can conclude that in this case such an agreement is neither informal nor soft law as it is meant to fully formally comply with the requirements for signing an international agreement. Accordingly, this also shows the intentions of the parties and primarily the ones coming from Israel, with the US support, that such agreements from the Abrahamic Accords series do tend to have some mandatory forms and be fully legal agree-

18 United Nations Mission for the Referendum in Western Sahara, 'Background' <https://minurso.unmissions.org/background> accessed 24 March 2026.

19 WA 2020.

20 U.S. Department of State, 'The Abraham Accords Declaration' (2020) <https://www.state.gov/wp-content/uploads/2021/01/Sudan-AA.pdf> accessed 24 March 2026.

21 U.S. Department of State, 'Abraham Accords Peace Agreement: Treaty of Peace, Diplomatic Relations and Full Normalization between the United Arab Emirates and the State of Israel' (2020) <https://www.state.gov/wp-content/uploads/2020/09/UAE_Israel-treaty-signed-FINAL-15-Sept-2020-508.pdf> accessed 24 March 2026.

ments. In the case of the United Arab Emirates this agreement is really of a constitutional character as it overrules the domestic regulation in order to accommodate this agreement. 'The Parties further undertake to adopt any legislation or other internal legal procedure necessary in order to implement this Treaty, and to repeal any national legislation or official publications inconsistent with this Treaty.'[22] We can conclude that while the agreements do not comply with some formal requirements the intentions are very clear, and where USA did not manage to secure the necessary form of an international agreement it did want the effects it produces. It was needed to put the Abrahamic Accords into the field of soft laws, which request for a certain behaviour but also lack the necessary legal enforcement mechanism, which actually perfectly works here.

Concerning the interpretation or disputes regarding Abrahamic Accords it is evident that they have a true soft law character where they can't be enforced by the signatory parties, but only alternatively by the authoritative power which has supported their creation, in this case the USA. We can also see that while not directly connected to Israel, the Washington Agreement also in some form belongs to the series of Abrahamic Accords, since it strengthens the position of the USA in the broader Mediterranean area, which is the final aim of the whole US procedure of making the Accords. Obviously the parties to such agreements have signed the accords with one another but have in fact given their promise to the USA, so it is probably that the USA will also have a priority to reconcile parties in case it is needed later. 'Any such dispute which cannot be settled by negotiation may be referred to conciliation or arbitration subject to the agreement of the Parties.'[23] While conciliation and arbitration are not explicitly quoted in all the agreements it can be presumed that this is or will be the potential way of dealing with future miss understandings. It is possible that the arbitration might happen on a forum, which is different from the one presumed or expected by the USA but considering its influence on both signatories.

The Accords were signed during the Trump presidency and this was not influencing their implementation, as he was present only as a witness ex officio. 'In recognition of this appreciation, the two countries have asked President Donald J. Trump to sign this document as a witness to their shared resolve and as the host of their historic meeting.'[24] Donald Trump as a Presi-

---

22 Ibid.

23 Ibid.

24 U.S. Department of State, 'Abraham Accords: Declaration of Peace, Cooperation, and Constructive Diplomatic and Friendly Relations' (2020) <https://www.state.gov/wp-co

dent of the USA had a very limited power to influence the parties personally, so the agreements were signed due to the interests and capacities of the USA primarily. The facts like the US withdrawal from Afghanistan have not much to do with the current government, as it is a long procedure that started or was planned years before. Regarding Kosovo and its Economic normalization as it has been supported for years by the USA and the EU as well. The support Serbia and Kosovo got from the USA and all the mutual promises and requirements are just a natural and logical flow of these processes. Therefore the mutual recognition of Israel and Kosovo, which both enjoy the unlimited support of the USA, is somewhat a logical outcome and to have these two countries cooperate and establish the highest level of diplomatic relations.

ntent/uploads/2020/09/Bahrain_Israel-Agreement-signed-FINAL-15-Sept-2020-508.pdf> accessed 24 March 2026.

CHAPTER 9

The Application of Informal Rules in the Russian Framework

1 The Russian Legislative Mechanisms and Their Understanding of Informal Rules

The Russian involvement in foreign politics is also being shaped more in line with the global trends of using soft power and only using hard power when it is deemed absolutely necessary. With the rise of its involvement in various global conflicts, for Russia, it is necessary to use as much soft power as possible, taking into consideration its recent full military capacity involvement in Ukraine. Russian diplomacy was very active before the war in Ukraine, but it is also very active now during the war. Interestingly, Russia does have the support of some states for this war, from which the most prominent one is coming from China. For every political and military support that Russia gets, it has to pay back in some way. So, it is essentially using its full military and global political capacity at the moment. 'Let us mention that the federal legislation distinguishes international treaties from political arrangements.'[1] It is not necessary to conclude formal treaties when Russia is in fact gaining support from some states, which is vital for its strategy in Ukraine and the support it gets in the UN and its Security Council as well. Russia is getting ready for a new divide on its Western borderline and is aiming to fix the borderline with the EU by making some new Republics in Ukraine.

Just before its engagement in Ukraine started, Russia changed the decades-long status quo situation in the Caucasus, it formed a new reality which was more acceptable to Azerbaijan while still keeping its dominance over Armenia. The new solution regarding Nagorno-Karabakh is described in a document called a 'Statement'[2] and at that time, agreed by the representatives of

1 Sergei Marochkin and Rustam Khalafyan, 'The Norms of International Soft Law in the Legal System of the Russian Federation' (2013) 6 Journal of Politics and Law 90.

2 President of Russian Federation, 'Statement by President of the Republic of Azerbaijan, Prime Minister of the Republic of Armenia and President of the Russian Federation' (2020) <http://en.kremlin.ru/events/president/news/64384> also available at <https://documents-dds-ny.un.org/doc/UNDOC/GEN/N20/307/34/PDF/N2030734.pdf?OpenElement> accessed 24 March 2026.

 | HTTPS://DOI.ORG/10.1163/9789004746091-011

Azerbaijan, Armenia and Russia in 2020. That 'Statement[3] was particularly made by the President of the Republic of Azerbaijan, Prime Minister of the Republic of Armenia and President of the Russian Federation'[4] and was the newest resolution regarding the hostilities in Nagorno-Karabakh. It has in many ways changed this conflict and wanted to unfreeze it, but also make Armenia more passable by the regional trade and infrastructure networks. While Russia has not blocked others from accessing this conflict and finding a solution, with the recent move, it looks like it does not want any other interference here any longer, but the Turkish. Together with Turkey, now Russia aims to have a greater cooperation in different sectors, including security as well. This is an interesting novelty since Turkey is a NATO member state and Russia is confronting it on different fronts, but this is not the only organization causing headaches to Russia recently. 'The Russian Government systematically adopts legal acts that stipulate the observance of decisions of the Organization for Security and Co-operation in Europe (OSCE).'[5] With the war in Ukraine, Russia is excluded from many organizations and its cooperation capacity is limited, which also endangers the enactment and respect for human rights, not just in Ukraine but also in Russia. In the long run, it is not possible to determine how and on what grounds there will be future cooperation between the West and Russia and how it will look like after the war in Ukraine concludes.

The decline in regard to human rights guarantees in Russia are obvious after the war in Ukraine started, but it is also evident in some other regions such as in Afghanistan after the Taliban came back to power. While the USA was aware that the situation in Afghanistan will not be good, it is more complex now to expect that Russia or China will be able to develop the level of human rights capacity, taking into consideration their previous and also present practices in this regard. 'Moscow follows a realpolitik line that is typical of Russian foreign policy and refrains from commenting on the domestic political situation or the human rights situation in Afghanistan.'[6] Russia supports China in Afghanistan and while China has a free hand in Afghanistan, it supports the decisions Russia will make regarding Ukraine.

3 Ibid.

4 Ibid.

5 Sergei Marochkin and Rustam Khalafyan, 'The Norms of International Soft Law in the Legal System of the Russian Federation' (2013) 6 Journal of Politics and Law 90.

6 Sabine Fischer and Angela Stanzel, 'Afghanistan: The West Fails – a Win for China and Russia? The Views from Beijing and Moscow' (2021) 50 SWP Comment <https://www.swp-berlin.org/publications/products/comments/2021C50_MoscowBeijing_Afghanistan.pdf> accessed 24 March 2026.

In any case, the role and application of international laws and standards should not be diminished in Russia and certainly could play an important role in the process of re-establishing the future relationship between Russia and the West. 'Recommendations of international organizations and their bodies play a definite role in the process of interpretation of domestic law.'[7] While Russia presently has not much interest to comply with the Western standards, it is likely possible that it will comply with the future solutions regarding Ukraine. In Ukraine, Russia will likely be ready to support a peace agreement, similar to the one in Nagorno-Karabakh, where after a war, a new political setting was achieved, and could represent the interests of Russia, the NATO member Turkey, and also be acknowledged by China. It is worth mentioning that as long as an agreement regarding Ukraine is not achieved and respected, be it in the form of soft or hard law, Ukraine will remain outside the reach of trade and development routes, running the risk of becoming a frozen conflict, establishing a new 'Frozen Curtain' on the frontiers between Europe and Asia.

2 Case Studies of Russian Informal Rules

One of the most important and recent soft law regulations regarding the involvement of the Russian Federation in post-conflict development is obviously the Statement[8] stemming from the Nagorno-Karabakh war in 2020. This war has produced, as its final outcome, an agreement agreed upon by the Armenian and Azerbaijani sides under the patronage of Russia. The agreement was bringing in a very new setting of the Nagorno-Karabakh conflict and, in some sense, satisfied the requests of both Azerbaijan and Turkey for a broader control over this territory. While dealing with many important issues, the agreement did not deal with the present or future status of the Nagorno-Karabakh Republic as it existed until 2024. 'While some secessionist forces, such as the one in Nagorno-Karabakh, may interpret the Kosovo precedent more broadly, as bestowing a positive right of secession on peoples, it is legally accurate to conclude that the ICJ Kosovo Advisory Opinion does not

7 Sergei Marochkin and Rustam Khalafyan, 'The Norms of International Soft Law in the Legal System of the Russian Federation' (2013) 6 Journal of Politics and Law 90.

8 President of Russian Federation, 'Statement by President of the Republic of Azerbaijan, Prime Minister of the Republic of Armenia and President of the Russian Federation' (2020) <http://en.kremlin.ru/events/president/news/64384> also available at <https://documents-dds-ny.un.org/doc/UNDOC/GEN/N20/307/34/PDF/N2030734.pdf?OpenElement> accessed 24 March 2026.

establish a positive right of secession.'[9] Also, as far as the entity is not part of the UN, we can't speak about full recognition or even partial recognition, as anyway, it is the only reality for some post-conflict societies or republics, so to say. While some parts of Nagorno-Karabakh remained outside the control of Azerbaijan by this agreement from 2020, the recent complete takeover of NK by Azerbaijan in 2023 opens the door for a more hard law-like regulation and future status determination for the NK inside the Azerbaijani constitutional framework. Obviously, the informally agreed Statement[10] of 2020 has widely opened the door for this change and the transformation of the NK future status points to a direction which is regulated fully by Azerbaijan and more by hard laws in the future.

Further, when we speak about other case studies where Russia had an active role previously, we necessarily come to Afghanistan, which has been in a stage of a big turmoil recently. Afghanistan is still very important to Russia strategically, since it stands on the road connecting it to its partners such as Iran and India. 'Hence, Afghanistan plays a vital role in Russia's constant geographic strategy formulation, which is mainly concerned with the dominance of Eurasia and former Soviet territory, which is vital for Russia's 'great power' identity.'[11] Although economically, Afghanistan is now more connected to China, its security still remains to some extent in the hands of Russia. Overall, in Asia, the Russian and Chinese interest together look like getting more and more aligned and their interests are at the moment unified and coordinated fully in the sense of both security and trade.

In the economic sense, the Russian and Chinese interests are also very similar, since Russia is a big producer of energy and has found a perfect match in China, which is a big user of energy with a constantly rising demand, in order to sustain its growing economy. 'One of Moscow's big hopes was for another gas pipeline from western Siberia to the Chinese market, which would reduce Moscow's reliance on Europe as a gas market.'[12] While Russia keeps its inter-

---

9 Milena Sterio, 'Self-Determination and Secession under International Law: Nagorno-Karabakh' (2016) 59 German YB Int'l L 81.

10 President of Russian Federation, 'Statement by President of the Republic of Azerbaijan, Prime Minister of the Republic of Armenia and President of the Russian Federation' (2020) <http://en.kremlin.ru/events/president/news/64384> also available at <https://documents-dds-ny.un.org/doc/UNDOC/GEN/N20/307/34/PDF/N2030734.pdf?OpenElement> accessed 24 March 2026.

11 Kaneshko Sangar, 'Afghanistan's Significance for Russia in the 21st Century: Interests, Perceptions and Perspectives' (2016) 12 Politics in Central Europe 59.

12 Mathew Burrows and Robert A. Manning, 'Kissinger's Nightmare: How an Inverted US-China-Russia May Be Game-Changer' (2015) 33 Valdai Papers <https://valdaiclub.com/files/11410/> accessed 24 March 2026.

ests and stake in the European energy markets, it also tries to control more the paths of energy leading to Europe by having good relations with Turkey as an energy transit country. While there are many interesting agreements to be researched regarding Russia and various countries, we will still keep researching the one concerning Nagorno-Karabakh as it existed until 2023.

3 The Application of Informal Rules in Russian Foreign Policy

The application of informal rules/soft law regulations by the Russian Federation are such that they completely align with its own interests and with the interests of its allies. While regarding security and specifically its involvement in the war in Ukraine, as a solo endeavour, its trade related interests are more intensified and broadly understood and discussed with its partners, from which obviously, the main role belongs to China. 'Russia, in turn, seems to have limited the activities that might directly harm Chinese economic interests.'[13] Russia, both technically and logistically, fully complies with the growing Chinese interests in transporting goods and is ready to further support it by opening new trade corridors where an important role belongs to various regions, from which one is the South Caucasus.

While full trade is limited due to sanctions imposed on Russia, it still succeeds in maintaining its dominant position as an energy trading great power, but now focusing more on the Asian markets than the European ones. 'And in the midst of the Ukraine crisis, amid calls for international isolation of Russia, Putin was received with open arms in Beijing and signed a long-awaited gas deal with China.'[14] While energy prices are rising, it is always possible to make a certain sale and the demand will simply always make ways for Russian gas to reach a consumer in either Europe or, now, more likely in Asia.

When it comes to trade and its rules amidst the war in Ukraine, it is obvious that Russia uses different tools to guarantee a stable income against the sanctions imposed on it by the West. This somewhat stable position also guarantees it a future important role in controlling various post-conflict territories within some important Asian trade routes. 'Moscow made the manipulation of these conflicts a key element of its foreign policy, and certainly linked its respective policies toward Ukraine, the South Caucasus and even Syria to one

13 Alexandra Martin, 'China in the Broader Black Sea Region' [2021] Globsec <https://www.globsec.org/sites/default/files/2021-03/China-in-the-Broader-black-sea-region-ver7-non print.pdf> accessed 24 March 2026.

14 Rajan Menon and Eugene Rumer, *Conflict in Ukraine: The Unwinding of the Post–Cold War Order* (Massachusetts Institute of Technology 2015).

another.'[15] As all the conflicts where the Russian engagement is visible are geographically close, it can be seen that they are part of the bigger network that Russia is building for decades. Also, the connection of Turkey to all the previous Russian regions of interest and the specific arrangement Russia has with Turkey makes a very interesting new fusion of common interests. While Russia and Turkey are not connected so tightly like Turkey and NATO, their interests have found some informal ways forward to tighten their common interests and such a connection, for now, looks stronger than the one Turkey has with its Western allies, at the moment. It is a question of the future to see how such a connection will look like and with a tendency to get even closer, considering the political situation and establishments in both Russia and Turkey.

The unfreezing of the situation around Nagorno-Karabakh and the opening of new trade corridors in the Caucasus while making new conflicts on the EU borders, shows how the trade priorities might function in the coming decades for Russia. Finally, the very quick and politically important dissolution of the Nagorno-Karabakh Republic in 2023 proves that Russian interests are being more quickly implemented in the domains under its control. In this regard, neither political promises nor human rights guarantees pose important and decision-making substances.

---

15 Svante Cornell, 'The Impact of the Ukraine and Syria Conflicts on the Geopolitics of the South Caucasus' in Kornely Kakachia, Stefan Meister and Benjamin Fricke (ed), *Geopolitics and Security: A New Strategy for the South Caucasus* (Konrad-Adenauer-Stiftung 2018).

CHAPTER 10

The Application of Informal Rules in the Chinese Framework

1 The Chinese Legislative Mechanisms and Their Understanding of Informal Rules

China is a very new player in the global politics concerning international development and investments, but in particular in the area of post-conflict development. While it has been quietly developing its agenda the biggest surprise was when China announced that it does have a plan for the war-torn Afghanistan. This plan came in a way of some agreements agreed between the neighbours of Afghanistan and regarding its development, we will mention here two documents – the Joint Statement[1] and the Tunxi Initiative.[2] These two documents, while being very political and declarative, do put in a lot of efforts with the aim to develop Afghanistan from various perspectives. The use of soft laws is not an unknown term in China. 'The range and variety of soft law used in China are much greater than those used in Europe.'[3] It can also be said that due to the structure of the political life in China, the discipline of citizens is very high and once something is a law, be it hard or soft, it is accordingly respected. When compared to the EU, the Chinese application of soft laws also aims to reaching a higher goal where it gets unified for the whole

1 Embassy of the People's Republic of China in the Kingdom of the Netherlands, 'Joint Statement of the Third Foreign Ministers' Meeting Among the Neighboring Countries of Afghanistan' (31 March 2022) <http://nl.china-embassy.gov.cn/eng/zgyw/202203/t20220331_10658230.htm> also accessible on <http://lawinfochina.com/display.aspx?id=8253&lib=tax&SearchKeyword=&SearchCKeyword=> accessed 24 March 2026.

2 Ministry of Foreign Affairs of the People's Republic of China, 'The Tunxi Initiative of the Neighboring Countries of Afghanistan on Supporting Economic Reconstruction in and Practical Cooperation with Afghanistan' (1 April 2022) <https://www.fmprc.gov.cn/mfa_eng/gjhdq_665435/2675_665437/2676_663356/2677_663358/202204/t20220401_10662024.html> also available on <https://lawinfochina.com/display.aspx?id=8251&lib=tax&SearchKeyword=&SearchCKeyword=> accessed 24 March 2026.

3 Francis Snyder, 'Three Worlds of Chinese Soft Law' in Mariolina Eliantonio, Emilia Korkea-aho and Oana Ştefan (ed), *EU Soft Law in the Member States: Theoretical Findings and Empirical Evidence* (Hart 2021).

 | HTTPS://DOI.ORG/10.1163/9789004746091-012

country, whereas in Europe every state can ignore some soft law requirements when they are not in its own best interests.

Since China is a big manufacturer of various products it also has a huge demand for raw materials and energy needed for their production. There are many resource-rich countries, which due to their low industrial development can't use the raw materials they own and are keen to sell them on the global market. Such countries usually do not have the necessary means to invest into the exploitation of resources, for which China with its various investment systems can help and thus benefit both the local societies and its own growing demands. There are many undeveloped countries and also countries which have previously struggled with some kind of conflicts, which are desperately in need of foreign investments, for which China is making very attractive arrangements. 'In a nutshell, the underlying connotation of soft power lies in the ability to make others meet their goals through attraction rather than coercion.'[4] Chinese investments are very certain and well-planned, they always develop projects in such a manner that they make sure the goods they are extracting and needing will ultimately reach China. Therefore the Belt and Road Initiative (BRI)[5] as a transportation network can serve the purpose of transporting goods from China, but also raw materials back into China.

BRI is a very complex framework of various international agreements where such agreements also have different forms, not rarely found also in a form of a soft law. Such a practice serves the final aim and the ultimate goal of China to make and complete the BRI transportation network as fast and as smooth as possible. 'The relationship among myriad forms of primary agreements is unclear and there is no central repository for BRI agreements.'[6] Various investments regarding the BRI are made in such a way that they benefit local states and China as well. In the chapters to come we will follow up on the most recent Chinese agreements concerning BRI and also its agreements touching upon the territories of post-conflict states such as Afghanistan primarily but also Nagorno-Karabakh and Kosovo.

4 Bei Feng & He Jiang, 'Strengthening China's Diplomatic Soft Power: Taking the Basic Categories of International Law as the Path' (2022) 3 Foundation for Law and International Affairs Review 82.

5 Office of the Leading Group for Promoting the Belt and Road Initiative, 'Belt and Road Portal' <https://eng.yidaiyilu.gov.cn/> accessed 24 March 2026.

6 Heng Wang, 'The Belt and Road Initiative Agreements: Characteristics, Rationale, and Challenges' (2021) 20 World Trade Review 282.

2 Case Studies of Chinese Informal Rules

China has been recently utilizing its soft power and soft regulations regarding its expansionist trade agenda. It seems that China is not interested in spreading its political power like some other states now and previously in the colonial era. Still there is one country in which China is ready to play with all stakes in, and that is Taiwan. A direct conflict over Taiwan is only a remote possibility[7] while Taiwan is under the protection of the USA similarly as North Korea is under the protection of China making some very complicated system of power balance on the Eastern borders of China. While it can't be foreseen when and how the dispute over Taiwan will be resolved, it is by now very visible how China is solving such disputes on its Western borderlands. 'China opposes any attempt to make Afghanistan the battlefield of international competition, especially the attempt to arbitrarily launch 'new Cold War' and proxy war in Afghanistan which threatens the interests of other countries.'[8] China overall needs peace in order to guarantee its stable export of industrial products and it would not be possible for China to survive in a position such as Russia today, under sanctions. China also needs a good relationship with everyone and while it tolerates both security and trade-related dominance of other countries in certain post-conflict regions it is still ready to invest in them as long as it feels safe to do so.

China does not want to confront any trade-related arrangements other influential countries have made but tries to find its own place and interests in investing and developing projects. It is very interesting to observe that while the USA and Russia have been engaged in various conflicts in Eastern Europe, China has been active in making investments and building up infrastructure projects. China has reached as far as Central and Eastern European Countries (CEEC) regarding not just to trade but also infrastructure projects which were, just a few years ago, the exclusive right of the EU, USA and Russia. 'To arrive at the above conclusions, one begins with the massive amounts of trade and investment China made in the CEEC under its BRI program.'[9] While

7 International Crisis Group, 'Risky Competition: Strengthening U.S.-China Crisis Management' (2022) 324 Asia Report <https://icg-prod.s3.amazonaws.com/324-us-china-crisis-management.pdf> accessed 24 March 2026.

8 Wang Yu, 'China Actively Upholds Multilateralism, Jointly Building a Community with a Shared Future for Mankind with Afghanistan' (24 February 2021) <https://af.china-embassy.gov.cn/eng/sgxw/202102/t20210224_10004691.htm> accessed 24 March 2026.

9 Ronald C. Brown, 'China's BRI in Central Eastern European Countries: "17+1" Connectivity, Divisiveness, Or Pathway to EU-CHINA FTA?' (2020) 22 San Diego International Law Journal 1.

China has been very successful in implementing some infrastructure projects in Africa and elsewhere, it is coming more under scrutiny under which conditions it offers such investments.

The democratic standards being implemented in both post-communist and post-conflict states in the EU Eastern borderlands are putting China under scrutiny of what and how it is implementing regarding its big infrastructure investments. 'It seems that Japan, with the help of the European Union (EU) and US, as well as other members of the QUAD (Australia, and India), could insert vital principles for infrastructure projects, such as "transparency," "accountability," and "debt sustainability."'[10] While many governments receiving Chinese investments are not particularly stable or democratic, it is necessary to have some level of outside control of who is investing, how such investments are being developed and what future democratic prospects such investment can endanger. Allowing outside actors, such as China, to penetrate into the post-conflict societies of the USA and the EU, prioritizes some post-conflict developments but also makes them more vulnerable and politically unstable. This aspect of development will be under future discussion where soft laws and regulations can again play an important role.

3 The Application of Soft Laws in the Chinese Foreign Policy and Development

The Chinese economic growth is also being followed by investments into the sphere of education, where Chinese students are attending all sorts of courses outside of China in order to accumulate knowledge and bring it back home to China. 'The realm of education is one in which China has pushed hard to project soft power.'[11] Therefore it is not coming as a surprise that China is becoming a leader in many new technologies where it is not just a place of production, but the place where innovations happen. Research and development of new technologies require funds, which China is able and willing to invest. China is also very willing to invest in its people and in particular students, which are then in return able to develop such projects and innovations, which are again very competitive on the global market. Also China is ready to trade with every-

10 Umirdinov Alisher, 'Generating a Reform of the BRI from the Inside: Japan's Contribution Via Soft Law Diplomacy' [2019] RIETI Discussion Paper Series <https://www.rieti.go.jp/jp/publications/dp/19e076.pdf> accessed 24 March 2026.

11 Jean-Marc F. Blanchard and Fujia Lu, 'Thinking Hard About Soft Power: A Review and Critique of the Literature on China and Soft Power' (2012) 36 Asian Perspective 565.

one, whereas Western countries frequently put on some democracy-related limitations regarding trade and cooperation.

With the rising number of post-conflict societies where democracy, human rights and investments guarantees are not secured, China succeeds to invest and benefit, while others are waiting for the endless implementation of standards. 'The above conceptual change is a good start for widening the scope of BRI participants, but is still limited to sovereign states.'[12] While it is interesting to research what is a sovereign state and how China understands it there are certainly no obstacles for its cooperation with the Taliban-led Afghanistan. While in the Western investment concept, it is not possible to invest into places where no legal mechanisms are functioning regarding investment protections, China finds a way in this regard and in the form of soft law agreements keeps itself on the safe side. We will now outline some of the most important agreements regarding Chinese relationship with Afghanistan and further also explain them more in detail. One agreement has a more declarative form and explains 'China's Position on the Afghan Issue'[13] and the other one, 'The Tunxi Initiative of the Neighboring Countries of Afghanistan on Supporting Economic Reconstruction in and Practical Cooperation with Afghanistan'[14] includes a broader number of countries from the neighbourhood of Afghanistan.

Regarding such agreements and declarations in a soft law form it is obvious that the enforcement mechanisms are missing and that the sole goodwill of the parties and in particular the Taliban regime is necessary in order to make them work. Here China is ready to go the extra mile and give such a level of support to the Taliban, which will in turn see their absolute interest and necessity to cooperate with China. Obviously the Western borders of China are very important since there is its gate and dry port for the trade with the West or the New Silk Road now popularly called BRI. It is not that China only needs safety on the BRI road, but it also needs a very good relationship with all the governments with which it cooperates in order to lower

12 Gong Hongliu, 'The Belt and Road Initiative (BRI): A China-Specific Approach for Global Governance' (2018) 8 Journal of WTO and China 36.

13 Ministry of Foreign Affairs of the People's Republic of China, 'China's Position on the Afghan Issue' <https://www.fmprc.gov.cn/eng/gjhdq_665435/2675_665437/2676_663356/2677_663358/202304/t20230412_11057785.html> accessed 24 March 2026.

14 Ministry of Foreign Affairs of the People's Republic of China, 'The Tunxi Initiative of the Neighboring Countries of Afghanistan on Supporting Economic Reconstruction in and Practical Cooperation with Afghanistan' (1 April 2022) <https://www.fmprc.gov.cn/mfa_eng/gjhdq_665435/2675_665437/2676_663356/2677_663358/202204/t20220401_10662024.html> also available on <https://lawinfochina.com/display.aspx?id=8251&lib=tax&SearchKeyword=&SearchCKeyword=> accessed 24 March 2026.

the risk of potential conflicts. Each kind of conflict can seriously endanger and deter business activities; accordingly a quick form of resolving them in some kind of dispute settlement centre is most necessary. 'The PRC's new International Commercial Court (to be based in PRC in Shenzhen and Xian, with Chinese judges having oversight of this court) may not be flexible enough to meet the diverse demands that might arise in efforts to apply soft law mechanisms and norms.'[15] While culturally different from many, China is also different regarding the Muslim-based traditions in Asia but also the Western capitalistic standards and concepts of trade and investments. Still one of the main clash points between civilizations or better to say East and West is the African continent, which has long been divided by great powers. Now in this new era of resource-hungry societies some new perspectives and also possible division lines are being drawn in this very rich continent regarding both raw materials and energy supplies.

It is finally also a challenge to see whether parties will, after accepting unfavourable terms in contracts with China, be ready to comply with Chinese Courts or its Arbitration mechanisms. Keeping in mind that the implementation of some final decisions over countries and especially legally unstable countries and post-conflict societies, it can't be guaranteed and is highly regime-dependent. 'From a long-term perspective, it is possible to build a new investment dispute settlement center under the BRI or even a dispute settlement center under the BRI with a wider scope of jurisdiction in the future as needed, provided that all conditions are available.'[16] Accordingly, China will need to set up a strong institution base for dispute resolutions. Here the main challenge will be how to enforce the reached decisions in post-conflict societies, which are also having unstable regimes, budgets and fragile governmental structures regarding the implementation and finalization of any infrastructure project and investment.

15 Ping Xiong and Roman Tomasic, 'Soft Law, State-Owned Enterprises and Dispute Resolution on PRC's Belt and Road – Towards an Emerging Legal Order?' (2019) 49 Hong Kong L.J. 1025.

16 Shi Jingxia & Dong Nuan, 'Investor-State Dispute Settlement under the BRI' (2021) 1 Wuhan University International Law Review 47.

CHAPTER 11

The Conflict Resolution and Reconciliation Capacity of Post-conflict Agreements

It is evident that a very important aspect of post-conflict agreements belongs to their conflict resolution and reconciliation capacity. While agreements do not precisely mention conflict resolution and reconciliation, they do focus on reaching them in their various ideas and outcomes. They certainly incorporate such a requirement in the soul of the relevant agreements. We can't speak about the agreements implementation in any form, forgetting or ignoring their conflict resolution and reconciliation capacity. 'As a general approach, reconciliation implies that in an ideal case everything which impacts on a relationship troubled by violence should bring in whatever may help to create normal and good relationships.'[1] When we are aiming at defining the level and capacity of such a good relationship, we must observe that it must be the one which is contrary and different to the one present at the moment. Conflicts therefore occur because the level of trust changes and certain injustices or violence are produced by various political regimes and become unbearable. 'Reconciliation addresses past violence and injustice, present reframing and encounter of the other and future possibilities of cooperation, peace and harmonious interaction.'[2] Such an interaction must be put in a completely new framework and serve the best interest of all citizens, while also respecting their possible differences and sufferings during the conflict.

As long as the agreements or their implementation does not offer a satisfactory level of reconciliation, we can't speak about the resolution of the conflict as such. 'Obviously, reconciliation is a major mechanism preventing the resumption of violent conflict.'[3] It is necessary that the level of reconciliation is such that parties simply see no future need to be in a conflict any longer. Whatsoever, they need to feel the necessity to cooperate to the extent

1 Martin Leiner, 'Conclusion: From Conflict Resolution to Reconciliation' in Martin Leiner and Christine Schliesser (ed), *Alternative Approaches in Conflict Resolution* (Palgrave Macmillan 2018).

2 Ibid.

3 Rafael Biermann, 'The Politics of Reconciliation in Former Yugoslavia-Assessing Progress Across the Region' in Carolina Rehrmann, Rafael Biermann and Philip Tolliday (ed), *Societies in Transition: The Caucasus and the Balkans between Conflict and Reconciliation* (Vandenhoeck & Ruprecht 2020).

HTTPS://DOI.ORG/10.1163/9789004746091-013

that the conflict is not a solution any longer and that it goes against the interests of all parties involved. In order to achieve this in a complex environment of post-conflict societies, it has to be agreed by all the stakeholders in a given situation. This usually means that the perpetrators of crimes, which are usually high-ranking officials and politicians, are either put on trial, or they are simply removed from their positions. One of the possible tools towards such reconciliation is to offer apologies and reconcile, but also to understand what wrongs they have done and finally forgive the other. This is a very hard and complex step as some high-ranking politicians and officials could be celebrated as heroes in their own societies for the crimes committed during the conflict. 'Although the "top-down" approach and institutional support is one of the preconditions for establishing contact and dialogue and for reaching reconciliation, the change of the state policy towards dealing with conflicts is usually a long-term task.'[4] Be it either a reconciliation coming from inside, like the South African case of Truth Commissions publicly admitting the wrongdoings or the classical justice based on being served by International Criminal Courts, it all has to be done on an equal and just basis. Therefore, reconciliation itself has to be a process, which, as its final outcome and goal, has the act of conflict resolution and rebuilding the relationships between people and their respective societies.

The correlation of justice to reconciliation is the key issue and while more the justice has been served and just solutions achieved during reconciliation, the more stable the societies will be and ready to cooperate and prosper altogether. Since justice can be seen differently from various perspectives, it is necessary to combine and understand various aspects of it in order not to harm the whole of the process. 'Reconciliation is about reconciling these different justice claims.'[5] Therefore, justice as a whole has to be seen and understood as a final solution where everyone has got the most, while it is not the maximum and at least has not harmed unnecessarily others, including their common future. Ultimately, everyone has to be a stakeholder in the peace process and defend it as a final outcome of their mutual efforts and understandings. 'Reconciliation is a process which is always threatened by the revi-

4 Vesna Nikolić-Ristanović and Sonja Ćopić, 'Dealing with Conflicts in a Post-conflict Society: A Restorative Initiative in Serbia' in Carolina Rehrmann, Rafael Biermann and Philip Tolliday (ed), *Societies in Transition: The Caucasus and the Balkans between Conflict and Reconciliation* (Vandenhoeck & Ruprecht 2020).

5 Martin Leiner, 'Conclusion: From Conflict Resolution to Reconciliation' in Martin Leiner and Christine Schliesser (ed), *Alternative Approaches in Conflict Resolution* (Palgrave Macmillan 2018).

talization of enmity.'[6] While it is hard to say when the reconciliation finishes, as there are efforts done even decades after the conflicts, it has to be understood that the process itself has to be done with due respect and common understandings of own needs, and also respecting the others. Timeframes regarding reconciliation are hard to be outlined and scheduled in advance; they have to be built up on the mutual consent of the parties and the respect of their own needs and constraints. 'It is, however, fundamental to highlight that reconciliation does not naturally become easier with time.'[7] Focusing on the process itself is the key, where special preparations have to be done for making bigger steps in the whole process. One of the key necessities to achieve that is when a certain group is able to get into the stadium where they are ready to forgive; then, forgiveness can come from both the inside and outside needs. Observers of reconciliation can be divided into two main groups: those who argue that forgiveness is an absolute condition for reconciliation and those who argue that forgiveness is not a prerequisite for successful reconciliation.[8] In theory, the process of reconciliation takes more than just the two sides in the conflict, there are the communities observing the process from outside and ultimately the whole of the human society is in fact trying to understand, correlate and learn from the whole process.

The process of reconciliation has to be done carefully and, finally, not serve the interests and viewpoints of outside observers but empower the victims and other people in the society which have suffered the most in order to be able to coop with future physical, emotional and survival challenges. 'Empowerment is also aimed at ownership, where the people involved take ownership of the process when it addresses their needs and is consistent with their ideals.'[9] Offering a just and fair compensation in many cases will not and

6 Martin Leiner, 'Setting the Stage: An Introductory Clarification of Concepts of East Central Europe' in Lily Gardner Feldman, Raisa Barash, Samuel Goda and André Zempelburg (ed), *The Former Soviet Union and East Central Europe between Conflict and Reconciliation* (Vandenhoeck & Ruprecht 2019).

7 Valérie Rosoux, 'Time and Reconciliation: Negotiating with Ghosts' in Natascha Mueller-Hirth and Sandra Rios Oyola (ed), *Time and Temporality in Transitional and Post-Conflict Societies* (Routledge 2018).

8 Samuel Goda, 'The OSCE and Reconciliation: Between Theory and Practice' in Lily Gardner Feldman, Raisa Barash, Samuel Goda and André Zempelburg (ed), *The Former Soviet Union and East Central Europe between Conflict and Reconciliation* (Vandenhoeck & Ruprecht 2019).

9 Marichen van der Westhuizen, 'Thoughts into Action: Creating a Long-Term Movement toward a Reconciled and Just Society' in Christo Thesnaar and Len Hansen (ed), *Unfinished Business? Faith Communities and Reconciliation in a Post-TRC Context* (African Sun Media 2020).

can't be expected, even monetary indemnifications are usually not enough and also the use of honest words and apologies can't do much in some instances. Therefore, it is hard to establish a general framework and amount for the indemnification of victims, while globally, conflicts happen daily and simply trying to solve them with monetary means is simply impossible. 'Reconciliation, on the other hand, has to be achieved with much less attention and fewer financial resources.'[10] All societies globally are interconnected and follow all the wrongdoings and sufferings of others; in their eyes, justice is many times seen differently. 'While a general definition of economic globalization is impossible because the data remain incomplete, clearly, reality is complex and the borders between interdependence and globalization are blurred.'[11] All societies have some sort of interdependence with one another and this complex system of relationships brings the notion of justice, compensation and reconciliation into a very vague and hardly explainable system universally.

It is necessary to bring reconciliation closer and be more universal, for what many times post-conflict peace agreements bring in is a definition or the establishment of a specific relationship between parties, which can be said that it is just in a given situation under the given circumstances. 'These forms of interstate cooperation have their roots and robustness in the management of external sovereignty, *i.e.* the management of interdependence.'[12] Accordingly it is not that a certain society needs apologies or guarantees from a certain perpetrator, but they want to have a universal declaration and acceptance of the new situation. Also, they can, in the future, fit back into their own society and into global standards of human rights and democratization of processes. In this given system of theoretical approaches, we evidently have to outline that the post-conflict agreements do have such characteristics and are able to serve as a tool for reconciliation in their very flexible nature. Post-conflict agreements inherently have the capacity for reconciliation and as we will see it in the following chapters, they do allow for a very high level of mutual understandings and cooperation capacities. Overall, reconciliation, in its legal notion, is a phase which can't be explained by post-conflict agree-

10 Martin Leiner, 'Creating Space for Truth: Reconciliation Studies and the 2014 TRC Re-Enactment' in Christo Thesnaar and Len Hansen (ed), *Unfinished Business? Faith Communities and Reconciliation in a Post-TRC Context* (African Sun Media 2020).

11 Wolfgang H. Reinicke and Jan Martin Witte, 'Interdependence, Globalization, and Sovereignty: The Role of Non-binding International Legal Accords' in Dinah Shelton (ed), *Commitment and Compliance: The Role of Non-Binding Norms in the International Legal System* (Oxford University Press 2000).

12 Ibid.

ments but can be certainly achieved by implementing them. Finally, we can argue that the best and most appropriate tools to achieve reconciliation today are in fact such non-formal agreements which are reached immediately after the conflict. They have incorporated a capacity for future changes from inside and also development potentials from the outside perspective.

1 Ways Forward in Reconciliation

When international organizations or the parties themselves try to find the best solution and the way forward in reconciliation, it is necessary to outline that no universality can be achieved in any aspect, whatsoever. While some could argue that courts or the now functioning ICC can bring justice and finally reconcile the societies, others will simply refute it. Maybe, a few decades ago, the importance and role of international courts and tribunals was seen differently, certainly that view has changed by now. 'But victims are also often put into threatening and traumatic situations by lawyers of the accused so that they usually do not feel free or safe to tell the truth.'[13] It looks like there are more arguments now against courts and tribunals; this statement is also supported by the fact that a huge number of countries also do not recognize the universal jurisdiction of the ICC. 'The quest for unity and social cohesion, reconciliation and social healing, justice and social solidarity can be served significantly by universities.'[14] Universities are also seen as institutions which have a significant number of professionals being involved in many aspects of human life and society; they can also serve the reconciliation role.

Universities are also capable of quickly setting up research groups which can be very interdisciplinary, experienced and unbiased. They are the places where different cultures, ideas and people meet and are able to discuss without the pressure of their peers or societies. 'Endorsement of separation attitudes of acculturation on a large scale shows that there is no solid background of reconciliation.'[15] As long as universities in post-conflict societies can't serve their role and bring young people together to study and research-

---

13 Martin Leiner, 'Creating Space for Truth: Reconciliation Studies and the 2014 TRC Re-Enactment' in Christo Thesnaar and Len Hansen (ed), *Unfinished Business? Faith Communities and Reconciliation in a Post-TRC Context* (African Sun Media 2020).

14 Nico Koopman, 'Churches, Universities and the Post-TRC Process: Impulses from a Consultation' in Christo Thesnaar and Len Hansen (ed), *Unfinished Business? Faith Communities and Reconciliation in a Post-TRC Context* (African Sun Media 2020).

15 Mimoza Telaku and Shifra Sagy, 'Perceptions of Collective Narratives and Acculturation Attitudes: The Case of Serbs and Albanians in Kosovo' in Lily Gardner Feldman, Raisa

ers to research, we are not able to speak about reconciliation success in any of its possible forms. One of the main obstacles for universities and their professors is that they have not taken part in military, war and other atrocities; hopefully, so their role and importance is more recognized. 'On the contrary, the rebels use the negotiations to gain a higher status, possibly equal to the government.'[16] The balance of power after conflicts is disturbed in various aspects and the society sees some figures as important, whereas they might be the biggest obstacles in finding a solution and implementing reconciliation between societies.

Finding the right balance to reconcile societies does not logically follow the fact that conflict leaders need to be reconciled as well. The conflict and its reconciliation part concern the society as a whole and does not focus or depend on its prominent individuals, in any form. Also, the establishment of guilt of some individuals does not necessarily mean or guarantee their punishment as perpetrators, and many times, has a completely opposite outcome after the conflict. All this makes reconciliation harder and longer while societies remain divided from inside and distanced from each other from outside. 'Finally, the international community did not attain its major goal to individualize guilt and avoid assigning collective responsibility.'[17] It is hard to measure who has done harm with or without their free will, intentions to do so or the amount of pressure which was exercised on someone or how they felt and were able to coop with such a pressure. People and societies from both inside and outside will always be divided, and the level and amount of such a division can't be measured before, during or after the conflict.

With the conflict in Ukraine, we can observe that while the Russian Government standpoints speak and call for unity, there are a big number of people, from which are many belonging to the younger generation, who are not ready to take part in the war and support the Russian government in any form. 'The OSCE offers the additional advantage of being inclusive – it is the only security organization in the Euro-Atlantic and Eurasian region that includes

---

Barash, Samuel Goda and André Zempelburg (ed), *The Former Soviet Union and East Central Europe between Conflict and Reconciliation* (Vandenhoeck & Ruprecht 2019).

16 Cesare Zucconi, 'Beyond Official Negotiations: The Experience of the Community of Sant'Egidio' in Martin Leiner and Christine Schliesser (ed), *Alternative Approaches in Conflict Resolution* (Palgrave Macmillan 2018).

17 Rafael Biermann, 'The Politics of Reconciliation in Former Yugoslavia-Assesing Progress Across the Region' in Carolina Rehrmann, Rafael Biermann and Philip Tolliday (ed), *Societies in Transition:The Caucasus and the Balkans between Conflict and Reconciliation* (Vandenhoeck & Ruprecht 2020).

both Russia and NATO member countries.'[18] While Russia has been criticized for its aggression in Ukraine, very little has been done to convince it to refrain from such activities. The expulsion of Russia from the Council of Europe[19] is another step which will make the final reconciliation harder, whereas the final solution will be of a concern not just to Ukraine but to the EU, Europe and the globe as a whole. Similarly, regarding Israel, the constant inability of the two communities to establish mutual rights and respects produces immense harm to both nations, and also to the global efforts of peace and nation building.

2 Friction in Post-conflict Agreements

One of the many aspects which have to be taken care of and are also indirectly included in the post-conflict agreements is definitely friction. Friction happens naturally in everyday life and is becoming more and more part of multicultural societies of today and accordingly, also applied to divided and post-conflict societies. 'Friction, as an analytical concept, highlights the imperfection of the connectivity between various agents and their ideas at the global and local level.'[20] It can be said that the more heterogeneous human societies are, they are becoming more influenced by friction and their research becomes more important today. In the peace agreements which are usually short and somewhat unclear, friction can happen in their various stadiums of implementation and it is completely unpredictable how, when and in which amount it will occur. Such a friction can sometimes nullify the impacts of intervention, produce adverse effects, or even in some cases, help to further peace, although not always in the manner expected by interveners.[21] It is not possible to include and implement some global or EU standards in post-conflict societies just because that is a requirement; sometimes, intercultural differences are so

18 Matthew Rojansky, 'Russian-Ukrainian Relations: Conflict Ad Reconciliation over Shared History' in Lily Gardner Feldman, Raisa Barash, Samuel Goda and André Zempelburg (ed), *The Former Soviet Union and East Central Europe between Conflict and Reconciliation* (Vandenhoeck & Ruprecht 2019).

19 Council of Europe, 'The Russian Federation Is Excluded from the Council of Europe' (16 March 2022) <https://www.coe.int/en/web/portal/-/the-russian-federation-is-excluded-from-the-council-of-europe> accessed 24 March 2026.

20 Susanne Buckley-Zistel, 'Frictional Spaces: Transitional Justice between the Global and the Local' in Annika Björkdahl and others (ed), *Peacebuilding and Friction: Global and local encounters in post-conflict societies* (Routledge 2016).

21 Annika Björkdahl and others, 'Conclusion: Peacebuilding and the Significance of Friction' in Annika Björkdahl and others (ed), *Peacebuilding and Friction: Global and local encounters in post-conflict societies* (Routledge 2016).

high that they produce resistance and completely opposite results. Even if on a state level or in some parts of the society, some standards are welcome, at other instances, they can be completely misunderstood. 'However, even if the state is scarcely present, local institutions seldom operate completely disconnected from the state.'[22] Local actors can be different than the central authorities and have different legal tradition; therefore, applying some standards in such contexts requires flexibility and more understanding.

The sole fact that something has been agreed does not guarantee its implementation or its potential immediate implementation in post-conflict contexts. There is a need to balance out the needs and requests of a certain part of the society and provide a guarantee for them that they will see an interest in the final implementation of the peace process. 'In many cases we see that more uncivil local actors – which are exclusivist and/or do not reject violence by definition – are the ones with the most local support, playing important roles in service provision or even building peace.'[23] The clash between various political ideas in the same group can be frequently outlined and seen after the conflict, as there is always a group which remains more radical and military-oriented. There are obviously so many perspectives which can't be all solved and seen from the international perspective of peace builders, with even many years of previous experience. 'Frictional peacebuilding occurs when local actors resist the liberal democratic peace by engaging in anti-pluralist and ethnically polarised politics oriented towards maintaining the status quo and fundamentally challenging the international liberal ideas….'[24] The challenge always remains and consists of the problems which have not been tackled before in history, for example of a society which has never been democratic is different from the one which once was so, and is now transitioning back to democracy in the given peace process. The Western understanding of friction can be seen in the fact that the economy can't give equally to everyone, while human and constitutional rights remain unchanged and guaranteed the same for everyone.

In the post-conflict societies, it is not the case that everyone has the same economic right, but neither the human nor minority rights can be guaranteed

22 Willemijn Verkoren and Mathijs van Leeuwen, 'The Imagined Agent of Peace: Frictions in Peacebuilding through Civil Society Strengthening' in Annika Björkdahl and others (ed), *Peacebuilding and Friction: Global and local encounters in post-conflict societies* (Routledge 2016).

23 Ibid.

24 Annika Björkdahl and Ivan Gusic, 'Sites of Friction: Governance, Identity and Space in Mostar' in Annika Björkdahl and others (ed), *Peacebuilding and Friction: Global and local encounters in post-conflict societies* (Routledge 2016).

fully to every individual. 'But what the concept of compound friction illustrates is that international actors cannot meddle in complex social systems without causing unpredicted effects.'[25] By acknowledging a certain social system and recognizing its existence, it is also recognized that it has been set up on a system of various inequalities. The friction of such inequalities and the recognition of such a system cause the inability of the society to further its reconciliation. 'Unsuccessful interventions may stem from the inflexibility of global liberal peace policies, limiting adaptation to local contexts.'[26] Friction due to the understanding of some standards between Western and other peacekeepers, including locals as well, is somewhat completely inconsistent. 'On the one hand, international peacebuilding holds far less power than is usually assumed.'[27] It is also important to note that no mechanism which can produce full and just reconciliation exists and that the idea of a magic wand does not exist.

We can observe many post-conflict societies which have been supported in many aspects, including financial means that have not produced the required advancements, as expected. The complex issue of friction and all the elements present in one conflict that make and shape it can't be foreseen in their full capacity. 'Friction cannot be designed into peacebuilding interventions in the way this has been attempted with concepts such as 'hybridity' and ownership.'[28] Accordingly, friction as a concept can't be measured in advance, neither can it be blamed on the local stakeholders who are coming out of the conflict. Friction is something that happens and grows with the implementation of peace agreements and follows the reconciliation efforts, it comes and goes unpredictably. Overall, friction is haunting both for the local and international stakeholders, while it is very hard to observe it or eradicate it as long it lasts and exists in the background of the peace-building, conflict resolution and reconciliation processes.

---

25 Gearoid Millar, 'Respecting Complexity: Compound Friction and Unpredictability in Peacebuilding' in Annika Björkdahl and others (ed), *Peacebuilding and Friction: Global and local encounters in post-conflict societies* (Routledge 2016).

26 Annika Björkdahl and others, 'Conclusion: Peacebuilding and the Significance of Friction' in Annika Björkdahl and others (ed), *Peacebuilding and Friction: Global and local encounters in post-conflict societies* (Routledge 2016).

27 Annika Björkdahl and Ivan Gusic, 'Sites of Friction: Governance, Identity and Space in Mostar' in Annika Björkdahl and others (ed), *Peacebuilding and Friction: Global and local encounters in post-conflict societies* (Routledge 2016).

28 Annika Björkdahl and others, 'Conclusion: Peacebuilding and the Significance of Friction' in Annika Björkdahl and others (ed), *Peacebuilding and Friction: Global and local encounters in post-conflict societies* (Routledge 2016).

3 Possible Ways Forward with the Concept of Friction in Post-conflict Agreements

In the framework of global post-conflict developments, there are very few rules which can be widely applied and their outcomes thoroughly guaranteed. One is certain though, it is that the concept of transitional justice or the time which needs to pass in order to achieve justice, or a more just society as its final outcome in the future. 'In other words, originating in concrete localities after the experience of two world wars, transitional justice has by now developed into a pervasive global norm.'[29] As every other idea, transitional justice has been also developing for decades in order to be able to transform post-conflicts societies and serve justice to the highest possible extent. Being a very broad idea itself, transitional justice includes many stakeholders, of which many are, between themselves, in friction, they refute each other by trying to achieve ultimately the same goal. Similar to different interests of states, other public or private organizations also have different understandings, practices and priorities.

One of the best examples of disparities, friction and the implementation of the ideas of transitional justice within the western understanding is visible in case of Afghanistan. The needs and interests of the Afghani society, where so much different and sometimes opposing ideas have been implemented by Western stakeholders, is that the society has turned back to its previous stadium of radical governance without any possible friction in this process. 'It appears that frictions, and new and unexpected outcomes developed from the process that resulted from the encounters between the structured and simplified perceptions of interveners, the suboptimal policies they produced, and the local Afghan responses.'[30] The most prominent and extreme form of friction in the peacebuilding process has therefore probably occurred in Afghanistan recently. It is not recommended that we come up with a conclusion that it was a complete misunderstanding between Western democracies and local elites in Afghanistan from the beginning. Also, we will be able to explain it later from the Chinese perspective of a future Afghanistan; its involvement looks smoother, with less possibility for friction.

---

29 Susanne Buckley-Zistel, 'Frictional Spaces: Transitional Justice between the Global and the Local' in Annika Björkdahl and others (ed), *Peacebuilding and Friction: Global and local encounters in post-conflict societies* (Routledge 2016).

30 Jaïr van der Lijn, 'Frictions in Illusionstan: Engagement between the "Global" and the "Local" in Afghanistan's Imagination-Building' in Annika Björkdahl and others (ed), *Peacebuilding and Friction: Global and local encounters in post-conflict societies* (Routledge 2016).

It is also very important to note that the Chinese practice of peacebuilding has by now gained experience from various regions, 'there has been increasing trade friction between China and a few African countries, primarily Egypt and South Africa'.[31] South Africa, being itself part of the BRICS, and Egypt, a potential future member, show that the geopolitical situation is changing and the border between East and West is constantly changing and is in permanent friction. 'The U.S.–China relationship has settled into an openly competitive dynamic in which decision-makers on both sides are more risk-tolerant and see the introduction of friction as necessary for achieving national objectives.'[32] Friction can also be seen as a confrontation of national interests of a certain state with the ideas promoted in post-conflict agreements, which many times do not represent the same needs and future development patterns. The USA–China trade friction is as prominent as much is the USA–Russia security friction present today, more than possibly any time before. All the frictions being present in some domestic politics are immediately projected to the involvements in other societies and very visible in post-conflict societies where the direction changes are the easiest to be observed. 'This is why friction cannot be described simply as a confrontation between actors, or as a function of structures, or as occurring between one intervention and the local setting.'[33] Friction can also produce conflicts on various levels, including trade, but also ultimately open warfare situations, in which again, we don't see the solution to the problem but the escalation, which is by now overly dangerous for the peacebuilding experiences we have developed so far.

31 Wei Liang, 'China's Soft Power in Africa: Is Economic Power Sufficient?' (2012) 36 Asian Perspective 667.

32 International Crisis Group, 'Risky Competition: Strengthening U.S.-China Crisis Management' (2022) 324 Asia Report <https://icg-prod.s3.amazonaws.com/324-us-china-crisis-management.pdf> accessed 24 March 2026.

33 Gearoid Millar, 'Respecting Complexity: Compound Friction and Unpredictability in Peacebuilding' in Annika Björkdahl and others (ed), *Peacebuilding and Friction: Global and local encounters in post-conflict societies* (Routledge 2016).

CHAPTER 12

Kosovo and Its Post-conflict Peace Agreements

Reaching an agreement regarding Kosovo was never easy and while no final agreement has been reached so far, the few partial agreements have also taken much more time than was the case in other ex-Yugoslav conflicts. The decades-long ambiguity regarding the future status of Kosovo is not solely connected to the Serbian and Kosovo sides but opens a broader disagreement in the whole UN and also sharply divides the EU. While The European Union Rule of Law Mission in Kosovo (EULEX)[1] has taken over many important state-building roles from the United Nations Interim Administration Mission in Kosovo (UNMIK).[2] it was never clear what, how and when it will finally achieve. 'Under the principle of conferral, the Union shall act only within the limits of the competences conferred upon it by the Member States in the Treaties to attain the objectives set out therein.'[3] While the divide in the UN itself was obvious, the separate viewpoints and interests were also present in the EU where the accession of Serbia and Kosovo is seen differently.

The EU had a more obvious aim to understand the new reality and also accept the mutual agreements between Serbia and Kosovo which could bring them closer to each other and more importantly closer to possible future EU integrations. In order to achieve any kind of cooperation between Serbia and Kosovo, there was an obvious need to make Serbia accept various forms and levels of cooperation with Kosovo, but also support the integration of four North Kosovo Serbian municipalities into the Kosovo legal framework. While Serbia was ready to discuss and accept some changes, it is still hesitant to accept the Kosovo independence overall, and only claims 'negotiation process with Pristina',[4] as it sees the agreements which are being concluded with

1 EULEX, 'EULEX Accountability' <https://www.eulex-kosovo.eu/?page=2,23> accessed 24 March 2026.

2 United Nations, 'United Nations Interim Administration Mission in Kosovo' <https://peacekeeping.un.org/en/mission/unmik> accessed 24 March 2026.

3 European Union, 'Consolidated Version of the Treaty on European Union, Article 5, OJ C 202, 7.6.2016' (2016) <https://eur-lex.europa.eu/eli/treaty/teu_2016/art_5/oj/eng> accessed 24 March 2026.

4 Office for Kosovo and Metohija, Government of the Republic of Serbia, 'Negotiation Process with Pristina' (2023) <https://www.kim.gov.rs/eng/pregovaracki-proces.php> accessed 24 March 2026.

its autonomous province and not with an independent state, which is also in line with The UN Security Council Resolution 1244.[5] While the UN itself can't exercise force to make parties agree, it still considers EU as a stakeholder to have more interests and influence in bringing the sides closer and supporting their mutual agreements.

The ultimate goal of the EU is to make Serbia and Kosovo agree about as many issues as possible, which will finally make them more connected and likely integrated into the EU more smoothly in the future. 'An implementation committee will be established by the two sides, with the facilitation of the EU.'[6] The most important aspect of the normalization process between Serbia and Kosovo is definitely the Brussels Agreement, signed in 2013.[7] While this agreement has made tremendous steps in regard to the inclusion of the Serbian minority into the Kosovo legal framework, it has, even after more than 10 years, still not been fully implemented. The two sides were not ready to change their standpoints; Serbia refuses to recognize the authorities in Kosovo while it refuses to officially form the Association/Community of Serbian municipalities. In a recent Agreement from Ohrid,[8] they have again outlined some commitments which were not signed in any manner on this occasion. 'This was on the one hand, because I think that one party, Kosovo, lacked flexibility on the substance, and on the other hand because [of] Serbia's previously stated principles not to sign although they were fully ready to implement.'[9] The most important point of disagreement is about who and how they can control the Serbian minority in North Kosovo. As was outlined before, the Serbian interest is 'including the possibility for financial support by Serbia and a direct communication channel for the Serbian community to the Govern-

5 United Nations, 'Resolution 1244 (1999)' (10 June 1999) <https://unmik.unmissions.org/sites/default/files/old_dnn/Res1244ENG.pdf> accessed 24 March 2026.

6 Brussels Agreement, 'First Agreement of Principles Governing the Normalization of Relations' (2013) <https://www.peaceagreements.org/media/documents/ag2022_5bdc31b326555.pdf> also available at <https://www.srbija.gov.rs/cinjenice/en/120394> and <https://gzk.rks-gov.net/ActDetail.aspx?ActID=8892&langid=2> accessed 24 March 2026. Further will be cited as BA 2013.

7 Ibid.

8 European Union External Action, 'Belgrade-Pristina Dialogue: Agreement on the path to normalisation between Kosovo and Serbia' (2023) <https://www.eeas.europa.eu/eeas/belgrade-pristina-dialogue-agreement-path-normalisation-between-kosovo-and-serbia_en> accessed 24 March 2026.

9 EEAS Press Team, 'Belgrade-Pristina Dialogue: Press Remarks by High Representative Josep Borrell after the Ohrid Meeting with President Vučić and Prime Minister Kurti' (2023) <https://www.eeas.europa.eu/eeas/belgrade-pristina-dialogue-press-remarks-high-representative-josep-borrell-after-ohrid-meeting_en> accessed 24 March 2026.

ment of Kosovo'.[10] The overall protection of national minorities and its shortcomings in Kosovo are not a surprise, when we know that other similar challenges of minority protection in EU and especially the ones coming from the Kosovo non-recognizing countries are still a very big challenge.

When we compare the USA standpoints regarding Kosovo, it is evident that they are more straightforward, since the USA was also one of the most important protagonists of the Kosovo independence. After the Brussels Agreement[11] was signed, it became evident that it was not fully implemented, and in order to show that USA supports it and the whole agenda of discussions and agreements, it has decided to bring together Serbia and Kosovo and make them sign an additional document, the Washington Agreement (WA).[12] This agreement is very specific since it has two similar but finally different versions and 'the leaders did not sign one agreement jointly.'[13] While the agreement is the same for both parties, its most important part is different and deals in specific with Israel. Serbia and Kosovo have therefore signed two different agreements, which can be seen as a promise towards the USA, and are coming together in a package with other similar agreements signed under the USA support in the framework of the Abrahamic Accords. These agreements are concerning mainly Israel and its Muslim neighbours in the MENA region. Although Serbia and Kosovo do not belong to this region geographically, potentially politically they do. 'The two parties signed two separate but nearly identical documents, essentially letters of intent to cooperate with each other and with the US on a limited set of issues.'[14] Probably the most important aspects of the WA are not concerning the mutual relationship between Serbia and Kosovo but rather their commitment to support USA in its endeavours and also their common determination to block Russian and Chinese influence by limiting their trade

10 EEAS Press Team, 'Belgrade-Pristina Dialogue: EU Proposal – Agreement on the Path to Normalisation between Kosovo and Serbia' (2023) <https://www.eeas.europa.eu/eeas/belgrade-pristina-dialogue-eu-proposal-agreement-path-normalisation-between-kosovo-and-serbia_en> accessed 24 March 2026.

11 BA 2013.

12 Washington Agreement, 'Economic Normalization' (2020) <https://www.peacefare.net/2020/09/04/much-ado-about-nothing/> also available at <https://exit.al/en/2020/09/04/kosovo-and-serbia-signed-separate-pledges-not-an-agreement/> accessed 24 March 2026. Further will be cited as WA 2020.

13 Paul Fraioli, 'The Kosovo–Serbia Normalisation Agreements' (2020) 26 Strategic Comments vii.

14 Branislav Stanicek, 'Belgrade-Pristina Dialogue: The Rocky Road towards a Comprehensive Normalisation Agreement' [2023] European Parliamentary Research Service <https://www.europarl.europa.eu/thinktank/en/document/EPRS_BRI(2025)779231> accessed 24 March 2026.

and investments possibilities in the respective territories. 'It is clear that the agreement reached in Washington is not legally binding, but instead represents a diplomatic moment of political signaling.'[15] In the coming chapters, we will explain in more detail how such non-formal agreements such as the WA can shape and reshape economic activities in a post-conflict society.

In this chapter, we plan to research two informal agreements achieved in the framework of the dialogue between Serbia and Kosovo, while in specific, we aim to see their conflict resolution and development potentials in this given post-conflict framework. There are many other agreements from which we have previously mentioned the Ohrid Agreement. 'Critics, among them Professor Daniel Serwer, observe that the agreement in Ohrid seems to be more process-focused, without ensuring a real engagement of the parties, given that they did not sign it and that it is not valid from the point of view of international law.'[16] The Ohrid Agreement[17] and any other similar and possible future agreements are therefore just steps to achieve the more important requirements from both the Brussels Agreement and the Washington Agreement, overall. This idea is overall known as the Franco-German treaty proposal, which is meant to bring back parties to the negotiation table again, but without any crucial changes in their mutual relationships. 'Kosovo and Serbia agree that the present Treaty shall not affect the bilateral and multilateral international treaties and agreements already concluded by them or relating to them.'[18] Accordingly, the most important aspects and changes in the mutual relationship between Serbia and Kosovo, but also possible constitutional changes to accommodate the new and innovative solutions, potentially from the Ohrid Agreement but also from both the BA and WA, are still to be seen. The most important aspects of such agreements remain and their inno-

---

15 Leonardo Dinic, 'Huawei Targeted by Trump's Recent Serbia-Kosovo Meeting?' (28 October 2020) <https://www.chinausfocus.com/finance-economy/huawei-targeted-by-trumps-recent-serbia-kosovo-meeting> accessed 24 March 2026.

16 Branislav Stanicek, 'Belgrade-Pristina Dialogue: The Rocky Road towards a Comprehensive Normalisation Agreement' [2023] European Parliamentary Research Service <https://www.europarl.europa.eu/RegData/etudes/BRIE/2021/689371/EPRS_BRI(2021)689371_EN.pdf(2021)689371_EN.pdf> accessed 24 March 2026.

17 European Union External Action, 'Belgrade-Pristina Dialogue: Agreement on the path to normalisation between Kosovo and Serbia' (2023) <https://www.eeas.europa.eu/eeas/belgrade-pristina-dialogue-agreement-path-normalisation-between-kosovo-and-serbia_en> accessed 24 March 2026.

18 Alexandra Brzozowski and Alice Taylor, 'LEAK: Franco-German Plan to Resolve the Kosovo-Serbia Dispute' (2022) <https://www.euractiv.com/section/enlargement/news/leak-franco-german-plan-to-resolve-the-kosovo-serbia-dispute/> accessed 24 March 2026.

vation- and implementation-related capacity will be further explained in more detail.

1 Development-Related Aspects

1.1 Trade Perspectives

One of the first aspects we are going to approach when talking about development is definitely the trade potentials for both Serbia and Kosovo as post-conflict societies. While these countries have as their major trade partner the EU, they are still more closely connected and legally integrated into the CEFTA[19] framework, which consists mainly of Western Balkan non-EU member states and Moldova. While the majority of CEFTA countries are found in the Western Balkans surrounded by EU member states, their biggest challenge is therefore on how to align their trade and policies to a greater extent. 'Three CEFTA members, Serbia Bosnia and Herzegovina (BiH) and Moldova, did not recognize Kosovo's independence.'[20] This proved to make trade and cooperation between Serbia and Kosovo a very complex issue. Such a pressure to promote trade and mutual relationships also puts the EU into a very challenging position. In fact, Kosovo and its customs were not recognized as such since the CEFTA accession documents were signed on its behalf by UNMIK.[21] In this regard, UNMIK or UNMIK-Kosovo was officially the member of CEFTA and was representing Kosovo. When Kosovo previously asked for the removal of UNMIK from its name in CEFTA, it failed. 'The request was refused, primarily on the ground that it was not submitted by UNMIK on behalf of Kosovo.'[22] Such a request to change its position and leave the UNMIK framework has only recently become possible. In general, the overall EU integration is only possible through the CEFTA framework. 'Considering their history, Kosovo

19 Central European Free Trade Agreement, 'About' <https://cefta.int/about/> accessed 24 March 2026.

20 Balkans Policy Research Group, 'Kosovo's Contested Representation in CEFTA: A Political and Legal Overview' [2021] Policy Report <https://balkansgroup.org/wp-content/uploads/2021/11/Kosovos-Contested-Representation-in-CEFTA-151021.pdf> accessed 24 March 2026.

21 United Nations, 'United Nations Interim Administration Mission in Kosovo' <https://peacekeeping.un.org/en/mission/unmik> accessed 24 March 2026.

22 Balkans Policy Research Group, 'Kosovo's Contested Representation in CEFTA: A Political and Legal Overview' [2021] Policy Report <https://balkansgroup.org/wp-content/uploads/2021/11/Kosovos-Contested-Representation-in-CEFTA-151021.pdf> accessed 24 March 2026.

does not want to be a vehicle to further Serbia's economic growth through a common market, since Serbia is already the biggest exporter among CEFTA countries.'[23] The prior name dispute inside CEFTA has now slowly outgrown to an open conflict between Serbia and Kosovo, where the latter imposes trade barriers which are completely outside the CEFTA Agreement, whereas UNMIK is not interfering due to their, by now, very limited mission capacities in Kosovo. All such challenges and trade blockages are not likely to change in the future even though Kosovo became a CEFTA member, representing itself directly, and not through its UNMIK mission any longer.

In general, the imposition of 100% import tax on goods originating from Serbia and Bosnia and Hercegovina[24] has been a very extreme solution by the Kosovo government to try to position itself better regarding trade inside CEFTA. Unfortunately, such acts are completely against all the relevant EU trade standards, and have been seen very critically by the EU as well. An interesting aspect of this trade ban was also that the relevant legislation imposing it has an Annex[25] where, among other products, Coca-Cola drink is not supposed to be taxed with 100% tax, when imported from Serbia to Kosovo. As a multinational company, Coca-Cola distributes on the market with a certain distribution key that is not able to accommodate the various possible future-specific requests of entities such as Kosovo, or to establish a production line there. It also shows how some multinational companies and the governments standing behind them are still above some post-conflict societies, which are respectively deemed to be independent in many other aspects.

As was outlined before, the whole process of Kosovo integration into the channels of regional and global trade do have to follow the trade patterns already established. This was once again outlined in the WA where the USA requested Kosovo to join the newly formed Mini-Schengen trade area, which it is very hesitant to do. 'Both parties will join the "mini-Schengen zone," announced by Serbia, Albania and North Macedonia in October 2019, and fully utilize its benefits.'[26] Lately, mini-Schengen was renamed Open Balkan[27]

---

23 Marko Savković and Bernard Nikaj, 'Opportunity Costs of the Kosovo-Serbia Stalemate' [2021] Sbunker <https://sbunker.org/wp-content/uploads/2023/12/3.-Opportunity-Cost-of-the-Dialogue-Between-Kosovo-and-Serbia1666958448.pdf> accessed 24 March 2026.

24 Republic of Kosovo, 'Odluku' (21 November 2018) <https://kryeministri.rks-gov.net/sr/blog/odluke-76-sednice-vlade-21-11-2018/> accessed 24 March 2026.

25 Ibid.

26 WA 2020.

27 Albanian Government, 'Important Cooperation Agreements Signed at Open Balkan Summit' (2 September 2022) <https://www.kryeministria.al/en/newsroom/nenshkruhen-marreveshje-te-rendesishme-bashkepunimi-ne-samitin-per-ballkanin-e-hapur-beograd/> accessed 24 March 2026.

and after initial successes, it is now facing various other challenges due to the renewed political disagreements in the region.

While the USA was very keen to encourage Kosovo connect and trade with its regional partners, it is less keen and supportive when it comes to trade with countries such as Russia or China. 'On this note, while Gazprom was enlisted on the respective sanctions decision by the Government of Kosovo, its branch in Serbia (NIS) was never explicitly sanctioned.'[28] It is evident that USA has an interest in making Kosovo independent of Russian and Chinese investments and while it succeeds in this regard, a bigger challenge is still the influence these two countries have towards Serbia. Contrary to this expectation, Serbia, similarly to the whole of the EU, is not able to make itself independent of the Russian energy resources. The rising demand on the energy market makes its independence, again hand in hand with the EU, lower with every move and new sanctions imposed by the EU on Russia. Therefore, one of the biggest challenges of Serbia and Kosovo as post-conflict societies is not how to maintain their sovereignty but how to balance their huge energy dependence; in this case, they again share the destiny of the EU overall and have not much influence or say in this regard.

When it comes to the Chinese influence regarding trade and development in the Balkans, it is necessary to note that as the majority of global trade happens with China, so is the case here. The trade imbalances and economic independence remain very challenging overall in the Balkans and Europe. 'Unlike in other parts of the globe, China cannot match the EU's economic and trading dominance in South-East Europe.'[29] The EU remains the biggest and most influential trading partner of the Balkan countries, but some changes regarding investments, infrastructure and overall future potentials are changing, with which we will deal in more detail in the following chapters.

28 Pëllumb Kallaba, 'Russian Interference in Kosovo: How and Why?' (2017) 9 Kosovar Centre for Security Studies <https://qkss.org/images/uploads/files/Russian_interference_in_Kosovo_finale_2_735070.pdf> accessed 24 March 2026.

29 Edward P. Joseph, 'From Crisis to Convergence: A Strategy to Tackle Balkans Instability at Its Source' [2022] Foreign Policy Institute and Wilson Center <https://www.wilsoncenter.org/publication/crisis-convergence-strategy-tackle-balkans-instability-its-source> accessed 24 March 2026.

1.2 Investment Possibilities

The peak of investments in Kosovo was in the Yugoslav times and after its independence, they did not come close to those successes back in the time. This was also the period when, as we can claim, rule of law was guaranteed and the complex bureaucratic measures were still serving to a great amount the interests of the people, not to say the working class. On the ashes of the Kosovo industry after the war, there were some notable investment successes and profitable enterprises formed, but overall the real ownership of the previous era companies and assets was never solved. 'In the case of Kosovo, the massive privatisation of public companies resulted in objections from both the UN Legal Advisor and the Serb Authorities.'[30] As in every post-conflict society, just as is the case with every post-colonial society, it is very hard to determine who remains as the owner of the assets and what is the legal basis.

Kosovo, overall, promises a good investment opportunity due to its cheap labour force and vicinity to the EU, with many trade related benefits when it comes to exporting. 'Turkey currently is the biggest investor in Kosovo with more than 900 Turkish companies operating.'[31] Due to the cultural and historic ties, Kosovo is a good place for Turkish investments also, and can be used as a good solution for outsourcing goods and labour outside the EU, keeping the high standards for goods and services required by the EU market. Most importantly, Turkey has an interest to keep itself active in various conflicts where it can also benefit economically or geo-strategically. Turkey is one of the biggest supporters of the Azerbaijani economy, which again brings us close to the idea and influence of great powers and their role in regional conflicts. Azerbaijan itself is present in Serbia and its Azvirt[32] Company has an important role in the Serbian infrastructure building. While Azerbaijan itself does not recognize Kosovo, there could be still some infrastructure development projects possible, according to mutual agreements and possible future political alignments.

---

30 Eric De Brabandere, *Post-conflict Administrations in International Law: International Territorial Administration, Transitional Authority and Foreign Occupation in Theory and Practice* (Martinus Nijhoff Publishers 2009).

31 Doğu Ergil, 'Turkey's Power and Influence on Kosovo' in David L. Phillips and Lulzim Peci (ed), *Threats and Challenges to Kosovo's Sovereignty* (Institute for the Study of Human Rights at Columbia University 2018).

32 SAKOM, 'Belgrade Bypass Was Built by Builders from Azerbaijan and China Together with Serbian Subcontractors' (4 July 2023) <https://sakom.org.rs/en/belgrade-bypass-was-built-by-builders-from-azerbaijan-and-china-together-with-serbian-subcontractors/> accessed 24 March 2026.

When it comes to big investments, and one of them is the building up of a railroad connection network through Serbia, connecting the port of Thessaloniki to Budapest, there is a very important Chinese interest[33] and investment in this region in this regard. Such a corridor can potentially open up new possibilities, and the race for Chinese investments[34] is already present in the area of Central and Eastern Europe (CEE), trying to, overall, be part of the future BRI transportation network leading towards the EU. 'Moreover, because of a lack of cohesion among them, CEE countries are competing with each other regarding possible investment from China.'[35] While Chinese investments are very straightforward and have an aim to quickly solve connection challenges or resource transportation issues, the EU investments, overall, are taking a much longer time and are bureaucratically more complex. Many times, the EU investments have various aspects, from which not all are economic but their political connotations are more important, which again brings challenges to the ruling elites in certain countries. 'Western donors have argued that China's unconditional financial aid is eroding the bargaining power of their agencies and that it undermines their efforts at improving good governance, human rights protection, and the rule of law in aid recipient countries.'[36] The CEE region is overall split between EU and non-EU member-states and the lack of investments, infrastructure and development projects are equally high in all of them. The inability of the EU to satisfy the big investment demands in CEE have left the door open for China, which is using the idea of free trade and investments by slowly penetrating more and more inside the EU, and is challenging its trade, investment and potentials in many countries, not just in the post-conflict ones.

In regard to post-conflict societies and the case of Serbia and Kosovo dialogue, there have been some very important aspects regarding China and its influence, in specific regarding Serbia where it is already dominating the telecommunications infrastructures development. 'That cooperation has not been disturbed shows the fact that Huawei opened its Digitalization and Innovation

33 Office of the Leading Group for Promoting the Belt and Road Initiative, 'Belt and Road Portal' <https://eng.yidaiyilu.gov.cn/> accessed 24 March 2026.

34 Ibid.

35 Sebastien Goulard, 'From 17+1 to 27+1 Mechanism?' (20 July 2021) <https://www.oboreurope.com/en/from-17-to-27-mechanism/> accessed 24 March 2026.

36 Svante E. Cornell and Niklas Swanström, 'Compatible Interests? The EU and China's Belt and Road Initiative' (2020) 1 SIEPS Swedish Institute for European Policy Studies <https://sieps.se/en/publications/2020/compatible-interests/> accessed 24 March 2026.

Center in Belgrade only 10 days after the Washington agreement was signed.'[37] While the WA itself has tried to limit Huawei's influence in Serbia, although not explicitly stating that, it became evident that the Serbian government simply has no capacities to limit it and is using fully the potentials of its cooperation with China. Overall, in regard to the telecommunications investments, except in Kosovo, in all post-conflict societies such as Nagorno-Karabakh and Afghanistan, there is an absolute dominance of China due to its approachable, cheap and competitive technology. Finally, China is supplying its telecommunication network components to Serbia and to some other EU member-states as well, such as Germany, for instance.

Kosovo and its privatization process and the sharing of the most important industrial and mining capacities in it, were not particularly mentioned in any of the Agreements. Mining was the most important sector of the economy in Kosovo, but for now, it remains unsolved and while many big cities in Kosovo have been built and developed on this sector, there is very little activity in this regard. Kosovo is famous for its mining industry and citizens of cities such as Titova Mitrovica (previously) or Zvechan would never be so developed if there is no mining in their vicinity. Therefore, the issue of economic activities and development is key for the existence of mining cities and communities around them and in our case, specifically the four Northern Serbian municipalities in Kosovo, while some changes and solutions in this regard can be also achieved by the future economic regulation or establishment of the A/C. 'The Association/Community will have full overview of the areas of economic development, education, health, urban and rural planning.'[38] Economic development can be achieved only by investments and solving the complex ownership issues, mainly regarding The Trepcha mining complex. Still, while there is no final solution regarding state property, its division and investment security, there is also no prosperity potential.

As previously mentioned, the investment need of this region is huge, and many important projects which could give it a chance to develop are still in the form of a plan. Investments are needed to develop various transportation routes which can give possibilities for further investments into industry and production. The Washington Agreement[39] has been explicitly giving its sup-

37 Stefan Vladisavljev, 'China's "Digital Silk Road" Enters the Western Balkans' [2021] Association for International Affairs (AMO) <https://chinaobservers.eu/wp-content/uploads/2021/06/CHOICE_policy-paper_digital-silk-road_A4_web_04.pdf> accessed 24 March 2026.

38 BA 2013.

39 WA 2020.

port to the development of the 'Belgrade-Pristina highway'[40] and also the 'Belgrade-Pristina rail agreement',[41] since both are necessary for Kosovo to connect it regionally and to the main roads leading towards the EU, other European countries and the world overall.

1.3 Infrastructure Development Potentials

Kosovo is a small landlocked country without big rivers, which could give it connectedness and transportation capacity but also permanent access to water. The Water Resources Management (WRM) is therefore very important in Kosovo and has been accordingly approached in its post-conflict agreements. 'The process of water management in Kosovo illustrates a serious disjunction between the technical aspects of WRM and its political implementation during a post-conflict reconstruction phase.'[42] Water is broadly seen as a very important resource which has not been approached and regulated on a global scale, but it does have its importance and capacity in post-conflict agreements. Researching potentials for water resource sharing management and the positive examples from Kosovo can develop research further and provide solutions for other similar cases in water-scarce regions globally and more importantly, border regions and post-conflict societies.

One of the most important water resources in Kosovo is actually coming from Serbia, so while the two governments were not able to agree about it before, it was one of the key points in the Washington Agreement, bringing a solution to water- and electricity sharing solutions to North Kosovo. 'Both parties will agree to work with the U.S. Department of Energy, and other appropriate U.S. Government entities, on a feasibility study for the purposes of sharing Gazivode/Ujmani Lake, as a reliable water and energy supply.'[43] Water from this source is also important for communal use, agriculture and industry where one of the biggest industries is the energy production facilities in Obilic. Securing water sources is very important in the framework of development of every post-conflict society, as has been also outlined before. Finally, the water management and the actual shortages also represent security concerns and not just simple economic needs. 'Physical water stress, inadequate investments in infrastructure, mismanagement of water resour-

40 Ibid.

41 Ibid.

42 Florian Krampe, 'Water for Peace? Post-conflict Water Resource Management in Kosovo' (2017) 52(2) Cooperation and Conflict 147.

43 WA 2020.

ces and national security issues make Kosovo water insecure.'[44] In any case, water bills, together with electricity bills payments, have also been one of the biggest challenges in regard to their non-payments on North Kosovo, and it is still to be seen how independent North Kosovo with its A/C can be and in what form it can be supported by Serbia in this regard.

After the global issue of water scarcity and recently, more hand in hand with it, is the coming of energy scarcity of not just post-conflict societies but overall. As we are researching countries outside the EU, it is evident that they have similar demands like the ones inside the EU, and finally exactly the same sources of energy supplies as well. With the crisis in Ukraine and the new modules of energy transportation, it is evident that such infrastructure projects also cause deep divisions inside the EU and are a key and strategic interest of every country and economy. 'The TurkStream pipeline, a downscaled version of the South Stream project that is to run through Bulgaria, Serbia, and Hungary, revived the allure of Russian investment in the region.'[45] Overall, every energy-related infrastructure investment project has some of its roots back in its Asian sources, where many times, they are somehow connected to Russia. At the moment, there are not so many options to source energy to Europe which would not include transit through Ukraine or Turkey. The rising demand to regulate energy transit is therefore, now and even more in the future, meant to be a part of post-conflict agreements in order to achieve energy stability in the EU as well.

The development and infrastructure sectors such as energy and telecommunications are seen as necessary and vital for every post-conflict society and, accordingly, their prioritized approach with possible future solutions have been included into the relevant agreements. 'Discussions on Energy and Telecoms will be intensified'[46] with an aim to bring the connectivity and also standardization of supplies more harmonized by the sides and included in other similar regional frameworks. Regarding electrical energy, the biggest challenge is the payment of electricity bills in North Kosovo and the final regulation of its transit.

---

44 Wolrd Bank, 'Water Security Outlook for Kosovo' [2018] World Bank Publications <https://documents1.worldbank.org/curated/en/496071548849630510/Water-Security-Outlook-for-Kosovo.pdf> accessed 24 March 2026.

45 Dimitar Bechev, 'Russia's Strategic Interests and Tools of Influence in the Western Balkans' [2019] NATO Strategic Communications Centre of Excellence <https://stratcomcoe.org/cuploads/pfiles/russias_strategic_interests_in_balkans_11dec.pdf> accessed 24 March 2026.

46 BA 2013.

In the sphere of oil and gas, an important supplies network is therefore leading from Russian sources while regarding telecommunications, the sourcing of equipment is focused on China, while both sources are seen accordingly as a security threat by the USA. 'Both parties will prohibit the use of 5G equipment supplied by untrusted vendors in their communications networks.'[47] This interesting solution from the WA is coming at the same time when USA has a conflict with Huawei at home, so it aims at spreading its standards and their applications towards its allied states. 'As Europe's largest economy, Germany is still heavily reliant on China for its telecoms networks,'[48] which evidently comes due to its efficiency, cost and applicability in the given provider networks. The removal of the Chinese 5G equipment from the USA might be smooth, while in regard to the EU, it is more problematic due to its cost, dependency and efficiency overall. In post-conflict societies, due to their limited financial abilities and a great demand for development in the telecommunications sector, it is hard to exclude competitiveness, just as we can see it in the case of Serbia.

1.4 Potentials for Future Development

The overall potential of Kosovo, in comparison to other similar post-conflict societies, is comparably higher due to the vicinity and support it gains from the EU. The Stabilisation and Association Agreement, among others, offers Kosovo a very prosperous trade potential, which is also noted by potential investors. Still, due to various unforeseen factors, the rule of law and the overall administration can be seen primarily as limiting factors for investments. Corruption is also one of the main reasons why international corporations are hesitant to invest into Kosovo. 'Although Kosovo, like many post-conflict cases, grew fast in the immediate post-conflict period, this was due to foreign assistance, remittances, the large international presence, and illegal activities.'[49] The unfinished privatizations of the most important sectors such as mining, smelters and other connected industries make the situation more complex, where investors can't find the most appropriate way to establish themselves permanently in Kosovo.

---

47 WA 2020.

48 Mathieu Pollet, 'Time to Cut Back on Huawei, German Minister Tells Telecoms Giants' (18 August 2023) <https://www.politico.eu/article/germany-interior-minister-nancy-faeser-huawei-china-telecoms/> accessed 24 March 2026.

49 Graciana del Castillo, *Rebuilding War-Torn States: The Challenge of Post-conflict Economic Reconstruction* (Oxford University Press 2008).

While some energy-rich post-conflict societies can easily achieve energy independence, at least, which could also guarantee them future potentials of development such as it is the case with Azerbaijan or Afghanistan, Kosovo being an energy producer, still can't use its potentials and is an energy-dependent country. So is the case with Serbia, which could also achieve more in regard to energy production, but its energy dependence, together with the whole Europe, is also very visible. In the WA, it was outlined even before the whole energy crisis in Europe has occurred, that 'both parties will diversify their energy supplies'[50] and this way try to be more independent of Russian resources. The overall dependence on energy from Russia and the telecommunications equipment from China are not a post-conflict specific thing, as they are common for all societies, while the ones in Europe are presently more vulnerable to such challenges.

A big potential lies also in transportation and the connectivity opportunities; in the Western Balkans, it is primarily with Serbia. It has a very prominent role and is perfectly finding its place as well in the Chinese ideas and investments regarding connectivity. 'The Digital Silk Road, which aims to connect countries along the maritime and terrestrial routes of the BRI through telecommunication networks, is another tool that gives China a key advantage over its competitors.'[51] China is not just dominant in regard to telecommunications in post-conflict societies but in all other societies, including the EU itself. The potentials of Chinese investments can be used to bring advancement to post-conflict societies, while some other more regulated and strict markets such as the EU or the USA will be hesitant to implement them.

When we speak about land transportation, we can also observe that the Western Balkans falls into this priority area, including Serbia, which was already receiving tremendous investments and developments in this regard. 'However, while these conditions may seem attractive, the spillover to the rest of the economy is sometimes limited as Chinese companies often provide their own workers and supplies, and rarely rely on local resources.'[52] It can easily happen that the country itself does not benefit much from it, just as is the case in Serbia. 'However, projects are frequently subcontracted to local companies, which in turn depend on political patronage of politically con-

50 WA 2020.

51 Philippe Le Corre, 'China's Rise as a Geoeconomic Influencer: Four European Case Studies' [2018] Carnegie Endowment for International Peace <https://carnegieendowment.org/files/WP_LeCorre_China_formatted_FINAL_WEB.PDF> accessed 24 March 2026.

52 Plamen Tonchev, 'China's Road: Into the Western Balkans' [2017] European Union Institute for Security Studies (EUISS) <https://www.iss.europa.eu/sites/default/files/EUISS Files/Brief%203%20China's%20Silk%20Road.pdf> accessed 24 March 2026.

nected owners.'[53] The opportunities, even including the big investment projects in some non-democratic countries never reach the market and its enterprises, and they are never able to openly compete for them. The profit is devoted, split and shared in a very small circle of people, which are interconnected with state politics and the ruling decision-making elites.

Such cases of investment potentials in post-conflict countries which have not yet reached a certain level of democracy can therefore be seen as a limiting factor to offer potentials to a broader circle of people, enterprises and ideas, which can ultimately offer advancement to the whole society. 'Large Chinese infrastructure projects are therefore often implemented through inter-governmental agreements, which open the door for lex specialis (special law) procedures that bypass public procurement law.'[54] These special laws do have their aim and also fit perfectly into the quickly rising investment potentials of post-conflict societies, but only once they are properly managed. Unfortunately, many times in developing societies, the opportunities are not given enough attention to and they are left to be regulated and achieved on the free market, while being very strictly limited in requirements and accessible only to a very limited circle of people. 'If a borrowing country defaults on its debts, a Chinese state-owned company, and by extension the Chinese government, could seize ownership of infrastructure that it originally constructed.'[55] Regarding seizing of property, there have been some cases in various societies, but still due to the very big influence and interference in countries like Kosovo or Nagorno-Karabakh by other influential states, such defaults and destabilization attempts are not likely to happen. Keeping in mind the influence and interests of China in Afghanistan, it is also not likely that it will have an interest to destabilize it by confiscations.

Overall, the potentials of post-conflict societies in connectivity and infrastructure are very important and in this case, considering the BRI initiative,[56]

53 Martin C. Steinwand, 'Foreign Aid and Political Stability' (2015) 32(4) Conflict Management and Peace Science 395.

54 Wouter Zweers, Vladimir Shopov, Frans-Paul van der Putten, Mirela Petkova and Maarten Lemstra, 'China and the EU in the Western Balkans: A Zero-Sum Game?' [2020] Clingendael Netherlands Institute of International Relations <https://www.clingendael.org/sites/default/files/2020-08/china-and-the-eu-in-the-western-balkans.pdf> accessed 24 March 2026.

55 Henrik Larsen, 'The Western Balkans between the EU, NATO, Russia and China' [2020] CSS Analyses in Security Policy <https://css.ethz.ch/content/dam/ethz/special-interest/gess/cis/center-for-securities-studies/pdfs/CSSAnalyse263-EN.pdf> accessed 24 March 2026.

56 Office of the Leading Group for Promoting the Belt and Road Initiative, 'Belt and Road Portal' <https://eng.yidaiyilu.gov.cn/> accessed 24 March 2026.

we can see how Serbia is benefiting from such projects. Still, if all the agreements are respected and Kosovo itself gets a better connectivity to Serbia, it can also be closer to the EU markets and have easier access to them. 'In addition, both parties will commit to a joint feasibility study on options for linking Belgrade-Pristina rail infrastructure to a deep sea port in the Adriatic',[57] where such an additional opportunity for Serbia and some other countries surrounding it, can also boost its own transportation capacity by reaching seaports which are so essential for global trade and development opportunities today.

2 Administration-Related Aspects of the Agreements

2.1 Relevant Challenges, in General

Administration-related challenges in Kosovo depend on many factors, while one of them is surely the instable North Kosovo, with its Serbian minority, which is hesitant to incorporate into the Kosovo institutions. While Serbia supports such disintegration or claims overall Kosovo as its territory, the Kosovo government, on its side, is also not doing much regarding human and minority rights guarantees in the North. 'A toxic environment is one of the key consequences of the unfinished Serbia – Kosovo relations.'[58] While the two governments are discussing and trying to reach a solution and agree, one of the most notable shortcomings is the (non) implementation of the relevant agreements. Such implementation challenges, law enforcement failures and the rule of law, overall, in Kosovo, is in fact not fully in the hands of Kosovo and its responsibility, but to some extent, belongs to the various and many international missions present in Kosovo since 1999. 'Kosovo institutions, in other words, were aware that the agreement cannot be realized without its partners (KFOR, EULEX, and the OSCE), because any exercise of sovereignty in that part without the involvement of KFOR would have been unsustainable.'[59] Accordingly, every agreement reached between the governments, be it in a soft or hard law form, needs enforcement or at least support towards its implementation. 'In total, about 80 percent of the Brussels agreements have

57 WA 2020.

58 Arben Hajrullahu, 'The EU's Ambiguous Integration Process for Kosovo' in David L. Phillips and Lulzim Peci (ed), *Threats and Challenges to Kosovo's Sovereignty* (Institute for the Study of Human Rights at Columbia University 2018).

59 Adem Beha, 'Disputes over the 15-Point Agreement on Normalization of Relations between Kosovo and Serbia' (2015) 43 Nationalities Papers 102.

been implemented.'[60] While many technical issues have been incorporated into the relationship between Kosovo and Serbia, the key points of such agreements are still missing, in specific, who and how they can assist Kosovo in regard to the establishment of the Association/Community of Serbian municipalities (A/C) and to what extent, or making it join the Open Balkan initiative[61] as was foreseen in the Washington Agreement.

The sole and most important request regarding administration is the request from Kosovo that Serbia recognizes its independence. Obviously, Serbia refuses to do this while it is recently, very engaged and open to agree about some state-like powers being transferred onto Kosovo without ultimately finally recognizing it *de iure*. Even if Serbia would recognize Kosovo, it will not be a final solution for many of its economic problems and challenges, also considering the fact that it would not make the EU as a whole agree to it. While EU overall has a status-neutral position towards Kosovo, some member states are not likely to change their standpoints, even if Serbia would recognize Kosovo after all. 'By delaying Kosovo's international recognition and by undermining its statehood, one could argue that the Brussels dialogue directly erodes Kosovo's external sovereignty.'[62] Kosovo has been seen and is trying to achieve EU integration steps even before getting a candidate-country status, and its EULEX mission[63] can indeed help a lot in such efforts.

One very critical moment where EU is not supporting Kosovo is its establishment of an embassy in 'Jerusalem',[64] which came after the mutual recognition of Israel and Kosovo and as a direct outcome of the Washington Agreement from 2020. The recognition of Israeli is indeed coming as a surprise, but it won't change the Serbian standpoint and neither will it change the Israeli standpoint regarding Palestine. Finally, none of the EU non-recognizer states have been influenced by such a move from Israel. It was not up to the EU to recognize Kosovo, is a repeated stance of the EU High Representative, and

60 Shpetim Gashi and Igor Novaković, 'Brussels Agreements Between Kosovo and Serbia: A Quantitative Implementation Assessment' [2020] Friedrich-Ebert-Stiftung <https://library.fes.de/pdf-files/bueros/belgrad/17009.pdf> accessed 24 March 2026.

61 Albanian Government, 'Important Cooperation Agreements Signed at Open Balkan Summit' (2 September 2022) <https://www.kryeministria.al/en/newsroom/nenshkruhen-marreveshje-te-rendesishme-bashkepunimi-ne-samitin-per-ballkanin-e-hapur-beograd/> accessed 24 March 2026.

62 Agon Demjaha, 'The Impact of Brussels Dialogue on Kosovo's Sovereignty' in David L. Phillips and Lulzim Peci (ed), *Threats and Challenges to Kosovo's Sovereignty* (Institute for the Study of Human Rights at Columbia University 2018).

63 EULEX, 'EULEX Accountability' <https://www.eulex-kosovo.eu/?page=2,23> accessed 24 March 2026.

64 Ambasadat, 'Jerusalem, Izrael' <https://ambasadat.net/izrael> accessed 24 March 2026.

furthermore, this issue belongs to the UN Security Council.[65] Even while there are various agreements that states are reaching in the framework of post-conflict development, it is still the UN Security Council which decides, and it is certain that it will still remain silent regarding both the Kosovo and Palestinian independence requests.

From the overall perspective of post-conflict societies and their possible and potential recognition, it can be noted that Kosovo is a very important case where many states have recognized it or have not recognized it due to their inner divides and possible secessionist movements. 'From a Russian perspective, the West has started to destroy the shared normative understanding as regards issues of secession and (non) recognition, and now Russia has started to ignore the established set of international legal rules as well.'[66] In fact, any UNSC permanent member-state can now support a certain territory and enforce its military supervision over it by claiming that it has a right to secession and self-determination. This issue of independence is additionally complicated by the ICJ decision regarding Kosovo[67] where it has missed the opportunity to foresee how independence can be exactly gained according to international law in such cases. Therefore the research, understanding and achievements in the dialogue between Serbia and Kosovo are important and also they can be seen as supported by the biggest number of states, including both recognizers and non-recognizers altogether.

The most important achievement which we are going to explain in this chapter is the future possible establishment of the Association/Community of Serbian Municipalities (A/C), as foreseen by the BA. 'There will be an Association/Community of Serb majority municipalities in Kosovo.'[68] This very complex administrative, possibly autonomous and self-administered form of Serbian autonomy in Kosovo is still to be formed and its real powers, whether executive or not, are yet to be formalized. 'The Community/Association will be created by statute.'[69] While there are many questions remaining, the major

65 Jeta Krasniqi, 'EU-Mediated Kosovo-Serbia Dialogue: A New Attempt or Resumption with the Old Approach?' [2020] Kosova Democratic Institute (KDI) and the Konrad Adenauer Foundation <https://kdi-kosova.org/wp-content/uploads/2020/10/Policy-Brief-20-07-24-EU-mediated-Kosovo-Serbia-dialogue-ENG.pdf> accessed 24 March 2026.

66 Stefan Oeter, 'The Kosovo Case – An Unfortunate Precedent' (2015) 75 ZaöRV 51.

67 International Court of Justice, 'Accordance with International Law of the Unilateral Declaration of Independence in Respect of Kosovo' (22 July 2010) <https://www.icj-cij.org/public/files/case-related/141/141-20100722-ADV-01-00-EN.pdf> accessed 24 March 2026.

68 BA 2013.

69 Ibid.

ones are who and according to what laws will make this statute, since the constitution of Kosovo does not foresee such an entity in Kosovo at all.

Regarding Serbia and its constitution, there is also no legal possibility for the A/C, but there is a very wide space regarding Kosovo, where it is still an autonomous province in Serbia and has certain constitutionally established administrative rights. The Serbian government is behaving and treating Kosovo as its province and according to the UN Security Council Resolution 1244,[70] it remains part of Serbia. While there are many practical challenges in North Kosovo and freedom of movement and property is still not fully established in its southern parts, one future common challenge is 'the Merdare Common Crossing Point facility',[71] which is directly connecting Serbia to Kosovo and remains fully outside the future borders of the A/C. Kosovo is accordingly pushing trade in this direction, since the taxes collected here do not belong to the special budget line, where taxes are paid when imported over North Kosovo crossings.

2.2 Autonomy Concerns

The most important questions regarding the future of both Kosovo and its Serbian minority, possibly inside the A/C in the future, are very challenging and complex. At the moment, no final solution has been achieved and so far, it is very hard to predict anything in this regard. There are many processes which are supporting the overall development of Kosovo, but even after more than two decades of independence, it still seems impossible to maintain them without the support of international stakeholders. 'Its importance notwithstanding, the excessive focus on whether the Berlin Process (and other international fora and processes) contribute to Kosovo's sovereignty tends to cloud other important issues, such as whether Kosovo itself adequately functions as a proper state internationally.'[72] While Serbia functions in a legal vacuum and is divided between European integrations and its partners on the East, Russia and China mainly, Kosovo remains under full control of its pro-Western politics. The agreements coming from various sides do not deal, in general, with the future of Kosovo but place it, or better to say leave it in the political limbo of a semi-recognized country, without giving it a possibility for its future

70 United Nations, 'Resolution 1244 (1999)' (10 June 1999) <https://unmik.unmissions.org/sites/default/files/old_dnn/Res1244ENG.pdf> accessed 24 March 2026.

71 WA 2020.

72 Ioannis Armakolas, 'Kosovo's Status Consolidation: Lessons from the Berlin Process' in David L. Phillips and Lulzim Peci (ed), *Threats and Challenges to Kosovo's Sovereignty* (Institute for the Study of Human Rights at Columbia University 2018).

representation inside the UN. 'The Agreement does not indicate whether Kosovo is a state or not, the parties are described as "sides" without further details, and there is no definition of how the Association/Community of Serbian municipalities should be organized, the cornerstone of the agreement, and what legal status it should have.'[73] The Brussels Agreement could be seen as a very good tool in advancing the resolution of this conflict, where its initial success has now turned into a total backlash, where the Serbian and Kosovo governments are still sitting together but not advancing in any direction forward.

While the Brussels Agreement was a more comprehensive one, the Washington Agreement has been a very declarative agreement; it was also titled and aimed as an agreement on economic normalization. In general, the Washington Agreement has still brought the biggest surprise and shock, to some extent, where the impossible has happened. Israel has recognized Kosovo without any prior sign or interest to do so; in fact, it was forced to align in this case to the general USA foreign policy in this regard, ignoring its local and regional interests. 'Hoti had said he was going to Washington to secure mutual recognition with Serbia, but instead, the paper he signed agreed instead to mutual recognition with Israel.'[74] This interesting phenomenon of international law is still going to remain as a research possibility, where actually not just post-conflict societies but also internationally recognized states such as Israel are forced to completely ignore their local policies and align them accordingly with some informal agreements. Interestingly, this agreement which deals with so many crucial issues can't be even accessed in any available registers of international treaties.

Regarding Serbia, the Washington Agreement was more of a declarative character, without asking much then, just to align its policies with the USA, while for Kosovo, there was a bigger challenge in it by requesting to 'join and fully utilize the Mini-Schengen Zone',[75] which it is still hesitant to do. This interesting regional cooperation agreement seems as a new CEFTA[76] in the Balkans, where Serbia and Kosovo still can't fully cooperate and understand the overall benefits and necessities of such agreements. CEFTA can be seen as an important tool to integrate post-communist countries into the EU and so

73 Florian Bieber, 'The Serbia-Kosovo Agreements: An Eu Success Story?' (2015) 40 Review of Central and East European Law 285.

74 Paul Fraioli, 'The Kosovo–Serbia Normalisation Agreements' (2020) 26 Strategic Comments vii.

75 WA 2020.

76 Central European Free Trade Agreement, 'About' <https://cefta.int/about/> accessed 24 March 2026.

the Mini Schengen, or by its new name Open Balkan,[77] bringing together societies of the divided Western Balkans, giving them a common possibility to join the EU, together.

One of the most important issues and challenges in regard to the overall Serbian constitutional framework is the transfer of the Serbian judicial bodies into the Kosovo system. 'The judicial authorities will be integrated and operate within the Kosovo legal framework.'[78] This solution from the BA is still to be challenged and explained by the Serbian Constitutional Court and its Constitution,[79] which is silent in this regard and the future of all the agreements and changes achieved in those agreements. All the requirements from the agreements, which are given outside the mandate of the Serbian government, could be potentially a case brought to the Court. They all will have to face final approval in both the Serbian Parliament and its Constitutional Court as well. The overall legality of all the documents signed and agreements reached regarding Kosovo can be easily approved by the Serbian authorities, as long as there is the Resolution 1244,[80] which ultimately guarantees Serbian sovereignty over Kosovo and is not likely going to be changed, even in the case if Serbia fully recognizes Kosovo.

2.3 Prospects for Democracy

The democratic potential of every post-conflict society is always limited in the beginning as a direct outcome of the cessation of the conflict. In regard to Kosovo, as a very specific case, we will aim to see how and when Kosovo becomes or can become a fully democratic country, following the established patterns from the EU. Democratic countries and, in specific, the post-conflict ones need to achieve some kind of consensus on their future, while the agreements to head in such directions are not always very clear. 'The Ahtisaari Plan was an extensive legal text that served as a framework for the declaration of

77 Albanian Government, 'Important Cooperation Agreements Signed at Open Balkan Summit' (2 September 2022) <https://www.kryeministria.al/en/newsroom/nenshkruhen-marreveshje-te-rendesishme-bashkepunimi-ne-samitin-per-ballkanin-e-hapur-beograd/> accessed 24 March 2026.

78 BA 2013.

79 The National Assembly of the Republic of Serbia, 'Constitution of The Republic of Serbia' (30 September 2006) <https://www.parlament.gov.rs/upload/documents/Constitution-%20of_Serbia_F.pdf> accessed 24 March 2026.

80 United Nations, 'Resolution 1244 (1999)' (10 June 1999) <https://unmik.unmissions.org/sites/default/files/old_dnn/Res1244ENG.pdf> accessed 24 March 2026.

independence.'[81] The Ahtisaari Plan was not a democratically agreed plan which could be accepted as a common goal and framework and while its initial idea was to establish the institutions, its final failure can be seen as an overall failure of an idea that one expert can solve such a complex case.

In Kosovo, it is not just the Ahtisaari Plan that was questionable, there is also the EULEX mission, which has many times proven not to be fit for the purpose, and due to various scandals, its overall mission was endangered as well. 'On the other hand, EULEX's legitimacy has been undermined by allegations of corruption among its staff as well as criticism over its reluctance to prosecute political elites allegedly involved in serious cases of organized crime and corruption.'[82] The overall idea of bringing Kosovo instantly into the level of EU democracies has failed not due to its own shortcomings but due to the EULEX failures and the overall weak management of international organizations. 'As a Rule of Law Mission with certain limited executive functions ensuring accountability is fundamental for EULEX Kosovo.'[83] In fact, EULEX can be seen as a mission which has all the necessary means, funds and tools to make all aspects and institutions of the Kosovo society advance, which is unfortunately not always the case. The possible failure or missed opportunity for EULEX can also be seen as a failure of the EU overall and in specific, its Common Security and Defence Policy (CSDP), which is very important now with the war in Ukraine and the never stopping refugee crisis on the EU external borders.

While the main aim of this work is to establish some patterns which can be used by the EU, UN, OSCE and other similar organizations, we can observe that such patterns are indeed very hard to establish and function. When it comes to the EU, we can observe that it tends to establish its own 'IKEA'[84] templates which can be applied in various post-conflict settings, although in the foreign missions, it is important to listen more to local stakeholders than to apply EU requirements and establish strong and authoritative institutions

81 Enver Hasani, 'The Role of the Constitutional Court in the Development of the Rule of Law in Kosovo' (2018) 43 Rev Cent & E Eur L 274.

82 Rok Zupančič, Nina Pejič, Blaž Grilj and Annemarie Peen Rodt, 'The European Union Rule of Law Mission in Kosovo: An Effective Conflict Prevention and Peace-Building Mission?' (2018) 20 Journal of Balkan and Near Eastern Studies 599.

83 EULEX, 'EULEX Accountability' <https://www.eulex-kosovo.eu/?page=2,23> accessed 24 March 2026.

84 Kari M. Osland & Mateja Peter, 'The Double Proximity Paradox in Peacebuilding: Implementation and Perception of the EU Rule of Law Mission in Kosovo' (2019) 28 European Security 493.

on both the local level and the ones having an international background in order to achieve sustainable law-making and its appropriate enforcement.

It is always more possible to achieve some democratic standards with foreign aid, support and assistance using various peace-making tools, agreements and other similar social interactions.

Although we have a large amount of various international stakeholders present in Kosovo, the overall situation is still not advancing and the democratic capacity of the society is still very low, specifically regarding its Serbian minority. 'The incompatible positions of the UN, EU, and OSCE towards Kosovo's status resulted in a lack of clarity, coordination, coherence, and exit strategy that weakened the efforts for state building in Kosovo.'[85] While the UN does not see Kosovo as an independent state, the EU has no consensus to see it as such and the OSCE lacks capacity to treat it as such, since the overall number of self-proclaimed states on the European continent is also rising at the moment. One of the main questions is what agreements can be achieved there which can be called democratic and serve the society and its democratic future, but still remain internationally a not fully recognized country. Sometimes, not only the terms and the specific points in the agreement are ambiguous, but also the very 'end result' (i.e. closer to Europe) is highly ambiguous.[86] One of the biggest challenges still faced by the EU is the question of how to treat Kosovo and other similar entities on its borders, while keeping its present democratic standards and the protection of human and minority rights.

It is necessary to research the most important democratic achievements in Kosovo, its post-conflict development and its agreements with Serbia altogether. The previously agreed future establishment of the A/C can be seen as a democratic institution and a step forward as was mutually agreed. Its implementation can further advance the democratic potential of Kosovo and the integration of its Serbian minority. 'The structures of the Association/Community will be established on the same basis as the existing statute of the Association of Kosovo municipalities, e.g. president, vice president, assembly, and council.'[87] While the framework for the establishment of the A/C in constitutional terms is missing, its initial form is more than clear and ready for implementation.

85 Gëzim Visoka, 'Kosovo: A Hybrid Negative Peace' in Paul R. Williams and Milena Sterio (ed), *Research Handbook on Post-conflict State Building* (Edward Elgar 2020).

86 Krenar Gashi, Vjosa Musliu and Jan Orbie, 'Mediation Through Recontextualization: The European Union and The Dialogue Between Kosovo and Serbia' (2017) 22 European Foreign Affairs Review 533.

87 BA 2013.

The Brussels Agreement has advanced and democratized the talks between the Serbian and Kosovo governments, where they have reached very important solutions, which are considered as milestones in the decades-long divisions and confrontations. It is not possible to advance and democratize Kosovo's society without the implementation of what has been agreed. 'The Association/Community will exercise other additional competences as may be delegated by the central authorities.'[88] While there are many open questions remaining, it is still deemed more appropriate that the Serbian minority decides on the relevant aspects of its life in Kosovo. The integration process and issues such as health care, education or university diplomas have still not been successfully solved. In this regard, there is a connection with the Washington Agreement, which requires that governments 'mutually recognize diplomas and professional certificates',[89] since the school system in Kosovo is separate and in the long run, the Kosovo state does not have capacities to establish the educational autonomy for its Serbian minority.

3 Security Concerns

3.1 Relevant Concerns, in General

The overall security of the EU and also the Western Balkans due to the refugee crisis and the permanent Serbia and Kosovo destabilization actions are altogether very complex and challenging. While the EU in fact does have the necessary tools to economically integrate countries, it still lacks the tools to permanently pacify them. 'Without a clear timeline and the credible promise of EU membership, the European Union no longer has sufficient gravitational pull to bring the two sides to a deal alone.'[90] While it is not just the EU interest present in this region but also the USA, Russia and as we have seen it recently, the Chinese influence as well. The outreach of the EU, and all other organizations present in Kosovo and broader, should be more interactive when they aim at achieving certain standards and human rights. 'In principle, the relaunch of the process of enlargement towards the Western Balkans could be a game-changer for the EU-facilitated dialogue between

88 Ibid.

89 WA 2020.

90 Heather A. Conley and Dejana Saric, 'The Serbia-Kosovo Normalization Process: A Temporary U.S. Decoupling' [2021] CSIS BRIEFS <https://csis-website-prod.s3.amazonaws.com/s3fs-public/publication/210527_Conley_Serbia_Kosovo_Normalization.pdf?VersionId=.21Hry3HPFOAwZTCoBbJaZjcVSMfTGqF> accessed 24 March 2026.

Serbia and Kosovo, and hence diminish Russia's strength in the region.'[91] While Russia has interestingly gained some support for its actions in Ukraine globally, there are also few states in Europe which support its actions in this regard, from which on the Western Balkans, the most prominent one is Serbia. Such support is evidently against EU policies and the EU is ready to push Serbia by various means, not to say punish it directly, in order to change its attitude. Regarding security, it can be outlined that as much influence Russia gains in Ukraine, the less influence Serbia will gain in Kosovo. Since Serbia is a Russian proxy in the region, the EU will not tolerate the rise of the Russian influence anywhere, and limit it wherever possible. The most important support Serbia gains from Russia is in fact in the UN, with its efforts of not letting Kosovo gain wider recognition, while the actual investments from Russia in Serbia are rather scarce. 'Still, Russia's attempts to discourage Serbia from seeking a compromise will not necessarily translate into real efforts to sabotage a deal if one is reached.'[92] So, even if a deal is reached or Serbia recognizes Kosovo, it will probably not change the Russian standpoints, as it is always ready to confront the West and has not much interest in a landlocked country such as Kosovo.

The difference between Kosovo and Armenia is that Armenia stands in the way of any possible form of unification of Turkish nations, what could be seen as a threat to Russia but also to China. In Kosovo, we can observe that the interests and strategical investments from Russia are not a priority, while it already has access and connections to the Serbian market. Russia is ready to economically support Serbia and also back it up in the form of cheap energy in an era of globally rising energy prices. While Russia is accordingly ready to punish other nations which are supporting Ukraine, including the EU as well, it is less likely and possible to punish Serbia in this regard. The security situation in all of these nations (Ukraine, Moldova and Georgia) clearly became worse as a result of Russia punishing them for their efforts to integrate with the EU.[93] Probably, the most rigorous punishment by Russia has been received by Armenia, where its influence over Nagorno-Karabakh has been almost

---

91 Maria Giulia Amadio Viceré, 'The Future Is Back: The EU, Russia and the Kosovo–Serbia Dispute' [2019] IAI PAPERS <https://www.iai.it/sites/default/files/iaip1919.pdf> accessed 24 March 2026.

92 Maxim Samorukov, 'A Spoiler in the Balkans? Russia and the Final Resolution of the Kosovo Conflict' [2019] Carnegie Endowment for International Peace <https://carnegieendowment.org/files/WP_Samorukov_Balkans_v2.pdf> accessed 24 March 2026.

93 Mikheil Sarjveladze, 'The South Caucasus in the Context of the EU-Russia Crisis' (2017) 28 Security Policy Working Paper <https://www.baks.bund.de/sites/baks010/files/working_paper_2017_28.pdf> accessed 24 March 2026.

entirely diminished, mainly due to its efforts to establish connections with Western States.

The overall Russian influence in the Western Balkans is visible in regard to trade divides and limitations, where Kosovo has implemented trade sanctions and a 100% tax on goods on its non-recognizing countries from the region. While Serbia is a permanent threat in the eyes of Kosovo, the Republic of Srpska entity in Bosnia and Herzegovina is a bigger challenge since it guarantees very high rights to the Serbian minority living in Bosnia. 'Putin seeks to "gather in the Russian lands" in the near abroad, and is content with its modest investment in maintaining frozen conflicts in Kosovo and Republika Srpska: a relatively low-cost stalemate is far preferable to a defeat especially when this stalemate raises the costs to the West, while maintaining Russia's stake in the region.'[94] The low level of Russian investments here is compensated with its security support for Serbs in both countries, where at a certain moment, they can gain also beneficial status in regard to energy trade.

It is hard to determine how long some Western Balkan countries can in fact support Russia and gain its security-, legal- and development-related support. Also, in regard to security and investments overall, it is very similar when we look at China and its newly established trade and investment interests in the Western Balkans. 'Other critics point out that, if the Balkan countries fail to repay the loans, China can request political favours or exercise unfavourable contractual clauses such as seizure of assets or even land/territory.'[95] The overall security dimension of both Russian and Chinese investments is very complex where they do not see it as a priority to develop regions which fall far from their sphere of interest; they are more keen to access resources and in the shortest and cheapest way manage their trade patterns. Russia needs a stable market for its energy in Europe while China needs a stable market for its goods where access to various raw materials can be seen as a plus.

Kosovo can overall be seen as a cradle of many present and future conflicts due to its sharp division lines in the international community and complex legal status. It can hardly be said that any post-conflict society had such an international turmoil as Kosovo, and so many various aspects regarding its future and development. Probably the most important legal aspect of a semi-

94 Mark Baskin, 'Unpacking Russia's Balkan Baggage' in David L. Phillips and Lulzim Peci (ed), *Threats and Challenges to Kosovo's Sovereignty* (Institute for the Study of Human Rights at Columbia University 2018).

95 Branislav Stanicek and Simona Tarpova, 'China's Strategic Interests in the Western Balkans' [2022] European Parliamentary Research Service <https://www.europarl.europa.eu/RegData/etudes/BRIE/2022/733558/EPRS_BRI(2022)733558_EN.pdf(2022)733558_EN.pdf> accessed 24 March 2026.

recognized Kosovo is its newly established diplomatic relationship and the recognition coming from Israel, as was a requirement from the WA. 'Kosovo [Pristina] and Israel agree to mutually recognize each other.'[96] This was one really crucial outcome of the Washington Agreement and is still to be debated how it can raise the security in the SEE borders or Europe and more importantly in The Middle East, with its forever lasting conflicts, and especially the Israeli–Palestine conflict.

Similarly to Israel and its problematic treatment of Palestine, it also remains to be seen how Kosovo treats its Serbian minority and the future establishment of the A/C, as was foreseen by the Brussel Agreement. 'The Community/Association shall have a representative role to the central authorities and will have a seat in the communities' consultative council for this purpose.'[97] This will bring a completely new viewpoint on relationships in a post-conflict state towards minorities, from which if successful, even states such as Israel and others can learn and advance their democratic capacities and protect human and minority rights to a greater and more acceptable extent.

3.2 Conflict Prevention Capacity

Conflict prevention is the main priority of all post-conflict agreements. It is also the biggest challenge for post-conflict societies and their future development. In regard Kosovo, we can outline that the legal challenges regarding its status and possible future UN membership start the moment when it has self-declared its independence. Even when the ICJ was dealing with Kosovo, it did not use the opportunity to define this complex issue, whereas it only supported the Kosovo independence as *de facto*. 'The Court was thus able to argue that, as the authors of the independence declaration were acting outside the legal framework of the U.N. interim administration, their declaration did not violate that framework and, as no legal prohibition of declarations of independence exists, the declaration did not violate general international law.'[98] It is complex to understand how the ICJ ignored all the UN Security Council Resolutions and while ignoring them, it has given a green light to every potential future secessionist nation. It can be concluded that such resolutions are just declarative and any act of a *de facto* state is not violating them since they

96 WA 2020.

97 BA 2013.

98 Richard Caplan, 'The ICJ's Advisory Opinion on Kosovo' (2010) 55 PEACEBRIEF <https://www.usip.org/sites/default/files/PB55%20The%20ICJs%20Advisory%20Opinion%20on%20Kosovo.pdf> accessed 24 March 2026.

are obviously not obliged to apply such Resolutions. This circle of independence declarations has continued and we have by now ended up in a situation where the world and its sovereign states are being torn apart widely, where the UN lacks capacity to respond or is not meant to respond at all?

The actual support Kosovo gets in regard to its independence is ultimately not enough for its prosperity and economic development and while it insists on its recognition, it completely ignores its economy and development needs. Serbia is also somehow limiting its prosperity and the EU integration due to its complex standpoints regarding Kosovo. 'The perceived irreconcilable differences over the status of Kosovo are seen as the main obstacle to normalization.'[99] In this regard, we can outline different viewpoints and while even the EU is split in regard to Kosovo's recognition, it can't be seen as an obstacle towards its development and its rising investment capabilities. Overall, the Serbian recognition would after all not bring much prosperity to Kosovo and the EU will, most likely, still remain divided in this regard. 'The main problem of the European Union relates to its inability to define and carry out a consistent policy towards Kosovo.'[100] It is hard to expect that the situation will get any better but in this case, Serbia is in a much better position since its economy is overall being supported by EU, Russia and even China recently. While the EU once again proved to be a very important player regarding economic development in the region, it still lacks enforcement power regarding security issues.

The permanent exclusion of the Western Balkans from the EU integration is due to the permanent conflicts which are harming not just the local nations but the EU as well. There is a huge pressure on all the conflicts in this region from the EU to achieve agreements and align their requests and demands with each other in a democratic way. When it comes to Kosovo, we have a series of talks, with relevant agreements achieved, which have in fact successfully brought many commonly agreed solutions and made cooperation between Serbia and Kosovo more viable. 'Agreements, therefore, signed merely between Belgrade and Pristina, under the auspices and pressure of Brussels are not enough to resolve the conflict sustainably.'[101] The overall divisions certainly can't be over-

99 Ahmeti Bardha and others, 'Serbia and Kosovo in 2035: Scenarios' [2018] Friedrich-Ebert-Stiftung <https://brussels.fes.de/fileadmin/public/editorfiles/events/2018/Q2/FES-Study.pdf> accessed 24 March 2026.

100 Vladimir Medović, 'The Potential and Limits of the European Union as a Mediator in the Dialogue Between Serbia and Kosovo*' (2022) 3 Istituto Affari Internazionali (IAI) Papers <https://www.iai.it/sites/default/files/iaip2203.pdf> accessed 24 March 2026.

101 Argyro Kartsonaki, 'Playing with Fire: An Assessment of the EU's Approach of Constructive Ambiguity on Kosovo's Blended Conflict' (2020) 22 Journal of Balkan and Near Eastern Studies 103.

come just by these two nations since there is already the status-neutral position of the EU and the sharp division lines in the UN regarding Kosovo. While many nations do not recognize Kosovo, it is also evident that Kosovo has a very hard time when trying to join various international organizations when it faces the lack of support from some of the members. 'Relations between the countries had reached the maximum irritation during the end of 2018, when as a result of the aggressive campaign of Serbia, Kosovo's membership in INTERPOL was impossible, but also earlier in UNESCO.'[102] In regard to such important international bodies, there is no clear agenda of which is the responsible entity regarding the application of post-conflict societies such as Kosovo, especially keeping in mind that EULEX is self-reducing its mandate and leaving some loopholes in the overall policing and law enforcement. The question remains whether it is a necessity, priority or of any importance to have post-conflict societies as members of international organizations, even before their UN membership.

While in general, we are unable to answer the question of what level of recognition a state needs in order to join international organizations and whether it is possible at all before becoming a UN member state. There are different standpoints in this regard and the bigger and more influential states such as the USA are able to establish exceptions to many long-established standards of laws and policies. In regard to Kosovo, as of 2020, a very complex agreement has been reached where both Serbia and Kosovo had in fact the requirement to align their economic, security and other aspects with the USA. 'For all these reasons, the description of the Washington Agreement as two separate legally binding declarations rather than a treaty or as just a political commitment seems plausible.'[103] The most important and also a very surprising move was in fact coming from one of the agreements in Washington signed by the Kosovo Prime Minister, having as an outcome a new mutual recognition reality between Kosovo and Israel. This is a very new way of solving the question of international recognitions where in fact Israel was not even a party to the given agreement or represented during the talks. On the

---

102 Eugen Cakolli, 'KOSOVO: Between Universal Non-Recognition and "Derecognitions"' [2020] Kosova Democratic Institute (KDI) and the Konrad Adenauer Foundation <https://www.kas.de/documents/286052/0/Policy+brief+20-09-13+Kosovo+Between+universal+non-recognition+and+derecognitions+(Eng).pdf/8245552b-5744–11b7-a1fb-429be14582c7+(Eng).pdf/8245552b-5744–11b7-a1fb-429be14582c7?version=1.0&t=1610102495727> accessed 24 March 2026.

103 Robert Muharremi, 'The "Washington Agreement" Between Kosovo and Serbia' (2021) 25 insights <https://www.asil.org/sites/default/files/ASIL_Insights_2021_V25_I4.pdf> accessed 24 March 2026.

other side, there was a similar surprising event when Serbia agreed to move its embassy to Jerusalem,[104] which is against the overall EU standpoint. The EU is not having embassies in Jerusalem and is not recognizing it as the capital city of Israel according to the UNSC Resolution 478 (1980), which calls on all UN member-states to withdraw their embassies from Jerusalem.

As both the WA and BA agreements have certain security connotations, it is important to outline the most important ones which also have the capacity to greatly influence other similar post-conflict societies and agreements. The most important breakthrough in this regard in the BA is the integration of the judicial system from North Kosovo to the overall Kosovo system, but more importantly regarding the security concerns was the integration of the police structures from North Kosovo. 'All police in northern Kosovo shall be integrated in the Kosovo Police framework.'[105] While police integration has occurred in its most simple form, the overall integration of all the Serbian security forces is still questionable, in specific regarding the recent clashes in North Kosovo and in particular in the Banjska village. When it comes to the WA, it has also outlined a very important and challenging issue of protecting religious places. The BA has requested the Kosovo authorities for the 'protection of religious sites and implementation of judicial decisions pertaining to the Serbian Orthodox Church, and continued restitution of Holocaust-era heirless and unclaimed Jewish property'.[106] These are very important requests, knowing that Kosovo is a predominantly Muslim country and that its democratic capacities are limited due to the constant indoctrination and threat of the radicalization of various groups in Kosovo.

3.3 Possible Terrorism-Related Concerns

Terrorism threat as the most important security threat is in the rise overall, and in specific in the EU neighbourhood. While the aim of this work is not to go too broad but to research and focus on societies on which EU in fact has or could have actual influence. One of the most important division lines of various policies in regard to security is very visible in Asia but also in Africa as well. 'There is concern in Mali that, unlike the UN's neutral approach to conflicts and crises, the EU's "principled pragmatism" focuses too much on protecting

---

104 WA 2020.
105 BA 2013.
106 WA 2020.

its own interest in containing migration flows to Europe.'[107] In general, both the Asian and African migration and refugee crises pose a threat to the overall EU security. Similarly to Asia, in Africa, the overall concerns interests and influences of regional and global influential state powers are different and many times challenged. 'This is also the case in Libya as well as in Syria, where Russia and Turkey (similar to Nagorno-Karabakh) have split the areas of conflict into zones of influence.'[108] What is interesting in this regard is that Russia, and Turkey as a NATO member, have aligned their security interests, which also guarantees and enables cooperation against security threats, which is an actual danger for both these two nations and the EU as well.

From the EU perspective, it is most important to have a common and previously aligned agenda for terrorist threats and their timely resolution mechanisms. With the rising number of post-conflict societies, there is a rising number of terrorist or diversion attacks, in parallel, as has been seen recently. Finally, terrorist attacks are not originating only from predominantly Muslim groups, as some media might interpret it. In conflicts between Ukraine and Russia, Serbia and Kosovo and finally in Nagorno-Karabakh, there were attacks from the other side which can fit into the definition of a terrorist attack, since it is always the last and ultimate way to fight the opposing side in war and also post-war time. In specific, regarding Kosovo, the dissatisfaction with agreements and their implementation has caused many different forms of clashes, including the attacks on Kosovo Police personnel and also on EULEX in North Kosovo. When balancing support to one or the other side, it has to be particularly established who will gain control over which aspect of life, so no dissatisfaction and resistance movements are therefore encouraged. 'There is more reason to assert that member states hold more power than the formal division of labour initially suggests, and that EU unity is not set in stone.'[109] While EU unity might not be set in stone, the interest overall

107 Loes Debuysere and Steven Blockmans, 'The EU's Integrated Approach to Crisis Response: Learning from the UN, NATO and OSCE' in Roger Mac Ginty, Sandra Pogodda, and Oliver P. Richmond (ed), The EU and crisis response (Manchester University Press 2021).

108 Sofia Maria Satanakis and Katrin Süss, 'The Shift in Turkey's Foreign Policy' (2021) 3 Austria Institut für Europaund Sicherheitspolitik <https://www.aies.at/download/2021/AIES-Fokus-2021-03.pdf> accessed 24 March 2026.

109 Wouter Zweers and Myrthe de Boon, 'Overcoming EU Internal Dividing Policy Brief Lines in the Belgrade-Pristina Dialogue' [2022] Clingendael <https://www.clingendael.org/sites/default/files/2022-04/Policy_brief_Overcoming_EU_internal_dividing_lines_Belgrado_Pristine_Dialogue.pdf> accessed 24 March 2026.

remains the same with also the very important establishment of human and minority rights, which requires the treatment of same problems and issues with the most appropriate and goal-oriented approaches.

The challenges posed in Kosovo, even 20 years after the initial conflict, are that the Kosovo Albanians were leading a guerrilla war against the Serbian state in Kosovo, in which they have also committed some war crimes. Since such war crimes were not solved by the ICTY initially, they have remained an obstacle to serving justice in Kosovo regarding the KLA and its prior activities. As a direct outcome of this, the establishment of a specialized court for war crimes investigation in Kosovo was formed. The Kosovo Specialist Chambers and Specialist Prosecutor's Office were established pursuant to an international agreement ratified by the Kosovo Assembly, a Constitutional Amendment and the Law on Kosovo Specialist Chambers and Specialist Prosecutor's Office.[110] 'These institutions are part of Kosovo's judicial system but are primarily staffed by international jurists and located in The Hague, Netherlands, to allay concerns over witness intimidation and political pressure.'[111] The overall evaluation of the work of various war crimes tribunals in the Balkans are not seen as reconciling, to an extent that mutual correlations and life can be established as was prior to the conflict, to an extent. Divisions regarding the future of Kosovo and, in specific, its limited sovereignty also raise the point whether it should have an army after all and with what aim. 'The Secretary apparently also suggested that if Kosovo was going to pursue the creation of a Kosovo army, it should be done in consultation with and with the support of all parties and communities.'[112] The creation of an army of a non-UN member-state in a sovereign territory of the other under the internationally supervised mandate by the UN would be a very interesting and both a legally and security-related challenging issue.

Regarding terrorism, we can find some relevant points in the agreements between Serbia and Kosovo, where in the BA, it was foreseen that 'members of other Serbian security structures will be offered a place in equivalent Kosovo

110 Kosovo Specialist Chambers & Specialist Prosecutor's Office, 'Kosovo Specialist Chambers & Specialist Prosecutor's Office' <https://www.scp-ks.org/en> accessed 24 March 2026.

111 Sarah E. Garding, 'Kosovo: Background and U.S. Policy' [2021] Congressional Research Service <https://sgp.fas.org/crs/row/R46175.pdf> accessed 24 March 2026.

112 Vincent L. Morelli, 'Kosovo: Background and U.S. Relations' [2018] Congressional Research Service <https://sgp.fas.org/crs/row/R44979.pdf> accessed 24 March 2026.

structures',[113] which would bring an even bigger division between the communities since the Serbian minority still can't see the aim and interest in developing Kosovo as an independent state. Such challenges pose threat to the overall peace and security where such persons can be seen as a threat but also be easily blamed for any conflict between the two communities in the future. In general, it is needed to balance more the institutions in Kosovo which are having a possibility to additionally divide and distance the two communities from each other.

The most important aspect regarding terrorism is the limitation of the activities of a terrorist group from the WA; in fact, it has not much connection to Kosovo or Serbia after all. The parties have agreed to 'designate Hizballah in its entirety as a terrorist organization',[114] which is an interest of the USA foreign policy, which sees this group as a threat to Israel and supported by Iran. The mutual recognition between Kosovo and Israel has also not caused much concern regarding Hezbollah or any similar group, as they are strictly regionally focused and have no direct concerns in Kosovo. Also, the recent attack in Banjska village is questionable since while Kosovo sees its actors as terrorists, Serbia sees them as fighters for the Serbian rights in Kosovo. The agreements did not deal with any other terrorist group in the region and also the more important issue of fighters going to war in foreign countries, whereas Balkan has been seen as an important ground to get mercenaries for conflicts which are active now and also the many previous ones, globally.

4 Human Rights and Democracy

4.1 Human and Minority Rights Aspects

The integration of minorities is one of the most complex and demanding issues in almost all post-conflict societies. In this regard, especially, it has to be taken into account what the presently new minority, which was previously the majority, might have committed breaches of human rights or possibly war crimes during the conflict. The challenge is how to integrate such minorities, which are seen as an enemy, and by doing so build future democratic societies. One of the most notable examples of such integration in Europe is the case

113 BA 2013.
114 WA 2020.

of Northern Ireland, whereas no one can claim that neither The Republic of Ireland nor The United Kingdom are not democratic societies or were not so at the beginning of the conflict. 'As a result many Catholic-nationalists felt unwelcome in Northern Ireland, and they perceived both real and imagined discrimination against them in employment, the distribution of public services, and political representation.'[115] The case of Northern Ireland is a valuable experience, since it in fact represents a conflict which has been concluded some 25 years ago. This time very closely corresponds to the date when the armed conflict ended in Kosovo, or better to say Yugoslavia, at that time. The Good Friday Agreement[116] in Northern Ireland could be seen as a very formal agreement, which has in fact brought back peace to Northern Ireland and while it was not a perfect and instant conflict resolution mechanism from this distance, it can be seen as a functioning and capacity building tool for both communities. An interesting fact is that the division lines were mainly present on religious grounds and the prosecution of a minority such as the Catholics, is hard to imagine in the EU, where they are present in a considerable number, but still it was the case.

When we look at Kosovo, we can observe that the conflict here also involves religion in some aspects, the Serbian Orthodox church is a minority religion in Kosovo and almost exclusively practiced by Serbs in Kosovo. 'The Orthodox Church often adheres to a narrative describing Byzantine, Serbian or Russian Christians as abandoned and sometimes betrayed and attacked by western Christianity'.[117] While there are many religious conflicts, also including the recent 'betrayal' of the Armenian Christians in Nagorno-Karabakh, it can be seen very differently, but the possibility to practice their religion freely in future in this region is also very questionable.

Another important aspect of minority rights is the management of their property rights, since in post-conflict societies, it can always be observed that properties of all kinds are shrinking in the hands of the minority groups. While there are some differences in regard to privatization of some companies where minorities can be excluded and through the central government, only a

115 Roger Mac Ginty, Orla T. Muldoon and Neil Ferguson, 'No War, No Peace: Northern Ireland after the Agreement' (2007) 28(1) Political Psychology 1.

116 Ireland, 'The Good Friday Agreement' <https://www.ireland.ie/en/25-years-of-the-good-friday-agreement/about-the-good-friday-agreement/> accessed 24 March 2026.

117 Martin Leiner, 'Setting the Stage: An Introductory Clarification of Concepts of East Central Europe' in Lily Gardner Feldman, Raisa Barash, Samuel Goda and André Zempelburg (ed), *The Former Soviet Union and East Central Europe between Conflict and Reconciliation* (Vandenhoeck & Ruprecht 2019).

limited number of people coming from a non-minority group potentially benefit. In Kosovo, there are many property-related challenges, where the most notable one is the non-existent guarantee for the use of private property by Serbs trying to resettle in certain areas after many years being in exile. A more important question for the government is the future ownership of big enterprises and the actual use of mineral resources found on the territory of Kosovo. 'They also indicate a recognition of the fact that the resolution of property rights issues is a central component of peacebuilding efforts and indispensable to economic revitalization and the stability of peacebuilding and democratization efforts.'[118] Overall, property rights have not been successfully managed in Kosovo; there is an even bigger challenge than property, which is the actual lack of employment possibilities.

There have been not so many foreign investments as one would expect to happen in a state where both the UN and the EU missions are present to such a great extent and with influence. While, for instance, EULEX can't be blamed for the lack of investments, it is not realistic to blame the Kosovo government either, since it financially, economically and structurally depends on the support coming from its foreign partners. 'EULEX had an almost non-existent bottom-up dimension, it adopted a highly technocratic approach, and experienced problems with accountability.'[119] The support that foreign investors are gaining in Kosovo, together with the support that the whole system can guarantee to small- and medium-sized enterprises, is far behind EU standards as one would expect after two decades of foreign-managed efforts in Kosovo state-building.

When we look into the Kosovo-related agreements, it can be observed that overall the BA is dealing to a very big extent with the specific minority rights which are supposed to be enjoyed by the Serbian Minority in Kosovo, after its actual integration into the Kosovo legal system. Apart from many previously explained rights, it can also be added that the Serbian judges acting in North Kosovo will be integrated into the Kosovo judiciary system in order to guarantee access to judicial protection in the Serbian language. There shall also be

---

118 Margaret Cordial and Knut Rosandhaug, 'The Response of the United Nations Interim Administration Mission in Kosovo to Address Property Rights Challenges' in Scott Leckie (ed), *Housing, Land, and Property Rights in Post-conflict United Nations and Other Peace Operations: A Comparative Survey and Proposal for Reform* (Cambridge University Press 2009).

119 Kari M. Osland and Mateja Peter, 'Securitisation of the EU Approach to the Western Balkans: From Conflict Transformation to Crisis Management' in Roger Mac Ginty, Sandra Pogodda, and Oliver P. Richmond (ed), *The EU and crisis response* (Manchester University Press 2021).

higher court instances, like the Appellate court, with the aim to guarantee the protection and judiciary support to the Serbian minority in their native language. 'A division of this Appellate Court, composed both by administrative staff and judges will sit permanently in northern Mitrovica (Mitrovica District Court).'[120] Such guarantees and institutional compositions are in fact rather normal for a democratic society, while the most important minority rights protection institution is still pending to be formed – it is the Association/Community of Serbian municipalities, with its presumable, enforcement capacities to oversee the important aspects of the everyday life of Serbs in Kosovo.

In regard to the Washington Agreement, it does not mention directly the formation of the A/C but instead insists on economic cooperation and the membership of Kosovo in the Mini Schengen Agreement (Open Balkan). Still, there is a long-standing issue the WA is dealing with, which is a very important human right and that is to 'expedite efforts to locate and identify the remains of missing persons',[121] which is a huge challenge for both societies, after the by now 25 years, since the conflict has ended. The issue of missing persons is also a key component for the overall reconciliation of two nations, but even as much as there is an interest in it, we still can't see the actual honest moves to do this and finalize this important post-conflict development milestone.

4.2 Democratic Potentials in the Agreements

The overall democratic potentials of a certain post-conflict society, and in this regard Kosovo, depends much on the support and recognition it gains from abroad. While the international community is divided in regard to the recognition of Kosovo, it also has to be taken into account, to a certain extent, when the resolution of the conflict is being dealt with and the exact solutions implemented. Also, to a certain extent, it is necessary to have some solutions or standards forced onto a society, be it Serbia or Kosovo, in order to have an environment where agreements are in fact being implemented and not just agreed on paper. The initial ideas of finding solutions for Kosovo and the agenda set in the Ahtisaari plan many years ago have unfortunately failed, and while it was set in stone for some, the others didn't want to accept such solutions coming from a one-sided approach. The point of departure is an argument that unilateral decisions and proposals, such as the Ahtisaari plan, had a largely negative impact on the relationship between the two par-

120 BA 2013.

121 WA 2020.

ties.[122] While many aspects of the Ahtisaari plan have been implemented, we are not sure if that has benefited the whole process of conflict resolution and reconciliation in Kosovo.

Politically, the communities in Kosovo are very divided and also inside certain entities, there are strong division lines when it comes to decision-making about their future role in Kosovo. In this regard, it can also be said that UNMIK and EULEX also have not done much to make people feel that they belong to a certain society or state, in this case Kosovo. 'The insistence of internationals, including those of EULEX, on an inclusive concept of peacebuilding has led to the scenario whereby some locals are invited to take part in projects solely to comply with donors requirement to ensure the inclusion of locals.'[123] Various approaches in this peacebuilding have led to many different standards being implemented, ultimately leading to a divide locally, regionally and internationally where no one can really define Kosovo and its present legal status.

It is hard to blame the lack of democratic potentials of the locals and their political organizations since even the more proficient institutions and mission such as the EULEX are not able to find the best way of implementing democratic standards, among which the most important one is definitely the rule of law. 'Broader political considerations not related to the primary objective of the mission were a source of constant frustration to EULEX staff and some openly stated that despite its heavy footprint, the EU was not serious about the rule of law in Kosovo.'[124] The EULEX mission and its courts have also missed the opportunity to judge the responsible persons for war crimes, which has then led to the establishment of the Kosovo Specialist Chambers Court, which is completely outside the EULEX framework and also represents the downgrading of its missions' capacities in this important aspect. In general, it is hard to say and claim one day in what aspects has EULEX served as a benchmark for its conflict resolution, since its mission is having a very passive stance in the times of rising interethnic conflicts in Kosovo.

Due to the many divisions in the EU, it can be observed that even the EU is struggling to implement some of its standards and procedures when it comes to accession policies. When the EU signed the Stabilization and Accession

122 Andrej Semenov, 'The Washington Agreement: A Supplementary Document to the EU Efforts in Kosovo?' (2021) 23 Insight Turkey 259.

123 Rok Zupančič and Nina Pejič, *Limits to the European Union's Normative Power in a Post-conflict Society: EULEX and Peacebuilding in Kosovo* (Springer 2018).

124 Kari M. Osland and Mateja Peter, 'Securitisation of the EU Approach to the Western Balkans: From Conflict Transformation to Crisis Management' in Roger Mac Ginty, Sandra Pogodda, and Oliver P. Richmond (ed), *The EU and crisis response* (Manchester University Press 2021).

Agreement (SAA), it was also not in the usual form, showing the lack of democratic capacity of such an agreement, which can be later seen as an obstacle to the integration of Kosovo into the EU. 'On the other hand, in contrast to all other SAAs, the SAA with Kosovo is concluded by the EU alone and not by the EU and its member-states.'[125] Such inner divides are also endangering Kosovo and its efforts to be a democratic society after all, while they make it as an exception which does not fit into the previously established patterns and standards of democratic accession to the EU. Also, in some similar situations, it can be stated that the divided societies and their 'reconciliation almost served as an accession condition for joining the EU',[126] which was the case in some previous practices in the EU until now.

When it comes to Serbia, it is evident how it influences and shapes the opinion of Serbs in Kosovo; such a relationship is very specific and due to the financial incentives that Kosovo Serbs are gaining from the Serbian state. The recent changes in the mutual relationship between the Serbian minority in Kosovo and the *de facto* Kosovo state were not discussed much on a local level but the solutions or better say what has to be achieved was dictated from Belgrade. This has also enabled the very smooth transfer of the Serbian institutions from North Kosovo into the system of The Republic of Kosovo. 'Accordingly, Vučić is not merely a thermometer reflecting the public's mood, but rather he is a thermostat leader with the ability to adjust their attitudes to accept Kosovo's recognition.'[127] The very big influence of the Serbian President on the Serbs in Kosovo dates back to the Milosevic era when Serbs were looking for an authority which could support them in their efforts in Kosovo. The role of Vučić and its final aim in regard to Kosovo independence is still questionable, while it is visible that he is ready to give certain favours, in exchange for the support his government is gaining from the EU.

Regarding the influence of Kosovo politicians, we can observe that they are not so authoritative and depend exclusively on the support from the EU and the USA. Interestingly, the ex-President of Kosovo Hashim Thaci has been one of the first accused persons by the KSC, and accordingly the work of this court

125 Peter Van Elsuwege, 'Legal Creativity in EU External Relations: The Stabilization and Association Agreement Between the EU and Kosovo' (2017) 22 European Foreign Affairs Review 393.

126 Valérie Rosoux, 'Time and Reconciliation: Negotiating with Ghosts' in Natascha Mueller-Hirth and Sandra Rios Oyola (ed), *Time and Temporality in Transitional and Post-conflict Societies* (Routledge 2018).

127 Leon Hartwell, 'The Serbia-Kosovo Dialogue: Ripe for Resolution?' [2021] Center for European Policy Analysis <https://cepa.org/wp-content/uploads/2021/05/CEPA-Serbia-Kosovo-5.10.21-V2.pdf> accessed 24 March 2026.

has therefore influenced directly the democratic potentials and capacities of the new Kosovo state. While the USA support is very important for Kosovo, it is actually just declarative and USA is ready to defend its priorities more than respect the democratic will of people of Kosovo in regard to their foreign relations. Kosovo was, to some extent, forced to accept some changes during the WA negotiations towards its foreign policies without even being able to discuss them in the government or decide on elections. The only real winner of these "negotiations" is the State of Israel because the only concrete point of the agreement is the one that states the mutual recognition of Israel and Kosovo, and that Serbia will move its embassy from Tel Aviv to Jerusalem.[128] Such moves are not typical for any democratic country where by signing an informal agreement, they completely change their understanding of the previously long-established foreign relationships they have maintained and prioritized.

Some new and innovative democratic standards have also been requested by the BA, while it has still outlined a very important democracy-related requirement regarding the integration of the police from North Kosovo into the system of The Republic of Kosovo. Before the BA, the four Serbian municipalities in North Kosovo were not under the full control of the police from Pristina. 'The Commander of this region shall be a Kosovo Serb nominated by the Ministry of Interior from a list provided by the four mayors on behalf of the Community/Association.'[129] While this can be seen as a very democratic solution after the recent conflicts, such as the one in Banjska village, this idea is not looking very realistic to be managed on a long run. The management and access to police forces and their democratic control are key in every post-conflict society and is representing a valuable democratic achievement.

Finally, regarding the WA and its solutions for democracy, there is a very important requirement of 'airline passenger screeneing'[130] since Kosovo is still seen as a country where potential terrorists can be recruited, although recently the EU allowed visa-free travel for Kosovo citizens into the EU. While guaranteeing the freedom of movement inside the EU as a beneficial and democratic achievement, it also puts pressure on the local development as some areas in Kosovo could probably depopulate due to the lack of investments and development potentials, just as was the case in many Eastern European countries after they joined the EU.

---

128 Chen Xin, 'Serbia External Relations Briefing: The Washington Agreement' (2020) 32 China-CEE Institute <https://china-cee.eu/wp-content/uploads/2020/10/2020er09_Serbia.pdf> accessed 24 March 2026.

129 BA 2013.

130 WA 2020.

CHAPTER 13

Nagorno-Karabakh and Its Post-conflict Peace Agreement

Probably the most important perspective of the effects and developments in post-conflict societies and the real enforcement capacity of informal agreements can be seen in the case of Nagorno-Karabakh (NK). While NK has never gained broader recognition as a state it has functioned for some two decades as a proxy of the Armenian state, for which it had until 2023 the full support of The Russian Federation. What has changed and how changes are managed in regard to post-conflict societies and their relevant agreements can be seen in the recent resolutions regarding the NK conflict. In 2023 Azerbaijan, as it has long waited, became a dominant military, political and finally law enforcement actor on its entire territory, finally including the territory of the NK as well. This also brings a new perspective and some challenges for the agreements reached in regard to the resolution of the crisis, which was supported by many and also 'the UN has supported the full implementation of a 9 November 2020 Trilateral Statement by the leaders of Armenia, Azerbaijan and Russia'[1] whose implementation is now questionable in many of its aspects. It can be claimed that this agreement ceased to exist, but in fact it has also regulated a much broader array of regional issues than the question of the NK itself. While many aspects of the agreement will be outdated some will still remain, as they represent the strategic and national interests of either Armenia or Azerbaijan. Also in this regard the Russian interests remain as they need a stable Caucasus region while the war in Ukraine still remains a top priority.

Together with the Russian interests in the region there is also the Chinese interest, and it is also requiring the peaceful resolution of conflicts in order to freely trade and lower the possibilities of disturbance. 'Since overland trade is twice as expensive as maritime trade, the inclusion of the South Caucasus in the geopolitical belt of China can be seen as part of a strategy that places

1 UN News, 'Armenia-Azerbaijan: UN Calls for "Credible and Durable" End to Fighting in Flashpoint Region' (21 September 2023) <https://news.un.org/en/story/2023/09/1141232> accessed 24 March 2026.

HTTPS://DOI.ORG/10.1163/9789004746091-015

geopolitical tactics above trade policy.'[2] All the changes in the region of South Caucasus are happening primarily because of geostrategic interests of some states where ultimately human and minority rights are not deemed to be one of the priorities after all. The final dissolution of The Nagorno-Karabakh Republic from 1 January 2024 shows that geostrategic interests are indeed a very important factor in every post-conflict society, and crucial in regard to any of its soft law agreement.

1 Development-Related Aspects

1.1 Trade Perspectives

Development was a very complex issue in NK as in every other post-conflict society. While we are trying to find parallels between various post-conflict societies and regions globally, it is more and more evident that every region has its very specific connotations, which in fact can't really always be properly understood. Still, like in Kosovo or Afghanistan, the region of NK has ended up in a country where it maybe did not really belong as an outcome of some post-colonial arrangements. Also similarly to Crimea this region can be disputed and arguments pro and contra can be very easily raised. Still our legal argumentation will not be going in this direction but will be aiming to determine what development aspects the recent statement[3] or agreement could have produced. Also in these new connotations some other development possibilities will be quoted. While the Statement from 2020 has been agreed by The President of the Republic of Azerbaijan, the Prime Minister of the Republic of Armenia and President of the Russian Federation have finally lost its main function. It can still be read and understood as a soft law in regard to the remaining still-pending issues between Armenia and Azerbaijan.

This agreement has brought in a new reality for both Armenia and Azerbaijan including the disputed territory of NK but some parts of Armenia proper as

2 Mikheil Sarjveladze, 'The South Caucasus in the Context of the EU-Russia Crisis' (2017) 28 Security Policy Working Paper <https://www.baks.bund.de/sites/baks010/files/working_paper_2017_28.pdf> accessed 24 March 2026.

3 President of Russian Federation, 'Statement by President of the Republic of Azerbaijan, Prime Minister of the Republic of Armenia and President of the Russian Federation' (2020) <http://en.kremlin.ru/events/president/news/64384> also available at <https://documents-dds-ny.un.org/doc/UNDOC/GEN/N20/307/34/PDF/N2030734.pdf?OpenElement> accessed 24 March 2026. Further will be quoted as Statement 2020.

well. The whole agreement actually brought in new opportunities regarding trade for everyone, including Armenia as well. 'Russia could not include Azerbaijan in the Eurasian Economic Union and Pakistan in the Collective Security Treaty Organization due to the veto of Armenia.'[4] While the Eurasian Economic Union[5] is a very formal organization, Russia needs to spread its influence and trade capacity in the region and in this case it does it in a more informal way. While formally this new agreement was a Statement[6] its background is a very important turning point where Azerbaijan finds itself obliged to follow up on policies and trade patterns, which will be more in line with Russian interests. Accordingly it will follow a path similar to Turkey, which is having very good relations with Russia while its relationship with the West has recently deteriorated. Overall trade patterns made by both Turkey and Azerbaijan will from now be more aligned with Russian interests due to the close political proximity and recent political and military favours it has done to them.

Regarding trade in the Caucasus, it falls inside a bigger and wider trade route, which is connecting Asia to Europe excluding territories of Russia and Iran, which both might find themselves under stricter sanctions soon. While getting this Caucasus corridor open it also remains under the influence of Russia in some way due to its political and security-related control regarding both Armenia and Azerbaijan, but is also a priority and a vital interest for Turkey. 'The Middle Corridor represents Turkey's vision for connecting China to Europe via Central Asia and the South Caucasus.'[7] As this project is called 'Caravanserai Project'[8] it has an aim to connect Turkic speaking people from Asia, which spans as far as the Xinjiang Uyghur Autonomous Region in Northwest China. There is a common and shared interest for both Turkey and China to have a safe and secure connection over Asia, which will ultimately also get Asian products closer to Europe. 'Chinese digital products and services, including those of Huawei, are much more affordable, faster, and come with greater regulatory flexibility compared with what other global tech suppliers offer,

4 Yılmaz, Salih, 'Land Swap Formula in the Nagorno-Karabakh Crisis Solution: Goble Plan and Lavrov Plan' (2022) 100 bilig 177.

5 EAEU, 'Eurasian Economic Union' <http://www.eaeunion.org/?lang=en#about> accessed 24 March 2026.

6 Statement 2020.

7 Feride Inan and Diana Yayloyan, 'New Economic Corridors in the South Caucasus and the Chinese One Belt One Road' [2020] The Economic Policy Research Foundation of Turkey <https://armenia-turkey.net/files/2020-04/oTvkVwhboZ2ysfXTVQniYEDv1I.pdf> accessed 24 March 2026.

8 Organization of Turkic States, 'Areas of Cooperation' <https://www.turkicstates.org/en/areas-of-cooperation-detail/3-customs-cooperation> accessed 24 March 2026.

thus making them attractive.'[9] Such telecommunication products are very much needed in various Asian states and also countries in the EU neighbourhood and the various post-conflict societies. Such societies, which see IT development as a quick way to make huge steps forward in the sense of economy and connectedness, are more than ready to cooperate with China in this and many other aspects.

When we speak about Chinese telecommunications equipment and especially Huawei and its products, we can observe that this company does have a particular focus on some post-conflict developments including Afghanistan, NK and also Kosovo where it was particularly mentioned in the Washington Agreement. Since in Afghanistan and NK, Huawei will invest and develop telecommunication networks in Kosovo it probably won't, but in Serbia it still has a chance and can cause a turning point. 'European actors see their trade deficits with China soaring and a lot of the promised infrastructure projects not materializing at all.'[10] While China faces a lot of political and administrative limitations in the EU neighbourhood by the EU it certainly has absolute freedom of investment in Asia, Middle East and now in the Caucasus area as well. 'For example, Huawei is taking part in projects to create "smart cities" in Karabakh.'[11] Therefore rising the production and export orientation of this post-conflict region can have a potential in the future as a place to produce, trade and export to the markets nearby and the broader World overall.

1.2 Investment Possibilities

When approaching the issue of investments in the post-conflict Caucasus and in particular the NK region, it is necessary to mention the will of Azerbaijan to invest tremendous resources into this region. The main aim of Azerbaijan is to show that it is a conflict solver and development-friendly country, while it is a question of who will settle here after the Armenians have left. In this regard it aims also to cooperate as much as possible with many foreign investors, and here a very prominent role will also belong to China. 'As Huawei gains a major role in building the digital backbone of the Karabakh region, its ability to

9 Vusal Guliyev, 'Azerbaijan's Digitalization Efforts, Revitalization of the Liberated Territories, and Role of China's Huawei' (2022) 3 Caucasus Strategic Perspectives 117.

10 Alexandra Martin, 'China in the Broader Black Sea Region' [2021] Globsec <https://www.globsec.org/sites/default/files/2021-03/China-in-the-Broader-black-sea-region-ver7-non print.pdf> accessed 24 March 2026.

11 Seymur Mammadov, 'Azerbaijan-China: 30 Years of Cooperation That Can Become an Example for the World' (2022) <https://www.chinadaily.com.cn/a/202204/02/WS62484315a310fd2b29e54ead.html> accessed 24 March 2026.

shape the region's high-tech landscape in the long term will grow exponentially.'[12] While this region for now stays off limits to the EU and US investors, due to the Russian influence it is more than ready to welcome Chinese investments.

Regarding the future Chinese investments in the Caucasus it is not likely that they will have any limitations, like it was previously mentioned regarding The Washington agreement in Kosovo or the Abrahamic Accords in which countries are accepting the US security dominance. Such an investment realm closely connected to the ban of Huawei, primarily from the USA but also from countries from its sphere of interest in the development of telecommunications sector. 'Chinese investments may not only help to develop other transportation routes but also help the region's countries, especially Azerbaijan, to build up non-oil export potential.'[13] As Azerbaijan needs to be well-connected to the world, due to its oil export it also aims to be connected to the world regarding the Asia to Europe trade route where it can't count solely on the routes via Georgia. While Georgian trade routes can be easily interrupted by Russia, which neither Azerbaijan nor Turkey can prevent, they need to have a fixed passage through Armenia, which can always remain open and under the control of Russia and Turkey as guarantors. Since the recently agreed corridor through Southern Armenia connecting Azerbaijan to Nakhichevan is looking more complex than initially, still there is the last alternative for Azerbaijan and it is to connect to Nakhichevan via Iran. This very new solution did not look possible for a long period of time but according to new discussions it is. 'Azerbaijan and Iran agreed to build a railroad in Iran that will link Azerbaijan with its exclave of Nakhchivan.'[14] This project could finalize the interconnectedness issues in the South Caucasus and satisfy the transportation needs of Azerbaijan and Iran but also Turkey and Russia.

A good relationship with neighbours is also necessary for investors because they want to make sure that products will be actually exported from a certain country and not fall under any kind of sanctions and blockades. Azerbaijan as every other oil exporting country wants to invest into future potentials for

12 Vusal Guliyev, 'Azerbaijan's Digitalization Efforts, Revitalization of the Liberated Territories, and Role of China's Huawei' (2022) 3 Caucasus Strategic Perspectives 117.

13 Anar Valiyev, 'Azerbaijan Through the Prism of BRI: China's Mounting Interests and Influence in the Region' (2019) 621 PONARS Eurasia Policy Memo <https://www.ponarseurasia.org/wp-content/uploads/attachments/Pepm621_Valiyev_Oct2019-1.pdf> accessed 24 March 2026.

14 TASS, 'Baku, Tehran Agree to Build Railroad to Nakhchivan across Iran' (6 October 2023) <https://tass.com/world/1686277> accessed 24 March 2026.

what it needs to stabilize its neighbourhood and have countries such as Russia and Iran support its development goals in the NK and broader. 'If Azerbaijan is to diversify its oil-based economy, it will need the EU – rather than Iran or Russia – for technology and know-how.'[15] EU is indeed an important trade partner of Azerbaijan in the oil sector which also makes it a favourable investment potential. EU and the USA could not any longer maintain any political leverage over Azerbaijan as they have also lost Turkey to Russia. Interestingly, Israel is well-connected to Azerbaijan as they have in common the disagreement, or in some cases conflict, with Iran. With such an aim of opposing Iran and having good relationships with Israel, Azerbaijan can also have some Abrahamic Accords-like arrangement with the USA, while the informal way of such agreements would also be a perfect match to maintain good relationships with Russia, at the same time.

Regarding Armenia, its potential for development are limited and fixed to Russian and alternatively Chinese investors. There are also prospects to have a good relationship with Iran, while the exports outside of its region remain a huge challenge for Armenia. 'Before the war, almost 40 per cent of de facto Nagorno-Karabakh's budget came from mining metals that were transported to Armenia for sale.'[16] While Armenia has lost NK and its resources we need to outline that the war with Azerbaijan was based purely on ethnic reasons and not regarding its resources.

1.3 Infrastructure Development Potentials

The infrastructure projects connecting East and West, but also North with the South are gaining new importance with the relevant perspectives for more and better connectedness. While the flow of goods through Russia via Ukraine is getting more burdensome there is a need to approach some alternatives. Such alternatives are aiming towards the Mediterranean Sea via Turkey, for which the opening of The NK frozen conflict and the better connectivity in the region was necessary. It is not only that the South Caucasus is important for reaching Europe, but it also has an important role in the North to South connectivity. 'Rebuilding relatively small sections of railway in Armenia and Azer-

15 Jana Kobzova and Leila Alieva, 'The EU and Azerbaijan: Beyond Oil' [2012] European Council on Foreign Relations Policy Memo <https://ecfr.eu/wp-content/uploads/ECFR57_EU_AZERBAIJAN_MEMO_AW.pdf> accessed 24 March 2026.

16 International Crisis Group, 'Improving Prospects for Peace after the Nagorno-Karabakh War' (2020) 91 Crisis Group Europe Briefing <https://www.crisisgroup.org/europe-central-asia/caucasus/nagorno-karabakh-conflict/b91-improving-prospects-peace-after-nagorno-karabakh-war> accessed 24 March 2026.

baijan would make much more viable the 7,200-kilometer (4,400-mile) International North-South Transport Corridor, a projected rail route stretching from Finland through Russia to the Persian Gulf and on to India.'[17] With the establishment of new trade routes and in particular the regional co-operations in the framework of BRICS[18] Russia, in particular, seeks better connectivity with Southern Asia towards India, the Gulf states and finally also towards Africa. In this North to South connectivity race Russia has an absolute priority since it does not fall under the Chinese BRI[19] plan but connects with very important Russian trading partners such as Iran and India.

When we look closer to the present divides in The South Caucasus we can see that Azerbaijan is a country consisting of two parts, divided by Armenia standing firmly between them. The connectivity between these two parts of Azerbaijan is definitely a priority for it but also for Turkey, which can reach Central Asia after a decades-long blockade of its border with Armenia. 'A high-quality fast road and rail link to and from Nakhichevan across Armenia's southern Meghri region was a goal of Azerbaijan even in Soviet times.'[20] While this link might be a state priority for Azerbaijan it is not until now that it gained importance becoming a priority for both Turkey and China, having a route which bypasses Russia proper. It is very important that Azerbaijan invests in infrastructure in this regard as it sees itself as a transportation hub between the East and West already.

Therefore, together with the establishment of the idea of connecting the two parts of Azerbaijan, this statement or the agreement between Armenia and Azerbaijan has also interestingly foreseen this connection. It came as a counteroffer for letting Armenia be connected to NK through a small Lachin corridor, which has lost its importance after the last Armenian refugee left NK in 2023. 'The Lachin Corridor (5 km wide), which will provide a connection between Nagorno Karabakh and Armenia.'[21] This solution that the Lachin Corridor will remain part of Azerbaijan, although controlled by Russian forces,

---

17 Thomas de Waal, 'In the South Caucasus, Can New Trade Routes Help Overcome a Geography of Conflict?' [2021] Carnegie Endowment for International Peace <https://carnegieendowment.org/files/de_Waal_South_Caucasus_Connectivity.pdf> accessed 24 March 2026.

18 BRICS, 'BRICS Information Portal' <http://infobrics.org/> accessed 24 March 2026.

19 Office of the Leading Group for Promoting the Belt and Road Initiative, 'Belt and Road Portal' <https://eng.yidaiyilu.gov.cn/> accessed 24 March 2026.

20 Thomas de Waal, 'The Nagorny Karabakh Conflict in Its Fourth Decade' (2021) 2 CEPS Working Document <https://www.ceps.eu/download/publication/?id=34122&pdf=WD 2021-02_The-Nagorny-Karabakh-Conflict-in-its-Fourth-Decade.pdf> accessed 24 March 2026.

21 Statement 2020.

made the idea of connecting two parts of Azerbaijan to some extent a realistic expectation. The same obligation to let the free movement between Azerbaijan and Nakhichevan viable has been included as an obligation of Armenia. 'The Republic of Armenia shall guarantee the security of transport connections between the western regions of the Republic of Azerbaijan and the Nakhichevan Autonomous Republic in order to arrange unobstructed movement of persons, vehicles and cargo in both directions.'[22] Such a road would not just benefit Azerbaijan but also Armenia and potentially be a part of the larger framework of the BRI[23] roads where goods can travel freely between East and West benefiting both countries. 'Trying to benefit from the Chinese-led Belt and Road Initiative (BRI), Baku seeks to secure a railroad/highway corridor via Armenia to the Azerbaijani exclave of Nakhchivan.'[24] It can be concluded that while a certain long-lasting conflict was gaining momentum the actual changes were made in the best interests of some more influential countries. Also it can happen that Azerbaijan never gets connected to Nakhichevan in this way. Still the world politics, the interests of other nations and finally the new priorities of Russia, China and Turkey could make this happen with some new perspectives.

1.4 Potentials for Future Developments

The overall prospects of trade, investments and infrastructure developments are very important in the South Caucasus and its vicinity. It would not be possible to broker a new more stable arrangement between Armenia and Azerbaijan without the obvious common interests of Russia and Turkey. Interestingly we can observe that by bringing closer the harsh division lines between them Russia has also managed to sideline Georgia as a transportation hub with which it is in conflict from earlier. 'Furthermore, a future prospect of opening up Armenia's borders with Turkey and Azerbaijan would enable a Caspian trade flow which would be a cost-effective alternative to the current and longer route over Georgia.'[25] Russia has managed to punish Georgia by this new constellation and also bring closer to its orbit countries

22 Ibid.

23 Office of the Leading Group for Promoting the Belt and Road Initiative, 'Belt and Road Portal' <https://eng.yidaiyilu.gov.cn/> accessed 24 March 2026.

24 Anar Valiyev, 'Karabakh After the 44-Day War: Russian Peacekeepers and Patterns' (2021) 705 PONARS Eurasia Policy Memo <https://www.ponarseurasia.org/wp-content/uploads/2021/08/Pepm705_Valiyev_August2021.pdf> accessed 24 March 2026.

25 Feride Inan and Diana Yayloyan, 'New Economic Corridors in the South Caucasus and the Chinese One Belt One Road' [2020] The Economic Policy Research Foundation of

which anyway largely depend on it. It can also be interesting to observe how this new trade route developments will influence Georgia and its new position in The Black Sea region, with a rising Russian dominance and especially occupying new territories in Ukraine.

Overall all the Caucasus states are in fact getting less space to move around since they are now being hold in a grip between Russia, Iran and Turkey. 'Yet, Russia has been using its role as a mediator for advancing its own interests rather than the actual conflict resolution.'[26] This also corresponds to the actual situation in Ukraine where Russia aims at spreading its influence rather than simply gaining and controlling territory or accessing resources. One of the main questions here is how will Russia transit gas through Ukraine to Europe, it can be easily answered by drawing some parallels from other regions and in particular the South Caucasus, as our case study. 'In 2007, when Tehran inaugurated gas supplies to neighboring Armenia, Russia's Gazprom immediately bought up the pipeline project within Armenia and built it with a small circumference to preclude its future use for transiting gas to European markets.'[27] The obvious changes towards a better connectivity in the region are not solely for the benefit of local, regional and global stakeholders. It necessarily implies the Russian dominance in the energy and transportation sector, leaving it as a sole controller of the transportation flows between Europe and Asia.

When the EU is searching for alternative oil suppliers and tries to limit its Russian imports it forgets that Russia is one step ahead. While starting the war in Ukraine it has counted on such developments and is now aiming at controlling the majority of gas supplies routes towards Europe. Russia has intensified cooperation with Azerbaijan in this regard before, during and after the conflict in NK and has by now established itself as a decision-making factor in the South Caucasus and broader. 'In other words, the EU's geo-economic- vital energy security interests are not guaranteed by Azerbaijan's oil/gas supplies, while Azerbaijan strategically depends on the EU as a key oil and gas export

Turkey <https://armenia-turkey.net/files/2020-04/oTvkVwhboZ2ysfXTVQniYEDv1I.pdf> accessed 24 March 2026.

26 Sadi Sadiyev Saleh and others, 'South Caucasus and a "New Great Game": The Communication of Competition in Securitised International Relations' (2021) 29 Journal of Contemporary European Studies 282.

27 Brenda Shaffer, 'European Union Energy Policy: The Role of the South Caucasus' in Kornely Kakachia, Stefan Meister and Benjamin Fricke (ed), *Geopolitics and Security: A New Strategy for the South Caucasus* (Konrad-Adenauer-Stiftung 2018).

and consumption market.'[28] Therefore the burden of securing gas supplies is now again placed on the EU, while Russia can now more easily request policy alignments which are corresponding to Russian interests from Azerbaijan after it has supported its takeover in the NK.

In this sense it is observable how informal rules are regulating the play in global political games where their application or non-application does produce some outcomes. 'Based on this logic, pipelines to take Caspian oil and gas across the Caucasus to European and other international energy markets became the centerpiece of U.S. policy in the region.'[29] Considering the USA withdrawal from Afghanistan the new order in the NK and the South Caucasus leaves very little space for the EU and USA common efforts to reshape its policies and contacts with this part of the world.

2 Administration-Related Aspects of the Agreement

2.1 Relevant Challenges in General

It is never easy to achieve and maintain some administration related solutions in post-conflict societies, in fact the administration with all of its constellations is many times the reason for the conflict to start. There are many different solutions in administering post-conflict societies, where UN also has a prominent role, we will deal with the territory of NK which has administered itself as a non-UN recognized country until 2024. As every post-conflict society or republic must have its own territory, so was the case with NK. The territory administered or controlled by the NK Republic was much bigger than its actual territory in the Soviet era. It has in fact controlled a big piece of Azerbaijani territory, which it has gained in the previous war and used it as a buffer zone ever since. This buffer zone was frequently attacked and also served as a soft borderline from the NK towards Azerbaijan proper. It was obvious that by controlling such a big piece of the Azerbaijani land no real peace and full

28 Khachatryan Hasmik, 'The Nagorno-Karabakh War: A New Reality in the South Caucasus and Its Implications for the EU' [2020] Institute of European Democrats <https://www.iedonline.eu/download/geopolitics-values/36-Khachatryan_The_Nagorno-Karabakh_war_A_new_reality_in_the_South_Caucasus_and_its_implications.pdf> accessed 24 March 2026.

29 Eugene Rumer, Richard Sokolsky and Paul Stronski, 'U.S. Policy Toward the South Caucasus: Take Three' [2017] Carnegie Endowment for International Peace <https://carnegieendowment.org/files/CP_310_Rumer_Sokolsky_Stronski_Caucusus_Final_Web.pdf> accessed 24 March 2026.

ceasefire can be achieved. 'Should Armenia give back six lands and territories and keep only "Lachin" land?'[30] This was one of the main question in the pre-2020 war era and while it was discussed, it was also not until the recent war and the new 'Settlement' Agreement that it has finally returned these territories to Azerbaijan. After the agreement has been reached, it became more obvious where the new borders of the NK could be, but without their recognition by Azerbaijan or a final definition of their overall status. Accordingly NK as a non-recognized republic or potential autonomous province in Azerbaijan would still remain unrecognized by the UN and the international community overall, with a more visible Russian influence over its final status. At least this was the case in 2020 after the introduction of the changes foreseen by the Statement agreement.

Russia in fact does not have an interest in losing NK or any similar territory in the South Caucasus as it has full control over them and aligns them with its own needs and interests. There are already two similar territories in Georgia, which are controlled by Russian military, probably in the same manner that the NK could have been controlled after the 2020 Agreement. Some corridors are sensitive because they cross the disputed territories of Abkhazia and South Ossetia, which are not named and the locations being only indicated by GPS coordinates.[31] In the case of NK Russia had no interest to recognize it or dispute it; it was perfectly happy with having full control over it after all.

The Armenian side or better to say NK Republic has been obliged to give up on all the territories conquered by Azerbaijan in the 2020 war, but also some which have been kept as strategical points in order to distance its capital Stepanakert from the actual contact line. 'The Agdam District shall be returned to the Republic of Azerbaijan.'[32] This district and city is considered to be very close to the capital Stepanakert; therefore it was treated accordingly as highly valuable in leaving the contact lines more distant. After the takeover of Shusha in 2020 just above Stepanakert the capital city, the whole of NK became completely exposed to the Azerbaijani military. This was the moment when Russians stepped in with an aim to save at least a piece of the once territorially much larger NK Republic. While the agreement did not speak about the future form of the NK it established and installed a Russian peacekeeping mission on

30 Ali Mortazavian and Mohammad Ghiacy, 'Regional and International Cooperation to Reduce-Nagorno – Karabakh Conflict' (2017) 10 J Pol & L 136.

31 Thomas de Waal, 'In the South Caucasus, Can New Trade Routes Help Overcome a Geography of Conflict?' [2021] Carnegie Endowment for International Peace <https://carnegieendowment.org/files/de_Waal_South_Caucasus_Connectivity.pdf> accessed 24 March 2026.

32 Statement 2020.

the contact lines between NK and Azerbaijan, making the actual territory of NK overall pending on their support. 'The peacemaking forces of the Russian Federation, namely, 1,960 troops armed with firearms, 90 armoured vehicles and 380 motor vehicles and units of special equipment, shall be deployed along the contact line in Nagorno-Karabakh and along the Lachin Corridor.'[33] At that moment it was not clear what administratively the NK Republic will be called, whether it will be a territory, country or republic; it will still be inside the Azerbaijani Republic with a possible Russian influence regarding its possible status.

2.2 Autonomy Concerns

When we try to define the status of the NK Republic before and in particular after the conflict of 2020 we can observe that it has considerably changed. From the previous Republic-like territorial status with a limited economic potential and the possibility to defend itself by being supported from Armenia and to some extent Russia, it became a very vulnerable territory after all. Due to the fact that Azerbaijan took the entire territory outside NK, which was previously a buffer zone, the military importance of NK has vanished instantly. While Armenia has actively participated in the signing of the final agreement the provisional government in NK has not been approached or participated in any form in this agreement. 'Although the fact that it has occurred without any formal concessions by Azerbaijan entails a significant loss of bargaining power for Armenia/Nagorno-Karabakh going forward.'[34] The fact that NK has not gained any prominent role or has been mentioned in the final agreement also entails its place in the Russian politics towards The South Caucasus. The territorial gains by Azerbaijan have been all acknowledged and also the peaceful transfer of other regions was noted and carefully calculated in the agreement. 'For Azerbaijan, the November 10 deal was considered a victory, not least because the document did not mention any status for Karabakh, thus confirming Azerbaijan's territorial integrity.'[35] In this regard it is not just that the status of NK has not been defined by any means but it also

33 Ibid.

34 Mark Anstey, Paul Meerts, Mikhail Troitskiy and I. William Zartman, 'The Conflict over Artsakh – Nagorno-Karabakh' (2020) 1 oPINion <https://assets.ctfassets.net/mvajnncmgvdq/1fPT78KfLANItgII8kRIbm/04dc0c24f46f468d7dce284a6e17fe1d/oPINion_Dez_2020.pdf> accessed 24 March 2026.

35 Anar Valiyev, 'Karabakh After the 44-Day War: Russian Peacekeepers and Patterns' (2021) 705 PONARS Eurasia Policy Memo <https://www.ponarseurasia.org/wp-content/uploads/2021/08/Pepm705_Valiyev_August2021.pdf> accessed 24 March 2026.

challenged the overall role of Armenia in all the Russian controlled organizations it is a member of, primarily the ones regarding trade and security. While the final status of the NK was not debated in the agreement it is also closely connected to the future mutual relationship of Russia and the two Caucasus states Armenia and Azerbaijan, while The NK Republic has ceased to exist after almost three decades of existence on 1 January 2024.

2.3 Prospects for Democracy

Prospects for democracy in the region of the South Caucasus, which borders Russia, Turkey and Iran are overall very limited. While some countries like Armenia and even more Georgia claim democratic statehoods, their actual implementation and development largely depends on their influential neighbours. In the agreement regarding NK any democracy-related requirements or even rights for the inhabitants of the NK or Azerbaijan, be it minority or the majority were not particularly mentioned. In general Azerbaijan itself has a very limited democratic capacity but due to its oil reserves it maintains a larger economic capacity, and with the possibility to develop the newly acquired lands from NK after all it does have the necessary development potential. 'In view of its democratic deficits, Azerbaijan has no interest in political transformation, but a strong interest in cooperating with the EU in the area of energy policy.'[36] While the EU is keen to cooperate in the energy sector with Azerbaijan, it has now no capacity to influence it in any form or require democracy-related prospects for the Azerbaijani society overall or the Armenian minority in the NK. With the full exclusion of any other side from the final NK Agreement, Russia has established itself as the dominant foreign policymaker in the region, whereas the lack of democracy and a strong position and the role of The Azerbaijani President are not something it is much concerned about. The Russian Federation also has a similar structure in the governing bodies where the President is able to establish its own viewpoint in any part of the social life, so criticizing Azerbaijan or Turkey would not make much sense.

Regarding Armenia we can also outline that it has not been consulted much or had any possibilities in the recent conflict; it was more a shock which should have been foreseen and solved in a democratic manner including The Republic of Armenia, NK and consultation with their foreign partners

36 Mikheil Sarjveladze, 'The South Caucasus in the Context of the EU-Russia Crisis' (2017) 28 Security Policy Working Paper <https://www.baks.bund.de/sites/baks010/files/working_paper_2017_28.pdf> accessed 24 March 2026.

altogether. 'At the same time, Armenia has also failed to be forthcoming in the negotiation process, pressured in large part by both the leadership in Stepanakert that has exerted significant influence over the government in Yerevan, as well as by pressure from the global Armenian Diaspora to hold out against any compromise solution.'[37] Apart from criticizing The Armenian Government as not being flexible enough to achieve an agreement, we can also outline their presumed role as a democratic society, which in fact should take into consideration the needs, requirements and demands from their own neighbours. It is very challenging to be positioned in a neighbourhood where no borders are open and where no agreements are being supported in this regard. The regional interests, priorities and co-operations are very important and as long as they are also in the interest of great states they should be accordingly maintained. As long as such interests change, no matter what the local democratic capacities are, such changes should be accommodated and approved using democratic means to the most extensive democratic means possible. It is now a matter of the future and the deals between Russia and the new future relationship between Armenia and Azerbaijan to see how NK will be established and whether Armenians will live in Azerbaijan after all.

3 Security Concerns

3.1 Relevant Concerns in General

The overall security concerns regarding NK are in general fitting into the global security and military intervention standards in post-conflict societies. Russia was in fact not ready to make steps and changes in its military regarding foreign interventions for decades. 'The most important case for Russia's counter-norm entrepreneurship in conflict was its campaign in Syria – its first major military intervention outside its own neighbourhood since Soviet times.'[38] It was not until the war in Syria that the Russian and Turkish interest have clashed directly but finally quickly got aligned back again; as an outcome of this 'friendship' they have also more easily reached an agreement regarding the changes in NK, which can be seen more as a favour to Turkey

37 Mark Anstey, Paul Meerts, Mikhail Troitskiy and I. William Zartman, 'The Conflict over Artsakh – Nagorno-Karabakh' (2020) 1 oPINion <https://assets.ctfassets.net/mvajnncmgvdq/1fPT78KfLANItgII8kRIbm/04dc0c24f46f468d7dce284a6e17fe1d/oPINion_Dez_2020.pdf> accessed 24 March 2026.

38 David Lewis, 'Contesting Liberal Peace: Russia's Emerging Model of Conflict Management' (2022) 98 International Affairs 653.

than to Azerbaijan overall. The strategic place of Turkey and its prior position of countering Russian interests has been changed and while Russia has seen a capacity in this regard it was also ready to give in return certain favours to Turkey. 'Moscow also moved to secure its control over regional energy supplies and transit infrastructure, countering EU and U.S. efforts to establish access to oil and natural gas supplies in Central Asia that bypassed Russia.'[39] While in the sense of security and military cooperation Russia and Turkey still stand on different sides they have come closer in regard to energy security, what also entails the energy supplies to Europe.

Turkey has also gained a lot by getting closer to Russia as it has interests in Europe both as an energy transit country and an important trading partner, but it also has similar interests towards the East specifically in regard to the Central Asian countries. 'It seems that after Turkey relinquished EU integration efforts, the country needs fresh coalitions that would be easiest to create within the Turkic world.'[40] Populistic governments are always in need of fresh coalitions, so is the case with Turkey, Russia and even Azerbaijan. Although Azerbaijan can mainly be thankful to Turkey for this huge change and territorial gains, which have in the end finally fully established the sovereignty of Azerbaijan on its entire territory. Azerbaijan itself remains divided from Turkey now for more than 100 years and needs also access to the Mediterranean and the EU markets, for what infrastructure has to be built in some way in the future. 'Turkey turned to Central Asia offering itself as a third partner with a shared ethnic background to diversify their external policy, capitalizing on the Central Asian republics' dissatisfaction with China's growing influence and Russia's grip.'[41] Accordingly while Russia and China are unable to reach Europe without Turkey, so is the case with Turkey, which needs a green light from both countries in order to establish better relationship with the Turkic countries in Central Asia, but primarily with Azerbaijan.

The sharing of Asia in this new era would never be possible without Turkey as it has a considerable soft power in regard to Turkic nations, which goes as far as the Chinese Western provinces. China also needs safety in this regard

39 Andrej Krickovic and Igor Pellicciari, 'From "Greater Europe" to "Greater Eurasia": Status Concerns and the Evolution of Russia's Approach to Alignment and Regional Integration' (2021) 12 Journal of Eurasian Studies 86.

40 Jakub Lachert, 'Nagorno-Karabakh as Part of Geopolitical Rivalry' [2021] Warsaw Institute <https://warsawinstitute.org/wp-content/uploads/2021/03/Nagorno-Karabakh-as-Part-of-Geopolitical-Rivalry-Jakub-Lachert-Warsaw-Institute-Special-Report-12.03.2021.pdf> accessed 24 March 2026.

41 Lilit Hayrapetyan, 'The Nagorno-Karabakh War of 2020 and the Change of the Regional Status Quo' (2022) 1 Przegląd Politologiczny 83.

and is keen to maintain a good relationship with Turkey and central Asian countries in order to have an undisturbed flow of goods towards Europe. The most important action of this new sharing of Asia is the exclusion of the USA and its interests as much as it is possible. The withdrawal of the USA from Afghanistan was an outcome, which perfectly fits into this new project of sharing Central Asia and limiting the US influence in this part of the world. The position of the USA and its European partners was quickly taken over by China, as it will also be in more detail explained in the following chapter dedicated exclusively to Afghanistan.

Another important Western-oriented country in the Caucasus is Georgia, which will not be able to sustain its Western support after it gets completely surrounded by Russian and Turkish common efforts and interests, potentially sharing and closing the Black Sea region between themselves. 'Thus, Russia was not only determined to teach the Georgians a lesson, which it claimed was borrowed from a Western playbook, but also to deter US geopolitical ambitions in the former Soviet republics.'[42] Overall the whole agreement regarding NK was in fact a way to punish the Western-oriented Armenian government, showing it and the whole nation that they have to pay a price for not following Russian policies. After punishing Georgia and keeping Armenia in a very tight grip we now turn to see what could be the plan of Russia in Ukraine, and its future conflict resolution terms.

While for many years it was evident that Ukraine is getting closer to the West it was not possible to see what final outcomes it will have regarding the Russian security plans in that regard. 'Thus, the differences in perceptions regarding the future of Donetsk and Lugansk between the West and the East are significant'.[43] It can't be foreseen now how and under what conditions the Russian War in Ukraine can be finished and it is necessary to see under what condition Russians are ready to stop it and let it, or not let it have back its normal life and development potentials. In fact, we can see that Russia is able and ready to be very efficient in this regard, as was also the case in NK where an agreement has been instantly concluded at the moment when Russia has seen that the changes it foresaw had been achieved, mainly by the relevant

42 Valur Ingimundarson, 'The "Kosovo Precedent": Russia's Justification of Military Interventions and Territorial Revisions in Georgia and Ukraine' [2022] LSE IDEAS <https://www.lse.ac.uk/ideas/Assets/Documents/updates/2022-SU-Valur-RussKosovo.pdf> accessed 24 March 2026.

43 Karina V. Korostelina, 'Reconciliation in Ukraine: Within and across the Boundary' in Lily Gardner Feldman, Raisa Barash, Samuel Goda and André Zempelburg (ed), *The Former Soviet Union and East Central Europe between Conflict and Reconciliation* (Vandenhoeck & Ruprecht 2019).

Azerbaijani military efforts. At that moment Russia decided to step in and that 'the Republic of Azerbaijan and the Republic of Armenia, hereinafter referred to as the "Parties," shall stop in their current positions.'[44] Therefore Russia at all costs aims to bring itself into a position where it can guarantee and maintain its dominant position; although it can come with certain security and military costs and interventions it does not lower its need to achieve such goals. The recent 2023 one-day war, or military intervention in NK by Azerbaijan, which finally ended the NK Republic could also be seen as a Russian agenda to punish and give a final message to the pro-Western Armenian Government and nation overall.

3.2 Conflict Prevention Capacity

When we approach the issue of conflict prevention and its overall importance on the European continent we can observe how Russia is in fact a key player in this regard. So while we speak about Russia it is hard to determine where it is placed in the overall framework of Europe and where its borders and interest are. 'The United States and Europe had a strategy for Central Europe, but they did not have a strategy for Russia.'[45] Russia is overall a bigger country than all of Europe and has more complex interests than just being a simple uninfluential country on the European borderlands. An important aspect of the EU is the development of Central European states and their security concerns, while with the EU and NATO membership they also get to the opposite side from Russia. 'The war in Ukraine has also demonstrated that 'neutrality', which was removed from the lexicon of post–Cold War security, persists as an item worthy of serious discussion.'[46] While in Europe there are no countries which have remained neutral and the war in Ukraine will finally show and draw hard borderlines between the East and West in Europe, once again. Ukraine will be possibly split and it is still to see how Turkey will behave and where it will lean regarding its security, military and overall economy concerns in the future.

While Turkey has benefited from both its Western and Eastern connections until now it is still to be challenged in this regard, or any time soon, and it will be asked to intervene against Russia in either military or trade related aspects.

---

44 Statement 2020.

45 Rajan Menon and Eugene Rumer, *Conflict in Ukraine: The Unwinding of the Post–Cold War Order* (Massachusetts Institute of Technology 2015).

46 Helena Rytövuori-Apunen, *Power and Conflict in Russia's Borderlands: The Post-Soviet Geopolitics of Dispute Resolution* (Bloomsbury Publishing 2020).

'As for Turkey, it cannot be assumed that Ankara, and President Erdogan personally, would be willing to make a major "civilisation break" with the West.'[47] Turkey has strong ties to the West and in particular to the EU and accordingly it depends on a common good relationship with them, which also necessarily entails trade aspects. Culturally Turkey might not be part of Europe but economically it does shape European economic activities with its overall Asian connections. When we speak about the potentials Central Asia has and its exploitation we necessarily have to turn again to Turkey, since apart from Russia and China it has the biggest potential to influence and shape them. 'Since the majority of Central Asian Muslims are Sunnis, Turkey has an advantage over Iran.'[48] Such an advantage Turkey can use for both strategical and trade concerns, where it can also establish common cultural and trade networks.

After all it would not be possible for Azerbaijan to make changes in regard to the NK conflict without Turkey, or making any agreement with Russia, which presumes the future land connection between Turkey towards Central Asia. Regarding such Turkish interests in Central Asia for now Russia has been a partner, but also it will require the support of Turkey in regard to its own agenda. With a common understanding and agreements regarding cooperation between Russia and Turkey in Western parts of Asia and between Russia and China in Central Asia, all three nations can benefit and reach a point in sharing future interests in Asia. 'Thus, Moscow is likely to tolerate an increased Chinese presence in the region as long as Beijing continues to accommodate Russia's geopolitical and security interests.'[49] While Russia is leaving Central Asia and focuses more on the EU borderlands and South Caucasus it aims to establish itself as a dominant force in this region combining security, trade and other aspects in regard to its own development agenda.

Conflict prevention and the overall control of all possible conflicts in its surroundings and throughout its borderlands are in the best interests and now also the priority of The Russian Federation, with the only exception being Ukraine where it actively maintains its division. When we talk about South Caucasus and the recent agreement in NK from 2020, we can see that

47 Kerim Has, Vali Kaleji and Sergey Markedonov, 'The Breakdown of the Status Quo and the International Dimension of the Nagorno-Karabakh Crisis' [2020] Valdai Discussion Club Report <https://valdaiclub.com/files/32745/> accessed 24 March 2026.

48 Mher Sahakyan, 'The New Great Power Competition in Central Asia: Opportunities and Challenges for the Gulf' [2021] AGDA Working Paper <https://hal.science/hal-03224546v1/document> accessed 24 March 2026.

49 Tracey German, 'Russia and the South Caucasus: The China Challenge' (2022) 74 Europe-Asia Studies 1596.

it is in fact a win-win situation for both Russia and Turkey and a still-pending frozen conflict like situation for both Armenia and Azerbaijan. It is in Kremlin's interest to freeze the Nagorno-Karabakh conflict to weaken both states, Azerbaijan and Armenia, and bring them back to Russia's orbit.[50] Both states will now depend on the goodwill of Russia and its actions, although with an important influence coming now also from Turkey. It is overall in the best interest of all the parties to change and start focusing on mutual cooperation and trade specific developments since the region is falling far back regarding development and its regional and global potentials.

When we look into the final solution reached and prescribed by The Statement of 2020 it is necessary to pay attention to the role of the observing Centre. 'For more efficient monitoring of the Parties' fulfilment of the agreements, a peacemaking centre shall be established to oversee the ceasefire.'[51] This Centre was in fact taking the role of some previously established monitoring practices in the framework of post-conflict societies. The Joint Russian–Turkish Centre for Controlling the Ceasefire in the Nagorno-Karabakh Conflict Zone which was established as a system of monitoring the implementation of the agreement between the Armenian and Azerbaijani sides in a conclusion of the 2020 war in Nagorno-Karabakh. Such a system of establishing a Peace Centre can be seen as a good solution and as it is run and controlled by states outside the conflict, namely Russia and Turkey, it can serve as a good example of finding solutions for the future. Now as the conflict in NK has ended with the dissolution of The Armenian NK Republic, it is necessary to see how such a centre can dissolve itself and conclude its mission while being not responsible to neither Armenia nor Azerbaijan as they were not active members in this centre after all. This centre finally did not live up to its mandate and in fact the conflict has been concluded without contacting it or any other previous forums of conflict resolution, such as the OSCE Minsk Group. 'Baku formally rejects the OSCE process, arguing that it has been rendered obsolete by Azerbaijan's November 2020 military victory.'[52] Azerbaijan in fact has no interest now to complicate its position and threaten itself by various human rights implementation requests by OSCE and similar organizations. Their military victory, although not solving the problem finally, is completely enough

50 Valeri Modebadze, 'The Escalation of Conflict between Armenians and Azerbaijanis and the Problems of Peaceful Resolution of the Nagorno-Karabakh War' (2021) 6 J Liberty & Int'l Aff 102.

51 Statement 2020.

52 International Crisis Group, 'Nagorno-Karabakh: Seeking a Path to Peace in the Ukraine War's Shadow' (2022) 93 Crisis Group Europe Briefing <https://icg-prod.s3.amazonaws.com/b093-seeking-a-path-to-peace_0.pdf> accessed 24 March 2026.

for the Azerbaijani government to claim that it has done the historic resolution of the conflict.

On the other side the NK has lost its previous potential to be a self-sufficient entity and its dissolution did not leave any capacity for the Armenians to remain in Azerbaijan. 'In the aftermath of Kosovo, Azerbaijan concluded that the international peacekeeping presence had in fact steered Kosovo toward independence.'[53] In this aspect our conclusion is that the UN and OSCE conflict resolution frameworks overall did not succeed in maintaining their capacity to prevent conflicts. The expectation that in Ukraine or any other similar Russian-controlled conflict the UN or the EU will be able to establish a mission is also very unlikely to happen. This brings in the idea and the possibility of concluding a Peace Agreement for Ukraine in an informal way and that way has also broken the peace process and given some opportunity for the conflict resolution and economic development possibilities in Ukraine.

3.3 Possible Terrorism-Related Concerns

The existence of terrorist groups of any kind or terrorist acts is not something that can be associated and placed generally in the conflict around NK. It is not that Armenia or Azerbaijan are using such methods of warfare; neither has Turkey been practising it in this case. Even if one party would use such methods the other one would immediately answer and the atrocities would get out of control. However, it is not the case with an open warfare where it can't be followed who and when will plan an attack all of a sudden. The control and limitation of the use of power under the indirect control of Russia and Turkey was the necessary tool to conclude the final agreement regarding NK. 'Criticism towards abuses of power is often considered by Russian courts as a sign of extremism, and the activities of many organizations in the North Caucasus and Moscow were banned because of charges of extremism'.[54] In the case of Azerbaijan the use of power, which it was allowed to use to that certain extent and patiently waiting for the moment to use it, fully has culminated in the act of letting it take over the territories which legally belong to it.

53 Nicu Popescu, *EU Foreign Policy and Post-Soviet Conflicts: Stealth Intervention* (Routledge 2011).

54 Fernando Avakian, 'Discursive Construction of the Islamic Threat in the Russian Federation in the Early 2000s: A Political Tool Hampering Reconciliation?' in Carolina Rehrmann, Rafael Biermann and Philip Tolliday (ed), *Societies in Transition:The Caucasus and the Balkans between Conflict and Reconciliation* (Vandenhoeck & Ruprecht 2020).

The situation where no terrorist acts were present in the NK before, during and after the conflict all point to the fact that the whole conflict was actually under a strict scrutiny. Overall no changes were possible on the field without the prior approval of regional powerful stakeholders. In a broader framework there have also been no terrorist atrocities when we look into a more complex relationship between Russia and Turkey previously. 'Since 2015 in Syria and later in Libya and Nagorno-Karabakh, Moscow and Ankara have actively supported opposing warring parties.'[55] It can be concluded that the use of terrorist groups is not something that can be logically assigned to all the conflicts in the Middle East but as an outcome of more complex historic, cultural and finally religious clashes between various interests in Asia and broader. 'On the other hand, the South Caucasus and Central Asia contain half of all the secular Muslim-majority states in the world.'[56] While the practice of having terrorist groups fighting the Russians or Soviets before was something characteristic for Central Asia and the Taliban movement in particular at that time, it is not the case any longer.

Both in the Soviet and post-Soviet era Russians did not have any actual threat coming from Azerbaijan even when they were more firmly supporting Armenia in the whole conflict. 'However, Azerbaijan had been one of the reliable partners of Moscow without any dissident movements.'[57] This shows that Russians indeed managed even before this final agreement was reached to control the requests and demands coming from Azerbaijani and have them patiently waiting for the right moment to come. Now as this right moment came and an agreement was concluded, Azerbaijan has had to do many complex foreign relations deals and apart from the Turkish support it has even secured the support of Israel. Interestingly while having an anti-Muslim sentiment Israel has supported a Muslim country against a Christian country. This close cooperation with Israel was not welcomed by Iran and its government but in particular the Azerbaijani group Hoseyniyun. 'The group, whose leaders are based in Iran, strongly criticizes the close relationship between Azerbaijan

55 Güney Yıldız, 'Turkish-Russian Adversarial Collaboration in Syria, Libya, and Nagorno-Karabakh' [2021] SWP Comment <https://www.swp-berlin.org/publications/products/comments/2021C22_Turkish-Russian_Collaboration.pdf> accessed 25 March 2026.

56 Svante Cornell, 'The Impact of the Ukraine and Syria Conflicts on the Geopolitics of the South Caucasus' in Kornely Kakachia, Stefan Meister and Benjamin Fricke (ed), *Geopolitics and Security: A New Strategy for the South Caucasus* (Konrad-Adenauer-Stiftung 2018).

57 Eva-Maria Auch, 'Conflict, Identity and Reconciliation in the South Caucasus' in Carolina Rehrmann, Rafael Biermann and Philip Tolliday (ed), *Societies in Transition: The Caucasus and the Balkans between Conflict and Reconciliation* (Vandenhoeck & Ruprecht 2020).

and Israel, and has even called for regime change in Azerbaijan.'[58] Therefore the overall security of Azerbaijan while in confrontation with Iran again strongly depends on good relationship with Russia, which can due to its good relationship with Iran guarantee Azerbaijani sovereignty and territorial integrity. In fact Azerbaijan is surrounded by countries which are not having a perfectly friendly relationship towards it, which is interestingly also true of Armenia, except for Iran, which has an excellent relationship with Armenia being a Christian country, which serves us with very complex geopolitical constellations.

To conclude, all these conflicts in the Caucasus apart from political concerns do not pose any direct threat to the EU since there is no migration crisis here or any irregular movement of people towards the EU. It can be rightly stated that the countries of the Southern Caucasus do not pose threats of irregular migration and there have not been increased requests for asylum in the EU.[59] Such migration-related concerns can be positively seen from the EU but also bring about the need to research how such conflicts are managed that migration does not happen while other similar conflicts in the MENA region produce huge migration waves towards the EU. The migration crisis which the EU is completely helpless to manage for decades also carries with it a possible source of terrorism threat, which is a real problem for its overall security.

4 Human Rights and Democracy

4.1 Human and Minority Rights Aspects

In the NK conflict and in its final agreement, human and minority rights were not prioritized and the previous sharp division lines between the Armenians and Azerbaijanis were maintained. Overall in the NK Republic and the two respective states confronting it over the issue of minorities has been long solved by not having them at all; simply Armenians and Azerbaijanis do not live next to each other and are not practising good neighbourly relations. The treatment of others is completely outside the EU or Western framework of

58 Middle East Institute, 'Azerbaijan's Hoseyniyun: The Prospects and Challenges of a Caucasus Hezbollah' (12 June 2023) <https://www.mei.edu/publications/azerbaijans-hoseyniyun-prospects-and-challenges-caucasus-hezbollah> accessed 25 March 2026.

59 Laure Delcour and Hrant Kostanyan, 'The Internal-External Nexus in the Eastern Partnership: Consequences of the EU's Crisis for the South Caucasus' in Kornely Kakachia, Stefan Meister and Benjamin Fricke (ed), *Geopolitics and Security: A New Strategy for the South Caucasus* (Konrad-Adenauer-Stiftung 2018).

human rights and minority protection. However, neither Russia nor Turkey really have the protection of minorities as their priority in this conflict and the economic cooperation with security concerns were the only priorities. "If Moscow's policies in the Baltic States reveal Russian behaviour at its most subtle, Russian power is at its most naked and abusive in the Transcaucasus.'[60] Russians have divided or at least supported the divisions in the Caucasus a few decades ago and even today they do not see any need and potential to change this situation.

In regard to the cruelty during the war there could be some concerns and also possible war crimes can be investigated, but it is finally not mentioned in the agreement and accordingly not planned at all. Russia is not looking friendly towards the International Criminal Courts after all, and it sees no need for any such court investigating in a post-conflict area under its dominance and control. Still to try to end the conflict and stop mutual accusations there has been an article regarding the exchange of the prisoners of war. 'The Parties shall exchange prisoners of war, hostages and other detained persons, and dead bodies.'[61] While the two states really demonize each other by all possible means and media information, it is also not a priority for Russia to stop such a behaviour after all.

In the sense of human rights, the agreement is not very detailed, but in fact it still does include some concerns regarding refugees and also includes the UNHCR in its implementation. 'Internally displaced persons and refugees shall return to the territory of Nagorno-Karabakh and adjacent areas under the supervision of the United Nations High Commissioner for Refugees.'[62] While there was a possibility that people will return, especially Armenians to the leftover territories of the NK Republic it is now less likely to happen after the recent exodus of Armenians from the NK in 2023. Will Azerbaijan be interested to bring some people back or attract other people to move into these areas by doing some planned development projects? We have explained some of the development-related concerns of the agreement before, but it is still to be seen finally how such passive areas of a post-conflict NK in Azerbaijan can be attractive to settle.

---

60 Sadi Sadiyev Saleh and others, 'South Caucasus and a "New Great Game": The Communication of Competition in Securitised International Relations' (2021) 29 Journal of Contemporary European Studies 282.

61 Statement 2020.

62 Ibid.

4.2 Democratic Potentials in the Agreement

The democratization potentials in the agreement or in the overall conflict over the NK have been off-topic for a long period of time and remained so. While the agreement itself was primarily dealing with military demarcation, it didn't include any requirement to help the parties achieve a democratic and mutually acceptable relationship. 'The peacemaking forces of the Russian Federation will be deployed for five years, a term to be automatically extended for subsequent five-year terms unless either Party notifies about its intention to terminate this clause six months before the expiration of the current term.'[63] Russia did not include the peacekeepers between the sides with an aim to divide them and risk losing the control over this conflict and region altogether. 'They did not leave Moldova, nor did they leave the two separatist entities in Georgia.'[64] The presence of Russian forces is meant to show that they are the masters of the game and the given situation; in fact no change is meant to happen without their knowledge and prior approval. Also if any of the sides would declare that Russian peacekeepers are not needed any longer it would certainly mean that it does not want the Russian involvement any longer and would probably cause a counter effect where Russians would support the other side. Exactly this is what has happened in 2023 as Russian peacekeepers left their positions and let Azerbaijan quickly takeover the entire territory of the NK Republic in a manner of hours.

Since Russians have actively taken part in the conflict and also included their military directly in the peacekeeping process, it was not foreseen that they might want to leave the territory of NK any time soon. While Russia overall maintains the same political framework like Azerbaijan, where a President has more power than the government itself, it is slightly different in Armenia. 'Not only did Russian action warn NATO member states of the risk of further eastward expansion, but it also humiliated a Western-leaning, vocally pro-democratic leader, punishing him with the loss of territory.'[65] Therefore any threats or democracy-like actions are not welcome by Russia as they actually try to include Western institutions and standards, which would limit the

63 Ibid.

64 András Rácz, 'In Russia's Hands: Nagorno-Karabakh after the Ceasefire Agreement' (2021) 8 EU Institute for Security Studies <https://www.iss.europa.eu/sites/default/files/EUISSFiles/Brief_8_2021.pdf> accessed 25 March 2026.

65 Heather Dehaan and Shalala Mammadova, 'War and Sovereignty: Lessons from Putin's War for the South Caucasus*' (2022) 78 KENNAN CABLE <https://www.wilsoncenter.org/publication/kennan-cable-no-78-war-and-sovereignty-lessons-putins-war-south-caucasus> accessed 25 March 2026.

broad working space of local political elites, usually controlled by Russia. In a broader sense of economic development and military cooperation Russia does not want to tolerate changes and hesitations from any of its allies. 'While Russian–Armenian cooperation was formed in a pragmatic manner that led to vassal-driven cooperation.'[66] In some sense the punishing of Armenia has shown that its overall well-being depends on Russia from one side, but also how it can hit hard the countries, which are hesitant regarding the implementation of Russian policies and agendas.

While Armenia wants to lower the Russian influence it is still questionable what support it can get and in specific what it can expect regarding the situation in the NK, in specific after the war and its total control by Azerbaijan. 'Armenia has also regarded the UN as bias due to early Security Council resolutions that stress the importance of territorial integrity.'[67] It is not possible that the wider Western community will support Armenia, although there were prominent examples of that; France did it for example. Also by knowing that Armenia is ultimately implementing the Russian agenda and is being part of the Russian framework in the South Caucasus, more than any other state, did not prevent some states to support it. Also Armenia has a very good relationships with Iran, which would again get fewer democracy-oriented countries support it in regard to any political decision in the NK or broader.

While the overall democratic capacity of Azerbaijan is very limited, its own sovereignty and independence is also limited to some extent due to the presence of some big and influential countries in its vicinity. Such countries like Russia, Turkey and Iran all belong to different economic integrations and military systems as well. 'Today, Azerbaijan is at the nexus of three major integration initiatives – the European Union, the Eurasian Economic Union and recently-established Belt and Road initiative (OBOR) initiative championed by China.'[68] All economic frameworks surrounding Azerbaijan do see it as part of their integration or at least cooperation process, while Azerbaijan only sees the idea of NK once again being reintegrated and under its control. For a long period of time Azerbaijan wanted to distance itself from Russia and it was not until Russia and Turkey came closer, so that Azerbaijan started again prioritizing its good relationship with Russia. Azerbaijan was unable to

66 Andrius Bivainis, 'Multi-Dimensional Assessment of the Second Nagorno-Karabakh War' (2022) 38 Security and Defence Quarterly 51.

67 Carey Cavanaugh, 'OSCE and the Nagorno-Karabakh Peace Process' (2016) 27 Sec & Hum Rts 422.

68 Anar Valiyev, 'Azerbaijan's Policy Toward EU Integration: Unrecognized Strategic Partner' in Kornely Kakachia, Stefan Meister and Benjamin Fricke (ed), *Geopolitics and Security: A New Strategy for the South Caucasus* (Konrad-Adenauer-Stiftung 2018).

advance its case under various forms of talks where the Western states were also included, so it was more than ready to accept any change which would be supported by Russia, but preferred the one coming from Russia and Turkey together. 'But cross-cutting and divergent interests within the Minsk Group suggest that the perceived deadlock relating to this misperceived frozen conflict also generates from the principals' internal co-optations of that soft law process.'[69] Azerbaijan finally did get back its full sovereignty and has considerably received something in return for falling back into Russian arms, which have in fact neither politically nor economically endangered its interests in the Western World for now.

Azerbaijan is still seen as a partner from the Western perspective, only that it will be more likely pressured by Russia in case something does not go as planned in relation to the Russian expansion in Europe. 'The war did not resolve the political status of Nagorno-Karabakh, however, and it upended the long-standing OSCE Minsk Group conflict resolution framework.'[70] When we talk about various organizations and their conflict resolution capacity such as OSCE, UN, EU and others it is necessary to mention their very limited conflict resolution capacity at the moment. As conflicts are not happening just as a free choice of some states or people they are more like pressed from above by an influential country, usually a UN Security Council permanent member state. 'Because international law currently does not establish a positive right of secession and merely tolerates select instances of successful secession, like the Kosovo case, the people of Nagorno-Karabakh do not have the right to secede from Azerbaijan, absent a peaceful negotiation.'[71] Accordingly, Kosovo together with NK represents some of the most notable conflicts, which although frozen are being changed and reshaped recently.

Finally as an Asian country although found in the Caucasus, which for the EU has a special interest, Azerbaijan does not feel like belonging to Europe and is more keen to establish friendly relationships with Turkey and recently with the framework of Turkic nations. 'It does not intend to adopt the EU's fundamental democratic values, nor does it need financial support from the

69 Christopher R. Rossi, 'Nagorno-Karabakh and the Minsk Group: The Imperfect Appeal of Soft Law in an Overlapping Neighborhood' (2017) 52 Texas International Law Journal 45.

70 Cory Welt, 'Azerbaijan and Armenia: The Nagorno-Karabakh Conflict' [2021] Congressional Research Service <https://sgp.fas.org/crs/row/R46651.pdf> accessed 25 March 2025.

71 Milena Sterio, 'Self-Determination and Secession under International Law: Nagorno-Karabakh' (2016) 59 German YB Int'l L 81.

EU due to its rich oil reserves.'[72] This independence also poses a very big challenge for the EU, as an oil-rich country such as Norway, Azerbaijan sees no interest in joining the EU. While Norway is overall a democratic country, it also sees no interest in doing so, and maintains higher human rights and social standards than the EU itself. It is not a surprise to see that Azerbaijan has no interest to implement any democratic standards as expected from the EU, and it is even more interesting to see that it even does not need to do so or is pressured by anyone in this regard. It is still a remaining challenge for the future to see what will happen to the Armenian minority in NK after it has been completely taken over politically and is now under the full control and sovereignty of the Azerbaijani Government.

72 András Rácz, 'War in Nagorno- Karabakh: A Two-Track Strategy for the EU' (2020) 30 DGAP Commentary <https://dgap.org/sites/default/files/article_pdfs/dgap-commentary-2020-30-en.pdf> accessed 25 March 2025.

CHAPTER 14

Afghanistan and Its Post-conflict Agreements

In a timeframe of almost half a century Afghanistan has been through many various influences, which have in fact all had the same aim and ultimately the same pathway of failure as their conclusion. The historic turning point when after Russia, USA and many other international stakeholders altogether have withdrawn with their agenda from Afghanistan China has stepped in, surprisingly or not. China tries to use the same pattern of enforcing its various aims such as political, economic and security-related ones mainly in order to benefit and create a common working pattern with Afghanistan. In the Chinese position[1] and framework of agreements regarding Afghanistan we can see that they focus mostly on security and development-related issues, which are actually the two biggest concerns for both China and Afghanistan together.

The agreements supported by China are coming in various forms and in line with the BRI (Belt and Road Initiative)[2] framework where China requests and asks for support and acknowledgement for its actual development solutions. An example for this is the 17+1 Initiative,[3] which brings together countries with the same development goals in the area of Eastern Europe with countries, which are both EU and non-EU member states equally. Similarly China is trying to group countries in the neighbourhood of Afghanistan to cooperate for their common goals and future overall. Regarding Afghanistan it is noteworthy to outline some agreements in various forms and formats; the first one is a Joint Statement on the Afghan Issue among the Neighbouring Countries of Afghanistan[4] and the second one is The Tunxi Initiative of Afgha-

1 Ministry of Foreign Affairs of the People's Republic of China, 'China's Position on the Afghan Issue' (12 April 2023) <https://www.fmprc.gov.cn/mfa_eng/gjhdq_665435/2675_665437/2676_663356/2677_663358/202304/t20230412_11057785.html> accessed 25 March 2025.

2 Office of the Leading Group for Promoting the Belt and Road Initiative, 'Belt and Road Portal' <https://eng.yidaiyilu.gov.cn/> accessed 25 March 2025.

3 One Belt One Road Europe, 'Greece and the New 17+1 Format' (18 April 2019) <https://www.oboreurope.com/en/greece-171-format/> accessed 25 March 2025.

4 Embassy of the People's Republic of China in the Kingdom of the Netherlands, 'Joint Statement of the Third Foreign Ministers' Meeting Among the Neighboring Countries of Afghanistan' (31 March 2022) <http://nl.china-embassy.gov.cn/eng/zgyw/202203/t20220331_10658230.htm> also accessible on <https://mofa.gov.pk/joint-statement-of-the-third-foreign-ministers-meeting-among-the-neighboring-countries-of-afghanistan> and on <http://lawinfochina.com/display.aspx?id=8253&lib=tax&SearchKeyword=&SearchCKeyword=> accessed 25 March 2025. Further it will be cited as JS 2022.

nistan's Neighboring Countries on Supporting Afghanistan's Economic Reconstruction and Practical Cooperation;[5] both focus on the most burning and vital problems of Afghanistan.

The Joint Statement is a much shorter version of the necessary achievements regarding Afghanistan incorporating the interests of China together with its neighbouring countries and also Afghanistan, while The Tunxi Initiative is a broader and more technical agreement. Regarding our research we will deal with the Joint Statement on the Afghan Issue among the Neighbouring Countries of Afghanistan (Joint Statement) as it is clearer and its headlines are leading us through the agenda of the most important developments, which need to be achieved altogether. To make any kind of help viable there is a need to regulate initial goals. The Tunxi Initiative is rich in content and will play an important role in promoting Afghanistan's peace, reconstruction, stability and development in the future.[6] It is interesting to note that even though the Western or US representatives were not taking part in concluding these agreements, their interests can be definitely found and covered in some aspects to a more or less satisfactory level. 'These two documents reflect the common political position of neighboring countries, and decide to provide material support for Afghanistan in key areas such as humanitarian assistance, interconnectivity, economy and trade, agricultural development, energy and power, and capacity building.'[7] It is noteworthy to mention that all the agreements concerning Afghanistan serve and mention the most important requirements, which come mainly from China. Interestingly all of its neighbours and other stakeholders as well can find an interest and benefit in the given agenda prescribed by these agreements.

What makes these agreements in particular interesting is the actual lack of Afghanistan's international recognition, or better to say its present Taliban

5 Ministry of Foreign Affairs of the People's Republic of China, 'The Tunxi Initiative of the Neighboring Countries of Afghanistan on Supporting Economic Reconstruction in and Practical Cooperation with Afghanistan' (1 April 2022) <https://www.fmprc.gov.cn/mfa_eng/gjhdq_665435/2675_665437/2676_663356/2677_663358/202204/t20220401_10662024.html> also available on <https://lawinfochina.com/display.aspx?id=8251&lib=tax&SearchKeyword=&SearchCKeyword=> accessed 25 March 2026. Further it will be cited as TUNXI 2022.

6 Ministry of Foreign Affairs of the People's Republic of China, 'Wang Yi Introduces the Important Consensus and Achievements of the Series of Meetings on the Afghan Issue' (1 April 2022) <https://www.fmprc.gov.cn/mfa_eng/gjhdq_665435/2675_665437/2676_663356/2678_663360/202204/t20220401_10663017.html> accessed 25 March 2026.

7 Ibid.

Government's recognition. 'On Afghanistan's path of returning to the mainstream international community and resume peaceful development and good neighborly relations, Tunxi is undoubtedly an important stop.'[8] Tunxi is in this case the name of the city where both the Joint statement and the Tunxi Agreements were made. Such agreements do not harm anyone and clearly serve as a tool to achieve future common goals without in fact agreeing in any form to the possible and potential human rights violations by the Taliban Government. Once again we need to outline that in fact the recognition of Afghanistan is not a priority for anyone at the moment but dealing with its humanitarian issues is. In such informal law agreements where a wide and broad number of countries agree we see the best solution in such a complex political and post-conflict context, where the conflict prevention is still a bigger stake than to achieve any kind of other political goals.

The Joint Statement turns to many different issues. It has 'Reaffirmed respect for the independence, sovereignty, territorial integrity and national unity of Afghanistan, support for the Afghan people in independently deciding the future of their country, and support for the basic principle of "Afghan-led and Afghan-owned".'[9] The ownership of the conflict or better to say this post-conflict constellation is transferred by China[10] to Afghanistan and again at this moment to its Taliban Government. Nothing that is not in their best interest is not agreed nor requested, therefore serving as a perfect tool to step by step achieve their common goals by the means of mutual development and conflict resolution. It is still a matter of the future to see how and to what extent the ideas from these agreements can be satisfied, but certainly the biggest achievement of these norms and requirements is that not a single country has or could have a negative comment to what has been agreed. Spoilers of any kind or form by trying to influence and change such agreements are not very likely to succeed or at least manage to change and rearrange the agreed terms, which are supported by so many neighbouring countries and ultimately led by China.

---

8 Lan Jianxue, 'Tunxi Foreign Ministers' Meeting May Kick off a New Journey for Afghanistan' (6 April 2022) <https://www.ciis.org.cn/english/COMMENTARIES/202204/t20220406_8500.html> accessed 25 March 2026.

9 Ibid.

10 Embassy of the People's Republic of China in the Islamic Republic of Afghanistan, 'China Plays an Active and Constructive Role in Afghan Peace and Reconciliation Process' (30 January 2021) <https://af.china-embassy.gov.cn/sgxw/202101/t20210131_1114515.htm> accessed 25 March 2026.

1 Development-Related Aspects

1.1 Trade Perspectives

The biggest turning point in the Afghan development after the shocking retake of the country by the Taliban is the almost unlimited support it gains from China. However, it does not come as a surprise, knowing that China was aiming to get access to some, or maybe all possible, Afghan resources which could be easily extracted and exported to China. Therefore China uses pretty much the same pattern as everywhere else, which has been proven to be shock resistant, namely the various Belt and Road Initiative (BRI)[11] legal mechanisms aimed as development tools. 'Many BRI legal issues fall outside the scope of WTO rules, FTAs, and BITs.'[12] The BRI is more like an idea and not a single project, it can differ from state to state and from situation to situation. 'All parties pledge to support Afghanistan's economic reconstruction in areas such as humanitarian assistance, connectivity, economy and trade, agriculture, energy and capacity building.'[13] It is not new that a powerful state wants to get resources from a country, as it was the case also earlier in Afghanistan or anywhere else on the globe during the colonial and post-colonial era as well.

Before any kind of extraction or transportation can happen there is a need to build the necessary infrastructure, or at least secure the available ones. The Chinese investors have been active in investing into Afghanistan even before. 'It is instructive that China's two biggest investments in the country so far are the Metallurgical Corporation of China's $3 billion investment in the Aynak copper field and the China National Petroleum Corporation's investment in the Amu Darya oil project have stalled, barely effectively running, let alone turning a profit.'[14] The Chinese hunger for resources can be most effectively satisfied from its neighbourhood also with the lowest possible cost. However, China wants to offer something in exchange, whereas it is hard to find the just compensation for a country where money for example means nothing and hunger threatens the citizens, among many other actual problems. 'China

---

11 Office of the Leading Group for Promoting the Belt and Road Initiative, 'Belt and Road Portal' <https://eng.yidaiyilu.gov.cn/> accessed 25 March 2026.

12 Heng Wang, 'The Belt and Road Initiative Agreements: Characteristics, Rationale, and Challenges' (2021) 20 World Trade Review 282.

13 TUNXI 2022.

14 Feng Zhang, 'China's New Engagement with Afghanistan after the Withdrawal' (2022) 2 LSE Public Policy Review 10.

will grant zero tariff treatment to 98 percent of the tariff lines of the Afghan products exported to China, and is willing to import more quality specialty products from Afghanistan.'[15] High quality products are being demanded by China and other markets as well; cheap products can be sourced out easier elsewhere whereas some specific products rise in both demand and final sales price.

In countries like Afghanistan production costs are very low and the regulations of any kind are completely absent; here it does not come as a surprise that some branches of agriculture like opium production increase for many years. 'Afghan opium production appears to have surged since 2016, partly due to the use of a new genetically modified poppy seed originating in China, where some opium is farmed legally for pharmaceutical purposes (China is one of the world's largest opiate consumers).'[16] This part of the Afghan economy concerns China more than any other country and presents both an economical and security challenge. China is not alone in such concerns; it hits harshly even countries being further located geographically but definitely the ones in its neighbourhood. 'Iran and Russia, however, have common interests on a number of important issues, ranging from stabilizing Afghanistan to combatting drug trafficking.'[17] China is not alone in these security and drug smuggling concerns and it can count also on its biggest regional (global)ally, The Russian Federation. 'It is also worth noting that, despite a difficult common history, Afghan elites mostly view Russia favourably, especially in regard to business cooperation.'[18] Even if the Afghan economy is maybe not having a prominent share in the global economy it does have its value for neighbouring

15 Ministry of Foreign Affairs of the People's Republic of China, 'Wang Yi Meets with Acting Foreign Minister of the Afghan Interim Government Amir Khan Muttaqi' (29 July 2022) <https://www.fmprc.gov.cn/mfa_eng/gjhdq_665435/2675_665437/2676_663356/2678_663360/202207/t20220729_10730548.html> accessed 25 March 2026.

16 Angela Stanzel, 'Fear and Loathing on the New Silk Road: Chinese Security in Afghanistan and Beyond' [2018] European Council on Foreign Relations <https://ecfr.eu/wp-content/uploads/ECFR-264-Chinese_Security_in_Afghanistan_2.pdf> accessed 25 March 2026.

17 Dmitri Trenin, Oleg Kulakov, Alexey Malashenko and Petr Topychkanov, 'A Russian Strategy for Afghanistan After the Coalition Troop Withdrawal' [2014] Carnegie Moscow Center <https://carnegieendowment.org/files/CMC_Article_Afganistan_Eng14.pdf> accessed 25 March 2026.

18 Józef Lang, 'Afghanistan: The View from Russia' (2014) 10 European Union Institute for Security Studies <https://www.files.ethz.ch/isn/182959/Alert_10-Afghanistan_view_from_Russia.pdf> accessed 25 March 2026.

countries, which are keen to develop it further and thus lower the instability from both inside and outside the country. 'The Afghan problem is also important for Russia's energy and hydrocarbon strategy in Eurasia, which is primarily about Russia's access to region's energy resources and control over the trade, transportation, and communication corridors.'[19] Still the most important aspect of trade in this region is its security dimension and in this regard Afghanistan is a key stakeholder.

For Russia the Afghan territory is vital for accessing Pakistan and more importantly India where Russia has even more interests. It has already been stressed that a peaceful, stable and prosperous Afghanistan serves the common interests of regional countries and Afghanistan, and it has expressed its readiness to jointly play a constructive role to this end.[20] However, there is an obvious need to secure the link from Afghanistan towards Europe, as China has it already elaborated in its BRI initiative. 'In the early 1990s, Afghanistan discussed possible natural gas supply arrangements with Hungary, then-Czechoslovakia, and several Western European countries, but these talks never progressed further.'[21] Coping with the imminent challenges regarding energy security, such ideas and even the more impossible ones are being evoked by the EU and its rising energy demands and also the possible future shortages.

1.2 Investment Possibilities

Investments in a post-conflict society are always problematic and considering the specific situation in Afghanistan, where human rights and democracy standards are very distant it is an even bigger challenge for any enterprise or multinational company. The regular standard requirements for development, which EU requires for investments, are not present in Afghanistan today. It is therefore not likely possible that any serious investment coming from the Western world can reach it in a normal and usual form as before. Still exceptions are possible and sometimes need to be made; the EU must switch from viewing Afghanistan solely as an intractable security challenge and focus

19 Kaneshko Sangar, 'Afghanistan's Significance for Russia in the 21st Century: Interests, Perceptions and Perspectives' (2016) 12 Politics in Central Europe 59.

20 JS 2022.

21 Nadeem Malik, 'Overview and Prospects for Energy Resources in Afghanistan: Measures for Improvement and Sustainable Development' (2009) 35 J Energy & Dev 141.

instead on unlocking the country's still-untapped potential as a hub for regional connectivity and a catalyst for region-wide economic growth and transformation. While EU standards are distant and also considering the geographical distance coming in combination with the political changes in the Afghan governance, there is truly very little to expect from possible EU investments.

Nevertheless there is China and it is wishing to continue its somewhat developed framework of investing in Afghanistan. 'Within the BRI framework, China will help Afghanistan to fully tap its geographic advantage as the heart of Asia and achieve economic self-sufficiency.'[22] Obviously no investments are happening in any country without a prior political decision to secure them in a matter of stabilizing the legal framework in which foreign investors can work and develop. In the Joint Statement parties expressed support for Afghanistan's efforts towards self-generated development and undertook to support the economic recovery of Afghanistan at both bilateral and multilateral levels. They have agreed to further and strengthen exchanges and cooperation with Afghanistan in such fields as trade and economy, energy, agriculture, finance, connectivity and infrastructure, to help Afghanistan build capacity for its self-generated development.[23] Since development can't be achieved without political stability it is necessary to have some basic cornerstones, which are permanently lacking in a framework of this post-conflict situation.

There should be some kind of legal document, which could be evoked in situations where enforcement mechanism fails or potentially could fail, just as there are the recent documents agreed for Afghanistan under its Chinese supervision. In the case of China the legal component is extremely flexible and at this moment when no stable Afghan government exists China actively encourages Chinese enterprises to invest in Afghanistan.[24] The almost unconditional support China gets from the Taliban officials is an answer to the present challenges, which are of course not about investments at all, but more about satisfying basic human needs in which China can offer instant help. The

22 Wang Yu, 'Ambassador Wang Yu published an article in Afghan media entitled "A Global Family: Building a China-Afghanistan Community with a Shared Future."' (2 October 2020) <https://af.china-embassy.gov.cn/sgxw/202010/t20201003_1114349.htm> accessed 25 March 2026.

23 JS 2022.

24 Yan Wei, 'The Cooperation Between China and Afghanistan Under the "Belt and Road Initiative"' (2018) 6 International Relations and Diplomacy 359.

Taliban government has concluded that Chinese enterprises are welcome[25] to invest, hoping that this opportunity to tap on its natural resources would secure support for other things as well. 'Chinese telecom giants, ZTE and Huawei, have been operating in Afghanistan since the early 2000s.'[26] Interestingly they were operating in the framework established and maintained by the USA and while the troublesome USA-Huawei relationship is now visible everywhere, in the case of Afghanistan it looks that Huawei remains.

Another aspect in which China has a counter partner is the oil and gas industry, as this area is dominated by Russia in the wider region of Asia. 'China National Petroleum Corporation (CNPC) was the first foreign oil company to invest in Afghanistan energy field, and it cooperated with Watan Oil & Gas of Afghanistan to explore the oil fields in northern Afghanistan.'[27] Even if Russia loses control over this industry it is still better than to let it be managed by the USA, in the end. The need to link Afghanistan to the global market is an expensive challenge but still looks possible in the mind of the Chinese government. At the moment it looks more viable to connect Afghanistan to China indirectly. 'Pakistan is the only country that can facilitate other Chinese objectives as well, such as the implementation of the BRI and consequent resource extraction from Afghanistan.'[28] If the energy capacity in all its richness gets somewhat extracted in Afghanistan it can in that case also compete with its Northern neighbours in satisfying the rising demands for energy of its Southern neighbours, mainly Pakistan and India but also China. It is hard to imagine that China can lead a green energy development in post-conflict countries such as Azerbaijan or Afghanistan, but the possibilities and demands definitely serve as an encouraging factor to do so.

---

25 Ministry of Foreign Affairs of the People's Republic of China, 'Wang Yi Holds Talks with Acting Deputy Prime Minister of Afghan Interim Government Mullah Abdul Ghani Baradar' (24 March 2022) <https://www.fmprc.gov.cn/mfa_eng/gjhdq_665435/2675_665437/2676_663356/2678_663360/202203/t20220325_10655539.html> accessed 25 March 2026.

26 Claudia Chia, Kunthavi Kalachelvam and Zheng Haiqi, 'Exploring China's Afghanistan Policy' (2021) 677 ISAS Insights <https://www.isas.nus.edu.sg/wp-content/uploads/2021/06/677.pdf> accessed 25 March 2026.

27 Yan Wei, 'The Cooperation Between China and Afghanistan Under the "Belt and Road Initiative"' (2018) 6 International Relations and Diplomacy 359.

28 Vinay Kaura, 'The Pakistan Factor in China's Afghanistan Policy: Emerging Regional Faultlines Amid US Withdrawal' [2021] The Middle East Institute <https://mei.edu/publication/pakistan-factor-chinas-afghanistan-policy-emerging-regional-faultlines-amid-us/> accessed 25 March 2026.

In the case of China the list of possibilities grows and targets some different fields of raw materials extraction, which are hugely demanded. In this case of lithium extraction the actual unregulated setting for mining in Afghanistan serves as a beneficial condition for investors while it also does not limit the access to sites by various environment protecting organizations. 'In theory, Afghanistan contains some $1 trillion worth of minerals, rare metals, oil, gas, precious stones, and other extractable resources.'[29] Such endless opportunities to extract resources and the limited regulations make Afghanistan an almost perfect heaven for investments, which is now in particular used by Chinese investors.

As one of the biggest challenges, and probably not the only one China might face, is the still unsafe and terrorism-threatened Afghan society where the Taliban are just stakeholders in the conflict. 'Investments are still risky because the Taliban faces their own security challenges by competing extremist organisations.'[30] When it comes to security challenges the Taliban are equally helpless as their Chinese allies in Xinjiang province and they both desperately need the help of Russia if not even the USA who was the master of the security game in Afghanistan before. Investments and security concerns go hand in hand and pose the most important challenge for developing post-conflict societies, not just in Afghanistan but to the same extent in Kosovo and Nagorno-Karabakh as well.

1.3 Infrastructure Development Potentials

As it was outlined many times earlier, infrastructure is the key for development of every society, be it developed, post-colonial or even post-conflict. 'Therefore regarding Afghanistan parties have reaffirmed commitment to deepen cooperation within such frameworks as the Belt and Road Initiative, as well as regional cooperation organizations, and to include Afghanistan in the regional connectivity, energy and transport networks, economic and trade systems, in order to help Afghanistan unleash its geographical advantages and economic

29 Vanda Felbab-Brown, 'A bri(dge) too far: The Unfulfilled promise and limitations of China's Involvement in Afghanistan' [2020] Global China: Regional influence and strategy <https://www.brookings.edu/wp-content/uploads/2020/06/FP_20200615_china_afghanistan_felbab_brown.pdf> accessed 25 March 2026.

30 Maryam Jami, Alamuddin Rizwan and Rajab Taieb, 'Sino–Afghan Security Relations beyond 2021' [2021] Friedrich Ebert-Stiftung (FES) Afghanistan and Institute of War and Peace Studies <https://library.fes.de/pdf-files/bueros/kabul/18638.pdf> accessed 25 March 2026.

potential.'[31] In colonial times the infrastructure development was closely connected to the extraction and transportation of resources and goods. 'China's Belt and Road Initiative today amounts to a $1 trillion chain of infrastructure development projects (or their promise) in 70 countries.'[32] Such an investment today is possible when we acknowledge its aim, which is again the transportation of goods from China and the necessary resources back to China.

Maybe Afghanistan is not the biggest market and opportunity for Chinese goods but certainly its resources are, therefore a compromise has been made and infrastructure developments will be introduced for a common goal and mutual benefit. 'BRI primary agreements largely emphasize project development, in contrast with many existing soft law instruments (like those in international financial law) that promote rule development.'[33] While the lack of rules and development potentials are obvious with the Taliban takeover it does not present an obstacle to the Chinese, who need for investing only a willing and cooperative government. Maybe the present cooperation potential is not crucial but with BRI agreements their future cooperation potential is also ensured. 'First, in 2008, the Chinese iron and steel corporation Metallurgical Group and Jiangxi Copper pledged to invest approximately US$4 billion to acquire 100 percent of the rights in the Afghan field Aynak, the second largest undeveloped copper deposit in the world.'[34] Interestingly since the old Silk Road era Afghanistan was not really considered as a crossroads country. 'In fact, Afghanistan is bypassed by two corridors of the BRI to its south and north, respectively: the China-Pakistan Economic Corridor and the China-Central Asia-West Asia economic corridor, which runs through the five Central Asian republics as well as Iran and Turkey.'[35] China has satisfied its needs for transport routes in the region but there is also Russia with its needs; in this regard it wants to connect with India, which is its trade and also main security partner in the Southern Asia region.

---

31 JS 2022.

32 Vanda Felbab-Brown, 'A bri(dge) too far: The Unfulfilled promise and limitations of China's Involvement in Afghanistan' [2020] Global China: Regional influence and strategy <https://www.brookings.edu/wp-content/uploads/2020/06/FP_20200615_china_afghanistan_felbab_brown.pdf> accessed 25 March 2026.

33 Heng Wang, 'The Belt and Road Initiative Agreements: Characteristics, Rationale, and Challenges' (2021) 20 World Trade Review 282.

34 Akram Umarov, 'Assessing China's New Policy in Afghanistan' (2017) 4 Central Asian Affairs 384.

35 Feng Zhang, 'China's New Engagement with Afghanistan after the Withdrawal' (2022) 2 LSE Public Policy Review 10.

The various roads and infrastructure developments are not just a win-win situation but more a triple win considering the biggest regional stakeholders. Afghanistan is willing to give play to its unique regional interconnectivity[36] as the Taliban officials have outlined it and therefore serve as a security guarantor for such investments and projects. 'Specifically, the Chinese government, while facing its own serious domestic poverty challenges and great needs in infrastructure, health care, and education, is willing to provide financial support that is disproportionate to its own level of economic development and relative to the contribution made by the industrialized countries.'[37] The regional disparities are probably more obvious in China than in some Western democracies and some of its regions are certainly more developed than many Western ones. There is another very important aspect of development and that is the telecommunications, where China is not just leading but is in a position to control the development of many societies in this regard globally. Telecommunication and the IT sector can offer much in return for some modest developments. At this time it is hard to predict how far the Afghan economy can reach with such developments, but certainly there is a huge demand for it as everywhere else. As outlined earlier, Huawei is a game changer on a global level so why it wouldn't be able to influence and into some extent help Afghanistan advance.

Another resource-related investment in Afghanistan, which now makes us turn from the US perspective more to the EU-Russia one, is definitely energy. Russia does not border Afghanistan but controls or at least does everything to control the energy sources in its neighbourhood accordingly. 'Russia is less relevant to the Afghan economy than are the Central Asian states, three of which supply half of Afghanistan's electricity, with the other half coming from Iran.'[38] Iran itself being under Western sanctions for a much longer period of time than Russia is now more than eager to cooperate with everyone. Specifically in the Russia–Chinese block it can help bridge its harsh international situation and help it economically but also in relation to its security

36 Xinhua, 'China, Afghanistan Pledge Orderly, Mutually Beneficial Cooperation' (25 March 2022) <http://english.www.gov.cn/statecouncil/wangyi/202203/25/content_WS623d1a7fc6d02e533532843b.html> accessed 25 March 2026.

37 Wei Liang, 'China's Soft Power in Africa: Is Economic Power Sufficient?' (2012) 36 Asian Perspective 667.

38 Ekaterina Stepanova, 'Russia's Approach to Afghanistan Following the Taliban Takeover' (2021) 724 PONARS Eurasia Policy Memo <https://www.ponarseurasia.org/wp-content/uploads/2021/11/Pepm724_Stepanova_Nov2021.pdf> accessed 25 March 2026.

concerns. 'An oil and gas pipeline from Iran passing through Afghanistan, Pakistan and into China has also been discussed.'[39] This is another multi-party opportunity where again the Asian neighbours together with Afghanistan can benefit and again stay completely out of the common US and EU interests in this important moment of rebuilding the Afghan infrastructure and economy.

1.4 Potentials for Future Development

Considering the underdevelopment of Afghanistan and compared to its abundant development potentials and opportunities, a balance is necessary to be achieved. It is also unknown, unclear and completely not understandable how the resources of Afghanistan have not until now been targeted in such a structural manner as the Chinese did it recently. 'Wang Yi said, on the premise of respecting Afghanistan's sovereignty, China is ready to carry out mutually beneficial cooperation with Afghanistan in an orderly manner, so as to help Afghanistan turn its resource advantage into a development advantage.'[40] From such an underdeveloped situation it can be clearly outlined that Afghanistan will face some advances with this recent Chinese involvement. In this regard, parties have urged the countries mainly responsible for the current predicament in Afghanistan to earnestly fulfil commitments on the economic recovery and future development of Afghanistan.[41] Now as always and in every situation before we pose the question of how in specific and at what costs, towards its environment primarily and what guarantees can the Chinese provide regarding any possible Afghani request? 'BRI primary agreements can be regarded as soft law because they provide for certain quasilegal obligations or law-like promises.'[42] It is necessary to understand the BRI in its wider framework, which will not be any different in the case of Afghanistan. However, such informal law-like promises are the ones without any kind of

---

39 Loro Horta, 'US Afghan Withdrawal: Enter China and Taliban?' (2021) 120 RSIS Commentary <https://rsis.edu.sg/wp-content/uploads/2021/08/CO21120.pdf> accessed 25 March 2026.

40 Ministry of Foreign Affairs of the People's Republic of China, 'Wang Yi Holds Talks with Acting Deputy Prime Minister of Afghan Interim Government Mullah Abdul Ghani Baradar' (24 March 2022) <https://www.fmprc.gov.cn/mfa_eng/gjhdq_665435/2675_665437/2676_663356/2678_663360/202203/t20220325_10655539.html> accessed 25 March 2026.

41 JS 2022.

42 Heng Wang, 'The Belt and Road Initiative Agreements: Characteristics, Rationale, and Challenges' (2021) 20 World Trade Review 282.

enforcement mechanism or a possibility to be requested, especially when they are coming from a UNSC permanent member state.

China is now not an any different UNSC permanent member state than its other four counterparts, although its post-conflict engagement is very new, while it aims to achieve pretty much the same goals using unenforceable informal and soft law like mechanisms overall. 'BRI primary agreements currently draw on soft law but adopt a focus on project development over rule development, unlike under existing soft law.'[43] Another important factor and difference in the Chinese standpoints is its tolerance towards the lack of domestic law enforcement, whereas as explained it does request the necessary political guarantees from the local political elites. Interestingly in the Afghani scenario the counteroffer from the Chinese towards the Taliban is their recognition, which might be of a historic importance and as such a key determinant in future activities of overthrowing governments, especially the West-supported ones. So if the Chinese agenda in Afghanistan succeeds it can be a very strong and hard building stone in the Asian system of regional interconnectedness. 'Primary agreements not only have legal implications but could also send political signals to domestic actors that the BRI is acceptable in host states, and thus advance a 'hardening' of the arrangements through secondary agreements.'[44] It is therefore not just the hardening that matters but the wider application of similar mechanisms, which from the economic perspective does not harm at all but poses a very strong security challenge.

It is a task for the future to see whether and how the Chinese will be able to eliminate some security challenges and having in mind the inability to fully cope and solve their local security threats and the notorious Uyghur minority issue. One solution offered and experimented by the Chinese is the famous system of citizens' control using sophisticated mechanisms, and in this great picture a key role is given to technology once again. Huawei and its further plans to pursue linkage with Afghanistan and Central Asia is key to the attempt of the Chinese dominance in the field of technology, which has also provoked the EU and US restrictions, respectively. China does not look like stopping here fully but only limiting its application in some specific jurisdictions. How will China manage to deal with various states and jurisdiction on the BRI road is still unknown, and the definitely very obvious lack of competence in intercultural communication brings it into a slightly uncomfortable situation. In the end, who will use whom and which party will be the first to

43 Ibid.
44 Ibid.

divert from the very soft law like BRI agreements, where remedies can again come back as a boomerang and pose a security threat in the end is not known. 'This might be rooted in the lack of cooperation experience between China and Afghanistan and the lack of a wide range of Afghan experts among the Chinese academic and policy community.'[45] Once an Agreement is signed, which is a very easy step, the second step is its implementation where the array of challenges is unlimited.

Considering the hardships of the Chinese in dealing with the cultural minority on their East makes another argument towards the request of a special attitude and behaviour in this regard. 'China and Russia don't have the soft power of a United States that can draw in hundreds of thousands of international students each year to enrol at its top-rated universities.'[46] Accordingly the list of challenges on the path of achieving development is very long. The already present lack of enforcement mechanisms is now coming together with the capacity to really deal with them in real life and the already persisting idea of communities who want to cooperate with both China and Russia but does not really want to fall under their influence or their respective way of life. It is probably most evident in the Afghani understanding of future where actually the youth plans its life according to EU standards and by risking their lives try to reach to the EU and form the already decades-long migration routes. 'Perhaps Afghanistan illustrates best the wrong path to dynamic growth and the consequences of it.'[47] It is another phenomena of Afghanistan that even the Syrian war has not produced such a problematic country and refugee crisis where it is not possible to either control or limit its consequences.

45 Akram Umarov, 'Assessing China's New Policy in Afghanistan' (2017) 4 Central Asian Affairs 384.

46 Mathew Burrows and Robert A. Manning, 'Kissinger's Nightmare: How an Inverted US-China-Russia May Be Game-Changer' (2015) 33 Valdai Papers <https://valdaiclub.com/files/11410/> accessed 25 March 2026.

47 Graciana del Castillo, 'Economic Reconstruction and Reforms in Post-Conflict Countries' in Arnim Langer and Graham K. Brown (ed), *Building Sustainable Peace: Timing and Sequencing of Post-Conflict Reconstruction and Peacebuilding* (Oxford University Press 2016).

2 Administration-Related Aspects of the Agreements

2.1 Relevant Challenges in General

In the administrative sense and regarding Afghanistan not much has been discussed seriously now or earlier apart from the Afghan claims to territories across the Durand Line, the contested Afghan–Pakistani border.[48] Also its situation of having minorities belonging to nations, which have their independent states on the North makes it a real challenge and a possible autonomy demand in the future. Still its partition could pose not just a local threat but a regional one including the Chinese problem of Uyghur separatism; therefore the Chinese have no interest in any changes, whatsoever. Although Afghanistan is often pictured as a prize in the 'great game' of nations,[49] the very tribal and nationally mixed composition of inhabitants makes it impossible for one force to dominate without any further foreign influence. Obviously now and also as it was the case earlier there is a need to regulate the most basic standards and requirements on what both the Afghanis and their neighbours can count on.

There have been prior attempts in the form of a Bonn process to approach the problem of administering Afghanistan, but since both the local government and its international supporter at that time, USA, have lost influence, such agreements can't produce any future standards. 'The formal Bonn process, however, was increasingly compromised over the course of its implementation as the informal sources of power and conflict in the country began to reassert themselves.'[50] Probably one of the biggest weaknesses of the Bonn Agreement was that not all the parties having a stake in the Afghan conflict were properly represented, which now with the Chinese involvement is not the case. The previous government, when considering its security concerns was never independent in fact and it was absolutely dependent on US forces regarding its security, which accordingly collapsed after their withdrawal. 'Before the Taliban took over, public spending was about 75 per cent financed by foreign donors; without such assistance, the vast majority of civil servants

48 Diana Janse, 'Russian Interests in Afghanistan' (2021) 1 SCEEUS Reports <https://www.ui.se/globalassets/ui.se-eng/publications/sceeus/russian-interests-in-afghanistan-sceeus-report-no1-2021.pdf> accessed 25 March 2026.

49 James Dobbins, Andrew Radin and Laurel E. Miller, 'Engage, Isolate, or Oppose: American Policy Toward the Islamic Emirate of Afghanistan' [2022] RAND Corporation <https://www.rand.org/pubs/perspectives/PEA1540-1.html> accessed 25 March 2026.

50 Naazneen H. Barma, *The Peacebuilding Puzzle: Political Order in Post-Conflict States* (Cambridge University Press 2017).

are not being paid.'[51] Now as this 'artificial' system of governance has failed it is to be seen how the new Taliban government can re-establish itself, at this time using a different form of governance than the one it was practising two decades ago.

The primary goal of the Chinese mainly and other countries as well is to maximally lower the security threat coming from Afghanistan, and at this time not just primarily from the Taliban themselves. 'Noted commitments and pledges made by Afghanistan to the international community that the territory of Afghanistan will not pose any threats to the neighboring countries and no place will be given to terrorist groups on the Afghan territory.'[52] In order to distract the Taliban from terrorism and help them fight other groups, which are not ready for a compromise, the Chinese are offering the best they can do, economic incentives. 'By promoting One Belt, One Road, the new generation of Chinese leaders is thus conceivably striving to implement some sort of a new Marshall Plan in Eurasia and to create a project similar to the Euro-Atlantic system on the Asian continent – but under Beijing's leadership.'[53] As the EU can influence and achieve political changes using economic tools the Chinese are convinced and also experienced enough to do the same.

Considering the very modest demands in Afghanistan and the low cost of resources for the Chinese this looks like a very viable solution, especially that by incorporating Afghanistan they benefit tremendously themselves as well. 'Afghanistan is ready to give play to its unique geographical advantages, participate in Belt and Road cooperation to a greater extent, and serve as a bridge for regional interconnectivity.'[54] This opportunity was not excluded in the previous decades, but now with the unprecedented Chinese expansion this idea is becoming a reality. If the Chinese are able to give a better offer to countries in Eastern Europe than the EU itself it is possible to repeat the same pattern in Afghanistan, but in this case they will have no political pressure at all.

---

51 International Crisis Group, 'Thinking Through the Dilemmas of Aid to Afghanistan' [2021] Watch List 2021 for the EU <https://icg-prod.s3.amazonaws.com/afghanistan.pdf> accessed 25 March 2026.

52 JS 2022.

53 Akram Umarov, 'Assessing China's New Policy in Afghanistan' (2017) 4 Central Asian Affairs 384.

54 Ministry of Foreign Affairs of the People's Republic of China, 'Wang Yi Holds Talks with Acting Deputy Prime Minister of Afghan Interim Government Mullah Abdul Ghani Baradar' (24 March 2022) <https://www.fmprc.gov.cn/mfa_eng/gjhdq_665435/2675_665437/2676_663356/2678_663360/202203/t20220325_10655539.html> accessed 25 March 2026.

2.2 Autonomy Concerns

The capacity-building efforts in Afghanistan are a very complex issue and the whole country can be seen as an ever-evolving system in a more and more turbulent world. There is a general comment on foreign involvement into post-conflict societies and the question posed is when does a country exit the stage of supervision and enter the stage of independence? 'Moreover, the Afghan government did not have the capacity necessary to absorb large inflows of aid – much of the money went to financing international consultants, who were not focused on transferring skills to their few Afghan counterparts and hence did not contribute to long-term capacity-building in the Afghan government.'[55] It is obvious that not just Kosovo, Nagorno-Karabakh, Afghanistan and many other similar countries are in a limbo; certainly there is a need to overall get involved in a post-conflict state building on a different and much more serious level.

The question of how to do post-conflict development or better to say how not to do it can be seen on the case of Afghanistan; the US involvement has lastly caused more harm than advanced the whole society as it is. As a last shot in Afghanistan and in order to pacify the demands regarding the involvement in Afghanistan, the USA has frozen the Afghani government assets, for what the Taliban and some foreign leaders have urged the United States to release those assets, which total around $7 billion.[56] It has come as a punishment for ordinary citizens and not the Taliban Government in general; also right now it is hard to imagine how and why to punish the Taliban once they are more than ready to cooperate with many, if not everyone. 'The UN Security Council has also recently omitted the word 'Taliban' from its statements regarding terrorist groups in Afghanistan.'[57] Further when it comes to China the Taliban are one of their key partners to fight terrorism equally inside Afghanistan and outside on its borders. China is in this case more concerned about the terrorist activities outside Afghanistan namely the East Turkestan Islamic Movement" (ETIM), an international terrorist organization designated by the UN Security Council, which not only poses a real threat to China's national security and

55 Naazneen H. Barma, *The Peacebuilding Puzzle: Political Order in Post-Conflict States* (Cambridge University Press 2017).

56 Clayton Thomas, 'Afghanistan: Background and U.S. Policy in Brief' [2022] Congressional Research Service <https://sgp.fas.org/crs/row/R45122.pdf> accessed 25 March 2026.

57 Ayesha Malik, 'The Islamic Emirate of Afghanistan and the Recognition of Governments under International Law' [2021] Research Society of International Law <https://rsilpak.org/wp-content/uploads/2021/10/afghanistan-taliban-recognition_rsil.pdf> accessed 25 March 2026.

territorial integrity, but also jeopardizes the domestic stability and long-term stability and security in Afghanistan.[58] In this regard China and other governments have agreed about the terrorist concern in Afghanistan in the following agenda. 'Expressed readiness to conduct counter-terrorism and security cooperation with Afghanistan to help it build counter-terrorism capacity.'[59] It is coming as a turning point where the former enemies are trying to cooperate with each other; but it also comes as a challenge and poses a real threat that some hard core terrorists will not be willing to pacify and will continue with their activities.

The remaining question for the future is to see how the Taliban will cope with such a challenge to have other organizations taking over their activities and ultimately how they will treat the pressure exercised on them and their governance activities. It is hard to expect and believe that the Taliban have the capacity to become the regional guarantor of security, but the gains they are facing are bigger and better than ever. Their autonomous rule can be legitimized and to some extent recognized by foreign governments in the future.

2.3 Prospects for Democracy

When it comes to state building, recognition and democracy it is hard to get and bring out some bright examples from the case of Afghanistan. 'Unfortunately, there is a dramatic discrepancy between what the international community has designed for Afghanistan and what is actually happening there.'[60] Overall it was a big challenge and also a big failure of the international community in its engagement. There is obviously a need to look for alternatives and the Chinese approach is definitely a prosperous one, if not the only alternative at the moment. Once again, we look at the post-conflict state building and whether there must be democracy and to what extent in such a post-conflict society. 'China hopes that Afghanistan will firmly and resolutely fulfill this commitment, which is necessary for Afghanistan to establish a positive image

58 Ministry of Foreign Affairs of the People's Republic of China, 'Wang Yi Meets with Acting Deputy Prime Minister of Afghan Taliban's Interim Government Mullah Abdul Ghani Baradar' (26 October 2021) <https://www.fmprc.gov.cn/mfa_eng/gjhdq_665435/2675_665437/2676_663356/2678_663360/202110/t20211026_10058258.html> accessed 25 March 2026.

59 JS 2022.

60 Mirza Sabawoon, 'The European Union's Strategy on Afghanistan. Selected Issues' (2019) 3 Central European Political Studies 181.

in the international arena and carry out normal international exchanges.'[61] There is an obvious need and urgency on the side of the Taliban to change and not to continue where they have stopped at the time of the US intervention. All the radical steps, which have been recently implemented into the Afghani society, can't stay and must go as the foreign governments send in aid and cooperate with its government.

It is not just about the standpoints of the Taliban and their relationship with locals, but also the request to respect foreign nationals and interests without pushing on them their standards and requirements. As it has been also outlined recently the parties have urged relevant Afghani parties to safeguard the security and legitimate rights and interests of foreign citizens and institutions in Afghanistan.[62] It is hard to predict how this balance will look like, but certainly it is possible to somehow pacify the opposing standpoints and bring in some developments without actually recognizing the Taliban and their still unclear and unstable governance. It is hard to expect any kind of democratic legitimacy and procedures necessary to make decisions in such turbulent times, but as long as the Taliban cooperate, their governance will not be jeopardized from outside. 'As already mentioned, however, the lack of democratic legitimacy would jeopardise the recognition of countless governments around the world and is not an established criterion under international law despite some state practice.'[63] In the framework of Central Asian states and the Chinese governance, democratic standards and governance legitimacy are not understood similarly as in the Western world. The prospects for Democracy have maybe been required from the previous structures and the USA in particular but its outcomes and the future requirements are less strict and maybe will need to give voice to some political powers, which were not present previously. The Taliban as seen today will therefore need to be ready to conform to the new, more democratic application of standards.

---

61 Ministry of Foreign Affairs of the People's Republic of China, 'Wang Yi Holds Talks with Acting Deputy Prime Minister of Afghan Interim Government Mullah Abdul Ghani Baradar' (24 March 2022) <https://www.fmprc.gov.cn/mfa_eng/gjhdq_665435/2675_665437/2676_663356/2678_663360/202203/t20220325_10655539.html> accessed 25 March 2026.

62 JS 2022.

63 Ayesha Malik, 'The Islamic Emirate of Afghanistan and the Recognition of Governments under International Law' [2021] Research Society of International Law <https://rsilpak.org/wp-content/uploads/2021/10/afghanistan-taliban-recognition_rsil.pdf> accessed 25 March 2026.

3 Security Concerns

3.1 Relevant Concerns in General

Security issues are the biggest concern in Afghanistan together with its permanent development and governance challenges. In a historical context, which can have some validity also today, one century ago under the Anglo-Russian Convention of 1907, the Russian and British empires agreed on spheres of influence, and Russia conceded Afghanistan to the British.[64] Afghanistan has always played a strategic role and safeguarded to some extent one empire from the other. But to what extent to govern Afghanistan and how much should it be controlled from outside is the main question, as it was also some two decades ago when the Americans aimed at reaching a permanent resolution; so it is today. The Bonn Agreement of December 2001 is officially an Agreement on Provisional Arrangements in Afghanistan Pending the Reestablishment of Permanent Government Institutions,[65] and was a key document in that era for why this past period of time has proved to be an unsuccessful effort. How and why the US system of peace implementation has failed is the right question to be posed. 'Here, responsibility lies with key US decisionmakers who believed they were masters of a technology-driven revolution in military affairs endowed with boundless power to reshape the nature of war.'[66] After having a similar fate like the Soviets and after spending a similar amount of time in Afghanistan it became evident that not just instant solutions are not possible, but the question still remained wide open of how to securitize Afghanistan. If the US government was not able to strengthen its capacity and support other organizations researching the legal, political and security concerns, they all remained silent towards a possible final outcome.

The Afghani government had to trust at this time the various independent institutions and their capacities. 'These so-called think tanks and foundations have seriously deviated from the spirit of scientific research and become the

64 Diana Janse, 'Russian Interests in Afghanistan' (2021) 1 SCEEUS Reports <https://www.ui.se/globalassets/ui.se-eng/publications/sceeus/russian-interests-in-afghanistan-sceeus-report-no1-2021.pdf> accessed 25 March 2026.

65 United Nations, 'Agreement on Provisional Arrangements in Afghanistan Pending the Reestablishment of Permanent Government Institutions (Bonn Agreement)' (5 December 2001) <https://peacemaker.un.org/sites/default/files/document/files/2024/05/af011205agreementprovisionalarrangementsinafghanistan28en29.pdf> accessed 25 March 2026.

66 Todd Greentree, 'What Went Wrong in Afghanistan?' (2021) 51 Parameters 7.

political and propaganda tools of the US and other Western countries.'[67] The war on information in Afghanistan has been now transferred to the war on who is going to be responsible for the Security Concerns in Afghanistan and whether it has been knowingly transferred from the USA into the hands of the Chinese. But before the Chinese have really stepped in, the USA knew exactly what to expect and what to leave behind. 'The unilateral US-Taliban negotiations had neither the Afghan government's presence nor the blessing of Washington's hesitant European allies.'[68] The US policy of forcing its allies to accept all its foreign policy agenda is gaining more and more critics in Europe, especially as the war in Ukraine continues posing a bigger security threat to Europe than any time before. The decision of not to intervene in Ukraine looks wise for both the USA and EU, but also it is in line with their departure from Afghanistan agenda and the non-interference into the Nagorno-Karabakh conflict recently.

Whereas the Chinese agenda of foreign relations is now completely different from the one supported by the USA and the EU, but also Russia previously. Such a course of action is not in line with the foreign policy strategy of Beijing, which prefers soft power to excessively harsh actions in achieving its goals[69] contrary to the already well-established practice of Russia to throw in a military intervention whenever it seems that it is possible and needed. China has stepped in as a completely non-aggressive stakeholder offering something in exchange for the favours it requests. 'Afghanistan hopes that China will support the Afghan side in enhancing its security capacity.'[70] The new Taliban government although gained power still faces many challenges; mainly it is the actual prominent problem of financing not just themselves but the whole of the country. It has reaffirmed its readiness to scale up joint efforts to combat

67 Wang Yu, 'The Truth about the Issues of Human Rights in Xinjiang' (9 July 2020) <https://af.china-embassy.gov.cn/sgxw/202007/t20200710_1114118.htm> accessed 25 March 2026.

68 Abdul Waheed Ahmad and Gabriella Lloyd, 'Lessons from Afghanistan for Western State-Building in a Multipolar World' [2022] Atlantic Council South Asia Center <https://www.atlanticcouncil.org/wp-content/uploads/2022/06/Lessons_From_Afghanistan.pdf> accessed 25 March 2026.

69 Akram Umarov, 'Assessing China's New Policy in Afghanistan' (2017) 4 Central Asian Affairs 384.

70 Ministry of Foreign Affairs of the People's Republic of China, 'Wang Yi Holds Talks with Acting Deputy Prime Minister of Afghan Interim Government Mullah Abdul Ghani Baradar' (24 March 2022) <https://www.fmprc.gov.cn/mfa_eng/gjhdq_665435/2675_665437/2676_663356/2678_663360/202203/t20220325_10655539.html> accessed 25 March 2026.

cross-border drug-related crime and protect people's health and social stability.[71] The drug-related issues came on even ground with the terrorism threats as a security concern in Afghanistan. In this case the stakeholders of fighting cross-border drug-related crimes are not just Asian countries but countries as far as Europe and even the EU itself.

3.2 Conflict Prevention Capacity

While one of the biggest shocks regarding Asian and global security recently came from Afghanistan, when the USA decided to leave this country, so it was a surprise when China swiftly responded and stepped in. The surprisingly high level of terrorist presence and threat from Afghanistan was not much influenced by these two acts. 'The U.S. government attests that these threats can be dealt with through an "over the horizon" approach, without a military presence in Afghanistan.'[72] Obviously the cost-to-benefit ratio had to be taken into account; where in this case costs were high or simply the benefits for leaving were maybe just more affordable? 'What is especially insidious in the US move is that by leaving Afghanistan, Washington was intentionally creating a gap to entice China to move in and devote more resources to its western borderlands.'[73] China is ready to deal with problems but more likely in an economic sense and not exactly in the security-related aspects. China can't afford to have an unstable country in its neighbourhood, which could do potential harm to its trade and business prospects. 'Ironically, if China fills the vacuum left by the US, it is to the benefit of all, including the US and its allies.'[74] The investments China will do and has already done in Afghanistan considering its cost-to-benefit ratio makes it logical that they support or in some sense sponsor Afghanistan, in the best possible manner.

---

71 JS 2022.

72 Kurita Masahiro, 'Great Power Politics over Afghanistan after the U.S. Withdrawal' [2022] NIDS East Asian Strategic Review <http://www.nids.mod.go.jp/english/publication/east-asian/pdf/2022/e01.pdf> accessed 25 March 2026.

73 Feng Zhang, 'China's New Engagement with Afghanistan after the Withdrawal' (2022) 2 LSE Public Policy Review 10.

74 Loro Horta, 'US Afghan Withdrawal: Enter China and Taliban?' (2021) 120 RSIS Commentary <https://rsis.edu.sg/wp-content/uploads/2021/08/CO21120.pdf> accessed 25 March 2026.

In other words, as much as they invest regarding both trade and security, so much they can expect in return. 'While China's economic prowess and infrastructure capabilities have been recognised, its BRI projects are criticised by the international community, which is wary that it ensnares countries in 'debt traps'.'[75] Even if the Chinese investors will own the whole of Afghanistan they are also responsible to feed its citizens and pacify them as well; the debt traps, which might occur in other parts of the globe, potentially can rise different concerns. On a short term owning something in a post-conflict setting might be beneficial but in the long run it can become too costly; such concerns as employment, environment and political instability can cause more harm in the future.

The security component is therefore always strongly connected to the more clear and controllable investment concerns. 'After years of heavily promoting its vast Belt and Road Initiative (BRI) as purely about development, China now seems to view security engagement as its primary concern.'[76] Although Chinese investments and in particular its political system were not targeted that much previously globally by terrorism as was the Western, this fact can change considering the recent confrontations with its Muslim Uyghur minority.

The conflict with Uyghur can destabilize China and its neighbour Muslim countries further to the West, where also Afghanistan belongs. 'The Afghan Taliban is a responsible government, and would like to reiterate to China and the whole world that it will never allow any terrorists to operate in Afghanistan, and will never allow anyone or any institution to use the Afghan territory to take actions against other countries, still less allow any forces to engage in activities that undermine China.'[77] China needs a safe Western borderland, which connects it to the world via land routes, as Russia also needs safe and secure Southern borderlands and that is why it has made extraordinary agree-

75 Claudia Chia, Kunthavi Kalachelvam and Zheng Haiqi, 'Exploring China's Afghanistan Policy' (2021) 677 ISAS Insights <https://www.isas.nus.edu.sg/wp-content/uploads/2021/06/677.pdf> accessed 25 March 2026.

76 Angela Stanzel, 'Fear and Loathing on the New Silk Road: Chinese Security in Afghanistan and Beyond' [2018] European Council on Foreign Relations <https://ecfr.eu/wp-content/uploads/ECFR-264-Chinese_Security_in_Afghanistan_2.pdf> accessed 25 March 2026.

77 Ministry of Foreign Affairs of the People's Republic of China, 'Wang Yi Holds Talks with Acting Deputy Prime Minister of Afghan Interim Government Mullah Abdul Ghani Baradar' (24 March 2022) <https://www.fmprc.gov.cn/mfa_eng/gjhdq_665435/2675_665437/2676_663356/2678_663360/202203/t20220325_10655539.html> accessed 25 March 2026.

ments previously with the Chechen separatists some years ago. The securitization of the Southern borders have allowed Russia to re-route trade from Europe towards the South, which became critical now at the time of the war in Ukraine. 'Over the past 20 years, Russia followed a realpolitik approach towards Afghanistan.'[78] Obviously Russia was not able to neither change nor influence the politics in Afghanistan; it can do so in former central Asian ex-Soviet Republics, but Afghanistan is a bigger challenge.

When we speak about business and agriculture it is hard to imagine a product that is on such a big demand in surrounding countries and coming from Afghanistan as is the opium extracted from poppy seeds. Although this trade is illegal it still does occur and all neighbouring countries including China, Russia and Iran all have their domestic drug use-related problems. They have all made further steps and encouraged relevant Afghani parties to take concrete actions against cultivation, production and illicit trafficking of narcotics in order to crack down on organized crime to free Afghanistan from the scourge of drugs.'[79] The drug use as a security concern is even higher after the US withdrawal, not that it was not present during its decades long intervention. 'Although these also involve the American Drug Enforcement Administration, Russia has severely criticised the US for its lack of commitment to eradicate poppy plantations.'[80] Although USA had no direct security threat from Afghani-made drugs use it can't be said for China, where apart from Uyghur separatism the drug use is of a direct concern and threat to the governance with a constant rise in drug users. 'China appreciates Afghanistan's firm attitude to the counter-narcotics issue, and is willing to assist Afghanistan in planting alternative crops.'[81] The support China is giving and the new trends they want to implement have a possibly very strong cultural concern, they

---

78 Rajab Taieb, Alamuddin Rizwan and Maryam Jami, 'Reluctant Reentrance? Russia and Afghanistan Post 2021' [2021] Friedrich Ebert-Stiftung (FES) Afghanistan and Institute of War and Peace Studies <https://library.fes.de/pdf-files/bueros/kabul/18642.pdf> accessed 25 March 2026.

79 JS 2022.

80 Józef Lang, 'Afghanistan: The View from Russia' (2014) 10 European Union Institute for Security Studies <https://www.files.ethz.ch/isn/182959/Alert_10-Afghanistan_view_from_Russia.pdf> accessed 25 March 2026.

81 Ministry of Foreign Affairs of the People's Republic of China, 'Wang Yi Meets with Acting Foreign Minister of the Afghan Interim Government Amir Khan Muttaqi' (29 July 2022) <https://www.fmprc.gov.cn/mfa_eng/gjhdq_665435/2675_665437/2676_663356/2678_663360/202207/t20220729_10730548.html> accessed 25 March 2026.

presumably still can't understand the demands and the way Afghani mindset can be changed.

In this regard and as in many others China can count on their Pakistani partners who have always had a good over-the-border relationship with Afghanistan. 'Despite its insistence on formalizing the Durand Line, Pakistan has leveraged the porous border to suit its strategic aims.'[82] The good relationship of Pakistan with Afghanistan is going back to the Soviet times, when Pakistan actually supported the anti-Soviet resistance movement from its territory. In any case, the closer cooperation of them will not be seen well from the strategic opponent of Pakistan in the region, India. While India has a good relationship with Russia, also the Chinese would need to improve their relationship with India after so many conflicts and as they are the biggest potential military opponents to the Chinese in the region but also an important member in the BRICS[83] organization.

Once again when trade is connected to the security concerns, as the formation of a security cooperation on India's Northern borders, where the biggest security threat it is receiving both from the Chinese and the Pakistani forces. India was about to invest in a long-term risk mitigation strategy[84] as the security threat will not pass in any case, but the good trade relationships are on the rise and are to be protected at all costs. India is also supporting together with Russia forces, which are not aligned with the government in Pakistan, and if balance, safety and security are to be achieved Russia and India are definitely stakeholders for this cause in Afghanistan as well.

3.3 Possible Terrorism-Related Concerns

The most important aspect to focus on the Chinese relationship with Afghanistan is definitely the terrorism threat. 'China defined "three evils" terrorism, separatism and religious extremism as its primary concerns in talks and meet-

82 Elizabeth Threlkeld and Grace Easterly, 'Afghanistan-Pakistan Ties and Future Stability in Afghanistan' (2021) 175 Peaceworks <https://www.usip.org/sites/default/files/2021-08/pw_175-afghanistan_pakistan_ties_and_future_stability_in_afghanistan.pdf> accessed 25 March 2026.

83 BRICS Information Portal, 'History of BRICS' (3 March 2023) <http://infobrics.org/page/history-of-brics/> accessed 25 March 2026.

84 Rudra Chaudhuri and Shreyas Shende, 'Dealing With the Taliban: India's Strategy in Afghanistan After U.S. Withdrawal' [2020] Carnegie Endowment for International Peace <https://carnegieendowment.org/files/Chaudhuri_Shende_-_Afghanistan.pdf> accessed 25 March 2026.

ings with Afghan officials.'[85] China can get the biggest gains in Afghanistan by demanding and lowering the prospects for terrorism inside Afghanistan, since separatism and religious extremism are also a concern for the Afghani Taliban inside their own country. 'The Afghan Taliban, which attaches great importance to China's security concerns, will resolutely honor its promise and never allow anyone or any force to use the Afghan territory to harm China.'[86] China was never the primary target of terrorists coming from Afghanistan; firstly they focused on the Soviets and then on the West in general and the USA. Interestingly the Pakistani government also had a similar security interest like their Afghani neighbours. 'Some claimed that without Islamabad's support, the Taliban could not have become as strong as they are today.'[87] Obviously the support in many different forms is key to commit terrorist acts, also once they have the territory on which they can freely move and train is given.

While Iran is considered as a country which supports terrorism, in this case, its activities do not target either Russia or China. 'Iran has not even been able to create an armed group in Afghanistan to defend its interests while it was able to organize Shia groups in Lebanon, Iraq, Syria, and Yemen.'[88] It is probably Iran who wants the most to have a stable neighbourhood where there will be no security risks for its own interests; therefore it is ready to make compromises similarly as China does. 'Iran and the United States collaborated in the defeating of the Taliban and the creation of a new Afghanistan government.'[89] Obviously the presence of the USA was not that big an issue for Iran as is the number of out-of-control terrorist organizations, which are ready to fight Iran as well, while it is also a Muslim country. So while presently fractions of the ex-Taliban combatants have various interests, they continue fighting, which poses the biggest security threat for everyone including the Taliban, which are interestingly seen now as an anti-terrorist actor.

85 Claudia Chia, Kunthavi Kalachelvam and Zheng Haiqi, 'Exploring China's Afghanistan Policy' (2021) 677 ISAS Insights <https://www.isas.nus.edu.sg/wp-content/uploads/2021/06/677.pdf> accessed 25 March 2026.

86 Ministry of Foreign Affairs of the People's Republic of China, 'Wang Yi Meets with Acting Deputy Prime Minister of Afghan Taliban's Interim Government Mullah Abdul Ghani Baradar' (26 October 2021) <https://www.fmprc.gov.cn/mfa_eng/gjhdq_665435/2675_665437/2676_663356/2678_663360/202110/t20211026_10058258.html> accessed 25 March 2026.

87 Loro Horta, 'US Afghan Withdrawal: Enter China and Taliban?' (2021) 120 RSIS Commentary <https://rsis.edu.sg/wp-content/uploads/2021/08/CO21120.pdf> accessed 25 March 2026.

88 Ghulam Faroq Keskin, Sayyad Sadri Alibabalu, and Mudassir Fatah, 'Russia's and Iran's Strategic Policies Towards the Afghanistan Crisis' (2020) 24 Trames 215.

89 Ibid.

All the neighbouring states and stakeholders had an easy goal to request changes, and they have called on the relevant Afghani parties to take more visible steps by making a clean break with all forms of terrorist forces. They requested them to monitor free movement of all terrorist organizations and to firmly fight and eliminate them including through dismantling of their training camps, to ensure that Afghanistan would never again serve as a breeding ground and safe haven or source of proliferation for terrorism.[90] The Taliban have overall changed their modus operandi and now functions as a formal governance structure where any other fraction trying to extend influence poses a threat. 'The Taliban later pledged to work with Russia, China and Iran to combat the Islamic State (IS) and drug trafficking.'[91] In order to maintain this situation of a lesser evil China, Iran, USA and Russia must support them in a sense that they can establish themselves as a government and be able to take responsibility for their own acts and also make certain human rights-related guarantees.

While the USA is not ready to commit and support the Taliban, China has showed its readiness to do so and will need the help of further stakeholders, which will most likely be Russia who wants to have a control over the security issues on the whole of the Asian continent, and even broader. 'To maintain its monopoly on security in Eurasia, the Kremlin must insert into Afghan matters.'[92] For Russia, it is perfect if there is a proxy dealing with Afghani matters since Russia also has its various challenges with the post-Soviet central Asian states, where it constantly has to defend its interest and secure the North Afghanistan borders. 'Traditionally, Russia supported anti-Taliban forces, such as the so-called Northern Alliance, whose political and military cadres were integrated into the post-9/11 democratic state.'[93] This imbalance of being permanently and for decades confronted with the Afghan majority Pashtu interests brought Russia into a harsh position at the negotiation table. China also has a complex position but the investment potentials, which could benefit everyone serve as a game changer and can be used for the benefit of everyone.

---

90 JS 2022.

91 Claudia Chia and Zheng Haiqi, 'Russia's Policy Overtures in Afghanistan' (2021) 694 ISAS Insights <https://www.isas.nus.edu.sg/wp-content/uploads/2021/11/694.pdf> accessed 25 March 2026.

92 Ibid.

93 Abdul Waheed Ahmad and Gabriella Lloyd, 'Lessons from Afghanistan for Western State-Building in a Multipolar World' [2022] Atlantic Council South Asia Center <https://www.atlanticcouncil.org/wp-content/uploads/2022/06/Lessons_From_Afghanistan.pdf> accessed 25 March 2026.

4 Human Rights and Democracy

4.1 Human and Minority Rights Aspects

The most challenging question regarding Afghanistan is the enforcement of human and minority rights, although the understanding of such rights is completely different here than in any other country. There were many attempts to influence and implement human rights in Afghanistan and one of the biggest efforts supporting it was also coming from the EU with the aim to raise them to an acceptable level. While now the enforcement of EU standards is questionable and even if the EU demands the Taliban will still have their own agenda and priorities. 'The Taliban appear to have an optimistic set of objectives for what they want from the EU and its member states: formal recognition, normalised diplomatic relations and unconditional aid to the country.'[94] Although the formal recognition is very far, the implementation of some standards might still be viable. The most important issue is the incorporation of minorities into the new governmental structures. 'The overwhelmingly Pashtu government formed by the Taliban in the Fall of 2021 involves five Tajiks and Uzbeks in high positions (vice-premier, head of general staff, and three ministers; two are former shadow provincial governors).'[95] Such efforts are not just to please the EU but also Russia who supports the inclusion and collaborates with the minorities from the North of Afghanistan.

When it comes to China and its standards for human and minority rights, they are again different from the ones in the EU, but have overall a very high inclusion and education level for women and female children. Such normative considerations are unlikely to influence the substance of China–Taliban relations insofar as they do not fundamentally affect Afghan or regional stability.[96] Although having different standards for Human Rights, which are for China and Afghanistan very distant from the EU and the overall Western understanding, they can still cooperate on some level and to some accept-

94 International Crisis Group, 'Thinking Through the Dilemmas of Aid to Afghanistan' [2021] Watch List 2021 for the EU <https://icg-prod.s3.amazonaws.com/afghanistan.pdf> accessed 25 March 2026.

95 Ekaterina Stepanova, 'Russia's Approach to Afghanistan Following the Taliban Takeover' (2021) 724 PONARS Eurasia Policy Memo <https://www.ponarseurasia.org/wp-content/uploads/2021/11/Pepm724_Stepanova_Nov2021.pdf> accessed 25 March 2026.

96 Jiayi Zhou, Fei Su and Jingdong Yuan, 'Treading Lightly: China's Footprint in a Taliban-Led Afghanistan' (2022) 8 SIPRI Insights on Peace and Security <https://www.sipri.org/sites/default/files/2022-11/sipriinsights_2208_china_and_afghanistan_2.pdf> accessed 25 March 2026.

able extent. 'China expects the Afghan side to continue to build an inclusive government, exercise prudent governance, and better safeguard the rights and interests of women and children, so as to demonstrate the tolerance and friendliness of Muslims.'[97] If a country or a government wants to advance the standards of that society they have to compete with other regional and global powers, where the discrimination of any kind is not a positive and expected standard of behaviour. 'The Taliban has also placed restrictions on female employment, which had represented around 20% of the workforce.'[98] The inclusion of women is not just a human right but an economy-related category as well. This kind of discrimination potentially divides the Afghani society from inside where not everyone shares the same standards as the Taliban and further encourages the emigration of people, causing the refugee crisis to continue as its direct outcome.

This has also been outlined in the meetings and the neighbouring states have expressed their appreciation for the efforts made, in particular Pakistan and Iran, on the issue of the Afghani refugees. They have called on the international community to provide continuous, sufficient and proportionate financial support for timely return of Afghan refugees with dignity and honour.[99] However, this is probably the toughest issue in the whole Afghan case and the constant flow of migrants from this country has caused the world to change overall and it can't be expected that after the US involvement, EU efforts and the new Chinese agenda there could be a real change to this problem in general.

4.2 Democratic Potentials in the Agreements

Without stabilizing Afghanistan in a legal and political context it is not likely possible that all the threats endangering it as a society will and could be neutralized. Regarding the overall democratization of the country, there was not much outlined until now; the Agreement from Tunxi has just outlined some basic cooperation concerns. It has expressed concern over the situation of the

97 Ministry of Foreign Affairs of the People's Republic of China, 'Wang Yi Holds Talks with Acting Deputy Prime Minister of Afghan Interim Government Mullah Abdul Ghani Baradar' (24 March 2022) <https://www.fmprc.gov.cn/mfa_eng/gjhdq_665435/2675_665437/2676_663356/2678_663360/202203/t20220325_10655539.html> accessed 25 March 2026.

98 Philip Loft, 'Aid to Taliban-Controlled Afghanistan' (2022) 9343 The House of Commons Library <https://researchbriefings.files.parliament.uk/documents/CBP-9343/CBP-9343.pdf> accessed 25 March 2026.

99 JS 2022.

Afghani refugees as well as the internally displaced people and support for the UN agencies in playing an active role in this regard.[100] Although not much has been achieved at the peak of the Afghani involvement by the international community, so at this critical moment, also not much is possible regarding democratization. In any case, the previous Afghani government and really any other similar government, which has been supported as a post-conflict and peacebuilding one was not without its own and specific shortcomings.

The level of involvement and support the previous government was receiving was tremendously high in regard to democratization potentials. All the countries, which have democratization as their priority need to revise their goals and tools to achieve them in many aspects they are active. 'In Haiti, Afghanistan, and Bosnia, the crisis of peacebuilding is simultaneously a crisis of democracy, as citizens grow increasingly disillusioned with electoral processes that seem to perpetually generate governments that are remote, indifferent, and often predatory.'[101] It is therefore very complex to make a solution where 'one size fits all' and as we are aiming at criticizing the UN and its Security Council we see how the world is inevitably divided both politically and culturally. 'Afghanistan belongs to the category of 'strong society and weak state'; the country cannot collect too many taxes on tribal society, especially Pashtun tribal society.'[102] A modern society can't function without taxes and the redistribution of wealth in some sense. It would be also very complex to tax the production and cultivation of, e.g. poppy seeds in Afghanistan, while the profits of this activity are considerable in the overall Afghan agricultural production and economy.

Although the drug production brings revenues it can't be used for development and infrastructure purposes, where the vast majority of the country could be better interconnected. 'With over 70% of the Afghan population residing in rural areas, the growing divide between Afghanistan's rural and urban populations was reinforced by the resistance of the Kabul-based government to devolve power and resources away from the centre.'[103] The lack of democratic capacity is in the case of Afghanistan in the core of the country and can't be changed by a simple intervention and sharing of the best practi-

100 JS 2022.

101 Timothy Donais, *Peacebuilding and Local Ownership: Post-Conflict Consensus-Building* (Routledge 2012).

102 Yan Wei, 'The Cooperation Between China and Afghanistan Under the "Belt and Road Initiative"' (2018) 6 International Relations and Diplomacy 359.

103 Viola Fee Dreikhausen, 'The EU Engagement in Afghanistan: Insights and Emerging Lessons' (2022) 7 European Union Institute for Security Studies <https://www.iss.europa.eu/sites/default/files/EUISSFiles/Brief_7_Afghanistan.pdf> accessed 25 March 2026.

ces. However, the real and honest sharing of know-how regarding democracy has probably never happened, and the foreign donors have just redistributed the funds between themselves and the Afghani agencies associated with them. This critique on the Western involvement and its shortcomings is widely used by both China and Russia. 'Moreover, China continues its aid programmes to even those countries on which the Western countries impose sanctions on grounds of failed democracy or non-compliance with international rules and regulations.'[104] This is exactly the case present in Afghanistan, where the Chinese are supporting by all possible means the not-recognized Taliban government and also invest huge amounts of resources in order to achieve a higher level of development than the USA did during its recent involvement. In some sense the Chinese are trying to buy peace and make sure that they will have a good relationship with Afghanistan, but also count on its Taliban government as a partner. 'China hopes and believes that the Afghan Taliban will make a clean break with the ETIM and other terrorist organizations, and take effective measures to resolutely crack down on them.'[105] China has at the moment the most to offer to Afghanistan and it is not hesitant to do so; its soft power is visible everywhere on the globe and while it dominates in Asia now it also spreads on other continents as well.

China and its BRI are likely to have a transformative effect on infrastructure development over large areas of the globe.[106] Probably one of the best experiences and cooperation frameworks is the one China has with Pakistan; they have already inter-combined the security and trade into one common policy for the benefit of both – 'A central part of the Belt and Road Initiative is the China–Pakistan Economic Corridor.'[107] In this regard it is possible to imagine that China will be in a position to enforce some of its demands on Afghani-

104 Amit Kumar Gupta, 'Soft Power of the United States, China, and India: A Comparative Analysis' (2013) 26(1/2) Indian Journal of Asian Affairs 37.

105 Ministry of Foreign Affairs of the People's Republic of China, 'Wang Yi Meets with Acting Deputy Prime Minister of Afghan Taliban's Interim Government Mullah Abdul Ghani Baradar' (26 October 2021) <https://www.fmprc.gov.cn/mfa_eng/gjhdq_665435/2675_665437/2676_663356/2678_663360/202110/t20211026_10058258.html> accessed 25 March 2026.

106 Ping Xiong and Roman Tomasic, 'Soft Law, State-Owned Enterprises and Dispute Resolution on PRC's Belt and Road – Towards an Emerging Legal Order?' (2019) 49 Hong Kong L.J. 1025.

107 Maryam Jami, Alamuddin Rizwan and Rajab Taieb, 'Sino–Afghan Security Relations beyond 2021' [2021] Friedrich Ebert-Stiftung (FES) Afghanistan and Institute of War and Peace Studies <https://library.fes.de/pdf-files/bueros/kabul/18638.pdf> accessed 25 March 2026.

stan, although any kind of democratization is presently not possible, neither is it a priority for China.

It is evident that the democratization as a standard is absolutely not a necessary requirement from the Chinese, and the simple adherence to their norms and rules is enough to gain their support and secure investments. 'Finally, Moscow will use the Afghanistan situation to confirm Russia's return to the global power competition and as an argument against the West's democratisation and human rights agendas.'[108] Russia will join China in blaming the West for all the failures in democratization processes in Afghanistan and in other similar post-conflict societies on the globe. This opportunity will also give Russia leverage over the West and its very critical involvement in Ukraine after all. While the efforts to implement democratization processes in Afghanistan are lost it serves as a valuable case study of what not to do, so we can prevent and maintain some basic level of democracy in such divided post-conflict societies.

108 Diana Janse, 'Russian Interests in Afghanistan' (2021) 1 SCEEUS Reports <https://www.ui.se/globalassets/ui.se-eng/publications/sceeus/russian-interests-in-afghanistan-sceeus-report-no1-2021.pdf> accessed 25 March 2026.

CHAPTER 15

Conclusion

Conflict resolution and the development capacities of soft laws in post-conflict peace settings inevitably have a very prominent role in the whole concept of their overall agenda of future development and reconciliation possibilities. The very tight connection line between soft laws, informal rules and political decisions has been researched in regard to their future potentials and possibilities, mainly in order to solve the given local challenges and also give as many guarantees as possible for the given societies' future development. In this regard, the importance of scrutinizing the three case studies in our work from various perspectives of development and conflict resolution are being also supported by different UN Security Council permanent member states' viewpoints. While the possibilities are unlimited, there are also many limiting factors where certain goals can't be achieved in the short run, but also many times unfortunately neither in the long run. It is therefore necessary to have a very clear picture of the possible and necessary agendas, which can be implemented in such post-conflict societies and also later potentially followed by other similar case studies globally. Our work has covered the research of post-conflict societies in regard to Kosovo, Nagorno-Karabakh and Afghanistan with their valuable research-related outcomes stemming from their informal agreements considering post-conflict development and conflict resolution.

When we look at the EU and its neighbourhood we can observe a rising number of conflicts, which are all limiting the development and conflict resolution capacities of local communities, but also of the EU. One of the most important research cases regarding the EU post-conflict development is definitely Kosovo, where it has been active in the post-conflict development and conflict resolution through its EULEX mission. EU has also supported the creation of many case-specific informal post-conflict documents between the governments in Belgrade and Pristina in order to reach a final and mutually acceptable solution. The focus of this work has been primarily on the First Agreement of Principles Governing the Normalization of Relations from 2013 also called The Brussels Agreement. It has to some extent outlined the most important achievements regarding the future mutual relationships between Serbia and Kosovo and the status of the Serbian minority, in specific in the four Serbian majority municipalities in North Kosovo. While there were many important advancements stemming from these agreements directly, they have

HTTPS://DOI.ORG/10.1163/9789004746091-017

still not been fully implemented. The biggest concern and obstacle in this regard is still the future formation of the Association/Community of Serbian municipalities with its possible enforcement capacities. While the Brussels Agreement has been supported by the EU and at that time EU member states were both France and the United Kingdom, we have observed how these two states see the development of post-conflict societies in the EU neighbourhood. Regarding Kosovo we have also researched an agreement coming from the US perspective, while it has supported the EU efforts generally, it has also outlined some of its specific requirements. Explicitly by the request of this agreement, Israel and Kosovo have mutually recognized each other, what has deeply changed the understanding of state sovereignty in the post-conflict settings overall. Now we are facing a completely different situation in Kosovo than the one EU is supporting and aiming at reconciling Serbia and Kosovo, also now finding a solution for the Israeli–Palestinian conflict became more challenging.

The relevant experiences regarding post-conflict societies are important to be researched and possibly applied in the future and in particular into the presently very actual conflict in Ukraine. Here we see that the EU is facing a new iron curtain being installed on its Eastern borders. While we are unable to research the overall development potentials in Ukraine after the war, we are certainly able to research the very valuable Russian perspective of conflict resolution mechanisms in the case of Nagorno-Karabakh. After the initial Agreement or Statement was achieved between Russia, Armenia and Azerbaijan in 2020 it was introducing various guarantees regarding the future situation in the Nagorno-Karabakh. A surprising change in this regard occurred in 2023, which has completely eradicated the existence of the Armenian-controlled Republic in Nagorno-Karabakh by 2024, and questioned the Russia-supported informal trilateral Agreement. Since the question of regulating the future status of the Armenian minority in Nagorno-Karabakh was to some extent settled in 2020, it is now unclear what status they will have if any in such a new constellation. We have also researched what potentials the resolution of this conflict has opened and how the needs for transportation and connectivity in this region can be revived in the future, for the benefit of all. Apart from Russia and its interests in this region of the South Caucasus we have also touched upon various other stakeholders where the key regional players are Turkey and Iran, but also China, which has an interest to develop further its BRI Initiative.

While we have researched China and its interests and influences in regard to Kosovo and the Nagorno-Karabakh conflicts, we have also added a more in depth research of its Afghanistan related potentials. Here we have focused on the most important influence and the agreements China has reached regarding Afghanistan and its new unrecognized Taliban government. The Chinese framework Agreements reached for the future development of Afghanistan have included also many of its neighbours, advancing that way the overall security, connectedness and development potentials around and in Afghanistan, but also in Central Asia. The Chinese agreements are covering many aspects concerning Chinese investments and development possibilities in Afghanistan primarily, but also their mutual efforts towards the BRI initiative. In this regard a prominent, but still limited, role is given to the protection of human and minority rights in Afghanistan and the overall interconnectivity of this requirement with the global security, development and conflict resolution concerns.

Finally, our research has aimed at giving answers to the many and various challenging questions regarding the most notable post-conflict societies and their relevant agreements reached recently in the framework and understanding of the UNSC permanent member states. The value of finding the legal paths necessary for development and reconciliation in post-conflict societies is even more valuable when we know that there are also new conflicts arising today. Such conflicts also need to be more critically approached and valuable solutions offered for the quick establishment and potentially the re-establishment of relationships with more democratic, human rights and development friendly solutions. While there are indeed conflicts lasting for years such as the one in Ukraine and the Israel–Palestinian conflict lasting for decades, they both pose a real threat to the idea of successful post-conflict resolution. Our work has aimed to offer new viewpoints and perspectives for possible future development ideas being based on informal agreements and their relevant conflict resolution capacities. Although such agreements have a limited enforcement capacity, they certainly pose a realistic opportunity for development potentials in post-conflict peace agreements.

Annex

1 Brussels Agreement Serbian Version

The Brussels Agreement (First Agreement of Principles Governing the Normalization of Relations) from 2013 Serbian[1] version.

First agreement of principles governing the normalization of relations

1. There will be an Association/Community of Serb majority municipalities in Kosovo. Membership will be open to any other municipality provided the members are in agreement.

2. The Community/Association will be created by statute. Its dissolution shall only take place by a decision of the participating municipalities. Legal guarantees will be provided by applicable law and constitutional law (including the 2/3 majority rule).

3. The structures of the Association/Community will be established on the same basis as the existing statute of the Association of Kosovo municipalities e.g. President, vice President, Assembly, Council.

4. In accordance with the competences given by the European Charter of Local Self Government and Kosovo law the participating municipalities shall be entitled to cooperate in exercising their powers through the Community/Association collectively. The Association/Community will have full overview of the areas of economic development, education, health, urban and rural planning.

5. The Association/Community will exercise other additional competences as may be delegated by the central authorities.

6. The Community/Association shall have a representative role to the central authorities and will have a seat in the communities consultative council for this purpose. In the pursuit of this role a monitoring function is envisaged.

7. There shall be one police force in Kosovo called the Kosovo Police. All police in northern Kosovo shall be integrated in the Kosovo Police framework. Salaries will be only from the KP.

8. Members of other Serbian security structures will be offered a place in equivalent Kosovo structures.

9. There shall be a Police Regional Commander for the four northern Serb majority municipalities (Northern Mitrovica, Zvecan, Zubin Potok and Leposavic). The Commander of this region shall be a Kosovo Serb nominated by the Ministry of Internal Affairs from a list provided by the four mayors on behalf of the Community/Association. The composition of the KP in the north will reflect the ethnic composition of the population of the four municipalities. (There will be another Regional Commander for the municipalities of Mitrovica South, Skenderaj and Vushtrri). The regional commander of the four northern municipalities will cooperate with other regional commanders.

10. The judicial authorities will be integrated and operate within the Kosovo legal framework.
The Appellate Court in Pristina will establish a panel composed of a majority of K/S judges to deal with all Kosovo Serb majority municipalities.

1 Brussels Agreement, 'First Agreement of Principles Governing the Normalization of Relations' (2013) <https://www.peaceagreements.org/media/documents/ag2022_5bdc31b326555.pdf> also available at <https://www.srbija.gov.rs/cinjenice/en/120394> accessed 26 June 2025.

The original Serbian version of this agreement is attached with a watermark of The Radio-Television of Serbia national broadcaster while its text is also available on the website of The Serbian Government.

A division of this Appellate Court, composed both by administrative staff and judges, will sit permanently in northern Mitrovica (Mitrovica District Court).
Each panel of the above division will be composed by a majority of K/S judges. Appropriate judges will sit dependant on the nature of the case involved.

11. Municipal elections shall be organised in the northern municipalities in 2013 with the facilitation of the OSCE in accordance with Kosovo law and international standards.

12. An implementation plan including time frame shall be produced by April 26. In implementing this agreement the principle of transparent funding will be addressed.

13. Discussions on Energy and Telecoms will be intensified by the two sides and completed by June 15.

14. It is agreed that neither side will block, or encourage others to block, the other side's progress in their respective EU paths.

15. An implementation committee will be established by the two sides, with the facilitation of the EU.

MA
I.D

I HEREBY CONFIRM THAT THIS IS THE TEXT PROPOSAL ON WHOSE ACCEPTANCE OR REFUSAL BOTH SIDES SHALL SUBMIT THEIR RESPECTIVE DECISIONS.

I.D

2 Brussels Agreement Kosovo Version

The Brussels Agreement (First Agreement of Principles Governing the Normalization of Relations) from 2013 Kosovo[2] version.

Republika e Kosovës
Republika Kosovo - Republic of Kosovo
Kuvendi - Skupština - Assembly

Law No. 04/L-199

ON RATIFICATION OF THE FIRST INTERNATIONAL AGREEMENT OF PRINCIPLES GOVERNING THE NORMALIZATION OF RELATIONS BETWEEN THE REPUBLIC OF KOSOVO AND THE REPUBLIC OF SERBIA

Assembly of Republic of Kosovo,

Based on Articles 18 and 65 of the Constitution of the Republic of Kosovo.

Approves

LAW ON RATIFICATION OF THE FIRST INTERNATIONAL AGREEMENT OF PRINCIPLES GOVERNING THE NORMALIZATION OF RELATIONS BETWEEN THE REPUBLIC OF KOSOVO AND THE REPUBLIC OF SERBIA

Article 1
Purpose

This law ratifies the First International Agreement of Principles Governing the Normalization of Relations between the Republic of Kosovo and the Republic of Serbia, initialled on April 19, 2013 by the Prime Minister of the Republic of Kosovo and the Prime Minister of the Republic of Serbia, endorsed by the Government of the Republic of Kosovo on 22 April, 2013, Decision Nr. 01/126, and by the Assembly of the Republic of Kosovo on 22 April, 2013, Resolution Nr. 04-R-10.

1

---

2 Brussels Agreement, 'First Agreement of Principles Governing the Normalization of Relations' (2013) <https://gzk.rks-gov.net/ActDetail.aspx?ActID=8892&langid=2> accessed 22 March 2026.

Article 2
Scope

Scope of this Law is the First International Agreement of Principles Governing the Normalization of Relations between the Republic of Kosovo and the Republic of Serbia, and this agreement constitutes integral part of this law. This law shall be implemented by the Republic of Kosovo with the assistance of the European Union, (EU), the North Atlantic Treaty Organization Forces in Kosovo, (KFOR), and the Organization for Security and Cooperation in Europe, (OSCE).

Article 3
Entry into force

This law enters into force immediately upon promulgation by the President of the Republic of Kosovo.

Law No. 04/L-199
27 June 2013

President of the Assembly of the Republic of Kosovo

____

Jakup KRASNIQI

2

In Kosovo, this agreement is promulgated in a form of a law and is treated as an International Agreement between two states.

First agreement of principles governing the normalization of relations

1. There will be an Association/Community of Serb majority municipalities in Kosovo. Membership will be open to any other municipality provided the members are in agreement.

2. The Community/Association will be created by statute. Its dissolution shall only take place by a decision of the participating municipalities. Legal guarantees will be provided by applicable law and constitutional law (including the 2/3 majority rule).

3. The structures of the Association/Community will be established on the same basis as the existing statute of the Association of Kosovo municipalities e.g. President, vice President, Assembly, Council.

4. In accordance with the competences given by the European Charter of Local Self Government and Kosovo law the participating municipalities shall be entitled to cooperate in exercising their powers through the Community/Association collectively. The Association/Community will have full overview of the areas of economic development, education, health, urban and rural planning.

5. The Association/Community will exercise other additional competences as may be delegated by the central authorities.

6. The Community/Association shall have a representative role to the central authorities and will have a seat in the communities consultative council for this purpose. In the pursuit of this role a monitoring function is envisaged.

7. There shall be one police force in Kosovo called the Kosovo Police. All police in northern Kosovo shall be integrated in the Kosovo Police framework. Salaries will be only from the KP.

8. Members of other Serbian security structures will be offered a place in equivalent Kosovo structures.

9. There shall be a Police Regional Commander for the four northern Serb majority municipalities (Northern Mitrovica, Zvecan, Zubin Potok and Leposavic). The Commander of this region shall be a Kosovo Serb nominated by the Ministry of Internal Affairs from a list provided by the four mayors on behalf of the Community/Association. The composition of the KP in the north will reflect the ethnic composition of the population of the four municipalities. (There will be another Regional Commander for the municipalities of Mitrovica South, Skenderaj and Vushtrri). The regional commander of the four northern municipalities will cooperate with other regional commanders.

10. The judicial authorities will be integrated and operate within the Kosovo legal framework.
The Appellate Court in Pristina will establish a panel composed of a majority of K/S judges to deal with all Kosovo Serb majority municipalities.

A division of this Appellate Court, composed both by administrative staff and judges, will sit permanently in northern Mitrovica (Mitrovica District Court).
Each panel of the above division will be composed by a majority of K/S judges.
Appropriate judges will sit dependant on the nature of the case involved.

11. Municipal elections shall be organised in the northern municipalities in 2013 with the facilitation of the OSCE in accordance with Kosovo law and international standards.

12. An implementation plan including time frame shall be produced by April 26. In implementing this agreement the principle of transparent funding will be addressed.

13. Discussions on Energy and Telecoms will be intensified by the two sides and completed by June 15.

14. It is agreed that neither side will block, or encourage others to block, the other side's progress in their respective EU paths.

15. An implementation committee will be established by the two sides, with the facilitation of the EU.

3 Washington Agreement Serbian Version

The Washington Agreement (Economic Normalization) from 2020 Serbian[3] version.

Economic Normalization

Serbia [Belgrade] and Kosovo [Pristina] agree to move forward with economic normalization by agreeing to the following:

- Both parties will implement the Belgrade-Pristina highway agreement previously signed on February 14, 2020.
- Both parties will implement the Belgrade-Pristina rail agreement previously signed on February 14, 2020.
    - In addition, both parties will commit to a joint feasibility study on options for linking Belgrade-Pristina rail infrastructure to a deep sea port in the Adriatic.
- Kosovo [Pristina] and Serbia [Belgrade] will work with the U.S. International Development Finance Corporation and EXIM on memorandums of understanding to operationalize the following:
    - The Peace Highway
    - The rail link between Pristina and Merdare
    - The rail link between Nis and Pristina
    - Providing financing to support loans required for small and medium-sized enterprises (SME's)
    - Additional bilateral projects.
    - An international, U.S. International Development Finance Corporation full-time presence in Belgrade, Serbia.
- Both parties will open and operationalize the Merdare Common Crossing Point facility.
- Both parties will join the "mini-Schengen zone," announced by Serbia, Albania, and North Macedonia in October 2019, and fully utilize its benefits.
- Both parties will mutually recognize diplomas and professional certificates.
- Both parties will agree to work with the U.S. Department of Energy, and other appropriate U.S. Government entities, on a feasibility study for the purposes of sharing Gazivode/Ujmani Lake, as a reliable water and energy supply.
- Both parties will diversify their energy supplies.
- Both parties will prohibit the use of 5G equipment supplied by untrusted vendors in their communications networks. Where such equipment is already present, both parties commit to removal and other mediation efforts in a timely fashion.
- Both parties will increase airline passenger screening, information-sharing between each other, and within the framework of broader U.S. cooperation in the Balkans, and commit to technology upgrades to combat illicit activities by implementing and operationalizing U.S.-provided screening and information systems, including PISCES, APIS, ATS-G, and SRTP.

---

3 Washington Agreement, 'Economic Normalization' (2020) <https://www.peacefare.net/2020/09/04/much-ado-about-nothing/> also available at <https://exit.al/en/2020/09/04/kosovo-and-serbia-signed-separate-pledges-not-an-agreement/> accessed 22 March 2026.

In Serbia, this agreement is officially not accessible although it was signed by the President of Serbia directly at the White House in 2020. The version signed by Serbia is different in the aspect that there is a specific paragraph requesting Serbia to move its Israeli Embassy to Jerusalem. The Agreement is part of a bigger series of agreements known as the Abrahamic Accords initiated during the American presidential campaign in September 2020.

- Both parties pledge to protect and promote freedom of religion, including renewed interfaith communication, protection of religious sites and implementation of judicial decisions pertaining to the Serbian Orthodox Church, and continued restitution of Holocaust-era heirless and unclaimed Jewish property.

- Both parties pledge to expedite efforts to locate and identify the remains of missing persons. Both parties commit to identifying and implementing long-term, durable solutions for refugees and internally displaced persons. Both parties commit to identify a point of contact to lead these efforts within their respective government ministries and coordinate between Belgrade and Pristina, and will provide an annual update on the number of cases resolved and pending.

- Both parties will work with the 69 countries that criminalize homosexuality to push for decriminalization.

- Both parties pledge to designate Hizballah in its entirety as a terrorist organization, and fully implement measures to restrict Hizballah's operations and financial activities in their jurisdictions.

- Kosovo [Pristina] will agree to implement a one-year moratorium seeking new membership into International Organizations. Serbia [Belgrade] will agree to a one-year moratorium of its de-recognition campaign, and will refrain from formally or informally requesting any nation or International Organization not to recognize Kosovo [Pristina] as an independent state. Both agreements to desist will take effect immediately.

- Serbia [Belgrade] agrees to open a commercial office, and a ministry of state offices, in Jerusalem on September 20, 2020 and move its Embassy to Jerusalem by July 1, 2021.

President Aleksandar Vucic
September 4, 2020

4 Washington Agreement Kosovo Version

The Washington Agreement (Economic Normalization) from 2020 Kosovo[4] version.

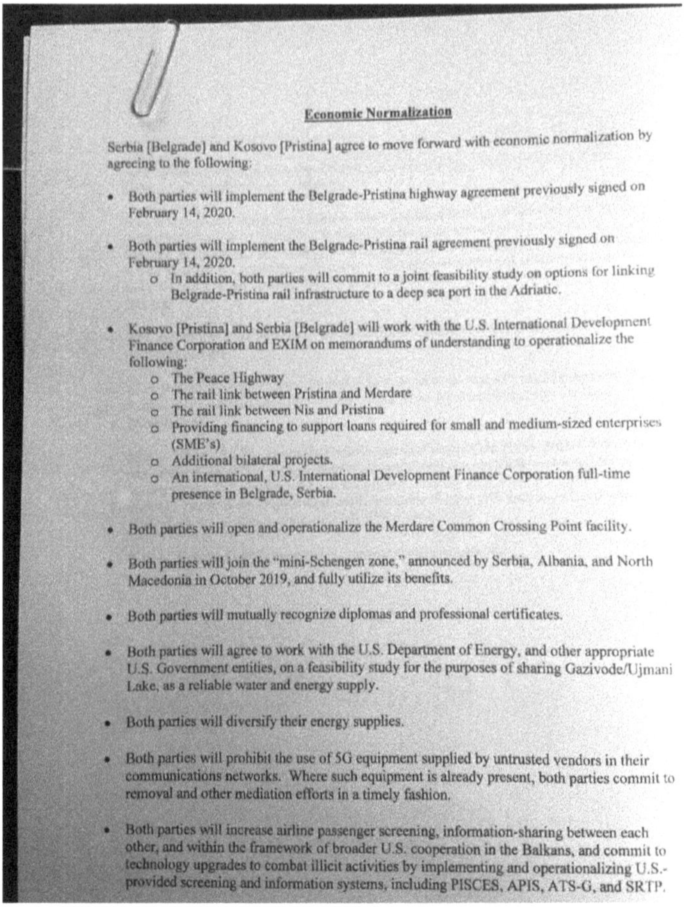

Economic Normalization

Serbia [Belgrade] and Kosovo [Pristina] agree to move forward with economic normalization by agreeing to the following:

- Both parties will implement the Belgrade-Pristina highway agreement previously signed on February 14, 2020.
- Both parties will implement the Belgrade-Pristina rail agreement previously signed on February 14, 2020.
  - In addition, both parties will commit to a joint feasibility study on options for linking Belgrade-Pristina rail infrastructure to a deep sea port in the Adriatic.
- Kosovo [Pristina] and Serbia [Belgrade] will work with the U.S. International Development Finance Corporation and EXIM on memorandums of understanding to operationalize the following:
  - The Peace Highway
  - The rail link between Pristina and Merdare
  - The rail link between Nis and Pristina
  - Providing financing to support loans required for small and medium-sized enterprises (SME's)
  - Additional bilateral projects.
  - An international, U.S. International Development Finance Corporation full-time presence in Belgrade, Serbia.
- Both parties will open and operationalize the Merdare Common Crossing Point facility.
- Both parties will join the "mini-Schengen zone," announced by Serbia, Albania, and North Macedonia in October 2019, and fully utilize its benefits.
- Both parties will mutually recognize diplomas and professional certificates.
- Both parties will agree to work with the U.S. Department of Energy, and other appropriate U.S. Government entities, on a feasibility study for the purposes of sharing Gazivode/Ujmani Lake, as a reliable water and energy supply.
- Both parties will diversify their energy supplies.
- Both parties will prohibit the use of 5G equipment supplied by untrusted vendors in their communications networks. Where such equipment is already present, both parties commit to removal and other mediation efforts in a timely fashion.
- Both parties will increase airline passenger screening, information-sharing between each other, and within the framework of broader U.S. cooperation in the Balkans, and commit to technology upgrades to combat illicit activities by implementing and operationalizing U.S.-provided screening and information systems, including PISCES, APIS, ATS-G, and SRTP.

---

4 Washington Agreement, 'Economic Normalization' (2020) <https://www.peacefare.net/2020/09/04/much-ado-about-nothing/> also available at <https://exit.al/en/2020/09/04/kosovo-and-serbia-signed-separate-pledges-not-an-agreement/> accessed 22 March 2026.

In Kosovo, this agreement is officially not accessible although it was signed by the Prime Minister of Kosovo directly at the White House in 2020. The version signed by Kosovo is very specific since in it it's stated that Kosovo and Israel agree to mutually recognize each other. This is an interesting precedent since Israel was not a party or signatory of neither the Serbian or the Kosovo version of this agreement. Further agreeing about a mutual recognition in an agreement named as Economic Normalization is also an interesting requirement.

- Both parties pledge to protect and promote freedom of religion, including renewed interfaith communication, protection of religious sites and implementation of judicial decisions pertaining to the Serbian Orthodox Church, and continued restitution of Holocaust-era heirless and unclaimed Jewish property.

- Both parties pledge to expedite efforts to locate and identify the remains of missing persons. Both parties commit to identifying and implementing long-term, durable solutions for refugees and internally displaced persons. Both parties commit to identify a point of contact to lead these efforts within their respective government ministries and coordinate between Belgrade and Pristina, and will provide an annual update on the number of cases resolved and pending.

- Both parties will work with the 69 countries that criminalize homosexuality to push for decriminalization.

- Both parties pledge to designate Hizballah in its entirety as a terrorist organization, and fully implement measures to restrict Hizballah's operations and financial activities in their jurisdictions.

- Kosovo [Pristina] will agree to implement a one-year moratorium seeking new membership into International Organizations. Serbia [Belgrade] will agree to a one-year moratorium of its de-recognition campaign, and will refrain from formally or informally requesting any nation or International Organization not to recognize Kosovo [Pristina] as an independent state. Both agreements to desist will take effect immediately.

- Kosovo [Pristina] and Israel agree to mutually recognize each other.

Prime Minister Avdullah Hoti
September 4, 2020

5 Kosovo Decision on 100% Import Duty on Serbian Goods (the Coca Cola Law)

The Kosovo Decision No 01/76 dated 21 November 2018 attached in its Serbian language version, which imposes a 100% import duty[5] on the goods imported from Serbia and Bosnia and Herzegovina. It also has an Annex quoting some goods which are excluded from this extensive taxation. The first item on the list is Coca Cola, a very popular drink produced by the famous Coca Cola Company.

Republika e Kosovës
Republika Kosova-Republic of Kosovo
Qeveria – Vlada – Government

Br. 01/76
Datum: 21.11.2018

Na osnovu člana 92 stav 4. i člana 93 stav (4) Ustava Republike Kosovo, člana 4 Pravilnika br. 02/2011 o oblastima administrativnih odgovornosti Kancelarije Premijera i ministarstava, izmenjenog i dopunjenog Pravilnikom br. 14/2017, Pravilnikom br. 15/2017 i Pravilnikom br. 16/2017, i Pravilnika br.07/2018, kao i člana 19 Pravilnika o radu Vlade Republike Kosova br. 09/2011, Vlada Republike Kosova je, na sednici održanoj 21. novembra 2018 godine, donela:

---

5 Republic of Kosovo, 'Odluku' (21 November 2018) <https://kryeministri.rks-gov.net/sr/blog/odluke-76-sednice-vlade-21-11-2018/> accessed 22 March 2026.

The imposition of 100% import duty on goods originating from Serbia, and Bosnia and Herzegovina is against the CEFTA Agreement. Initially, there were some goods exempted from this taxation, and among others it was the drink Coca Cola which was imported from Serbia. There were also other products from various multinational companies which just showed how (in)dependent post-conflict states were from multinational companies and their products.

ODLUKU

1. Nameće se mera carine od 100% na uvoz proizvoda poreklom iz Srbije i Bosne i Hercegovine.
2. Bez obzira na poreklo robe iz stava 1. ove odluke, mera od 100% se ne odnosi na poznate trgovačke robne marke drugih zemalja koje su proizvedene u Srbiji i Bosni i Hercegovini, koje su deo aneksa u prilogu ove odluke.
3. Obavezuje se Carina Republike Kosovo da zaustavi uvoz i pristup tržištu svih proizvoda koji na etiketi ili njihovoj deklaraciji imaju sadržaj: Uvoznik / distributer / predstavnik / proizvođač / ili na drugi način, za i na "Kosovo i Metohiju", "Kosovo UNMIK", "Kosovo 1244", "Kosovo Rezolucija 1244", kao i one u kojima se koriste samo imena gradova bez naziva države, ili bilo koji drugi naziv u suprotnosti sa ustavnim imenom Republike Kosovo.
4. Obavezuje se MTI – Tržišna inspekcija i opštinski inspektori da obavežu sve ekonomske operatere da uklone sa tržišta sve proizvode koji na etiketi ili njihovoj deklaraciji imaju sadržaj: uvoznik / distributer / zastupnik / proizvođač / ili na drugi način, za i na "Kosovo i Metohiju", "Kosovo UNMIK", "Kosovo 1244", "Kosovo Rezolucija 1244", kao i one na kojima se koriste samo imena gradova bez naziva država, ili bilo koji drugi nazivi koji su u suprotnosti sa ustavnim imenom Republike Kosovo.
5. Obavezuju se Carina Kosova, Agencija za hranu i veterinu i druge relevantne institucije da primenjuju iste mere protiv Srbije i Bosne i Hercegovine u pogledu dokumenata i sertifikata potrebnih za trgovinu (dokumenta i potvrde se odnose na analizu ispitivanja, laboratorijske analize, sanitarne i fitosanitarne sertifikate, barkodove kosovskih proizvoda).
6. Obavezuje se Ministarstvo finansija, Carina Kosova, Agencija za hranu i veterinu i druge relevantne institucije na sprovođenje ove odluke, u skladu sa važećim zakonskim propisima.
7. Sa ovom odlukom se ukida se odluka Vlade Republike Kosovo **br. 01/74** od 06. 11.2018 dana.
8. Ova odluka stupa na snagu danom potpisivanja.

Ramush HARADINAJ

____

Premijer Republike Kosovo

Dostavlja se:
- Zamenicima Premijera
- svim ministarstvima (ministrima)
- Generalnom sekretaru KPR-a
- Arhivi Vlade

Br	Naziv subjekta	Brend	Proizveden u	
1	Coca Cola HBC	Coca cola	Srbiji	
2	Ymalko	Ytong (Xella)blok	Srbiji	
3	Meridian Corporation	Rouch-Bravo	Srbiji	
4	Elkos SHPK	Henkel/Persil	Srbiji	
5	Lactalis shpk	Dukat	Bosni	
6	Meridian Corporation	Tuborg	Srbiji	
7	Gorenje Niti-Tiki	Gorenje	Srbiji	
8	Delfin LTD	Meggle	Bosni	
9	Fluidi	Jaffa – Nealkoholno piće	Srbiji	Jaffa - PIJE JO ALKOOLIKE

6 Nagorno-Karabakh Statement

The Statement[6] by President of the Republic of Azerbaijan, Prime Minister of the Republic of Armenia and President of the Russian Federation.

6 President of Russian Federation, 'Statement by President of the Republic of Azerbaijan, Prime Minister of the Republic of Armenia and President of the Russian Federation' (2020) <http://en.kremlin.ru/events/president/news/64384> also available at <https://documents-dds-ny.un.org/doc/UNDOC/GEN/N20/307/34/PDF/N2030734.pdf?OpenElement> accessed 22 March 2026.

This tripartite agreement or statement has ended the very intensive Second Nagorno-Karabakh War with an Azerbaijani dominance in NK and some very interesting and complex regional solutions. The statement and the war itself have lasted during the peak of the Corona virus Pandemic and the US Presidential elections in 2020. The requirements from this statement have never fully been implemented, and the Nagorno-Karabakh Republic has officially ceased to exist in 2024. Also, interestingly when in 2022 Russia attacked Ukraine, the long-lasting corona pandemics has lost priority and slowly faded away while the Russian invasion became the most important global issue in the years to come.

United Nations S/2020/1104

Security Council

Distr.: General
11 November 2020

Original: English

Letter dated 10 November 2020 from the Permanent Representative of the Russian Federation to the United Nations addressed to the President of the Security Council

I have the honour to bring to your attention a statement by the President of the Republic of Azerbaijan, the Prime Minister of the Republic of Armenia and the President of the Russian Federation on a complete ceasefire and termination of all hostilities in the area of the Nagorno-Karabakh conflict, signed on 9 November 2020 (see annex).

I should be grateful if you would circulate the present letter and its annex as a document of the Security Council.

(*Signed*) Vassily **Nebenzia**

Annex to the letter dated 10 November 2020 from the Permanent Representative of the Russian Federation to the United Nations addressed to the President of the Security Council

[Original: English and Russian]

Statement by President of the Republic of Azerbaijan, Prime Minister of the Republic of Armenia and President of the Russian Federation

We, President of the Republic of Azerbaijan Ilham Aliyev, Prime Minister of the Republic of Armenia Nikol Pashinyan and President of the Russian Federation Vladimir Putin, state the following:

1. A complete ceasefire and termination of all hostilities in the area of the Nagorno-Karabakh conflict is declared starting 12:00 am (midnight) Moscow time on November 10, 2020. The Republic of Azerbaijan and the Republic of Armenia, hereinafter referred to as the "Parties," shall stop in their current positions.

2. The Agdam District shall be returned to the Republic of Azerbaijan by November 20, 2020.

3. The peacemaking forces of the Russian Federation, namely, 1,960 troops armed with firearms, 90 armoured vehicles and 380 motor vehicles and units of special equipment, shall be deployed along the contact line in Nagorno-Karabakh and along the Lachin Corridor.

4. The peacemaking forces of the Russian Federation shall be deployed concurrently with the withdrawal of the Armenian troops. The peacemaking forces of the Russian Federation will be deployed for five years, a term to be automatically extended for subsequent five-year terms unless either Party notifies about its intention to terminate this clause six months before the expiration of the current term.

5. For more efficient monitoring of the Parties' fulfilment of the agreements, a peacemaking centre shall be established to oversee the ceasefire.

6. The Republic of Armenia shall return the Kalbajar District to the Republic of Azerbaijan by November 15, 2020, and the Lachin District by December 1, 2020. The Lachin Corridor (5 km wide), which will provide a connection between Nagorno-Karabakh and Armenia while not passing through the territory of Shusha, shall remain under the control of the Russian Federation peacemaking forces.

As agreed by the Parties, within the next three years, a plan will be outlined for the construction of a new route via the Lachin Corridor, to provide a connection between Nagorno-Karabakh and Armenia, and the Russian peacemaking forces shall be subsequently relocated to protect the route.

The Republic of Azerbaijan shall guarantee the security of persons, vehicles and cargo moving along the Lachin Corridor in both directions.

7. Internally displaced persons and refugees shall return to the territory of Nagorno-Karabakh and adjacent areas under the supervision of the United Nations High Commissioner for Refugees.

8. The Parties shall exchange prisoners of war, hostages and other detained persons, and dead bodies.

9. All economic and transport connections in the region shall be unblocked. The Republic of Armenia shall guarantee the security of transport connections between the western regions of the Republic of Azerbaijan and the Nakhchivan

Autonomous Republic in order to arrange unobstructed movement of persons, vehicles and cargo in both directions. The Border Guard Service of the Russian Federal Security Service shall be responsible for overseeing the transport connections.

As agreed by the Parties, new transport links shall be built to connect the Nakhchivan Autonomous Republic and the western regions of Azerbaijan.

7 Joint Statement for Afghanistan

The Joint Statement[7] of the Third ForeignMinisters' Meeting Among the Neighbouring Countries of Afghanistan.

Joint Statement of the Third Foreign Ministers' Meeting among the Neighboring Countries of Afghanistan

The third Foreign Ministers' Meeting Among the Neighboring Countries of Afghanistan was held in Tunxi, Anhui Province in China on 31 March 2022. Foreign Ministers or senior representatives of seven countries, namely China, Iran, Pakistan, Russia, Tajikistan, Turkmenistan and Uzbekistan, attended the meeting.

President Xi Jinping of the People's Republic of China sent a congratulatory message to the meeting. UN Secretary-General Antonio Guterres delivered remarks via video link.

In a candid and pragmatic atmosphere of mutual understanding, the parties had comprehensive, in-depth and constructive discussions on the situation in Afghanistan and on cooperation regarding Afghanistan, and declared the following:

1. Political and Diplomatic Fields

Reaffirmed respect for the independence, sovereignty, territorial integrity and national unity of Afghanistan, support for the Afghan people in independently deciding the future of their country, and support for the basic principle of 'Afghan-led and Afghan-owned'.

7 Embassy of the People's Republic of China in the Kingdom of the Netherlands, 'Joint Statement of the Third Foreign Ministers' Meeting Among the Neighboring Countries of Afghanistan' (31 March 2022) <http://nl.china-embassy.gov.cn/eng/zgyw/202203/t20220331_10658230.htm> also accessible on <http://lawinfochina.com/display.aspx?id=8253&lib=tax&SearchKeyword=&SearchCKeyword=> accessed 22 March 2026.

The Joint Statement is a very general document which is politically determining and supporting Afghanistan by its neighbours. It is regulating the general understanding of the situation in Afghanistan by its neighbouring countries and is fully accessible on the internet on the above given links. The Taliban Government in Afghanistan is not a signatory of the Joint statement.

Urged the countries mainly responsible for the current predicament in Afghanistan to earnestly fulfill commitments on the economic recovery and future development of Afghanistan.

Stressed that a peaceful, stable and prosperous Afghanistan serves the common interests of regional countries and Afghanistan, and expressed readiness to jointly play a constructive role to this end.

Noted the importance to achieve national reconciliation in Afghanistan through dialogue and negotiation, and to establish a broad-based and inclusive political structure, adopt moderate and sound domestic and foreign policies, and grow friendly relations with all countries, especially its neighbours, and *emphasized* the necessity for all sides to strengthen dialogue and communication with Afghanistan for the above purposes.

Noted the importance of taking necessary continuing steps in Afghanistan on ensuring women's rights and children's education, among others, and *called for* further actions to be taken to improve people's livelihood, safeguard the fundamental rights of all Afghans, including ethnic groups, women and children.

Reaffirmed opposition to attempts at politicizing humanitarian assistance, and *reiterated* respect and support for the central role of Afghanistan in distributing and using humanitarian assistance to be rendered by international community and international organizations to the people of Afghanistan.

2. Economic and Humanitarian Fields

Expressed deep concern over the humanitarian situation, economic and livelihood plight in Afghanistan and announced readiness to provide further humanitarian assistance to the people of Afghanistan.

Expressed appreciation of and support for the key role of the UN in providing humanitarian assistance to Afghanistan, and *called on* the international community in particular the UN agencies and relevant members of the UN Security Council to step up emergency humanitarian assistance to the people of Afghanistan.

Followed with concern the spread of COVID-19 and shortages of medicine and medical equipment in Afghanistan, and *expressed* readiness to help Afghanistan enhance capacity in health care and COVID-19 containment.

Expressed support for Afghanistan's efforts toward self-generated development, and undertook to support the economic recovery of Afghanistan at both bilateral and multilateral levels, open up ports further, and strengthen exchanges and cooperation with Afghanistan in such fields as trade and economy, energy, agriculture, finance, connectivity and infrastructure, to help Afghanistan build capacity for self-generated development.

Reaffirmed commitment to deepen cooperation within such frameworks as the Belt and Road Initiative, as well as regional cooperation organizations, and to include Afghanistan in the regional connectivity, energy and transport networks, economic and trade systems, in order to help Afghanistan unleash its geographical advantages and economic potential.

3. Counter-Terrorism and Security

Noted commitments and pledges made by Afghanistan to the international community that the territory of Afghanistan will not pose any threats to the neighbouring countries and no place will be given to terrorist groups on the Afghan territory.

Stressed terrorism as a key factor affecting stability in Afghanistan, condemned all forms of violence and terrorist attacks, and ***reiterated*** that ISIS, Al-Qaeda, ETIM, TTP, BLA, Jondollah, Jaish-Al-Adl, Jamaat Ansarullah, IMU and other terrorist organizations must not be given any place on the Afghan territory.

Called on relevant Afghan parties to take more visible steps to make a clean break with all forms of terrorist forces, monitor free movement of all terrorist organizations, and to firmly fight and eliminate them including through dismantling of their training camps, to ensure that Afghanistan would never again serve as a breeding ground, safe haven or source of proliferation for terrorism.

Urged relevant Afghan parties to safeguard the security and legitimate rights and interests of foreign citizens and institutions in Afghanistan.

Reaffirmed readiness to strengthen counter-terrorism and security cooperation among neighbouring countries, build a united front against terrorism. Noted the initiative of the Republic of Tajikistan on 'security belt' around Afghanistan. Tighten border control, prevent terrorist forces from fleeing across borders, and stay committed to safeguarding security and stability in the region.

Expressed readiness to conduct counter-terrorism and security cooperation with Afghanistan to help it build counter-terrorism capacity.

Encouraged relevant Afghan parties to take concrete actions against cultivation, production and illicit trafficking of narcotic drugs in order to crack down on organized crime to free Afghanistan from the scourge of drugs.

Reaffirmed readiness to scale up joint efforts to combat cross-border drug-related crime and protect people's health and social stability.

4. Refugees

Expressed concern over the situation of the Afghan refugee as well as internally displaced people and support for UN agencies in playing an active role in this regard.

Expressed appreciation of the efforts made by the regional countries, in particular Pakistan and Iran, on the issue of Afghan refugees and ***called on*** the international community to provide those countries with continuous, sufficient and proportionate financial support for timely return of Afghan refugees with dignity and honour.

5. Institution Building

Announced the launch of a mechanism for regular consultations among special envoys (special representatives) for Afghanistan of the neighbouring countries and three working groups namely political and diplomatic, economic and humanitarian, security and stability, to follow up on the outcomes of the foreign ministers' meetings among the neighbouring countries of Afghanistan.

Expressed appreciation and gratitude to the Chinese side for hosting the 3rd Foreign Ministers' Meeting at the high organizational level, supported Uzbekistan to convene the 4th Foreign Ministers' Meeting in first quarter of 2023 in Tashkent.

8 The Tunxi Initiative for Afghanistan

The Tunxi Initiative[8] of the Neighbouring Countries of Afghanistan on Supporting Economic Reconstruction in and Practical Cooperation with Afghanistan.

The Tunxi Initiative of the Neighboring Countries of Afghanistan on Supporting Economic Reconstruction in and Practical Cooperation with Afghanistan

The Third Foreign Ministers' Meeting Among the Neighboring Countries of Afghanistan was held in Tunxi, Anhui Province in China on 31 March 2022. Foreign ministers or high-level representatives of China, Iran, Pakistan, Russia, Tajikistan, Turkmenistan and Uzbekistan were present.

All parties at the meeting note that with the end of long years of war in Afghanistan, the country is now struggling with serious economic and livelihood difficulties as well as challenges across sectors. All parties pledge to support Afghanistan's economic reconstruction in areas such as humanitarian assistance, connectivity, economy and trade, agriculture, energy and capacity building.

1 Humanitarian Assistance

All parties decide to provide further humanitarian assistance to Afghanistan, and call on the international community to give more support to Afghanistan, to help it restore cash liquidity and avoid humanitarian disaster.

1. China will speed up delivering its commitment of providing Afghanistan with emergency humanitarian assistance such as food, winter supplies,

---

8 Ministry of Foreign Affairs of the People's Republic of China, 'The Tunxi Initiative of the Neighboring Countries of Afghanistan on Supporting Economic Reconstruction in and Practical Cooperation with Afghanistan' (1 April 2022) <https://www.fmprc.gov.cn/mfa_eng/gjhdq_665435/2675_665437/2676_663356/2677_663358/202204/t20220401_10662024.html> also available on <https://lawinfochina.com/display.aspx?id=8251&lib=tax&SearchKeyword=&SearchCKeyword> accessed 22 March 2026.

The Tunxi Initiative is a much more detailed agreement made by the neighbouring countries of Afghanistan on supporting economic reconstruction in and practical cooperation with Afghanistan. It is fully accessible on the internet on the above given links. The Taliban Government in Afghanistan is not a signatory of the Tunxi Initiative.

COVID-19 vaccines and medical equipment, and is ready to provide additional humanitarian assistance through bilateral and multilateral channels.

2. China will continue to provide Afghanistan with vaccines, medical equipment, medicine and other anti-epidemic supplies, carry out cooperation in Traditional Chinese Medicine, support the operation of Afghanistan's medical and health systems, and help Afghanistan fight COVID-19.

3. Iran has sent more than 30 humanitarian aid shipments including food, medicine and health items to help the people in different cities of Afghanistan, and is consulting and coordinating with the Afghan side to send new supportive shipments.

4. Iran will continue to provide emergency fuel and food and other necessary daily-life items to the people of Afghanistan.

5. Pakistan announced in-kind humanitarian assistance package of Rs. 5 billion (around $30 million). Pakistan has provided more than 13,000 tonnes of humanitarian aid to Afghanistan under Pak–Afghan Cooperation Forum and provided three consignments of wheat to Afghanistan. Pakistan has also been channelizing humanitarian assistance from various philanthropic organizations of Pakistan.

6. Pakistan is also acting as a channel to facilitate the flow of international humanitarian assistance to Afghanistan, including providing transit facility for Indian wheat to Afghanistan on an exceptional basis for humanitarian purposes and facilitating the UN Humanitarian Air Service (UNHAS) airbridge between Islamabad and Kabul.

7. Pakistan hosted 17th Extraordinary Session of OIC-CFM in Islamabad on 19 December 2021 where, inter alia, the following was decided:

a. Establishment of a Humanitarian Trust Fund for Afghanistan (formalized during the 48th OIC Council of Foreign Ministers meeting in Islamabad)
b. Appointment of Ambassador Tarig Ali Bakheet as Special Envoy of the Secretary General of the OIC for Afghanistan
c. OIC General Secretariat, together with Islamic Development Bank and the Humanitarian Trust Fund, to devise a roadmap in concert with UN system organizations for unlocking financial and banking channels
d. OIC General Secretariat, in concert with World Health Organization and other relevant stakeholders, shall secure vaccines and medical supplies for COVID-19
e. Launching an Afghanistan Food Security Programme, under the aegis of Islamic Organization for Food Security (IOFS)

8. Pakistan continues to provide free COVID-19 vaccination for all Afghans entering Pakistan, works with the Bill Gates Foundation for the eradication

of Polio in Afghanistan, and is allowing Afghan patients and their attendants entry into Pakistan to enable their treatment in hospitals across Pakistan.

9. Russia stands ready to continue its humanitarian assistance to the people of Afghanistan.

10. Tajikistan will continue to provide its logistics means, in particular through the six bridges across Tajik–Afghan border, to deliver humanitarian assistance to the people of Afghanistan. Tajikistan will maintain the functioning of border crossing point Panji Poyon for transporting food and other vital products to the people of Afghanistan.

11. Tajikistan will also continue to offer medical services to the citizens of Afghanistan residing in Tajik–Afghan border areas.

12. Turkmenistan will continue to provide humanitarian support to Afghanistan on a systematic basis, which is expressed in the construction of medical and educational institutions on the territory of the neighbouring country, preferential supplies of electricity, training of Afghan students in educational institutions of Turkmenistan, regularly sending of humanitarian convoys to Afghanistan, and other types of help and assistance.

13. Turkmenistan will continue to send humanitarian cargoes to Afghanistan with food, textile and household products, medicines and medical supplies, as well as oil products.

14. Turkmenistan from its own resources will supply medicines to the medical centre built by Turkmenistan in the province of Faryab and the maternity hospital in the Turgundi city of the province of Herat.

15. Uzbekistan expressed readiness to use the capabilities of the international transport and logistics hub in the city of Termez for the delivery of humanitarian cargo to Afghanistan.

2 Connectivity

All parties recognize the importance of connectivity to the sustainable development of Afghanistan as a 'land-locked country', and stand ready to leverage their respective strengths to support Afghanistan in, based on the existing transportation networks with neighbouring countries, exploring step by step new convenient channels to strengthen ' hard connectivity' of infrastructure and 'soft connectivity' of rules and standards with neighbouring countries.

All parties are ready to strengthen cooperation in the implementation of transport agreements developed within the framework of the UN's Economic and Social Commission for Asia and Pacific (ESCAP).

16. China supports the extension of the China–Pakistan Economic Corridor and the China–Central Asia–West Asia Economic Corridor to Afghanistan, and is ready to promote synergy between the Belt and Road Initiative and the development strategies of Afghanistan, and support the smooth operation of the China–Afghanistan freight train services, to help Afghanistan better integrate into the regional economic integration process.

17. Iran has paved the way for Afghanistan to connect to the world markets by the Khaf–Herat railway and plans to complete the railway and extend it to Central Asian countries via Mazar-e-Sharif to help Afghanistan get rid of landlock limitations.

18. Iran is developing the port of Chabahar and will continue to develop the infrastructure of Chabahar port and its land and sea transit routes along with road projects such as the Mahiroud–Farah road undertaken by Iran in order to help strengthen the situation and transit position of Afghanistan.

19. Pakistan with its renewed focus on 'geo-economics' feels that the dividends of 'regional' connectivity cannot be realized without enduring peace in Afghanistan and will continue to support efforts contributing to regional connectivity.

20. Pakistan believes that Afghanistan can be connected with the CPEC project for enhanced connectivity, which will benefit the entire region, especially Central Asia, for trade and commerce.

21. Agreement between Uzbekistan and Pakistan for Transit Trade (AUPTT) has been made operational and test run of four consignments under this arrangement has already materialized from Karachi to Tashkent through Afghanistan. Movement of trucks under TIR has been successfully operationalized between Pakistan and Uzbekistan via Afghanistan.

22. Pakistan is undertaking a number of connectivity projects with Afghanistan such as completion of Torkham–Jalalabad Road project and revival of road bus service between Pakistan and Afghanistan.

23. Russia supports development of transport connectivity between Central Asian countries and Afghanistan, Pakistan and other regional states and purposes in this regard to use capacities of Russian-Afghan joint transport companies 'ASTRAS' and 'AFSOTR'.

24. Tajikistan will further develop and construct the rail road and cargo center in the Free Economic Zone 'Panj' on the border area with Afghanistan with the view to increase transit trade.

25. Turkmenistan will contribute to the development of the transport, transit and communication system of Afghanistan, the intensification of the transit of cargo and passenger flows, by maintaining the operation of the railways along the route Atamyrat–Imamnazar–Akina–Andkhoy, which is designed to

connect the countries of the region with further access to the railway network of China. Turkmenistan is also interested in the further implementation of the transport project – the construction of the Turgundi–Herat railway with a length of 173 kilometres.

26. Turkmenistan intends to continue to promote the project of the transport corridor Turkmenistan–Afghanistan–Pakistan, as well as the implementation of the project of fibre optic line construction along the above route.

27. Turkmenistan will continue to promote the implementation of the Lapis Lazuli transit and transport corridor, established in the framework of the Agreement signed between Turkmenistan, Afghanistan, Azerbaijan, Georgia and Turkey. The successful implementation of this project will be a significant contribution to the development of interregional trade and economic relations, including the socio-economic condition of Afghanistan.

28. Turkmenistan will continue to maintain the uninterrupted operation of the Imamnazar–Akina and Serhetabat–Turgundi fibre optic lines, which are aimed at ensuring international transit flows, and will increase the speed of data transfer, as well as will guarantee a reliable communication link between Turkmenistan and Afghanistan.

29. Uzbekistan is ready to strengthen regional interconnectedness through the implementation of construction projects such as the 'Termez–Mazar-i-Sharif–Kabul–Peshawar' railway line.

30. Uzbekistan will continue to actively participate in the restoration of infrastructure facilities, in particular, the international airport in Mazar-i-Sharif.

31. Uzbekistan is ready to take an active part in the construction of large infrastructure projects in Afghanistan, such as the construction of roads, roadside infrastructure, bridges and tunnels.

3 Economy and Trade

All parties expressed willingness to assist Afghanistan on its efforts toward self-generated development, and encourage Afghanistan to formulate future economic development plans based on its own national conditions and enhance internal driving force for development.

All parties agree to explore the establishment of an economic cooperation belt around Afghanistan to improve Afghanistan's external development environment. All parties call on Afghanistan to create a favourable business environment for foreign enterprises.

All parties encourage the use of local currencies in bilateral trade and investment to lower transaction costs and facilitate trade and investment.

All parties are ready to strengthen communication with Afghanistan on trade policies, explore the signing of trade facilitation agreements, formulate transitional preferential trade arrangements, reduce taxes and fees on trade with Afghanistan, streamline customs clearance procedures such as commodity declaration and quality inspection, and improve Afghanistan's level of trade facilitation.

32. China pledges to continue to provide development assistance to Afghanistan for small and medium livelihood projects to benefit Afghan people.

33. China supports its enterprises in investing and starting businesses in Afghanistan when the security situation permits, and in resuming projects such as the Aynak Copper Mine and the Amu Darya Oilfield in due course. China supports its enterprises to help Afghanistan improve its mobile network, and explore and develop mineral resources.

34. Iran is pursuing the expansion of bilateral trade and economic exchanges with Afghanistan by different tools including development of joint border markets and continues to remove trade obstacles through different ways including reduction of existing tariffs based on agreements with Afghan side.

35. Iran declares its readiness to assist in the exploration and extraction of mines, including the reserves in joint borders areas, and to provide technical assistance as well as joint investment to Afghanistan in this field.

36. Pakistan has taken initiative to facilitate transit trade through operationalizing five border crossing points with Afghanistan. To ease issues in trade with Afghanistan, Pakistan revised customs processes and implemented other facilitative measures, including put in place a facilitative visa regime for Afghan people.

37. Pakistan has allowed export of several items to Afghanistan in Pakistani Rupees via land routes to facilitate Afghanistan's economy. A regime of Temporary Admission Documents (TAD) for commercial vehicles of Afghanistan and Pakistan has been agreed to facilitate movement of goods.

38. Pakistan has reduced/waived off customs duty on Afghanistan's perishable items such as fruits and vegetables being exported to Pakistan, and offered Afghanistan the opportunity to establish cold storage facilities close to border crossing points to assist trade in fruits and vegetables.

39. Russia expresses its support to national and joint Russian–Afghan businesses to start economic and trade activities in Afghanistan. Russia supports its companies to develop Afghanistan's oil and gas fields and realize mined products on mutual agreed conditions.

40. Turkmenistan will develop trade and economic ties with Afghanistan, and continue to implement new joint projects in such important areas as energy, transport and communications, involving Afghan companies to these projects.

In particular, Turkmenistan will promote the implementation of the construction of the transnational gas pipeline Turkmenistan–Afghanistan–Pakistan–India (TAPI), which is an important aspect of trade and economic cooperation, and which will ensure the development and restoration of the social and economic infrastructure of Afghanistan.

41. Uzbekistan takes an active part in the development of cross-border trade. For these purposes, the construction of the Termez International Trade Center is being carried out in the border zone with Afghanistan.

42. Uzbekistan is interested in increasing mutual trade with Afghanistan. To this end, the issue of establishing a preferential regime in mutual trade is being worked out with the Afghan side.

4 Agriculture

All parties note that agriculture is Afghanistan's pillar industry, encourage Afghanistan to vigorously develop agriculture and raise food self-sufficiency, and stand ready to provide necessary support for Afghanistan's agricultural development.

43. China supports Afghanistan in cultivating cotton, pepper, sunflower seeds and other agricultural products and exporting them to China, and will continue to facilitate the export of Afghan specialty agricultural products including pine nut, saffron, almond and pomegranate to China.

44. China stands ready to, as needed by Afghanistan, provide seeds, fertilizers and agricultural materials and machinery to Afghanistan, and support the development of high-value-added agricultural industries such as greenhouse planting to help Afghan farmers raise income.

45. China supports Afghanistan in strengthening agricultural infrastructure.

46. Iran declares its readiness to present to Afghanistan side a list of its agricultural and livestock needs to be produced in Afghanistan in order to be exported to Iran.

47. Pakistan is desirous of deepening agriculture cooperation with Afghanistan and continues to engage with Afghan side to explore ways and means for agriculture.

48. Pakistan can provide all possible technical assistance and capacity building opportunities to Afghanistan in the field of agriculture and livestock.

49. Pakistan and Afghanistan can enhance cooperation in agri-research, imports/exports of agricultural products, market access and potential areas of trade in livestock, red meat and fisheries.

50. Russia will develop cooperation with Afghanistan in the areas of mutual interest, in particular to promote the comprehensive agricultural development of Afghanistan, ensure food security, facilitate export of Russian agricultural products, and facilitate mutual access to agricultural products. Russia supports its enterprises to export livestock and agricultural products to Afghanistan on Afghanistan's market demands.

51. Uzbekistan will continue to supply Afghanistan with food products, flour and grain, as well as essential goods.

5 Energy

All parties recognize that accelerating energy infrastructure development is crucial to Afghanistan's economic development and improvement of living standards, and stand ready to make joint efforts to improve Afghanistan's energy infrastructure.

52. China is ready to continue discussions with Afghanistan on solar power station and other projects based on Afghanistan's needs and security condition, etc.

53. Iran declares its readiness to increase the current level of electricity export to Afghanistan, welcomes constructing power plants inside the country and also exporting technical and engineering services for all shapes of energy including renewable ones.

54. Pakistan supports energy infrastructure projects for the integration of regional countries in terms of economic development, infrastructure and improvement in livelihoods.

55. Pakistan is working on mega projects such as CASA-1000 and TAPI to augment energy cooperation with Central Asia through Afghanistan.

56. Russia stands ready to consider conduction of analysis with other interested parties of Afghanistan's crucial infrastructure (power, water supply, road system etc.) with a view to develop a coordinated reconstruction plan.

57. Tajikistan stands ready to ensure its continuous supply of electricity to Afghanistan on discounted rate as part of assistance for Afghanistan economic reconstruction, in particular to the Northern provinces and to the capital Kabul.

58. Tajikistan supports other multinational energy projects and emphasized the importance of completion of the CASA-1000 project which will serve as the vivid example of greater interregional cooperation and connectivity between Central and South Asia.

59. Turkmenistan intends to continue providing reliable energy supply to the northern provinces of Afghanistan, in particular, along the route of the Kerki–Shibergan power lines.

60. Furthermore, Turkmenistan will promote the realization of the project of construction of the Turkemenistan–Afghanistan–Pakistan (TAP) power transmission line, laid in parallel with the TAPI gas pipeline, together with the Afghan and Pakistani sides. The project will serve as an important part of the energy infrastructure of Afghanistan, helping it on its path to economic recovery.

61. Uzbekistan is ready to accelerate the implementation of the 'Surkhan–Puli-Khumri' power transmission line construction project.

62. Uzbekistan will continue the uninterrupted supply of electricity to Afghanistan, and also expresses its readiness to increase the volume of electricity supplied.

63. The Uzbek side expresses its readiness to participate in joint exploration of minerals and in projects for their development and production.

6 Capacity Building

All parties recognize that sufficient professional and technical talents is an important underpinning for Afghanistan's future development, stand ready to provide support to this end, and call on outstanding Afghan talents to contribute to the country's development and rejuvenation.

64. China pledges to further strengthen human resource development cooperation with Afghanistan for the cultivation of talents in key areas such as governance, health, poverty reduction and alleviation, disaster prevention and mitigation and trade and investment.

65. China is ready to work with other neighbours of Afghanistan to provide joint training programs for Afghanistan.

66. Iran has announced its readiness to provide Afghanistan people with bilateral or multilateral training courses in various fields such as health and treatment, empowerment of women and girls, technical training and other needed area inside Afghanistan or any other country.

67. Pakistan has offered technical and capacity building training in various sectors such as health, economy, banking, aviation and information technol-

ogy to Afghanistan. Pakistan has been considering positively scholarships for Afghan students.

68. Russia pledges to further provide scholarships to Afghan civilian students.

69. Tajikistan will continue to create favourable conditions to those Afghan students studying in its higher education institutions, as well as allocate annual scholarships to the citizens of Afghanistan.

70. Turkmenistan will continue to provide quotas for the education of Afghan students in educational institutions of Turkmenistan, training specialists in the fields of transport, energy and healthcare.

71. Uzbekistan expressed its readiness to organize courses for the training of specialists in the field of agriculture and irrigation on the basis of the Educational Center in Termez.

72. Uzbekistan will continue to train professional personnel, improve the skills of specialists and expand the list of professions on the basis of the Educational Center in the city of Termez to train Afghan youth.

All parties call on the international community as well as relevant regional and international financial institutions to provide financing support for Afghanistan's reconstruction and development.

Bibliography

Books

Arsham Kuftinec, Sonja 'Theatrical Facilitation in Post-war Societies: The Case of Bosnia' in Carolina Rehrmann, Rafael Biermann and Philip Tolliday (ed), Societies in Transition: The Caucasus and the Balkans between Conflict and Reconciliation (Vandenhoeck & Ruprecht 2020).

Auch, Eva-Maria, 'Conflict, Identity and Reconciliation in the South Caucasus' in Carolina Rehrmann, Rafael Biermann and Philip Tolliday (ed), Societies in Transition: The Caucasus and the Balkans between Conflict and Reconciliation (Vandenhoeck & Ruprecht 2020).

Avakian, Fernando 'Discursive Construction of the Islamic Threat in the Russian Federation in the Early 2000s: A Political Tool Hampering Reconciliation?' in Carolina Rehrmann, Rafael Biermann and Philip Tolliday (ed), Societies in Transition: The Caucasus and the Balkans between Conflict and Reconciliation (Vandenhoeck & Ruprecht 2020).

Barma, Naazneen H. The Peacebuilding Puzzle: Political Order in Post-conflict States (Cambridge University Press 2017).

Bernath Julie, Dit Fatogoma Adou Djané and Jones Briony, 'Understanding "Resistance" to Transitional Justice' in Martin Leiner and Christine Schliesser (ed), Alternative Approaches in Conflict Resolution (Palgrave Macmillan 2018).

Biermann, Rafael 'The Politics of Reconciliation in Former Yugoslavia-Assesing Progress across the Region' in Carolina Rehrmann, Rafael Biermann and Philip Tolliday (ed), Societies in Transition: The Caucasus and the Balkans between Conflict and Reconciliation (Vandenhoeck & Ruprecht 2020).

Boyle, Michael J. Violence after War: Explaining Instability in Post-conflict States (Johns Hopkins University Press 2014).

Brummer, Chris, Soft Law and the Global Financial System: Rule Making in the 21st Century (Cambridge University Press 2015).

Castillo, Graciana del, Rebuilding War-Torn States: The Challenge of Post-conflict Economic Reconstruction (Oxford University Press 2008).

Dam-de Jong, Daniella, International Law and Governance of Natural Resources in Conflict and Post-conflict Situations (Cambridge University Press 2015).

De Brabandere, Eric, Post-conflict Administrations in International Law: International Territorial Administration, Transitional Authority and Foreign Occupation in Theory and Practice (Martinus Nijhoff Publishers 2009).

Donais, Timothy, Peacebuilding and Local Ownership: Post-conflict Consensus-Building (Routledge 2012).

Eliantonio Mariolina, Korkea-aho Emilia and Ştefan Oana (ed), EU Soft Law in the Member States: Theoretical Findings and Empirical Evidence (Hart 2021).

Falkner Gerda, Treib Oliver, Hartlapp Miriam and Leiber Simone, Complying with Europe: EU Harmonisation and Soft Law in the Member States (Cambridge University Press 2005).

Ford, Jolyon, Regulating Business for Peace: The United Nations, the Private Sector and Post-conflict Recovery (Cambridge University Press 2015).

Goda, Samuel 'The OSCE and Reconciliation: Between Theory and Practice' in Lily Gardner Feldman, Raisa Barash, Samuel Goda and André Zempelburg (ed), The Former Soviet Union and East Central Europe between Conflict and Reconciliation (Vandenhoeck & Ruprecht 2019).

Goldbarsht, Doron, Global Counter-Terrorist Financing and Soft Law: Multi-layered Approaches (Edward Elgar 2020).

Grießer, Emanuel, '„Soft Law" in der Europäischen Union und Österreich' (Dissertation zur Erlangung des Akademischen Grades Dr.iur, Leopold-Franzens-Universität 2016).

Klimenko, V. Ekaterina, 'Russianin the Aftermath of the Chechen Conflict: Fostering Tolerance as Reconciliation Strategy' In Carolina Rehrmann, Rafael Biermann and Philip Tolliday (ed), Societies in Transition: The Caucasus and the Balkans between Conflict and Reconciliation (Vandenhoeck & Ruprecht 2020).

Knauff, Matthias, 'Soft Law Im Europäischen Und Internationalen Verwaltungsrecht' in Wolfgang Kahl und Markus Ludwigs (ed), Band 2: Grundstrukturen des europäischen und internationalen Verwaltungsrechts (CF Müller 2021).

Knauff, Matthias, Der Regelungsverbund : Recht Und Soft Law Im Mehrebenensystem (Mohr Siebeck 2010).

Koopman, Nico, 'Churches, Universities and the Post-TRC Process: Impulses from a Consultation' in Christo Thesnaar and Len Hansen (ed), Unfinished Business? Faith Communities and Reconciliation in a Post-TRC Context (African Sun Media 2020).

Korostelina, Karina V. 'Reconciliation in Ukraine: Within and across the Boundary' in Lily Gardner Feldman, Raisa Barash, Samuel Goda and André Zempelburg (ed), The Former Soviet Union and East Central Europe between Conflict and Reconciliation (Vandenhoeck & Ruprecht 2019).

Leiner, Martin, 'Conclusion: From Conflict Resolution to Reconciliation' in Martin Leiner and Christine Schliesser (ed), Alternative Approaches in Conflict Resolution (Palgrave Macmillan 2018).

Leiner, Martin, 'Creating Space for Truth: Reconciliation Studies and the 2014 TRC Reenactment' in Christo Thesnaar and Len Hansen (ed), Unfinished Business? Faith Communities and Reconciliation in a Post-TRC Context (African Sun Media 2020).

Leiner, Martin, 'Introduction to Negotiation' in Martin Leiner and Christine Schliesser (ed), Alternative Approaches in Conflict Resolution (Palgrave Macmillan 2018).

Leiner, Martin, 'Setting the Stage: An Introductory Clarification of Concepts of East Central Europe' in Lily Gardner Feldman, Raisa Barash, Samuel Goda and André Zempelburg (ed), The Former Soviet Union and East Central Europe between Conflict and Reconciliation (Vandenhoeck & Ruprecht 2019).

Marquier, Julia 'Soft law : das Beispiel des OSZE-Prozesses ; ein Beitrag zur völkerrechtlichen Rechtsquellenlehre' (Inaugural-Dissertation zur Erlangung des Grades eines Doktors der Rechte, Rheinische Friedrich-Wilhelms-Universität 2003).

Menon Rajan and Rumer Eugene, Conflict in Ukraine: The Unwinding of the Post–Cold War Order (Massachusetts Institute of Technology 2015).

Nikolić-Ristanović Vesna and Ćopić Sonja, 'Dealing with Conflicts in a Post-conflict Society: A Restorative Initiative in Serbia' in Carolina Rehrmann, Rafael Biermann and Philip Tolliday (ed), Societies in Transition: The Caucasus and the Balkans between Conflict and Reconciliation (Vandenhoeck & Ruprecht 2020).

Nußberger, Angelika, 'Hard Law or Soft Law – Does It Matter?: Distinction between Different Sources of International Law in the Jurisprudence of the ECtHR' in Anne van Aaken and Iulia Motoc (ed), The European Convention on Human Rights and General International Law (Oxford Academic 2018).

Petersmann, Ernst-Ulrich, 'From Integration through Law to Global Community Law? between Arbitration, Adjudication, and Judicial Overreach' in Giuliana Ziccardi Capaldo (ed), The Global Community Yearbook of International Law and Jurisprudence 2020 (Oxford University Press 2021).

Philpott, Daniel, The Politics of Past Evil : Religion, Reconciliation, and the Dilemmas of Transitional Justice (University of Notre Dame Press 2006).

Popescu, Nicu, EU Foreign Policy and Post-Soviet Conflicts: Stealth Intervention (Routledge 2011).

Rijsbergen, Marloes van, Legitimacy and Effectiveness of ESMA's Soft Law (Edward Elgar 2021).

Rojansky, Matthew, 'Russian-Ukrainian Relations: Conflict Ad Reconciliation over Shared History' in Lily Gardner Feldman, Raisa Barash, Samuel Goda and André Zempelburg (ed), The Former Soviet Union and East Central Europe between Conflict and Reconciliation (Vandenhoeck & Ruprecht 2019).

Rytövuori-Apunen, Helena, Power and Conflict in Russia's Borderlands: The Post-Soviet Geopolitics of Dispute Resolution (Bloomsbury Publishing 2020).

Saul, Matthew, Popular Governance of Post-conflict Reconstruction: The Role of International Law (Cambridge University Press 2014).

Scholz, Sebastian 'Integration Durch Soft Law – Eine Rechtsstaatliche Herausforderung' in Jörn Axel Kämmerer, Markus Kotzur and Jacques Ziller (ed), Integration und Desintegration in Europa (Nomos 2019).

Schuessler, Rudolf, 'Justice in Negotiations and Conflict Resolution' in Martin Leiner and Christine Schliesser (ed), Alternative Approaches in Conflict Resolution (Palgrave Macmillan 2018).

Senden, Linda, Soft Law in European Community Law (Hart Publishing 2004).

Sommer, Marie-Christin, 'Die Bedeutung des internationalen Soft Law der Vereinten Nationen und des Europarates für den deutschen Strafvollzug : am Beispiel des Vollzugs der Freiheitsstrafe an erwachsenen Männern' (Dissertation, Friedrich-Schiller-Universität Jena 2022).

Telaku Mimoza and Sagy Shifra, 'Perceptions of Collective Narratives and Acculturation Attitudes: the Case of Serbs and Albanians in Kosovo' in Lily Gardner Feldman, Raisa Barash, Samuel Goda and André Zempelburg (ed), The Former Soviet Union and East Central Europe between Conflict and Reconciliation (Vandenhoeck & Ruprecht 2019).

Westhuizen, Marichen van der, 'Thoughts into Action: Creating a Long-Term Movement toward a Reconciled and Just Society' in Christo Thesnaar and Len Hansen (ed), Unfinished Business? Faith Communities and Reconciliation in a Post-TRC Context (African Sun Media 2020).

Zucconi, Cesare, 'Beyond Official Negotiations: The Experience of the Community of Sant'Egidio' in Martin Leiner and Christine Schliesser (ed), Alternative Approaches in Conflict Resolution (Palgrave Macmillan 2018).

Zupančič Rok and Pejič Nina, Limits to the European Union's Normative Power in a Post-conflict Society: EULEX and Peacebuilding in Kosovo (Springer 2018).

Articles

Aas Rustad Siri and Malmin Binningsbø Helga "A Price Worth Fighting for? Natural Resources and Conflict Recurrence" (2012) 49 (4) Journal of Peace Research 531.

Abbott W. Kenneth and Snidal Duncan 'Hard and Soft Law in International Governance' (2000) 54 International Organization 421.

Adinolfi, Giovanna 'Soft Law in International Investment Law and Arbitration' (2021) 1 The Italian Review of International and Comparative Law 86.

Andone Corina and Coman-Kund Florin 'Persuasive Rather than "Binding" EU Soft Law? An Argumentative Perspective on the European Commission's Soft Law Instruments in Times of Crisis' (2022) 10 The Theory and Practice of Legislation 22.

Andone Corina and Greco Sara 'Evading the Burden of Proof in European Union Soft Law Instruments: The Case of Commission Recommendations' (2018) 31 Int J Semiot Law 79.

Ballard J., Megan 'Post-conflict Property Restitution: Flawed Legal and Theoretical Foundations' (2010) 28 Berkeley Journal of International Law 462.

Baylis, Elena "The International Law Commission's Soft Law Influence" (2019) 13 FIU L. Rev. 1007.
Beard, Jack M. 'Soft Law's Failure on the Horizon: The International Code of Conduct for Outer Space Activities' (2017) 38 U. Pa. J. Int'l L. 335.
Beha, Adem "Disputes over the 15-Point Agreement on Normalization of Relations between Kosovo and Serbia" (2015) 43 Nationalities Papers 102.
Bernstorff, Jochen von 'New Responses to the Legitimacy Crisis of International Institutions: The Role of "Civil Society" and the Rise of the Principle of Participation of "The Most Affected" in International Institutional Law' (2021) 32 EJIL 125.
Bieber, Florian 'The Serbia-Kosovo Agreements: An Eu Success Story?' (2015) 40 Review of Central and East European Law 285.
Bivainis, Andrius 'Multi-dimensional Assessment of the Second Nagorno-Karabakh War' (2022) 38 Security and Defence Quarterly 51.
Blanchard F. Jean-Marc and Lu Fujia 'Thinking Hard about Soft Power: A Review and Critique of the Literature on China and Soft Power' (2012) 36 Asian Perspective 565.
Block-Lieb, Susan 'Soft and Hard Strategies: The Role of Business in the Crafting of International Commercial Law' (2019) 40 Mich. J. Int'l L. 433.
Blutman, László 'In the Trap of a Legal Metaphor: International Soft Law' (2010) 59 The International and Comparative Law Quarterly 605.
Boyle E., Alan 'Some Reflections on the Relationship of Treaties and Soft Law' (1999) 48 The International and Comparative Law Quarterly 901.
Brown C., Ronald 'China's BRI in Central Eastern European Countries: "17+1" Connectivity, Divisiveness, Or Pathway to EU-CHINA FTA?' (2020) 22 San Diego International Law Journal 1.
Brown Scott A.W. 'The EU's 'strategic partnership' with China in a post-Brexit world: Recalibrating internal dynamics and facing up to external challenges' (2020) 4 Europe and the World: A Law Review 1.
Çalı Başak 'Costello Cathryn and Cunningham Stewart 'Hard Protection through Soft Courts? Non-Refoulement before the United Nations Treaty Bodies' (2020) 21 German Law Journal 355.
Cavanaugh, Carey 'OSCE and the Nagorno-Karabakh Peace Process' (2016) 27 Sec & Hum Rts 422.
Craig, Elizabeth 'From Soft to Hard Law? Culture, Identity, and Language Issues within the Northern Ireland Bill of Rights Process' (2010) 56 Focaal – Journal of Global and Historical Anthropology 35.
Cubie, Dug 'An Analysis of Soft Law Applicable to Humanitarian Assistance: Relative Normativity in Action?' (2011) 2 International Humanitarian Legal Studies 177.
Daly, Stephen 'The Rule of (Soft) Law' (2021) 32 King's Law Journal 3.

Druzin, Bryan H. 'Why Does Soft Law Have Any Power Anyway?' (2017) 7 Asian Journal of International Law 361.

Eliantonio Mariolina and Stefan Oana 'Soft Law Before the European Courts: Discovering a "Common Pattern"?' (2018) 37 Yearbook of European Law 457.

Feng Bei and Jiang He 'Strengthening China's Diplomatic Soft Power: Taking the Basic Categories of International Law as the Path' (2022) 3 Foundation for Law and International Affairs Review 82.

Fraioli, Paul 'The Kosovo–Serbia Normalisation Agreements' (2020) 26 Strategic Comments vii.

Freeland Steven and Nakarada Pecujlic Anja 'How Do You like Your Regulation – Hard or Soft? The Antarctic Treaty and the Outer Space Treaty Compared' (2018) 30 National Law School of India Review 11.

Gabriel, Henry Deeb 'The Use of Soft Law in the Creation of Legal Norms in International Commercial Law: How Successful Has It Been' (2019) 40 Mich J Int'l L 413.

Galbraith Jean and Zaring David 'Soft Law as Foreign Relations Law' (2014) 99 Cornell Law Review 735.

Gashi Krenar, Musliu Vjosa and Orbie Jan 'Mediation through Recontextualization: The European Union and the Dialogue between Kosovo and Serbia' (2017) 22 European Foreign Affairs Review 533.

Gentile, Giulia 'Ensuring Effective Judicial Review of EU Soft Law via the Action for Annulment before the EU Courts: A Plea for a Liberal-Constitutional Approach' (2020) 16 European Constitutional Law Review 466.

German, Tracey 'Russia and the South Caucasus: The China Challenge' (2022) 74 Europe-Asia Studies 1596.

Greentree, Todd "What Went Wrong in Afghanistan?" (2021) 51 Parameters 7.

Guliyev, Vusal 'Azerbaijan's Digitalization Efforts, Revitalization of the Liberated Territories, and Role of China's Huawei' (2022) 3 Caucasus Strategic Perspectives 117.

Guzman T. Andrew and Meyer L. Timothy 'International Soft Law' (2010) 2 Journal of Legal Analysis 171.

Gyeney, Laura 'Hard and Soft Law in EU's Integration Policy' (2018) 1 Hungarian Y.B. Int'l L. & Eur. L. 149.

Hasani, Enver 'The Role of the Constitutional Court in the Development of the Rule of Law in Kosovo' (2018) 43 Rev Cent & E Eur L 274.

Hayrapetyan, Lilit 'The Nagorno-Karabakh War of 2020 and the Change of the Regional Status Quo' (2022) 1 Przegląd Politologiczny 83.

Hongliu, Gong 'The Belt and Road Initiative (BRI): A China-Specific Approach for Global Governance' (2018) 8 Journal of WTO and China 36.

Hrnčiříková, Miluše 'The Meaning of Soft Law in International Commercial Arbitration' (2016) 16 International and Comparative Law Review 97.

Hultman Lisa, Kathman D. Jacob and Shannon Megan 'United Nations Peacekeeping Dynamics and the Duration of Post-civil Conflict Peace' (2016) 33 (3) Conflict Management and Peace Science 231.

Jawad Khushal and Saidi Zahid Ullah 'Obstacles to Implementing Foreign Law: A Comparative Study of Afghan and French Laws' (2024) 1 Al-Taqwa Journal of Social Sciences 30 DOI https://doi.org/10.63476/atjss.v1i1.52.

Jingxia Shi and Nuan Dong 'Investor-State Dispute Settlement under the BRI' (2021) 1 Wuhan University International Law Review 47.

Kartsonaki, Argyro 'Playing with Fire: An Assessment of the EU's Approach of Constructive Ambiguity on Kosovo's Blended Conflict' (2020) 22 Journal of Balkan and Near Eastern Studies 103.

Keskin Ghulam Faroq, Alibabalu Sayyad Sadri, and Fatah Mudassir 'Russia's and Iran's Strategic Policies towards the Afghanistan Crisis' (2020) 24 Trames 215.

Kessing, Peter Vendel 'Soft Law Instruments Regulating Armed Conflict: Are International Human Rights Standards Reflected' (2018) 12 Hum Rts & Int'l Legal Discourse 79.

Knauff, Matthias 'Coronavirus and Soft Law in Germany: Business as Usual?' (2021) 12 European Journal of Risk Regulation 45.

Krampe, Florian 'Water for Peace? Post-conflict Water Resource Management in Kosovo' (2017) 52 (2) Cooperation and Conflict 147.

Krickovic Andrej and Pellicciari Igor 'From "Greater Europe" to "Greater Eurasia": Status Concerns and the Evolution of Russia's Approach to Alignment and Regional Integration' (2021) 12 Journal of Eurasian Studies 86.

Krisch, Nico 'The Decay of Consent: International Law in an Age of Global Public Goods' (2014) 108 The American Journal of International Law 1.

Kumar Gupta, Amit 'Soft Power of the United States, China, and India: A Comparative Analysis' (2013) 26 (1/2) Indian Journal of Asian Affairs 37.

Láncos, Petra Lea 'A Hard Core under the Soft Shell: How Binding Is Union Soft Law for Member States?' (2018) 24 European Public Law 755.

Lewis, David 'Contesting Liberal Peace: Russia's Emerging Model of Conflict Management' (2022) 98 International Affairs 653.

Liang, Wei 'China's Soft Power in Africa: Is Economic Power Sufficient?' (2012) 36 Asian Perspective 667.

Lim, Kong Soon "Soft Law Instruments on Arctic Investment and Sustainable Development" (2020) 56 Polar Record 1.

Linos Katerina and Pegram Tom "The Language of Compromise in International Agreements" (2016) 70 International Organization 587.

Mac Ginty Roger, Muldoon Orla T. and Ferguson Neil 'No War, No Peace: Northern Ireland after the Agreement' (2007) 28 (1) Political Psychology 1.

MacMahon, Paul 'Soft Adjudication' (2017) 69 Administrative Law Review 529.

Mahr, Ewa 'Differences in the Local Perception of EULEX and KFOR in Their Security-Related Tasks' (2021) 30 European Security 43.

Malik, Nadeem 'Overview and Prospects for Energy Resources in Afghanistan: Measures for Improvement and Sustainable Development' (2009) 35 J Energy & Dev 141.

Mariański Michał 'The potential role of soft law rules and the French concept of regulations with the force of law (ordonnance) in achieving sustainable development goals' (2024) 66 Studia Prawnoustrojowe 301.

Marmor, Andrei 'Soft Law, Authoritative Advice and Non-Binding Agreements' (2019) 39 Oxford Journal of Legal Studies 507.

Marochkin Sergei and Khalafyan Rustam 'The Norms of International Soft Law in the Legal System of the Russian Federation' (2013) 6 Journal of Politics and Law 90.

Marshall, Brooke 'The Hague Choice of Law Principles, CISG, and PICC: A Hard Look at a Choice of Soft Law' (2018) 66 American Journal of Comparative Law 175.

Méndez Reátegui Rubén and Sumar Albujar Oscar 'Rule of Law Versus Soft Rule of Law' (2020) 109 Revista de Derecho Político 373.

Modebadze, Valeri 'The Escalation of Conflict between Armenians and Azerbaijanis and the Problems of Peaceful Resolution of the Nagorno-Karabakh War' (2021) 6 J Liberty & Int'l Aff 102.

Mortazavian Ali and Ghiacy Mohammad 'Regional and International Cooperation to Reduce- Nagorno - Karabakh Conflict' (2017) 10 J Pol & L 136.

Müller, Patrick "Normative Power Europe and the Israeli- Palestinian Conflict: The EU's Peacebuilding Narrative Meets Local Narratives" (2019) 28 European Security 251.

Oeter, Stefan 'The Kosovo Case – An Unfortunate Precedent' (2015) 75 ZaöRV 51.

Olsson, Ilhami Alkan 'Four Competing Approaches to International Soft Law' (2013) 58 Scandinavian Studies In Law 177.

Osland Kari M. and Peter Mateja 'The Double Proximity Paradox in Peacebuilding: Implementation and Perception of the EU Rule of Law Mission in Kosovo' (2019) 28 European Security 493.

Pečarič, Mirko 'Soft Law – The Intermediate Stage between Freedom and Control' (2022) 13 Danube 42.

Petropoulou Ionescu Danai and Eliantonio Mariolina 'Democratic Legitimacy and Soft Law in the EU Legal Order: A Theoretical Perspective' (2021) 17 (1) Journal of Contemporary European Research 43.

Roberts, Anthea Elizabeth 'Traditional and Modern Approaches to Customary International Law: A Reconciliation' (2001) 95 The American Journal of International Law 757.

Rossi, Christopher R. 'Nagorno-Karabakh and the Minsk Group: The Imperfect Appeal of Soft Law in an Overlapping Neighborhood' (2017) 52 Texas International Law Journal 45.

Rossi, Matthias "Soft Law Im Europarecht" (2020) 1 Zeitschrift für Gesetzgebung 1.
Ruys Tom and Rodríguez Silvestre Felipe 'Illegal: The Recourse to Force to Recover Occupied Territory and the Second Nagorno-Karabakh War' (2021) 32 EJIL 1287.
Sabawoon, Mirza 'The European Union's Strategy on Afghanistan. Selected Issues' (2019) 3 Central European Political Studies 181.
Sadiyev Saleh Sadi others 'South Caucasus and a "New Great Game": The Communication of Competition in Securitised International Relations' (2021) 29 Journal of Contemporary European Studies 282.
Sangar, Kaneshko 'Afghanistan's Significance for Russia in the 21st Century: Interests, Perceptions and Perspectives' (2016) 12 Politics in Central Europe 59.
Schwarcz L., Steven 'Soft Law as Governing Law' (2020) 104 Minnesota Law Review 2471.
Semenov, Andrej "The Washington Agreement: A Supplementary Document to the EU Efforts in Kosovo?" (2021) 23 Insight Turkey 259.
Song Ke and Ma Xuechan 'Individual Opinions as an Agent of International Legal Development?' (2022) 13 Journal of International Dispute Settlement 54.
Steinwand C., Martin 'Foreign Aid and Political Stability' (2015) 32 (4) Conflict Management and Peace Science 395.
Sterio, Milena 'Self-Determination and Secession under International Law: Nagorno-Karabakh' (2016) 59 German YB Int'l L 81.
Swain, Ashok 'Water and Post-conflict Peacebuilding' (2016) 61 (7) Hydrological Sciences Journal 1313.
Terpan, Fabien 'Soft Law in the European Union – The Changing Nature of EU Law' (2015) 21 European Law Journal 68.
Umarov, Akram 'Assessing China's New Policy in Afghanistan' (2017) 4 Central Asian Affairs 384.
Van Elsuwege, Peter 'Legal Creativity in EU External Relations: The Stabilization and Association Agreement between the EU and Kosovo' (2017) 22 European Foreign Affairs Review 393.
Veneziano, Anna 'The Soft Law Approach to Unification of International Commercial Contract Law: Future Perspectives in Light of Unidroit's Experience' (2013) 51 Vill. L. Rev. 521.
Von Schomberg, Rene 'The Precautionary Principle: Its Use within Hard and Soft Law' (2012) 2 EJRR 147.
Wang, Heng 'The Belt and Road Initiative Agreements: Characteristics, Rationale, and Challenges' (2021) 20 World Trade Review 282.
Wei, Yan 'The Cooperation between China and Afghanistan under the "Belt and Road Initiative"' (2018) 6 International Relations and Diplomacy 359.
Wessel, Ramses A. 'Normative Transformations in EU External Relations: The Phenomenon of "Soft" International Agreements' (2021) 44 West European Politics 72.

Xiong Ping and Tomasic Roman 'Soft Law, State-Owned Enterprises and Dispute Resolution on PRC's Belt and Road – Towards an Emerging Legal Order?' (2019) 49 Hong Kong L.J. 1025.

Yılmaz, Salih 'Land Swap Formula in the Nagorno-Karabakh Crisis Solution: Goble Plan and Lavrov Plan' (2022) 100 bilig 177.

Zhang, Feng 'China's New Engagement with Afghanistan after the Withdrawal' (2022) 2 LSE Public Policy Review 10.

Zupančič Rok, Pejič Nina, Grilj Blaž and Peen Rodt Annemarie 'The European Union Rule of Law Mission in Kosovo: An Effective Conflict Prevention and Peace-Building Mission?' (2018) 20 Journal of Balkan and Near Eastern Studies 599.

Cases

Accordance with International Law of the Unilateral Declaration of Independence in Respect of Kosovo, Advisory Opinion [2010] ICJ Reports 2010 403.

Application of the International Convention on the Elimination of All Forms of Racial Discrimination (Azerbaijan v Armenia), Provisional Measures [2021] ICJ Reports 2021 405.

Case Concerning Right of passage over Indian Territory (Portugal v India) Merits [1960] ICJ Reports 1960 6.

Corfu Channel case, Judgment [1949] IC J Reports 1949 4.

Gabčikovo-Nagymaros Project (Hungary/Slovakia), Judgment [1997] ICJ Reports 1997 7.

Military and Paramilitary Activities in and against Nicaragua (Nicaragua v United States of America), Provisional Measures Order [1984] ICJ Reports 1984 169.

Request for Interpretation of the Judgment of 23 May 2008 in the Case concerning Sovereignty over Pedra Branca/Pulau Batu Puteh, Middle Rocks and South Ledge (Malaysia/Singapore) (Malaysia v Singapore), Order [2018] ICJ Reports 2018 288.

Western Sahara, Advisory Opinion [1975] ICJ Reports 1975 12.

Internet Articles

Ahmad Abdul Waheed and Lloyd Gabriella 'Lessons from Afghanistan for Western State-Building in a Multipolar World' [2022] Atlantic Council South Asia Center <https://www.atlanticcouncil.org/wp-content/uploads/2022/06/Lessons_From_Afghanistan.pdf>.

Ahmeti Bardha and others, 'Serbia and Kosovo in 2035: Scenarios' [2018] Friedrich-Ebert-Stiftung <https://brussels.fes.de/fileadmin/public/editorfiles/events/2018/Q2/FES-Study.pdf>.

Amadio Viceré, Maria Giulia 'The Future Is Back: The EU, Russia and the Kosovo–Serbia Dispute' [2019] IAI PAPERS <https://www.iai.it/sites/default/files/iaip1919.pdf>.

Anstey Mark, Meerts Paul, Troitskiy Mikhail and Zartman I. William 'The Conflict over Artsakh – Nagorno-Karabakh' (2020) 1 oPINion <https://assets.ctfassets.net/mvajnncmgvdq/1fPT78KfLANItgII8kRIbm/04dc0c24f46f468d7dce284a6e17fe1d/oPINion_Dez_2020.pdf>.

Balkans Policy Research Group, 'Kosovo's Contested Representation in CEFTA: A Political and Legal Overview' [2021] Policy Report <https://balkansgroup.org/wp-content/uploads/2021/11/Kosovos-Contested-Representation-in-CEFTA-151021.pdf>.

Bechev, Dimitar 'Russia's Strategic Interests and Tools of Influence in the Western Balkans' [2019] NATO Strategic Communications Centre of Excellence <https://stratcomcoe.org/cuploads/pfiles/russias_strategic_interests_in_balkans_11dec.pdf>.

Buckley, Joanna 'Can the EU Be More Effective in Afghanistan?' [2010] Centre for European Reform <https://www.cer.org.uk/sites/default/files/publications/attachments/pdf/2011/pb_afhganistan_27apr10-223.pdf>.

Burrows Mathew and Manning A. Robert 'Kissinger's Nightmare: How an Inverted US-China-Russia May Be Game-Changer' (2015) 33 Valdai Papers <https://valdaiclub.com/files/11410/>.

Cakolli, Eugen 'KOSOVO: Between Universal Non-Recognition and "Derecognitions"' [2020] Kosova Democratic Institute (KDI) and the Konrad Adenauer Foundation <https://www.kas.de/documents/286052/0/Policy+brief+20-09-13+Kosovo+Between+universal+non-recognition+and+derecognitions+(Eng).pdf>.

Caplan, Richard 'The ICJ's Advisory Opinion on Kosovo' (2010) 55 PEACEBRIEF <https://www.usip.org/sites/default/files/PB55%20The%20ICJs%20Advisory%20Opinion%20on%20Kosovo.pdf>.

Chaudhuri Rudra and Shende Shreyas 'Dealing with the Taliban: India's Strategy in Afghanistan after U.S. Withdrawal' [2020] Carnegie Endowment for International Peace <https://carnegieendowment.org/files/Chaudhuri_Shende_-_Afghanistan.pdf>.

Chauvet Lisa, Collier Paul and Duponchel Marguerite 'What Explains Aid Project Success in Post-conflict Situations?' (2010) 5418 Policy Research Working Paper <https://documents1.worldbank.org/curated/en/713121468323979859/pdf/WPS5418.pdf>.

Chia Claudia and Haiqi Zheng 'Russia's Policy Overtures in Afghanistan' (2021) 694 ISAS Insights <https://www.isas.nus.edu.sg/wp-content/uploads/2021/11/694.pdf>.

Chia Claudia, Kalachelvam Kunthavi and Haiqi Zheng 'Exploring China's Afghanistan Policy' (2021) 677 ISAS Insights <https://www.isas.nus.edu.sg/wp-content/uploads/2021/06/677.pdf>.

Conley A. Heather and Saric Dejana 'The Serbia-Kosovo Normalization Process: A Temporary U.S. Decoupling' [2021] CSIS BRIEFS <https://csis-website-prod.s3.amazonaws.com/s3fs-public/publication/210527_Conley_Serbia_Kosovo_Normalization.pdf?VersionId=.21Hry3HPFOAwZTCoBbJaZjcVSMfTGqF>.

Cornell E., Svante and Swanström Niklas 'Compatible Interests? The EU and China's Belt and Road Initiative' (2020) 1 SIEPS Swedish Institute for European Policy Studies <https://sieps.se/en/publications/2020/compatible-interests/>.

Dehaan Heather and Mammadova Shalala 'War and Sovereignty: Lessons from Putin's War for the South Caucasus*' (2022) 78 KENNAN CABLE <https://www.wilsoncenter.org/sites/default/files/media/uploads/documents/KI_220616_Cable%2078-V1r1.pdf>.

Dobbins James, Radin Andrew and Miller E. Laurel 'Engage, Isolate, or Oppose: American Policy toward the Islamic Emirate of Afghanistan' [2022] RAND Corporation <https://www.rand.org/pubs/perspectives/PEA1540-1.html>.

Dreikhausen, Viola Fee 'The EU Engagement in Afghanistan: Insights and Emerging Lessons' (2022) 7 European Union Institute for Security Studies <https://www.iss.europa.eu/sites/default/files/EUISSFiles/Brief_7_Afghanistan.pdf>.

Felbab-Brown, Vanda 'A bri(dge) too far: The Unfulfilled promise and limitations of China's Involvement in Afghanistan' [2020] Global China: Regional influence and strategy <https://www.brookings.edu/wp-content/uploads/2020/06/FP_20200615_china_afghanistan_felbab_brown.pdf>.

Fischer Sabine and Stanzel Angela 'Afghanistan: The West Fails – a Win for China and Russia? The Views from Beijing and Moscow' (2021) 50 SWP Comment <https://www.swp-berlin.org/publications/products/comments/2021C50_MoscowBeijing_Afghanistan.pdf>.

Garding E. Sarah 'Kosovo: Background and U.S. Policy' [2021] Congressional Research Service <https://sgp.fas.org/crs/row/R46175.pdf>.

Gashi Shpetim and Novaković Igor 'Brussels Agreements between Kosovo and Serbia: A Quantitative Implementation Assessment' [2020] Friedrich-Ebert-Stiftung <https://library.fes.de/pdf-files/bueros/belgrad/17009.pdf>.

Hartwell, Leon 'The Serbia-Kosovo Dialogue: Ripe for Resolution?' [2021] Center for European Policy Analysis <https://cepa.org/wp-content/uploads/2021/05/CEPA-Serbia-Kosovo-5.10.21-V2.pdf>.

Has Kerim, Kaleji Vali and Markedonov Sergey, 'The Breakdown of the Status Quo and the International Dimension of the Nagorno-Karabakh Crisis' [2020] Valdai Discussion Club Report <https://valdaiclub.com/files/32745/>.

Horta, Loro 'US Afghan Withdrawal: Enter China and Taliban?' (2021) 120 RSIS Commentary <https://rsis.edu.sg/wp-content/uploads/2021/08/CO21120.pdf>.

Immenkamp Beatrix and Latici Tania 'Security Situation in Afghanistan: Implications for Europe' [2021] European Parliamentary Research Service <https://www.europarl.europa.eu/RegData/etudes/BRIE/2021/698771/EPRS_BRI(2021)698771_EN.pdf>.

Inan Feride and Yayloyan Diana 'New Economic Corridors in the South Caucasus and the Chinese One Belt One Road' [2020] The Economic Policy Research Foundation of Turkey <https://armenia-turkey.net/files/2020-04/0TvkVwhb0Z2ysfXTVQniYEDv1I.pdf>.

Ingimundarson, Valur 'The "Kosovo Precedent": Russia's Justification of Military Interventions and Territorial Revisions in Georgia and Ukraine' [2022] LSE IDEAS <https://www.lse.ac.uk/ideas/Assets/Documents/updates/2022-SU-Valur-RussKosovo.pdf>.

International Crisis Group, 'Improving Prospects for Peace after the Nagorno-Karabakh War' (2020) 91 Crisis Group Europe Briefing <https://www.crisisgroup.org/europe-central-asia/caucasus/nagorno-karabakh-conflict/b91-improving-prospects-peace-after-nagorno-karabakh-war>.

International Crisis Group, 'Nagorno-Karabakh: Seeking a Path to Peace in the Ukraine War's Shadow' (2022) 93 Crisis Group Europe Briefing <https://icg-prod.s3.amazonaws.com/b093-seeking-a-path-to-peace_0.pdf>.

International Crisis Group, 'Risky Competition: Strengthening U.S.-China Crisis Management' (2022) 324 Asia Report <https://icg-prod.s3.amazonaws.com/324-us-china-crisis-management.pdf>.

International Crisis Group, 'Thinking through the Dilemmas of Aid to Afghanistan' [2021] Watch List 2021 for the EU <https://icg-prod.s3.amazonaws.com/afghanistan.pdf>.

Jami Maryam, Rizwan Alamuddin and Taieb Rajab 'Sino–Afghan Security Relations beyond 2021' [2021] Friedrich Ebert-Stiftung (FES) Afghanistan and Institute of War and Peace Studies <https://library.fes.de/pdf-files/bueros/kabul/18638.pdf>.

Janse, Diana 'Russian Interests in Afghanistan' (2021) 1 SCEEUS Reports <https://www.ui.se/globalassets/ui.se-eng/publications/sceeus/russian-interests-in-afghanistan-sceeus-report-no1-2021.pdf>.

Joseph, P. Edward 'From Crisis to Convergence: A Strategy to Tackle Balkans Instability at Its Source' [2022] Foreign Policy Institute and Wilson Center <https://www.wilsoncenter.org/publication/crisis-convergence-strategy-tackle-balkans-instability-its-source>.

Kallaba, Pëllumb 'Russian Interference in Kosovo: How and Why?' (2017) 9 Kosovar Centre for Security Studies <https://qkss.org/images/uploads/files/Russian_interference_in_Kosovo_finale_2_735070.pdf>.

Karl, Fiona 'Rechtsschutz Gegen Soft Law Der EU' [2023] Geprägte Freiheit <https://journals.ub.uni-heidelberg.de/index.php/hfst/article/view/92640/87248>.

Kaura, Vinay 'The Pakistan Factor in China's Afghanistan Policy: Emerging Regional Faultlines Amid US Withdrawal' [2021] The Middle East Institute <https://mei.edu/publication/pakistan-factor-chinas-afghanistan-policy-emerging-regional-faultlines-amid-us/>.

Khachatryan, Hasmik 'The Nagorno-Karabakh War: A New Reality in the South Caucasus and Its Implications for the EU' [2020] Institute of European Democrats <https://www.iedonline.eu/download/geopolitics-values/36-Khachatryan_The_Nagorno-Karabakh_war_A_new_reality_in_the_South_Caucasus_and_its_implications.pdf>.

Kobzova Jana and Alieva Leila 'The EU and Azerbaijan: Beyond Oil' [2012] European Council on Foreign Relations Policy Memo <https://ecfr.eu/wp-content/uploads/ECFR57_EU_AZERBAIJAN_MEMO_AW.pdf>.

Kolarz, Stefania 'The European Union's Engagement with the "de-Facto States" in the Eastern Partnership' (2020) 8 EU Diplomacy Papers <https://www.coleurope.eu/sites/default/files/research-paper/edp_8_2020_kolarz_0.pdf>.

Krasniqi, Jeta 'EU-Mediated Kosovo-Serbia Dialogue: A New Attempt or Resumption with the Old Approach?' [2020] Kosova Democratic Institute (KDI) and the Konrad Adenauer Foundation <https://kdi-kosova.org/wp-content/uploads/2020/10/Policy-Brief-20-07-24-EU-mediated-Kosovo-Serbia-dialogue-ENG.pdf>.

Lachert, Jakub 'Nagorno-Karabakh as Part of Geopolitical Rivalry' [2021] Warsaw Institute <https://warsawinstitute.org/wp-content/uploads/2021/03/Nagorno-Karabakh-as-Part-of-Geopolitical-Rivalry-Jakub-Lachert-Warsaw-Institute-Special-Report-12.03.2021.pdf>.

Lang, Józef 'Afghanistan: The View from Russia' (2014) 10 European Union Institute for Security Studies <https://www.files.ethz.ch/isn/182959/Alert_10-Afghanistan_view_from_Russia.pdf>.

Larsen, Henrik 'The Western Balkans between the EU, NATO, Russia and China' [2020] CSS Analyses in Security Policy <https://css.ethz.ch/content/dam/ethz/special-interest/gess/cis/center-for-securities-studies/pdfs/CSSAnalyse263-EN.pdf>.

Le Corre, Philippe 'China's Rise as a Geoeconomic Influencer: Four European Case Studies' [2018] Carnegie Endowment for International Peace <https://carnegieendowment.org/files/WP_LeCorre_China_formatted_FINAL_WEB.PDF>.

Loft, Philip 'Aid to Taliban-Controlled Afghanistan' (2022) 9343 The House of Commons Library <https://researchbriefings.files.parliament.uk/documents/CBP-9343/CBP-9343.pdf>.

Malik, Ayesha 'The Islamic Emirate of Afghanistan and the Recognition of Governments under International Law' [2021] Research Society of International Law

<https://rsilpak.org/wp-content/uploads/2021/10/afghanistan-taliban-recognition_rsil.pdf>.

Martin, Alexandra 'China in the Broader Black Sea Region' [2021] Globsec <https://www.globsec.org/sites/default/files/2021-03/China-in-the-Broader-black-sea-region-ver7-nonprint.pdf>.

Masahiro, Kurita 'Great Power Politics over Afghanistan after the U.S. Withdrawal' [2022] NIDS East Asian Strategic Review <http://www.nids.mod.go.jp/english/publication/east-asian/pdf/2022/e01.pdf>.

Medović, Vladimir 'The Potential and Limits of the European Union as a Mediator in the Dialogue between Serbia and Kosovo' (2022) 3 Istituto Affari Internazionali (IAI) Papers <https://www.iai.it/sites/default/files/iaip2203.pdf>.

Molnár-Gábor, Fruzsina 'Soft Law: Bindung Ohne Fesseln?' [2022] Weich & Hart <https://heiup.uni-heidelberg.de/journals/rupertocarola/article/view/24585/18481>.

Morelli L., Vincent 'Kosovo: Background and U.S. Relations' [2018] Congressional Research Service <https://sgp.fas.org/crs/row/R44979.pdf>.

Muharremi, Robert 'The "Washington Agreement" between Kosovo and Serbia' (2021) 25 insights <https://www.asil.org/sites/default/files/ASIL_Insights_2021_V25_I4.pdf>.

Rácz, András 'In Russia's Hands: Nagorno-Karabakh after the Ceasefire Agreement' (2021) 8 EU Institute for Security Studies <https://www.iss.europa.eu/sites/default/files/EUISSFiles/Brief_8_2021.pdf>.

Rácz, András 'War in Nagorno- Karabakh: A Two-Track Strategy for the EU' (2020) 30 DGAP Commentary <https://dgap.org/sites/default/files/article_pdfs/dgap-commentary-2020-30-en.pdf>.

Rumer Eugene, Sokolsky Richard and Stronski Paul 'U.S. Policy toward the South Caucasus: Take Three' [2017] Carnegie Endowment for International Peace <https://carnegieendowment.org/files/CP_310_Rumer_Sokolsky_Stronski_Caucusus_Final_Web.pdf>.

Sahakyan, Mher 'The New Great Power Competition in Central Asia: Opportunities and Challenges for the Gulf' [2021] AGDA Working Paper https://hal.science/hal-03224546v1/document.

Samorukov, Maxim 'A Spoiler in the Balkans? Russia and the Final Resolution of the Kosovo Conflict' [2019] Carnegie Endowment for International Peace <https://carnegieendowment.org/files/WP_Samorukov_Balkans_v2.pdf>.

Sarjveladze, Mikheil 'The South Caucasus in the Context of the EU-Russia Crisis' (2017) 28 Security Policy Working Paper <https://www.baks.bund.de/sites/baks010/files/working_paper_2017_28.pdf>.

Satanakis Sofia Maria and Süss Katrin 'The Shift in Turkey's Foreign Policy' (2021) 3 Austria Institut für Europaund Sicherheitspolitik <https://www.aies.at/download/2021/AIES-Fokus-2021-03.pdf>.

Savković Marko and Nikaj Bernard 'Opportunity Costs of the Kosovo-Serbia Stalemate' [2021] Sbunker <https://sbunker.org/wp-content/uploads/2023/12/3.-Opportunity-Cost-of-the-Dialogue-Between-Kosovo-and-Serbia1666958448.pdf>.

Stanicek Branislav and Tarpova Simona 'China's Strategic Interests in the Western Balkans' [2022] European Parliamentary Research Service <https://www.europarl.europa.eu/RegData/etudes/BRIE/2022/733558/EPRS_BRI(2022)733558_EN.pdf>.

Stanicek, Branislav 'Belgrade-Pristina Dialogue: The Rocky Road towards a Comprehensive Normalisation Agreement' [2023] European Parliamentary Research Service <https://www.europarl.europa.eu/thinktank/en/document/EPRS_BRI(2025)779231>.

Stanzel, Angela 'Fear and Loathing on the New Silk Road: Chinese Security in Afghanistan and Beyond' [2018] European Council on Foreign Relations <https://ecfr.eu/wp-content/uploads/ECFR-264-Chinese_Security_in_Afghanistan_2.pdf>.

Stepanova, Ekaterina 'Russia's Approach to Afghanistan Following the Taliban Takeover' (2021) 724 PONARS Eurasia Policy Memo <https://www.ponarseurasia.org/wp-content/uploads/2021/11/Pepm724_Stepanova_Nov2021.pdf>.

Taieb Rajab, Rizwan Alamuddin and Jami Maryam 'Reluctant Reentrance? Russia and Afghanistan Post 2021' [2021] Friedrich Ebert-Stiftung (FES) Afghanistan and Institute of War and Peace Studies <https://library.fes.de/pdf-files/bueros/kabul/18642.pdf>.

Thomas, Clayton 'Afghanistan: Background and U.S. Policy in Brief' [2022] Congressional Research Service <https://sgp.fas.org/crs/row/R45122.pdf>.

Threlkeld Elizabeth and Easterly Grace 'Afghanistan-Pakistan Ties and Future Stability in Afghanistan' (2021) 175 Peaceworks <https://www.usip.org/sites/default/files/2021-08/pw_175-afghanistan_pakistan_ties_and_future_stability_in_afghanistan.pdf>.

Tonchev, Plamen 'China's Road: Into the Western Balkans' [2017] European Union Institute for Security Studies (EUISS) <https://www.iss.europa.eu/sites/default/files/EUISSFiles/Brief%203%20China's%20Silk%20Road.pdf>.

Trenin Dmitri, Kulakov Oleg, Malashenko Alexey and Topychkanov Petr 'A Russian Strategy for Afghanistan after the Coalition Troop Withdrawal' [2014] Carnegie Moscow Center <https://carnegieendowment.org/files/CMC_Article_Afganistan_Eng14.pdf>.

Umirdinov, Alisher 'Generating a Reform of the BRI from the Inside: Japan's Contribution via Soft Law Diplomacy' [2019] RIETI Discussion Paper Series <https://www.rieti.go.jp/jp/publications/dp/19e076.pdf>.

Valiyev, Anar 'Azerbaijan through the Prism of BRI: China's Mounting Interests and Influence in the Region' (2019) 621 PONARS Eurasia Policy Memo <https://www.ponarseurasia.org/wp-content/uploads/attachments/Pepm621_Valiyev_Oct2019-1.pdf>.

Valiyev, Anar 'Karabakh after the 44-Day War: Russian Peacekeepers and Patterns' (2021) 705 PONARS Eurasia Policy Memo <https://www.ponarseurasia.org/wp-content/uploads/2021/08/Pepm705_Valiyev_August2021.pdf>.

Vladisavljev, Stefan 'China's "Digital Silk Road" Enters the Western Balkans' [2021] Association for International Affairs (AMO) <https://chinaobservers.eu/wp-content/uploads/2021/06/CHOICE_policy-paper_digital-silk-road_A4_web_04.pdf>.

Waal, Thomas de 'In the South Caucasus, Can New Trade Routes Help Overcome a Geography of Conflict?' [2021] Carnegie Endowment for International Peace <https://carnegieendowment.org/files/de_Waal_South_Caucasus_Connectivity.pdf>.

Waal, Thomas de 'The Nagorny Karabakh Conflict in Its Fourth Decade' (2021) 2 CEPS Working Document <https://www.ceps.eu/download/publication/?id=34122&pdf=WD2021-02_The-Nagorny-Karabakh-Conflict-in-its-Fourth-Decade.pdf>.

Watkins Andrew and Sharan Timor 'Europe's Engagement in Afghanistan Post-2021: Uncertainty, Pragmatism, and Continued Partnership' [2020] Friedrich Ebert-Stiftung (FES) Afghanistan <https://library.fes.de/pdf-files/bueros/kabul/16900.pdf>.

Welt, Cory 'Azerbaijan and Armenia: The Nagorno-Karabakh Conflict' [2021] Congressional Research Service <https://sgp.fas.org/crs/row/R46651.pdf>.

Wolrd Bank, 'Water Security Outlook for Kosovo' [2018] World Bank Publications <https://documents1.worldbank.org/curated/en/496071548849630510/Water-Security-Outlook-for-Kosovo.pdf>.

Xin, Chen 'Serbia External Relations Briefing: The Washington Agreement' (2020) 32 China-CEE Institute <https://china-cee.eu/wp-content/uploads/2020/10/2020er09_Serbia.pdf>.

Yıldız, Güney 'Turkish-Russian Adversarial Collaboration in Syria, Libya, and Nagorno-Karabakh' [2021] SWP Comment <https://www.swp-berlin.org/publications/products/comments/2021C22_Turkish-Russian_Collaboration.pdf>.

Zhou Jiayi, Su Fei and Yuan Jingdong 'Treading Lightly: China's Footprint in a Taliban-Led Afghanistan' (2022) 8 SIPRI Insights on Peace and Security <https://www.sipri.org/sites/default/files/2022-11/sipriinsights_2208_china_and_afghanistan_2.pdf>.

Zweers Wouter and Boon Myrthe de 'Overcoming EU Internal Dividing Policy Brief Lines in the Belgrade-Pristina Dialogue' [2022] Clingendael <https://www.clingendael.org/sites/default/files/2022-04/Policy_brief_Overcoming_EU_internal_dividing_lines_Belgrado_Pristine_Dialogue.pdf>.

Zweers Wouter, Shopov Vladimir, Putten Frans-Paul van der, Petkova Mirela and Lemstra Maarten 'China and the EU in the Western Balkans: A Zero-Sum Game?' [2020] Clingendael Netherlands Institute of International Relations <https://www.clingendael.org/sites/default/files/2020-08/china-and-the-eu-in-the-western-balkans.pdf>.

Internet Web Pages

Afisi, Oseni Taiwo 'Neocolonialism' <https://iep.utm.edu/neocolon/>.

Albanian Government, 'Important Cooperation Agreements Signed at Open Balkan Summit' (2 September 2022) <https://www.kryeministria.al/en/newsroom/nenshkruhen-marreveshje-te-rendesishme-bashkepunimi-ne-samitin-per-ballkanin-e-hapur-beograd/>.

Ambasadat, 'Jerusalem, Izrael' <https://ambasadat.net/izrael>.

BRICS Information Portal, 'History of BRICS' (3 March 2023) <http://infobrics.org/page/history-of-brics/>.

BRICS, 'BRICS Information Portal' <http://infobrics.org/>.

Brussels Agreement, 'First Agreement of Principles Governing the Normalization of Relations' (2013) <https://www.peaceagreements.org/media/documents/ag2022_5bdc31b326555.pdf> and https://gzk.rks-gov.net/ActDetail.aspx?ActID=8892&langid=2>.

Brzozowski Alexandra and Taylor Alice, 'LEAK: Franco-German Plan to Resolve the Kosovo-Serbia Dispute' (2022) <https://www.euractiv.com/section/enlargement/news/leak-franco-german-plan-to-resolve-the-kosovo-serbia-dispute/>.

Byrd, William 'Afghanistan's Frozen Foreign Exchange Reserves: What Happened, What's Next' (1 March 2022) <https://www.usip.org/publications/2022/03/afghanistans-frozen-foreign-exchange-reserves-what-happened-whats-next>.

Central European Free Trade Agreement, 'About' <https://cefta.int/about/>.

Council of Europe, 'The Russian Federation Is Excluded from the Council of Europe' (16 March 2022) <https://www.coe.int/en/web/portal/-/the-russian-federation-is-excluded-from-the-council-of-europe>.

Dinic, Leonardo 'Huawei Targeted by Trump's Recent Serbia-Kosovo Meeting?' (28 October 2020) <https://www.chinausfocus.com/finance-economy/huawei-targeted-by-trumps-recent-serbia-kosovo-meeting>.

EAEU, 'Eurasian Economic Union' <http://www.eaeunion.org/?lang=en#about>.

EEAS Press Team, 'Belgrade-Pristina Dialogue: EU Proposal - Agreement on the Path to Normalisation between Kosovo and Serbia' (2023) <https://www.eeas.europa.eu/eeas/belgrade-pristina-dialogue-eu-proposal-agreement-path-normalisation-between-kosovo-and-serbia_en>.

EEAS Press Team, 'Belgrade-Pristina Dialogue: Press Remarks by High Representative Josep Borrell after the Ohrid Meeting with President Vučić and Prime Minister Kurti' (2023) <https://www.eeas.europa.eu/eeas/belgrade-pristina-dialogue-press-remarks-high-representative-josep-borrell-after-ohrid-meeting_en>.

Embassy of the People's Republic of China in the Islamic Republic of Afghanistan, 'Speech by Ambassador Wang Yu on Afghan Peace and Post-peace' (18 November 2020) <http://af.china-embassy.gov.cn/eng/zagx/202011/t20201119_1199994.htm>.

Embassy of the People's Republic of China in the Islamic Republic of Afghanistan, 'China Plays an Active and Constructive Role in Afghan Peace and Reconciliation Process' (30 January 2021) <https://af.china-embassy.gov.cn/sgxw/202101/t20210131_1114515.htm>.

EULEX, 'EULEX Accountability' <https://www.eulex-kosovo.eu/?page=2,23>.

Eurofound, 'Soft Law' <https://www.eurofound.europa.eu/observatories/eurwork/industrial-relations-dictionary/soft-law>.

European Commission, 'Country Responsible for Asylum Application (Dublin Regulation)' (23 September 2020) <https://home-affairs.ec.europa.eu/policies/migration-and-asylum/asylum-eu/determining-member-state-responsible-asylum-application_en>.

European Parliament, 'Kosovo: MEPs Welcome Lifting Tariffs on Goods from Serbia and Bosnia and Herzegovina' (4 February 2020) <https://www.europarl.europa.eu/news/en/press-room/20200402IPR76410/meps-welcome-lifting-tariffs-on-goods-from-serbia-and-bosnia-and-herzegovina>.

European Parliament, 'The Precautionary Principle: Definitions, Applications and Governance' (9 December 2015) <https://www.europarl.europa.eu/thinktank/en/document/EPRS_IDA(2015)573876>.

European Union Rule of Law Mission in Kosovo, 'About EULEX' <https://www.eulex-kosovo.eu/?page=2,60>.

European Union, 'Consolidated Version of the Treaty on European Union, Article 5, OJ C 202, 7.6.2016' (2016) <https://eur-lex.europa.eu/eli/treaty/teu_2016/art_5/oj/eng>.

Goulard, Sebastien 'From 17+1 to 27+1 Mechanism?' (20 July 2021) <https://www.oboreurope.com/en/from-17-to-27-mechanism/>.

International Center on Conflict and Negotiation, 'Conflict Resolution Documents for Nagorno-Karabakh Conflict' (2023) <http://iccn.ge/index.php?article_id=331&clang=1>.

International Court of Justice, 'Accordance with International Law of the Unilateral Declaration of Independence in Respect of Kosovo' (22 July 2010) <https://www.icj-cij.org/public/files/case-related/141/141-20100722-ADV-01-00-EN.pdf>.

International Court of Justice, 'How the Court Works' (2023) <https://www.icj-cij.org/how-the-court-works>.

Ireland, 'The Good Friday Agreement' <https://www.ireland.ie/en/the-good-friday-agreement/>.

Jianxue, Lan 'Tunxi Foreign Ministers' Meeting May Kick off a New Journey for Afghanistan' (6 April 2022) <https://www.ciis.org.cn/english/COMMENTARIES/202204/t20220406_8500.html>.

Kosovo Specialist Chambers & Specialist Prosecutor's Office, 'Kosovo Specialist Chambers & Specialist Prosecutor's Office' <https://www.scp-ks.org/en>.

Mammadov, Seymur 'Azerbaijan-China: 30 Years of Cooperation That Can Become an Example for the World' (2022) <https://www.chinadaily.com.cn/a/202204/02/WS62484315a310fd2b29e54ead.html>.

Middle East Institute, 'Azerbaijan's Hoseyniyun: The Prospects and Challenges of a Caucasus Hezbollah' (12 June 2023) <https://www.mei.edu/publications/azerbaijans-hoseyniyun-prospects-and-challenges-caucasus-hezbollah>.

Ministry of Foreign Affairs of the People's Republic of China, 'China's Position on the Afghan Issue' (12 April 2023) <https://www.fmprc.gov.cn/mfa_eng/gjhdq_665435/2675_665437/2676_663356/2677_663358/202304/t20230412_11057785.html>.

Ministry of Foreign Affairs of the People's Republic of China, 'China's Position on the Afghan Issue' <https://www.fmprc.gov.cn/eng/gjhdq_665435/2675_665437/2676_663356/2677_663358/202304/t20230412_11057785.html>.

Embassy of the People's Republic of China in the Kingdom of the Netherlands, 'Joint Statement of the Third Foreign Ministers' Meeting among the Neighboring Countries of Afghanistan' (31 March 2022) <http://nl.china-embassy.gov.cn/eng/zgyw/202203/t20220331_10658230.htm> also accessible on <http://lawinfochina.com/display.aspx?id=8253&lib=tax&SearchKeyword=&SearchCKeyword=>.

Ministry of Foreign Affairs of the People's Republic of China, 'The Tunxi Initiative of the Neighboring Countries of Afghanistan on Supporting Economic Reconstruction in and Practical Cooperation with Afghanistan' (1 April 2022) <https://www.fmprc.gov.cn/mfa_eng/gjhdq_665435/2675_665437/2676_663356/2677_663358/202204/t20220401_10662024.html>.

Ministry of Foreign Affairs of the People's Republic of China, 'Wang Yi Meets with Acting Deputy Prime Minister of Afghan Taliban's Interim Government Mullah Abdul Ghani Baradar' (26 October 2021) <https://www.fmprc.gov.cn/mfa_eng/gjhdq_665435/2675_665437/2676_663356/2678_663360/202110/t20211026_10058258.html>.

Ministry of Foreign Affairs of the People's Republic of China, 'Wang Yi Holds Talks with Acting Deputy Prime Minister of Afghan Interim Government Mullah Abdul Ghani Baradar' (24 March 2022) <https://www.fmprc.gov.cn/mfa_eng/gjhdq_665435/2675_665437/2676_663356/2678_663360/202203/t20220325_10655539.html>.

Ministry of Foreign Affairs of the People's Republic of China, 'Wang Yi Introduces the Important Consensus and Achievements of the Series of Meetings on the Afghan

Issue' (1 April 2022) <https://www.fmprc.gov.cn/mfa_eng/gjhdq_665435/2675_665437/2676_663356/2678_663360/202204/t20220401_10663017.html>.

Ministry of Foreign Affairs of the People's Republic of China, 'Wang Yi Meets with Acting Foreign Minister of the Afghan Interim Government Amir Khan Muttaqi' (29 July 2022) <https://www.fmprc.gov.cn/mfa_eng/gjhdq_665435/2675_665437/2676_663356/2678_663360/202207/t20220729_10730548.html>.

O'Donnell, Lynne 'The Water Wars Are Coming to Central Asia' (31 July 2023) <https://foreignpolicy.com/2023/07/31/afghanistan-uzbekistan-water-war-central-asia/>.

Office for Kosovo and Metohija, Government of the Republic of Serbia, 'Negotiation Process with Pristina' (2023) <https://www.kim.gov.rs/eng/pregovaracki-proces.php>.

Office of the High Representative, 'General Information' <https://www.ohr.int/about-ohr/general-information/>.

Office of the Leading Group for Promoting the Belt and Road Initiative, 'Belt and Road Portal' <https://eng.yidaiyilu.gov.cn/>.

One Belt One Road Europe, 'Greece and the New 17+1 Format' (18 April 2019) <https://www.oboreurope.com/en/greece-171-format/>.

Organization of Turkic States, 'Areas of Cooperation' <https://www.turkicstates.org/en/isbirligi-alanlari#3-customs-cooperation>.

Pollet, Mathieu 'Time to Cut Back on Huawei, German Minister Tells Telecoms Giants' (18 August 2023) <https://www.politico.eu/article/germany-interior-minister-nancy-faeser-huawei-china-telecoms/>.

Pompeo R., Michael 'The United States Further Restricts Huawei Access to U.S. Technology' (17 August 2020) <https://2017-2021.state.gov/the-united-states-further-restricts-huawei-access-to-u-s-technology/>.

President of Russian Federation, 'Statement by President of the Republic of Azerbaijan, Prime Minister of the Republic of Armenia and President of the Russian Federation' (2020) <http://en.kremlin.ru/events/president/news/64384>.

Republic of Kosovo, 'Odluku' (21 November 2018) <https://kryeministri.rks-gov.net/sr/blog/odluke-76-sednice-vlade-21-11-2018/>.

SAKOM, 'Belgrade Bypass Was Built by Builders from Azerbaijan and China Together with Serbian Subcontractors' (4 July 2023) <https://sakom.org.rs/en/belgrade-bypass-was-built-by-builders-from-azerbaijan-and-china-together-with-serbian-subcontractors/>.

TASS, 'Baku, Tehran Agree to Build Railroad to Nakhchivan across Iran' (6 October 2023) <https://tass.com/world/1686277>.

The National Assembly of the Republic of Serbia, 'Constitution of the Republic of Serbia' (30 September 2006) <https://www.parlament.gov.rs/upload/documents/Constitution_%20of_Serbia_F.pdf>.

Ukraine, Russian Federation, United Kingdom of Great Britain and Northern Ireland and United States of America, 'Memorandum on security assurances in connection with Ukraine's accession to the Treaty on the Non-Proliferation of Nuclear Weapons' (1994) Budapest, 5 December 1994, No. 52241 <https://treaties.un.org/Pages/showDetails.aspx?objid=0800000280401fbb>.

U.S. Department of State, 'Abraham Accords Peace Agreement: Treaty of Peace, Diplomatic Relations and Full Normalization between the United Arab Emirates and the State of Israel' (2020) <https://www.state.gov/wp-content/uploads/2020/09/UAE_Israel-treaty-signed-FINAL-15-Sept-2020-508.pdf>.

U.S. Department of State, 'Abraham Accords: Declaration of Peace, Cooperation, and Constructive Diplomatic and Friendly Relations' (2020) <https://www.state.gov/wp-content/uploads/2020/09/Bahrain_Israel-Agreement-signed-FINAL-15-Sept-2020-508.pdf>.

U.S. Department of State, 'Joint Declaration' (2020) <https://www.state.gov/wp-content/uploads/2021/01/Joint-Declaration-US-Morrocco-Israel.pdf>.

U.S. Department of State, 'The Abraham Accords Declaration' (2020) <https://www.state.gov/wp-content/uploads/2021/01/Sudan-AA.pdf>.

U.S. Department of State, 'The Abraham Accords Declaration' (2020) <https://www.state.gov/wp-content/uploads/2020/10/Abraham-Accords-signed-FINAL-15-Sept-2020-508-1.pdf>.

UN News, 'Armenia-Azerbaijan: UN Calls for "Credible and Durable" End to Fighting in Flashpoint Region' (21 September 2023) <https://news.un.org/en/story/2023/09/1141232>.

United Nations Mission for the Referendum in Western Sahara, 'Background' <https://minurso.unmissions.org/background>.

United Nations, 'Agreement on Provisional Arrangements in Afghanistan Pending the Re-establishment of Permanent Government Institutions (Bonn Agreement)' (12 May 2001) <https://peacemaker.un.org/afghanistan-bonnagreement2001>.

United Nations, 'Resolution 1244 (1999)' (10 June 1999) <https://unmik.unmissions.org/sites/default/files/old_dnn/Res1244ENG.pdf>.

United Nations, 'Secretary-General Deeply Concerned about Continued Clashes in Sudan, Strongly Condemns Deaths, Injuries of Civilians' (16 April 2023) <https://press.un.org/en/2023/sgsm21764.doc.htm>.

United Nations, 'Statute of the International Court of Justice' (18 April 1946) <https://www.icj-cij.org/statute>.

United Nations, 'United Nations Interim Administration Mission in Kosovo' <https://peacekeeping.un.org/en/mission/unmik>.

United Nations, 'United Nations Security Council' <https://www.un.org/securitycouncil/>.

Washington Agreement, 'Economic Normalization' (2020) <https://www.peacefare.net/2020/09/04/much-ado-about-nothing/< also available at <https://exit.al/en/2020/09/04/kosovo-and-serbia-signed-separate-pledges-not-an-agreement/>.

Xinhua, 'China, Afghanistan Pledge Orderly, Mutually Beneficial Cooperation' (25 March 2022) <http://english.www.gov.cn/statecouncil/wangyi/202203/25/content_WS623d1a7fc6d02e533532843b.html>.

Yu, Wang 'Ambassador Wang Yu published an article in Afghan media entitled "A Global Family: Building a China-Afghanistan Community with a Shared Future." (2 October 2020) <https://af.china-embassy.gov.cn/sgxw/202010/t20201003_1114349.htm>.

Yu, Wang 'China Actively Upholds Multilateralism, Jointly Building a Community with a Shared Future for Mankind with Afghanistan' (24 February 2021) <https://af.china-embassy.gov.cn/eng/sgxw/202102/t20210224_10004691.htm>.

Yu, Wang 'China and Afghanistan: Together for a Community of Shared Future Featuring Peace, Development and Prosperity' (29 October 2020) <http://af.china-embassy.gov.cn/eng/zagx/202010/t20201030_1199959.htm>.

Yu, Wang 'The Truth about the Issues of Human Rights in Xinjiang' (9 July 2020) <https://af.china-embassy.gov.cn/sgxw/202007/t20200710_1114118.htm>.

Index

www.ingramcontent.com/pod-product-compliance
Ingram Content Group UK Ltd.
Pitfield, Milton Keynes, MK11 3LW, UK
UKHW022219051026
15624UKWH00001B/235

9 789004 746084